'Every summer I teach a course on politics and popular culture and assign Andrew Heywood's *Political Ideologies*. The book provides a clear introduction to the "isms" that shape how most of us think about politics, including, in the new edition, populism. The book hits the sweet spot of being accessible to newcomers and illuminating for more advanced students.'

– **Nicholas Tampio**, *Fordham University, USA*

'This brand new edition of Andrew Heywood's *Political Ideologies* reflects the challenges and developments of our times: it includes a chapter on populism, a feminism chapter comprising intersectionality, trans theory and queer theory, an in-depth analysis of postcolonialism, case studies on contemporary issues and a discussion about the future prospects of each ideology. An indispensable tool for learning and teaching.'

– **Andrea Schapper**, *University of Stirling, UK*

'A rare book which helps teachers not only inform but also inspire students to discover their place among competing ideologies. Heywood's orderly presentation provides readers with excellent access to a wide range of ideological identities.'

– **John Uhr**, *Australian National University, Australia*

'*Political Ideologies* represents an excellent resource that continues to be of interest to both staff and students. Heywood sets out and develops a clear understanding of the ideologies that continue to shape contemporary politics and society.'

– **Michael Kyriacou**, *University of East Anglia, UK*

'*Political Ideologies* reflects considerable scholarship but communicates this in a clear and accessible way. The format, including tables and boxes that compare ideologies, is exceptionally reader-friendly. The tracking of the evolution of ideologies is particularly good, and helps students (and others!) make sense of the bewildering forest of labels that litter the political landscape today. This is a book that students will actually read!'

– **Jennifer Leigh Bailey**, *Norwegian University of Science and Technology, Norway*

'Andrew Heywood's book remains one of the best introductions to the study of political ideologies. Its main strength lies in the author's ability to explain complex ideas in an engaging and accessible way, while the 'Political Ideologies in Action' features encourage the reader to reflect on the relationship between political ideas and contemporary issues.'

– **Judi Atkins**, *Aston University, UK*

'This book is essential reading as a core text in political ideologies. It explores in detail the origins, key concepts, variants and tensions within ideologies, and this new edition provides even more extensive consideration of the most recent developments in ideology such as populism and trans and queer theory. A key attractive feature is the way the book relates ideology to current themes such as decolonising the curriculum, nationalism and the pandemic, anarchism and cyberspace. In short, this is a well-written, comprehensive, up-to-date and above all stimulating text.'

– **Paul Flenley**, *University of Portsmouth, UK*

'I teach an introductory course with many general education students. Consequently, I was looking for a text that was above all highly accessible and engaging without sacrificing content. *Political Ideologies* meets both goals by succinctly outlining foundational material and building meaningful points of comparison across the traditions with ample opportunity to address finer nuances and draw connections to recent events.'

– **Peter Doerschler**, *Bloomsburg University of Pennsylvania, USA*

SEVENTH EDITION

POLITICAL IDEOLOGIES

AN INTRODUCTION

ANDREW HEYWOOD

macmillan
international
HIGHER EDUCATION

RED GLOBE
PRESS

This edition published 2021 by

RED GLOBE PRESS

Previous editions published under the imprint PALGRAVE

Red Globe Press in the UK is an imprint of Macmillan Education Limited, registered in
England, company number 01755588, of 4 Crinan Street, London, N1 9XW.

Red Globe Press® is a registered trademark in the United States,
the United Kingdom, Europe and other countries.

ISBN 978-1-352-01194-4 hardback
ISBN 978-1-352-01183-8 paperback

This book is printed on paper suitable for recycling and made from fully
managed and sustained forest sources. Logging, pulping and manufacturing
processes are expected to conform to the environmental regulations of the
country of origin.

A catalogue record for this book is available from the British Library.

A catalog record for this book is available from the Library of Congress.

Commissioning Editor: Peter Atkinson

Assistant Editor: Becky Mutton

Cover Designer: Laura De Grasse

Senior Production Editor: Amy Brownbridge

Marketing Manager: Amy Suratia

BRIEF CONTENTS

CONTENTS

LIST OF ILLUSTRATIVE MATERIAL

KEY FIGURES

KEY CONCEPTS

PERSPECTIVES ON . . .

TENSIONS WITHIN . . .

POLITICAL IDEOLOGIES IN ACTION

FIGURES

TOUR OF THE BOOK

This book contains a number of pedagogical features to help you understand each ideology discussed, the key thinkers and concepts associated with them, the differences between them and the tensions within them.

At the start of each chapter...

Chapter previews highlight the broad nature of the ideology and give a taste of the discussion to follow in the chapter.

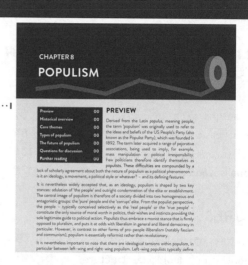

CHAPTER 8

POPULISM

Preview	00
Historical overview	00
Core themes	00
Types of populism	00
The future of populism	00
Questions for discussion	00
Further reading	00

PREVIEW

Derived from the Latin *populus*, meaning people, the term 'populism' was originally used to refer to the ideas and beliefs of the US People's Party (also known as the Populist Party), which was founded in 1892. The term later acquired a range of pejorative associations, being used to imply, for example, mass manipulation or political irresponsibility. Few politicians therefore identify themselves as populists. These difficulties are compounded by a lack of scholarly agreement about both the nature of populism as a political phenomenon – is it an ideology, a movement, a political style or whatever? – and its defining features.

It is nevertheless widely accepted that, as an ideology, populism is shaped by two key stances: adulation of 'the people' and outright condemnation of the elite or establishment. The central image of populism is therefore of a society divided into two homogeneous and antagonistic groups: the 'pure' people and the 'corrupt' elite. From the populist perspective, the people – typically conceived selectively as the 'real people' or the 'true people' – constitute the only source of moral worth in politics, their wishes and instincts providing the sole legitimate guide to political action. Populists thus embrace a monist stance that is firmly opposed to pluralism, and puts it at odds with liberalism in general and liberal democracy in particular. However, in contrast to other forms of pro-people illiberalism (notably fascism and communism), populism is essentially reformist rather than revolutionary.

It is nevertheless important to note that there are ideological tensions within populism, in particular between left-wing and right-wing populism. Left-wing populists typically define

Within each chapter...

Definitions of key terms, highlighted in the text, appear on the page where they are used, instead of in a separate glossary.

Environmentalism: A concern about the natural environment and particularly about reducing environmental degradation: a policy orientation rather than an ideological stance.

Humanism: A philosophy that gives moral priority to the achievement of human needs and ends.

Key figure boxes offer biographical details about the major thinkers and their influence on each ideological tradition, as well as highlighting their key writings.

KEY FIGURE

JAMES LOVELOCK (BORN 1919)

A UK atmospheric chemist, inventor and environmental thinker, Lovelock is best known as the inventor of the 'Gaia hypothesis'. This proposes that the Earth is best understood as a complex, self-regulating, living 'being', implying that the prospects for humankind are closely linked to whether the species helps to sustain, or threaten, the planetary ecosystem. Lovelock was also the first person to alert the world to the global presence of CFCs in the atmosphere, and he is, controversially, a supporter of nuclear power.

Colin McPherson/Corbis Entertainment/Getty Images

KEY CONCEPT

PRAGMATISM

Pragmatism, broadly defined, refers to behaviour that is shaped in accordance with practical circumstances and goals, rather than principles or ideological objectives. As a philosophical tradition, associated with 'classical pragmatists' such as William

disputes that seeks to clarify the mea[...] and hypotheses by identifying [...] consequences. The benefits of pragm[...] are that it allows policies and politi[...] be judged 'on their merits' (on th[...] works'), and that it prevents ideolog[...] divorced from reality and turning in[...] thinking. Critics, however, equate p[...]

Key concept boxes provide extended explanations of important ideas that underpin the ideologies under discussion.

Perspectives on...features
consider rival perspectives on
important political themes.

Political ideologies in action features draw
on important and contemporary case
studies to illustrate how each ideology
plays out in the real world

PERSPECTIVES ON ... IDEOLOGY

LIBERALS, particularly during the Cold War period, have viewed ideology as an officially
sanctioned belief system that claims a monopoly of truth, often through a spurious claim to be
scientific. Ideology is therefore inherently repressive, even totalitarian; its prime examples are
communism and fascism.

CONSERVATIVES have traditionally regarded ideology as a manifestation of the arrogance of
rationalism. Ideologies are elaborate systems of thought that are dangerous or unreliable
because, being abstracted from reality, they establish principles and goals that lead to repression,
or are simply unachievable. In this light, socialism and liberalism are clearly ideological.

SOCIALISTS, following Marx, have seen ideology as a body of ideas that conceal the
contradictions of class society, thereby promoting false consciousness and political passivity
among subordinate classes. Liberalism is the classic ruling-class ideology. Later Marxists adopted

POLITICAL IDEOLOGIES IN ACTION ...
DECOLONIZING THE CURRICULUM

EVENTS: In March 2015, the first protests
took place in the student-led Rhodes Must Fall
campaign. The campaign was initially directed
against a statue at the University of Cape Town
that commemorated Cecil Rhodes, the British
mining magnate and prime minister of Cape
Colony from 1890 to 1896. Although the
statue was removed in April 2015, the protest
movement spread to other universities, both
within South Africa and elsewhere in the world.
The Rhodes Must Fall in Oxford campaign called
on Oriel College, Oxford University, to take
down the statue of Rhodes that sits overlooking
the High Street, but this demand was rejected
in January 2016. The protesters objected to the
statues on the grounds that they glorified a man
who was an architect of apartheid and had been
deeply implicated in the racist and bloody history
of British colonialism.

SIGNIFICANCE: The Rhodes Must Fall protests
were linked to the wider goal of 'decolonizing the

Those who argue that the decolonization agenda
urgently needs to be applied to political ideologies
claim that, as a product of the Enlightenment,
ideology is intrinsically a part of the Western
intellectual tradition, so separating it from non-
Western cultures (Chinese, Indian, African, Islamic
and so on). Such thinking is consolidated by the
tendency of liberalism to operate as an ideology
of Western domination. Not only do liberals insist
that their values and institutions are universally

Getty Images Europe/Getty

TENSIONS WITHIN ... CONSERVATISM (1)

Neoliberalism	VS	Neoconservatism
classical liberalism	↔	traditional conservatism
atomism	↔	organicism
radicalism	↔	traditionalism
libertarianism	↔	authoritarianism
economic dynamism	↔	social order

Tensions within...features
highlight key points
of tension within each
ideology.

At the end of each chapter...

QUESTIONS FOR DISCUSSION

- How does the Marxist concept of ideology differ
  from the mainstream concept?
- Is ideology necessarily false? If so, why?
- Can 'socially unattached' intellectuals rise above
  ideology?
- Are all political ideas ideological, or only some of
  them?
- To what extent do ideologies differ in terms of
  their conceptual structure?
- What is the distinction between political ideology
  and political theory?

- How should the political spectrum be presented,
  and why?
- What is new about the 'new' ideologies?
- To what extent has ideological commitment
  become a lifestyle choice?
- Does the rise of 'new' ideologies mean that the
  old ones are now defunct?
- To what extent does the left/right divide aid our
  understanding of political ideologies?
- How should the political spectrum be presented,
  and why?
- Are ideologies destined never to end?

Questions for discussion encourage you
to reflect on some of the key issues and
debates relating to each ideology, either on
your own or within a group setting.

FURTHER RESOURCES

Ball, T., Dagger, R. & O'Neill, D. *Ideals and Ideologies:
A Reader* (2019). A broad anthology of important
writings, both classic and contemporary, covering
all major ideological traditions.

Freeden, M., Sargent, L. & Stears, M. *The Oxford
Handbook of Political Ideologies* (2015). Dozens of
experts collaborate to bring the key developments
and recent research in political ideology.

Further resources provide a list of useful
texts and online resources to extend your
study of ideologies beyond the book.

At the end of the book...

BIBLIOGRAPHY

Acton, Lord (1956) *Essays on Freedom and Power.*
London: Meridian.

Adams, I. (1989) *The Logic of Political Belief: A
Philosophical Analysis.* London and New York:
Harvester Wheatsheaf.

Adib-Moghaddam, A. (ed.) (2014) *Introduction to
Khomeini.* New York: Cambridge University
Press.

Adonis, A. and Hames, T. (1994) *A Conservative
Revolution? The Thatcher– Reagan Decade in
Perspective.* Manchester: Manchester University
Press.

Ball, T., Dagger, R.
Ideologies and
and New York

Ball, T., Dagger, I
and Ideologies
Routledge.

Baradat, L. P. (2
Origins and i
River, NJ: Pren

Barber, B. (2003) *Ji*
and Tribalism
London: Corg

There is a full
bibliography, and
in the index entries
material in boxes
are in bold, and the
on-page definitions
are in italics.

INDEX

Note: page numbers that are in **bold** type refer to figures, tables
italics refer to on-page definitions.

PREFACE TO THE SEVENTH EDITION

The world of political ideologies never ceases to surprise. The election of Donald Trump as US president in November 2016, and the referendum vote in the UK in favour of Brexit earlier in the year, thus appeared to come out of the blue. In both cases, the forces of mainstream conservatism were supplemented by an upsurge in populist nationalism that far exceeded the predictions of most pundits. In part, this was because the rise of populism – which, albeit to different degrees, affected most developed states as well as some developing states – threatened to reverse the dominant ideological trend of the post-1945 period: the onward march of liberalism. Nevertheless, it remains unclear whether resurgent populism is destined to be an ongoing trend, or merely a temporary one. This uncertainty occurs not least because other ideological developments have also recently come to the fore, such as the campaign for racial justice, associated with the Black Lives Matter movement, to say nothing about the myriad (and often contradictory) ideological ramifications of the Covid-19 pandemic since 2020.

The seventh edition of *Political Ideologies* has been systematically revised and updated throughout. It differs from the previous edition in a number of significant ways. The coverage of populism has been expanded by the inclusion of a separate chapter on the subject (Chapter 8). The chapter on Islamism has been replaced by one on the broader topic of fundamentalism (Chapter 12). The focus of the concluding chapter has shifted from the end-of-ideology debate (now incorporated into Chapter 1) to the topic of why ideologies matter, and to what extent (Chapter 12). The feminism chapter has been revised to include a consideration of modern approaches to gender and sexuality, including intersectionality, trans theory and queer theory (Chapter 9). The multiculturalism chapter has been restructured to analyse postcolonialism in greater depth (Chapter 11). All the 'Political Ideologies in Action' features have been updated to focus on contemporary, rather than historical, issues. Each of the substantive chapters now includes a concluding section reflecting on the future prospects of the ideology in question.

I would like to thank all those at Red Globe Press who have contributed to the production of the book, particularly Lloyd Langman and Peter Atkinson, whose suggestions and feedback throughout the process were unfailingly encouraging, constructive and insightful. I would also like to thank Matt Laing for his contribution to the Further Reading sections, as well as the anonymous reviewers who commented on the book at various points in its development. Discussions with friends and colleagues, notably Karen and Doug Woodward, Angela and David Maddison, Barbara and Chris Clarkson, Kate and Barry Taylor, Gill and Collin Spraggs, and Gill Walton, also helped to sharpen the ideas and arguments advanced here. The book is dedicated to my wife, Jean, without whose advice, encouragement and support none of the editions of this book would have seen the light of day.

UNDERSTANDING POLITICAL IDEOLOGIES

PREVIEW

All people are political thinkers. Whether they know it or not, people use political ideas and concepts whenever they express their opinion or speak their mind. Everyday language is littered with terms such as 'freedom', 'fairness', 'equality', 'justice' and 'rights'. In the same way, words such as 'conservative', 'liberal', 'socialist', 'communist' and 'fascist' are regularly employed by people either to describe their own views, or those of others. However, even though such terms are familiar, even commonplace, they are seldom used with any precision or a clear grasp of their meaning. What, for instance, is 'equality'? What does it mean to say that all people are equal? Are people born equal; should they be treated by society as if they are equal? Should people have equal rights, equal opportunities, equal political influence, equal wages? Similarly, words such as 'socialist' or 'fascist' are commonly misused. What does it mean to call someone a 'fascist'? What values or beliefs do fascists hold, and why do they hold them? How do socialist views differ from those of, say, liberals, conservatives or anarchists? This book examines the substantive ideas and beliefs of the major political ideologies.

This introductory chapter reflects on the nature of political ideology. It does so by examining the life and (sometimes convoluted) times of the concept of ideology, the structure of ideological thought, the differences between so-called 'classical' ideologies and 'new' ideologies, the extent to which ideologies conform to a left/right divide, and the question of whether ideology has or could come to an end. (Chapter 13 discusses how and why political ideologies matter.)

VIEWS OF POLITICAL IDEOLOGY

This book is primarily a study of political ideologies, rather than an analysis of the nature of ideology. Much confusion stems from the fact that, though obviously related, 'ideology' and 'ideologies' are quite different things to study. To examine 'ideology' is to consider a particular *type* of political thought, distinct from, say, political science or political philosophy. The study of political ideology thus involves reflection on questions about the nature, role and significance of this category of thought, and about which sets of political ideas and arguments should be classified as ideologies. For instance, is ideology true or false, liberating or oppressive, or inevitable or merely transitory? Similarly, are green ideology and multiculturalism, by virtue of their relatively narrow focus, ideologies in the same sense as liberalism and socialism, both of which offer a comprehensive vision of the desired future?

On the other hand, to study 'ideologies' is to be concerned with analysing the *content* of political thought, to be interested in the ideas, doctrines and theories that have been advanced by and within the various ideological traditions. For example, what can liberalism tell us about freedom? Why have socialists traditionally supported equality? How do anarchists defend the idea of a stateless society? Why have fascists regarded struggle and war as healthy? In order to examine such 'content' issues, however, it is necessary to consider the overarching 'type' of political thought we are dealing with. Before discussing the characteristic ideas and doctrines of the so-called ideologies, we need to reflect on why these sets of ideas have been categorized as ideologies. More importantly, what does the categorization tell us? What can we learn about, for instance, liberalism, socialism, feminism and fascism from the fact that they are classified as ideologies?

The first problem confronting any discussion of the nature of ideology is that there is no settled or agreed definition of the term, only a collection of rival definitions. As David McLellan (1995) commented, 'Ideology is the most elusive concept in the whole of the social sciences.' Few political terms have been the subject of such deep and impassioned controversy. This has occurred for two reasons. In the first place, as all concepts of ideology acknowledge a link between theory and practice, the term uncovers highly contentious debates about the role of ideas in politics and the relationship between beliefs and theories on the one hand, and material life or political conduct on the other. Second, the concept of ideology has not been able to stand apart from the ongoing struggle between and among political ideologies. For much of its history, the term 'ideology' has been used as a political weapon, a device with which to condemn or criticize rival sets of ideas or belief systems. Not until the second half of the twentieth century was a neutral and apparently objective concept of ideology widely employed, and even then disagreements persisted over the social role and political significance of ideology. Among the meanings that have been attached to ideology are the following:

- a political belief system

- an action-orientated set of political ideas

- the ideas of the ruling class

- the world-view of a particular social class or social group

- political ideas that embody or articulate class or social interests

- ideas that propagate false consciousness among the exploited or oppressed

- ideas that situate the individual within a social context and generate a sense of collective belonging

- an officially sanctioned set of ideas used to legitimize a political system or regime

- an all-embracing political doctrine that claims a monopoly of truth

- an abstract and highly systematic set of political ideas.

The origins of the term are nevertheless clear. The word 'ideology' was coined during the French Revolution by Antoine Destutt de Tracy (1754–1836), and was first used in public in 1796. For de Tracy, *idéologie* referred to a new 'science of ideas', literally an *idea*-ology. With a rationalist zeal typical of the **Enlightenment**, he believed that it was possible to uncover the origins of ideas objectively, and proclaimed that this new science would come to enjoy the same status as established sciences such as biology and zoology. More boldly, since all forms of enquiry are based on ideas, de Tracy suggested that ideology would eventually come to be recognized as the queen of the sciences. However, despite these high expectations, this original meaning of the term has had little impact on later usage, which has been influenced by both Marxist and non-Marxist thinking.

Marxist views

The career of ideology as a key political term stems from the use made of it in the writings of Karl Marx (see p. 76). Marx's use of the term, and the interest shown in it by later generations of Marxist thinkers, largely explains the prominence ideology enjoys in modern social and political thought. Yet the meaning Marx ascribed to the concept is very different from the one usually accorded it in mainstream political analysis. Marx used the term in the title of his early work *The German Ideology* ([1846]1970), written with his lifelong collaborator Friedrich Engels (1820–95). This also contains Marx's clearest description of his view of ideology:

> The ideas of the ruling class are in every epoch the ruling ideas, i.e. the class which is the ruling material force of society, is at the same time the ruling intellectual force. The class which has the means of material production at its disposal, has control at the same time over the means of mental production, so that thereby, generally speaking, the ideas of those who lack the means of mental production are subject to it. (Marx and Engels, [1846]1970)

Marx's concept of ideology has a number of crucial features. First, ideology is about *delusion* and mystification: it perpetrates a false or mistaken view of the world, what Engels later referred to as **'false consciousness'**. Marx used ideology as a critical concept, the purpose of which is to unmask a process of systematic mystification. His own ideas he classified as scientific, because they were designed to accurately uncover the workings of history and society. The contrast between ideology and science, between falsehood and truth, was thus vital to Marx's use of the term. Second, ideology is linked to the *class system*. Marx believed that the distortion implicit in ideology stems from the fact that it reflects the interests and perspective on society of the ruling class. The ideology of a capitalist society is therefore **bourgeois ideology**. The ruling class is unwilling to recognize itself as an oppressor and, equally, is anxious to reconcile the oppressed to their oppression. The class system is thus presented upside down, a notion Marx conveyed through the image of the camera obscura, the inverted picture

Enlightenment: An intellectual movement that reached its height in the eighteenth century and challenged traditional beliefs in religion, politics and learning in general in the name of reason and progress.

False consciousness: A Marxist term denoting the delusion and mystification that prevents subordinate classes from recognizing the fact of their own exploitation.

Bourgeois ideology: A Marxist term denoting ideas and theories that serve the interests of the bourgeoisie by disguising the contradictions of capitalist society.

that is produced by a camera lens or the human eye. Liberalism, which portrays rights that can only be exercised by the propertied and privileged as universal entitlements, is therefore the classic example of ideology.

Third, ideology is a manifestation of *power*. In concealing the contradictions on which capitalism, in common with all class societies, is based, ideology serves to hide from the exploited proletariat the fact of its own exploitation, and thereby upholds a system of unequal class power. Ideology literally constitutes the 'ruling' ideas of the age. Finally, Marx treated ideology as a *temporary* phenomenon. Ideology will only continue so long as the class system that generates it survives. The proletariat – in Marx's view, the 'grave digger' of capitalism – is destined not to establish another form of class society, but rather to abolish class inequality altogether by bringing about the collective ownership of wealth. The interests of the proletariat thus coincide with those of society as a whole. The proletariat, in short, does not need ideology because it is the only class that needs no illusions.

Later generations of Marxists showed, if anything, a greater interest in ideology than did Marx himself. This largely stems from the fact that Marx's confident prediction of capitalism's doom proved to be highly optimistic, encouraging later Marxists to focus on ideology as one of the factors explaining the unexpected resilience of the capitalist mode of production. However, important shifts in the meaning of the term also took place. In particular, all classes came to be seen to possess ideologies. For Lenin and most later Marxists, ideology therefore came to refer to the distinctive ideas of a particular social class, ideas that advance its interests regardless of its class position. However, as all classes – the proletariat as well as the bourgeoisie – have an ideology, the term was robbed of its negative or pejorative connotations.

The Marxist theory of ideology was perhaps developed furthest by Antonio Gramsci (see p. 5). Gramsci ([1935]1971) argued that the capitalist class system is upheld not simply by unequal economic and political power, but by what he termed the '**hegemony**' of bourgeois ideas and theories. Hegemony means leadership or domination and, in the sense of ideological hegemony, it refers to the capacity of bourgeois ideas to displace rival views and become, in effect, the common sense of the age. Gramsci highlighted the degree to which ideology is embedded at every level in society: in its art and literature; in its education system and mass media; in everyday language; and in popular culture. This bourgeois hegemony, Gramsci insisted, could only be challenged at the political and intellectual level, which means through the establishment of a rival 'proletarian hegemony', based on socialist principles, values and theories.

The capacity of capitalism to achieve stability by manufacturing legitimacy was also a particular concern of the Frankfurt School, a group of mainly German neo-Marxists who fled the Nazis and later settled in the USA. Its most widely known member, Herbert Marcuse (see p. 94), argued in *One-Dimensional Man* (1964) that advanced industrial society has developed a 'totalitarian' character through the capacity of its ideology to

Hegemony: The ascendency or domination of one element of a system over others; for Marxists, hegemony implies ideological domination.

manipulate thought and deny expression to oppositional views. According to Marcuse, even the tolerance that appears to characterize liberal capitalism serves a repressive purpose, in that it creates the impression of free debate and argument, thereby concealing the extent to which indoctrination and ideological control take place.

KEY FIGURE

ANTONIO GRAMSCI (1891–1937)

An Italian Marxist and revolutionary, Gramsci tried to redress the emphasis within orthodox Marxism on economic and material factors. In his major work, *Prison Notebooks* (1929–35), Gramsci rejected any form of 'scientific' determinism by stressing, through the theory of 'hegemony' (the dominance of bourgeois ideas and beliefs), the importance of political and intellectual struggle. While he did not ignore the 'economic nucleus', he argued that bourgeois assumptions and values needed to be overthrown by the establishment of a rival 'proletarian hegemony'.

Dea Picture Library/De Agostini/Getty Images

Non-Marxist views

One of the earliest attempts to construct a non-Marxist concept of ideology was undertaken by the German sociologist Karl Mannheim (1893–1947). Like Marx, he acknowledged that people's ideas are shaped by their social circumstances, but, in contrast to Marx, he strove to rid ideology of its negative implications. In *Ideology and Utopia* ([1929]1960), Mannheim portrayed ideologies as thought systems that serve to defend a particular social order, and that broadly express the interests of its dominant or ruling group. Utopias, on the other hand, are idealized representations of the future that imply the need for radical social change, invariably serving the interests of oppressed or subordinate groups. He further distinguished between 'particular' and 'total' conceptions of ideology. 'Particular' ideologies are the ideas and beliefs of specific individuals, groups or parties, while 'total' ideologies encompass the entire *Weltanschauung*, or 'world-view', of a social class, society or even historical period. In this sense, Marxism, liberal capitalism and Islamism can each be regarded as 'total' ideologies. Mannheim nevertheless held that all ideological systems, including utopias, are distorted, because each offers a partial, and necessarily self-interested, view of social reality. However, he argued that the attempt to uncover objective truth need not be abandoned altogether. According to Mannheim, objectivity is strictly the preserve of the 'socially unattached intelligentsia', a class of intellectuals who alone can engage in disciplined and dispassionate enquiry because they have no economic interests of their own.

The subsequent career of the concept was marked deeply by the emergence of totalitarian dictatorships in the interwar period, and by the heightened ideological tensions of the Cold War of the 1950s and 1960s. Liberal theorists in particular portrayed the regimes that developed in Fascist Italy, Nazi Germany and Stalinist Russia as historically new and uniquely oppressive systems of rule, and highlighted the role played by 'official' ideologies in suppressing debate and criticism, and promoting regimented obedience. Writers as different as Karl Popper (1945), Hannah Arendt (1951), J. L. Talmon (1952), Bernard Crick (1962) and the 'end of ideology' theorists examined in the final section of this chapter, came to use the term 'ideology' in a highly restrictive manner, seeing fascism and communism as its prime examples. According to this usage, ideologies are 'closed' systems of thought, which, by claiming a monopoly of truth, refuse to tolerate opposing ideas and rival beliefs. Ideologies are thus 'secular religions'; they possess a 'totalizing' character and serve as instruments of social control, ensuring compliance and subordination. However, not all political creeds are ideologies by this standard. For instance, liberalism, based as it is on a fundamental commitment to freedom, tolerance and diversity, is the clearest example of an 'open' system of thought (Popper, 1945).

A distinctively conservative concept of ideology can also be identified. This is based on a long-standing conservative distrust of abstract principles and philosophies, born out of a sceptical attitude towards rationalism (see p. 26) and progress. The world is viewed as infinitely complex and largely beyond the capacity of the human mind to fathom. The foremost modern exponent of this view was Michael Oakeshott (see p. 55). 'In political activity', Oakeshott argued in *Rationalism in Politics* (1962), 'men sail a boundless and bottomless sea'. From this perspective, ideologies are seen as abstract systems of thought, sets of ideas that are destined to simplify and distort social reality because they claim to explain what is, frankly, incomprehensible. Ideology is thus equated with dogmatism: fixed or doctrinaire beliefs that are divorced from the complexities of the real world. Conservatives have therefore rejected the 'ideological' style of politics, based on attempts to reshape the world in accordance with a set of abstract principles or pre-established theories. Until infected by the highly ideological politics of the New Right (see p. 62), conservatives had preferred to adopt what Oakeshott called a 'traditionalist stance', which spurns ideology in favour of pragmatism, and looks to experience and history as the surest guides to human conduct.

KEY CONCEPT
PRAGMATISM

Pragmatism, broadly defined, refers to behaviour that is shaped in accordance with practical circumstances and goals, rather than principles or ideological objectives. As a philosophical tradition, associated with 'classical pragmatists' such as William James (1842–1910) and John Dewey (1859–1952), pragmatism is a method for settling metaphysical disputes that seeks to clarify the meaning of concepts and hypotheses by identifying their practical consequences. The benefits of pragmatism in politics are that it allows policies and political assertions to be judged 'on their merits' (on the basis of 'what works'), and that it prevents ideology from becoming divorced from reality and turning into mere wishful thinking. Critics, however, equate pragmatism with a lack of principle or a tendency to follow public opinion rather than lead it.

Since the 1960s, however, the term 'ideology' has gained a wider currency through being refashioned according to the needs of conventional social and political analysis. This has established ideology as a neutral and objective concept, the political baggage once attached to it having been removed. Martin Seliger (1976), for example, defined an ideology as 'a set of ideas by which men posit, explain and justify the ends and means of organized social action, irrespective of whether such action aims to preserve, amend, uproot or rebuild a given social order'. An ideology is therefore an action-orientated system of thought. So defined, ideologies are neither good nor bad, true nor false, open nor closed, liberating nor oppressive – they can be all these things.

The clear merit of this social-scientific concept is that it is inclusive, in the sense that it can be applied to all 'isms', to liberalism as well as Marxism, to conservatism as well as fascism, and so on. The drawback of any negative concept of ideology is that it is highly restrictive. Marx saw liberal and conservative ideas as ideological but regarded his own as scientific; liberals classify communism and fascism as ideologies but refuse to accept that liberalism is also one; traditional conservatives condemn liberalism, Marxism and fascism as ideological but portray conservatism as merely a 'disposition'. However, any neutral concept of ideology also has its dangers. In particular, in offloading its political

PERSPECTIVES ON . . . IDEOLOGY

LIBERALS, particularly during the Cold War period, have viewed ideology as an officially sanctioned belief system that claims a monopoly of truth, often through a spurious claim to be scientific. Ideology is therefore inherently repressive, even totalitarian; its prime examples are communism and fascism.

CONSERVATIVES have traditionally regarded ideology as a manifestation of the arrogance of rationalism. Ideologies are elaborate systems of thought that are dangerous or unreliable because, being abstracted from reality, they establish principles and goals that lead to repression, or are simply unachievable. In this light, socialism and liberalism are clearly ideological.

SOCIALISTS, following Marx, have seen ideology as a body of ideas that conceal the contradictions of class society, thereby promoting false consciousness and political passivity among subordinate classes. Liberalism is the classic ruling-class ideology. Later Marxists adopted a neutral concept of ideology, regarding it as the distinctive ideas of any social class, including the working class.

FASCISTS are often dismissive of ideology as an over-systematic, dry and intellectualized form of political understanding based on mere reason rather than passion and the will. The Nazis preferred to portray their own ideas as a *Weltanschauung* or 'world-view', and not as a systematic philosophy.

FEMINISTS, particularly from the Marxist feminist tradition, have seen ideology as a means of legitimizing the subordination of women in a patriarchal society. Ideology therefore has an intrinsically sexist character, apparent in the tendency to view supposedly male qualities and attributes as the human norm.

ECOLOGISTS have tended to regard all conventional political doctrines as part of a super-ideology of industrialism. Ideology is thus tainted by its association with arrogant humanism and growth-orientated economics – liberalism and socialism being its most obvious examples.

FUNDAMENTALISTS have treated key religious texts as ideology, on the grounds that, by expressing the revealed word of God, they provide a programme for comprehensive social reconstruction. Secular ideologies, by contrast, are rejected because they are not founded on religious principles and so lack moral substance.

baggage the term may be rendered so bland and generalized that it loses its critical edge completely. If ideology is interchangeable with terms such as 'belief system', 'world-view', 'doctrine' or 'political philosophy', what is the point of continuing to pretend that it has a separate and distinctive meaning?

CONTOURS OF IDEOLOGY

Any short or single-sentence definition of ideology is likely to provoke more questions than it answers. Nevertheless, it provides a useful and necessary starting point. In this book, ideology is understood as the following:

> An ideology is a more or less coherent set of ideas that provides the basis for organized political action, whether this is intended to preserve, modify or overthrow the existing system of power. All ideologies therefore have the following features.

They:

(a) advance an account of the existing order, usually in the form of a 'world-view'
(b) outline a model of the desired future, a vision of the 'good society'
(c) explain how political change can and should be brought about – how to get from (a) to (b). (See Figure 1.1.)

This definition is neither original nor novel, and is entirely in line with the social-scientific usage of the term. It nevertheless draws attention to some of the important and distinctive features of the phenomenon of ideology. In the process, it also highlights differences between political theory or philosophy and political ideologies as contrasting approaches to the study of political thought. Political theory considers ideas and concepts that have been central to political thought. Traditionally, this has taken the form of a history of political thought, focusing on a collection of 'major' thinkers – from, for instance, Machiavelli to Rawls – and a canon of 'classic' texts. As it studies the ends and means of political action, political theory is clearly concerned with ethical or **normative** questions, such as 'Why should I obey the state?' and 'What should be the limits of individual freedom?' This approach has about it the character of literary analysis: it is primarily interested in examining what major thinkers said, how they developed and justified their views and the intellectual context in which they worked.

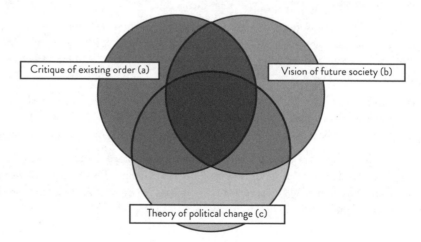

Figure 1.1   **Features of ideology**

Political ideologies differ from political theory in at least three respects. First, rather than focusing primarily on particular ideas and concepts – the state, authority, equality, justice and so on – or on the work of key thinkers, political ideologies look, first and foremost, at contrasting perspectives on political thought; each ideology thus offers a distinctive approach to political understanding. Composed of a particular configuration of ideas, doctrines and theories, these approaches provide a context in which political concepts, as well as the work of political thinkers, can be analysed. Ideologies can therefore be treated as frameworks within which the search for political knowledge takes place, otherwise known as paradigms (see p. 268).

Normative: The prescription of values and standards of conduct; what 'should be' rather than what 'is'.

Second, whereas political theory deals with ethical or normative questions (creating a sharp contrast between political theory and supposedly value-free political science), ideologies straddle the boundaries between

descriptive and normative thought, so blurring the distinction between what 'is' and what 'ought to be'. This reflects the fact that the ideologies contain both descriptive understanding about the workings of the existing order ((a) above) and normative or prescriptive beliefs about the nature of the future society ((b) above). Third, although political theory examines the ends and means of political action, ideologies go further. They are concerned with ideas that seek to change the world, action-orientated ideas that link (b) and (c) in the list above. Ideologies are thus not political philosophies but, rather, applied political philosophies.

Nevertheless, to view political ideologies as applied political philosophies is to suggest that they have a clarity of shape and internal consistency that they invariably lack; ideologies are only *more* or *less* coherent. Their apparent shapelessness stems in part from the fact that ideologies are not hermetically sealed systems of thought; instead, they are, typically, fluid sets of ideas that overlap with other ideologies and shade into one another. This not only fosters ideological development but also leads to the emergence of hybrid ideological forms, such as conservative nationalism (see pp. 137–9), socialist feminism (see pp. 196–7) and liberal multiculturalism (see pp. 237–8). Moreover, each ideology contains a range of divergent, even rival, traditions and viewpoints. Not uncommonly, disputes between supporters of the same ideology are more passionate and bitter than arguments between supporters of rival ideologies, because what is at stake is the true nature of the ideology in question – what is 'true' socialism, 'true' liberalism or 'true' anarchism?

Such conflicts, both between and within ideological traditions, are made more confusing by the fact that they are often played out with the use of the same political vocabulary, each side investing terms such as 'freedom', 'democracy', 'justice' and 'equality' with their own meanings. This highlights the problem of what W. B. Gallie (1955–6) termed 'essentially contested concepts'. These are concepts about which there is such deep controversy that no settled or agreed definition can ever be developed. In this sense, the concept of ideology is certainly 'essentially contested', as indeed are the other terms examined in the 'Perspectives on …' boxes found in this book.

Clearly, however, there must be a limit to the incoherence or shapelessness of ideologies. There must be a point at which, by abandoning a particularly cherished principle or embracing a previously derided theory, an ideology loses its identity or, perhaps, is absorbed into a rival ideology. Could liberalism remain liberalism if it abandoned its commitment to liberty? Would socialism any longer be socialism if it developed an appetite for violence and war? One way of dealing with this problem, following Michael Freeden (1996), is to highlight the morphology, the form and structure, of an ideology in terms of its key concepts, in the same way that the arrangement of furniture in a room helps us to distinguish between a kitchen, a bedroom, a lounge, and so on. Each ideology is therefore characterized by a cluster of core, adjacent and peripheral concepts, not all of which need be present for a theory or a doctrine to be recognized as belonging to that ideology. A kitchen remains a kitchen over time despite the relatively recent concept of an open plan kitchen or a dining area.

However, ideologies may be either 'thick' or 'thin', in terms of the configuration of their conceptual furniture. Whereas liberalism, conservatism and socialism are based on a broad and distinctive set of values, doctrines and beliefs, others, such as anarchism and feminism, are more thin-centred, often having

Descriptive: An account of something that is devoid of value judgements, focusing just on what 'is'.

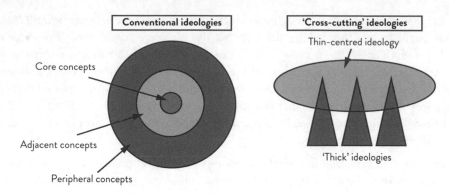

Figure 1.2   Contrasting ideological structures

a 'cross-cutting' character, in that they incorporate elements from 'thicker' ideological traditions (see Figure 1.2). This also explains why there is (perhaps unresolvable) debate and confusion about whether nationalism and multiculturalism in particular are ideologies in their own right or merely embellishments to other, 'host', ideologies.

FROM 'CLASSICAL' TO 'NEW' IDEOLOGIES?

Ideology may have been an inseparable feature of politics since the late eighteenth century (it is often traced back to the 1789 French Revolution), but its content has changed significantly over time, with the rate of ideological transformation having accelerated since the 1960s. New ideologies have emerged, some once-potent ideologies have faded in significance, and all ideologies have gone through a process of sometimes radical redefinition and renewal. Political ideology arose out of a transition from feudalism to industrial capitalism. In simple terms, the earliest, or 'classical', ideological traditions – notably liberalism, conservatism and socialism – developed as contrasting attempts to shape emergent industrial society. While liberalism championed the cause of individualism, the market and, initially at least, minimal government, conservatism stood in defence of an increasingly embattled *ancien régime*, and socialism advanced the quite different vision of a society based on community, equality and cooperation.

As the nineteenth century progressed, each of these ideologies acquired a clearer doctrinal character, and came to be associated with a particular social class or stratum of society. Simply put, liberalism was the ideology of the rising middle class, conservatism was the ideology of the aristocracy or nobility, and socialism was the ideology of the growing working class. In turn, political parties developed to articulate the interests of these classes and to give expression to the various ideologies. These parties therefore typically had a programmatic character.

The central theme that emerged from ideological argument and debate during this period was the battle between two rival economic philosophies: capitalism and socialism. This reflected the choice between market-based economic organization and state-centric economic organization. Political ideology thus had a strong economic focus. The battle lines between capitalism and socialism were significantly sharpened by the 1917 Russian Revolution, which created the world's first socialist state. Indeed, throughout what is sometimes called the 'short' twentieth century (from the outbreak of World War I in

1914 to the fall of communism in 1989–91), and particularly during the Cold War period (1945–90), international politics was structured along ideological lines, as the capitalist West confronted the communist East.

However, since around the 1960s, the ideological landscape has been transformed. Not only have major changes occurred within established or classical ideologies (for instance, in the rise of the New Left (see p. 94) and the New Right (see p. 62), but a series of so-called 'new' political ideologies have also emerged. The most significant of these are set out in Figure 1.3. The designation of these ideologies as 'new' can nevertheless be misleading, as each of them has roots that stretch back to the nineteenth century, if not beyond. New ideologies typically have a complex and ambiguous relationship with classical ideologies. This stems from the fact that these ideologies evolved both by applying established ideological thinking to new or more modern issues or concerns, or by opening up fresh ideological terrain that in some ways goes *beyond* the parameters of established ideological thinking (as in the case of radical feminism (see pp. 197–8) or deep ecology (see pp. 221–2)). New ideologies are thus new in the sense that they have given particular areas of ideological debate – gender equality, environmental sustainability, cultural diversity and so on – a prominence they never previously enjoyed. In the process, they have altered the focus and sometimes the terms of ideological debate. This has happened in at least three ways:

'Classical' ideologies	'New' ideologies
Liberalism	Feminism
Conservatism	Green ideology
Socialism	Multiculturalism
Nationalism	Fundamentalism
Anarchism	Populism (?)
Fascism (?)	Postcolonialism

Figure 1.3 'Classical' and 'new' ideologies

- First, there has been a shift away from economics and towards culture. Liberalism, conservatism and socialism were primarily concerned with issues of economic organization, or at least their moral vision was grounded in a particular economic model. By contrast, and in their various ways, new ideologies are more interested in culture than in economics: their primary concerns tend to be orientated around people's values, beliefs and ways of life, rather than economic well-being or even social justice. This has happened, in part, because the ideological gulf between capitalism and socialism has narrowed markedly, market-based economic arrangements (of one kind or another) having become almost universal.

- Second, fuelled by the general trend towards diversity, there has been a shift from social politics to identity politics (see p. 232). Identity links the personal to the social, in seeing the individual as 'embedded' in a particular cultural, social, institutional and ideological context, but it also highlights the scope for personal choice and self-definition, reflecting a general social trend towards **individualization**. In this sense, new ideologies such as feminism, green ideology and fundamentalism provide individuals with a range of ideological options rather than offering worked-out sets of

Individualization: The process through which people are encouraged to see themselves as individuals, possibly at the expense of their sense of social/moral responsibility.

political solutions that 'fit' their social position. This means that political activism has become, in effect, a lifestyle choice.

Universalism: The belief that it is possible to uncover certain values and principles that are applicable to all people and all societies, regardless of historical, cultural and other differences.

● Third, classical ideologies have been subjected to greater critical scrutiny as a result of the trend towards 'decolonizing the curriculum'. This has been reflected not only in the increasing significance of postcolonialism (see pp. 227–9), but also in the reappraisal of key political thinkers such as Immanuel Kant (see p. 23). Closely associated with Enlightenment thinking and '**universalist**' claims about our rights and obligations, Kant's

POLITICAL IDEOLOGIES IN ACTION . . .
DECOLONIZING THE CURRICULUM

EVENTS: In March 2015, the first protests took place in the student-led Rhodes Must Fall campaign. The campaign was initially directed against a statue at the University of Cape Town that commemorated Cecil Rhodes, the British mining magnate and prime minister of Cape Colony from 1890 to 1896. Although the statue was removed in April 2015, the protest movement spread to other universities, both within South Africa and elsewhere in the world. The Rhodes Must Fall in Oxford campaign called on Oriel College, Oxford University, to take down the statue of Rhodes that sits overlooking the High Street, but this demand was rejected in January 2016. The protesters objected to the statues on the grounds that they glorified a man who was an architect of apartheid and had been deeply implicated in the racist and bloody history of British colonialism.

Getty Images Europe/Getty

SIGNIFICANCE: The Rhodes Must Fall protests were linked to the wider goal of 'decolonizing the curriculum'. The term decolonization usually refers to the post-World War II dismantlement of the European colonial empires. In this context, however, it refers to the process through which the cultural and ideological legacy of colonial rule is challenged, especially in the realm of education. Commonly called 'decolonizing the mind', this involves interrogating the attitudes and assumptions that have sustained racial and civilizational hierarchies and broadening our intellectual vision to include a wider range of perspectives. For many, this requires that the under-representation of people of colour and other marginalized groups in the arena of scholarship is rectified, ending the domination of 'male, pale and stale' voices.

Those who argue that the decolonization agenda urgently needs to be applied to political ideologies claim that, as a product of the Enlightenment, ideology is intrinsically a part of the Western intellectual tradition, so separating it from non-Western cultures (Chinese, Indian, African, Islamic and so on). Such thinking is consolidated by the tendency of liberalism to operate as an ideology of Western domination. Not only do liberals insist that their values and institutions are universally applicable, and are therefore destined to prevail worldwide, but significant omissions (such as those about the brutal and exploitative nature of colonial rule and the racist assumptions that this rule was based upon) conceal the darker side of liberal hegemony. Nevertheless, over time, political ideologies have been increasingly effective in giving expression to non-Western (and sometimes anti-Western) views and voices. In the post-World War II period, this was evident in the emergence of African socialism, Arab socialism and Chinese communism. More recently, it has occurred through the rise of, for example, postcolonial nationalism, pluralist multiculturalism (see pp. 237–8) and various forms of religious fundamentalism (see Chapter 12).

contribution must now be reassessed in the light of remarks he made on colonial practices and slavery that suggested that he regarded these practices as tolerable, if not as necessary moments in the process of cultural and historical progress. Kant has also come to be viewed as a 'scientific racist' for writings in which he sought intellectually to establish the cultural superiority of white Europeans over Asians and Africans.

LEFT, RIGHT AND BEYOND

An additional way of categorizing political ideologies is on the basis of their position on the left–right political spectrum. The origins of the terms 'left' and 'right' in politics date back to the French Revolution and the seating arrangements of radicals and aristocrats at the first meeting of the Estates General in 1789. The left/right divide therefore originally reflected the stark choice between revolution and reaction. The terms have subsequently been used to highlight a divide that supposedly runs throughout the world of political thought and action, helping both to provide insight into the nature of particular ideologies and to uncover relationships between political ideologies more generally. Left and right are usually understood as the poles of a political spectrum, enabling people to talk about the 'centre-left', the 'far-right' and so on. This is in line with a linear political spectrum that travels from left-wing to right-wing, as shown in Figure 1.4. However, the terms left and right have been used to draw attention to a variety of distinctions.

Left   **Right**

Communism   Socialism   Liberalism   Conservatism   Fascism

Figure 1.4   Linear spectrum

Stemming from their original meanings, left and right have been used to sum up contrasting attitudes to political change in general, left-wing thinking welcomes change, usually based on a belief in **progress**, while right-wing thinking resists change and seeks to defend the **status quo**. Inspired by works such as Adorno et al.'s *The Authoritarian Personality* (1950), attempts have been made to explain ideological differences, and especially rival attitudes to change, in terms of people's psychological needs, motives and desires (Jost et al., 2003). In this light, conservative ideology, to take one example, is shaped by a deep psychological aversion to uncertainty and instability (an idea examined in Chapter 3). An alternative construction of the left/right divide focuses on different attitudes to economic organization and the role of the state. Left-wing views thus support intervention and collectivism (see p. 80), while right-wing views favour the market and individualism (see p. 24). Bobbio (1996), by contrast, argues that the fundamental basis for the distinction between left and right lies in differing attitudes to equality, left-wingers advocate greater equality while right-wingers treat equality as either impossible or undesirable. This may also help to explain the continuing relevance of the left/right divide, as the 'great problem of inequality' remains unresolved at both national and global levels.

Progress: Moving forward; the belief that history is characterized by human advancement underpinned by the accumulation of knowledge and wisdom.

Status quo: The existing state of affairs.

As a means of providing insight into the character of political ideologies and how they relate to one another, the traditional linear political spectrum nevertheless has a range of drawbacks. For instance, as all ideologies contain rival, or even contradictory, elements, locating them clearly on a linear political spectrum against a single criterion can be notoriously difficult. Anarchism, for instance, can be seen as either ultra-left-wing or ultra-right-wing, since it encompasses both anarcho-communist and anarcho-capitalist tendencies. It has also been argued that the ideologies that are traditionally placed at the extreme wings of the linear spectrum may have more in common with one another than they do with their 'centrist' neighbours. During the Cold War period in particular, it was widely claimed that communism and fascism resembled one another by virtue of a shared tendency towards totalitarianism (see p. 159). Such a view led to the idea that the political spectrum should be horseshoe-shaped, not linear (see Figure 1.5).

Figure 1.5   Horseshoe spectrum

Moreover, as political ideologies manifest themselves differently in different geographical contexts, it may be impossible to assign them an agreed left/right identity. Thus, while in the European context populism is predominantly associated with anti-immigrant and xenophobic political projects, giving it a distinctively right-wing character, in Latin America populism has been linked, historically, to state interventionist economic policies and the use of left-wing-orientated rhetoric.

A final drawback is that, as ideological debate has developed and broadened over the years, the linear spectrum has seemed increasingly simplistic and generalized, the left/right divide capturing only one dimension of a more complex series of political interactions. This has given rise to the idea of the two-dimensional spectrum, with, as pioneered by Eysenck (1964), a liberty/authority vertical axis being added to the established left/right horizontal axis (see Figure 1.6).

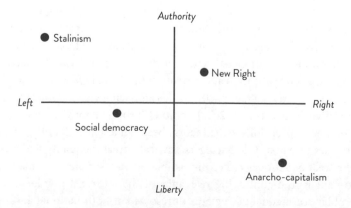

Figure 1.6   Two-dimensional spectrum

Nevertheless, a growing body of thought suggests that contemporary political ideologies have gone beyond the left/right divide. This may apply in the case of new ideologies, which, by virtue of their focus on issues of culture and identity rather than economic organization, no longer easily relate to the left/right battle between socialism and capitalism. For Anthony Giddens, sociological developments associated with the advance of globalization (see p. 21) have exhausted both left-wing and right-wing ideological tradition. In this view, the tendency for people's lives to be shaped increasingly by developments that occur, and events that happen, at a great distance from them has created societies that are so fluid and complex that they have, effectively, outgrown the major ideological traditions. Politics, therefore, has gone beyond left and right, a trend that has been particularly evident in the 'hollowing out' of parliamentary socialism since the 1990s.

However, instead of the emergence of an interconnected and interdependent world leading to ideological exhaustion, globalization may be in the process of replacing the left/right divide with one based on the gulf between 'open' and 'closed' political leanings (see Figure 1.7). People with 'open' political attitudes generally favour globalization, are tolerant or welcoming of cultural diversity, sympathize with an inclusive view of national identity, and typically support liberal social norms and values. By contrast, people with 'closed' attitudes are suspicious of, or oppose, globalization, fear cultural diversity, are drawn to an exclusive view of national identity, and usually support conservative social norms and values.

Open		Closed
Outward looking	v	Inward looking
Inclusive	v	Exclusive
Diversity	v	Homogeneity
Cosmopolitanism	v	Nationalism
Social liberalism	v	Social conservatism
Free trade	v	Protectionsim
Pooled sovereignty	v	State sovereignty

Figure 1.7   The open/closed divide

KEY FIGURE

ANTHONY GIDDENS (BORN 1938)

A UK social theorist, Giddens was an adviser to Tony Blair in the early years of 'new' Labour. His theory of 'structuration' reinvigorated social theory by setting out to transcend the conventional dualism of structure and agency. In works including *Beyond Left and Right* (1994), *The Third Way* (1998) and *The Runaway World* (1999), Giddens sought to remodel social democracy in the light of the advent of late modernity, taking into account developments such as globalization, de-traditionalization and increased social reflexivity.

Jeff Morgan 12/Alamy Stock Photo

THE END OF IDEOLOGY?

Is it possible to envisage ideology coming to an end? Or, for better or for worse, has ideology become a permanent feature of politics? The notion of the 'end of ideology' was particularly fashionable in the 1950s and 1960s. The most influential statement of this position was advanced by Daniel Bell. Bell (1960) was impressed by the fact that, after World War II, politics in the West was characterized by broad agreement among major political parties and the absence of ideological division or debate. Fascism and communism had both lost their appeal, while the remaining parties disagreed only about which ideologies could best be relied on to deliver economic growth and material prosperity. In effect, economics had triumphed over politics. Politics had been reduced to technical questions about 'how' to deliver affluence, and had ceased to address moral or philosophical questions about the nature of the 'good society'. To all intents and purposes, ideology had become an irrelevance.

KEY FIGURE

Jane Reed/ Harvard University News Office

DANIEL BELL (1919–2011)

A US academic and essayist, Bell drew attention, in *The End of Ideology* (1960), to the exhaustion of rationalist approaches to social and political issues, also warning, in the afterword to the 1988 edition, against the tyranny of utopian end-states. He helped to popularize the idea of 'post-industrialism', highlighting the emergence of 'information societies' dominated by a new 'knowledge class'. In *The Cultural Contradictions of Capitalism* (1976), Bell analysed the tension between capitalism's productivist and consumerist values and tendencies.

However, the process to which Bell drew attention was not the 'end of ideology' so much as the emergence of a broad ideological consensus among major parties, and therefore the suspension of ideological debate. In the immediate postwar period, representatives of the three major Western ideologies – liberalism, socialism and conservatism – came to accept the common goal of managed capitalism. This goal, however, was itself ideological – for example, it reflected an enduring faith in market economics, private property and material incentives, tempered by a belief in social welfare and economic intervention. In effect, an ideology of 'welfare capitalism' or 'social democracy' had triumphed over its rivals, although this triumph proved to be only temporary.

The 1960s witnessed the rise of more radical New Left ideas, reflected in a revival of interest in Marxist and anarchist thought and the growth of 'new' ideologies such as feminism and ecologism. The onset of economic recession in the 1970s provoked renewed interest in long-neglected, free-market doctrines and stimulated the development of New Right theories, which also challenged the postwar consensus. Finally, the 'end of ideology' thesis focused attention exclusively on developments in the industrialized West and ignored the fact that in the 1950s and 1960s communism remained firmly entrenched in the Soviet Union, Eastern Europe, China and elsewhere, and that revolutionary political movements were operating in Asia, Africa and parts of Latin America.

A broader perspective was adopted by Francis Fukuyama (see p. 17) in his essay 'The End of History' (1989), later developed into *The End of History and the Last Man* (1992). Unlike Bell, Fukuyama did not suggest that political ideas had become irrelevant, but that one particular set of ideas, Western liberalism, had triumphed over all its rivals. Fascism had been defeated in 1945, and Fukuyama clearly believed that the collapse of communist rule in Eastern Europe in 1989 marked the passing of Marxism-Leninism as an ideology of world significance. By the 'end of history', Fukuyama meant that the history of ideas had ended, and with it, fundamental ideological debate. Throughout the world there was, he argued, an emerging agreement about the desirability of liberal democracy (see p. 44), in the form of a market or capitalist economy and an open, competitive political system.

PERSPECTIVES ON . . . HISTORY

LIBERALS see history as progress, brought about as each generation advances further than the last through the accumulation of knowledge and understanding. Liberals generally believe that this will happen through gradual or incremental reform, not through revolution.

CONSERVATIVES understand history in terms of tradition and continuity, allowing little scope for progress. The lessons of the past provide guidance for present and future conduct. Reactionary conservatives believe that history is marked by decline, and wish to return to an earlier and preferred time.

SOCIALISTS are committed to a progressive view of history, which places heavy emphasis on the scope for social and personal development. Marxists believe that class conflict is the motor of history and that a classless, communist society is history's determinant end-point.

FASCISTS generally view history as a process of degeneration and decay, a decline from a past 'golden age'. They nevertheless subscribe to a cyclical theory of history that holds out the possibility of national rebirth and regeneration, usually through violent struggle and war.

FUNDAMENTALISTS have an ambivalent attitude towards history. Although they are strongly inclined to see the present as morally and spiritually corrupt in comparison with an idealized past, they conceive of social regeneration in modernist terms, thus rejecting conservative traditionalism.

KEY FIGURE

Thomas Trutschel/Photothek/
Getty Images

FRANCIS FUKUYAMA (BORN 1952)

A US social analyst and political commentator, Fukuyama's essay, 'The End of History?' (1989), argued that the Eastern European revolutions indicated that the history of ideas had ended with the recognition of liberal democracy as the 'final form of human government'. In *Trust* (1996) and *The Great Disruption* (1999), he discussed the relationship between economic development and social cohesion, highlighting contrasting forms of capitalist development. His other writings include *The Origins Of Political Order* (2011), *Political Order and Political Decay* (2014) and *Identity* (2018).

Without doubt, the Eastern European revolutions of 1989–91, which gave greatly renewed impetus to the process of democratization (see p. 18), and the dramatic reform of surviving communist regimes such as China profoundly altered the worldwide balance of ideological debate. However, it is far less certain that this process amounted to the 'end of history'. In particular, no sooner had the 'end of history' thesis been proclaimed than ideological forces that have little or nothing to do with Western liberalism started to rise to the surface. The first indication of this was the eruption of ethnic violence across much of former Yugoslavia during the 1990s, which suggested that the successor ideology to fallen communism may be nationalism rather than liberalism. Further evidence of the strengthening of non-liberal and anti-liberal forces was provided by the rise of religious fundamentalism in its various forms. This encouraged some to argue that world politics in the twenty-first century would witness, not the global triumph of liberalism, but a deepening 'clash of civilizations' (Huntington, 1996).

KEY CONCEPT

DEMOCRATIZATION

Democratization refers to the process of transition from authoritarianism to liberal democracy. Democratization encompasses three, sometimes overlapping, processes. (1) The breakdown of the old regime; this usually involves a loss of legitimacy and the faltering loyalty of the police and military. (2) 'Democratic transition' witnesses the construction of new liberal-democratic structures and processes. (3) 'Democratic consolidation' sees these new structures and processes becoming so embedded in the minds of elites and the masses that democracy becomes 'the only game in town' (Przeworski, 1991).

◎ QUESTIONS FOR DISCUSSION

- How does the Marxist concept of ideology differ from the mainstream concept?
- Is ideology necessarily false? If so, why?
- Can 'socially unattached' intellectuals rise above ideology?
- Are all political ideas ideological, or only some of them?
- To what extent do ideologies differ in terms of their conceptual structure?
- What is the distinction between political ideology and political theory?

- How should the political spectrum be presented, and why?
- What is new about the 'new' ideologies?
- To what extent has ideological commitment become a lifestyle choice?
- Does the rise of 'new' ideologies mean that the old ones are now defunct?
- To what extent does the left/right divide aid our understanding of political ideologies?
- How should the political spectrum be presented, and why?
- Are ideologies destined never to end?

◎ FURTHER READING

Ball, T., Dagger, R. & O'Neill, D. *Ideals and Ideologies: A Reader* (2019). A broad anthology of important writings, both classic and contemporary, covering all major ideological traditions.

Freeden, M., Sargent, L. & Stears, M. *The Oxford Handbook of Political Ideologies* (2015). Dozens of experts collaborate to bring the key developments and recent research in political ideology.

Ingersoll, D., Matthews, R. & Davison, A., *The Philosophic Roots of Modern Ideology* (2016). Comprehensively charts the intellectual evolution of major ideological traditions, and relevant contemporary debates, with analysis focused around key figures and texts.

Žižek, S. *The Pervert's Guide to Ideology* (2012). A unique and thought-provoking documentary in which one of the world's foremost philosophers looks at how ideological thought subtly underpins all aspects of modern life and culture.

The Political Compass, www.politicalcompass.org. A long-running website that asks questions to map people on a two-dimensional ideological spectrum, as well as linking to further reading. Find out where you sit!

CHAPTER 2

LIBERALISM

PREVIEW

The term 'liberal' has been in use since the fourteenth century but has had a wide variety of meanings. The Latin *liber* referred to a class of free men; in other words, men who were neither serfs nor slaves. It has meant generous, as in 'liberal' helpings of food and drink; or, in reference to social attitudes, it has implied openness or open-mindedness. It also came to be associated increasingly with the ideas of freedom and choice. The term 'liberalism', to denote a political allegiance, made its appearance much later: it was not used until the early part of the nineteenth century, being first employed in Spain in 1812. By the 1840s, the term was widely recognized throughout Europe as a reference to a distinctive set of political ideas. However, it was taken up more slowly in the UK. Although the Whigs, a long-established parliamentary faction, started to call themselves Liberals during the 1830s, the first distinctly Liberal government was not formed in the UK until W. E. Gladstone was appointed premier and established his first ministry.

The central theme of liberal ideology is a commitment to the individual and the desire to construct a society in which people can satisfy their interests and achieve fulfilment. Liberals believe that human beings are, first and foremost, individuals, endowed with reason. This implies that each individual should enjoy the maximum possible freedom consistent with a like freedom for all. However, although individuals are entitled to equal legal and political rights, they should be rewarded in line with their talents and their willingness to work. Liberal societies are organized politically around the twin principles of constitutionalism and consent, designed to protect citizens from the danger of government tyranny. Nevertheless, there are significant differences between classical liberalism and modern liberalism. Classical liberalism is characterized by a belief in a 'minimal' state, whose function is limited to the maintenance of domestic order and personal security. Modern liberalism, in contrast, accepts that the state should help people to help themselves.

HISTORICAL OVERVIEW

Liberalism was a product of the breakdown of **feudalism** in Europe, and the growth, in its place, of a market or capitalist society. In many respects, liberalism reflected the aspirations of the rising middle classes, whose interests conflicted with the established power of absolute monarchs and the landed aristocracy. Liberal ideas were radical: they sought fundamental reform and even, at times, revolutionary change. The English Revolution of the seventeenth century, and the American Revolution of 1776 and French Revolution of 1789 each embodied elements that were distinctively liberal, even though the word 'liberal' was not at the time used in a political sense. Liberals challenged the absolute power of the monarchy, supposedly based on the doctrine of the '**divine right** of kings'. In place of **absolutism**, they advocated constitutional and, later, representative **government** (discussed later in the chapter, in relation to liberal democracy). Liberals criticized the political and economic privileges of the landed aristocracy and the unfairness of a feudal system in which social position was determined by the 'accident of birth'. They also supported the movement towards freedom of conscience in religion and questioned the authority of the established church.

Feudalism: A system of agrarian-based production that is characterized by fixed social hierarchies and a rigid pattern of obligations.

Divine right: The doctrine that earthly rulers are chosen by God and thus wield unchallengeable authority; divine right is a defence for monarchical absolutism.

Absolutism: A form of government in which political power is concentrated in the hands of a single individual or small group, in particular, an absolute monarchy.

Government: The machinery through which collective decisions are made on behalf of the state, usually comprising a legislature, executive and judiciay.

Classical liberalism: A tradition within liberalism that seeks to maximize the realm of unconstrained individual action, typically by establishing a minimal state and a reliance on market economics.

Modern liberalism: A tradition within liberalism that provides (in contrast to classical liberalism) a qualified endorsement for social and economic intervention as a means of promoting personal development.

The nineteenth century was in many ways the liberal century. As industrialization spread throughout Western countries, liberal ideas triumphed. Liberals advocated an industrialized and market economic order 'free' from government interference, in which businesses would be allowed to pursue profit and states encouraged to trade freely with one another. Such a system of market-based industrial capitalism developed first in the UK, from the mid-eighteenth century onwards, and subsequently spread to North America and throughout Europe, initially into Western Europe and then, more gradually, into Eastern Europe. From the twentieth century onwards industrial capitalism exerted a powerful appeal for developing states in Africa, Asia and Latin America, especially when social and political development was defined in essentially Western terms. However, developing-world states have sometimes been resistant to the attractions of liberal capitalism because their political cultures have emphasized community rather than the individual. In such cases, they have provided more fertile ground for the growth of ideologies such as socialism, nationalism or religious fundamentalism, rather than Western liberalism.

Liberalism has undoubtedly been the most powerful ideological force shaping the Western political tradition. Nevertheless, historical developments since the nineteenth century have clearly influenced the nature and substance of liberal ideology. The character of liberalism changed as the rising middle classes succeeded in establishing their economic and political dominance. The radical, even revolutionary, edge of liberalism faded with each liberal success. Liberalism thus became increasingly conservative, standing less for change and reform, and more for the maintenance of existing – largely liberal – institutions. Liberal ideas, too, could not stand still. From the late nineteenth century onwards, the progress of industrialization led liberals to question, and in some ways to revise, the ideas of early liberalism. Whereas early or **classical liberalism** (sometimes called 'nineteenth-century liberalism') had been defined by the desire to minimize government interference in the lives of its citizens, **modern liberalism** (sometimes called 'twentieth-century liberalism') came to be associated with welfare provision and economic management. As a result, some commentators argued that liberalism was an incoherent ideology, embracing contradictory beliefs, notably about the desirable role of the **state**.

The Cold War period (1945–90) witnessed the consolidation of liberalism within the US-led capitalist West, even though its global ambitions were firmly resisted within the Soviet-led communist East and across much of what became known as the Third World. This consolidation was evident in two ways. The first was the spread of Western liberal democracy (see p. 44). A wave of democratization (see p. 18) occurred between 1943 and 1962, and involved countries such as West Germany, Italy, Japan and India; with a further wave of democratization starting in 1974, and affecting Greece, Portugal, Spain and much of Latin America. The second way in which liberalism was consolidated was through the 'silent revolution', which, beginning in the 1960s and affecting advanced industrialized countries in particular, saw the seemingly irresistible spread of liberal values in areas ranging from gender relations, homosexuality and religious observance to capital punishment and cultural diversity.

The end of the Cold War had yet more significant implications for liberalism, encouraging some to declare that it amounted to the 'liberal moment' in world affairs. The overthrow of communist regimes across Eastern Europe sparked a new and more dramatic process of democratization, with the formation of governments through multiparty elections and the adoption of market-based economic reforms becoming substantially more common. This created a situation in which, whereas in 1973 only 45 out of the 151 states then comprising the world community exhibited some of the key features of liberal-democratic governance, by 2003, 63 per cent of states, accounting for more than 70 per cent of the world's population, displayed these characteristics. In this context, 'end of history' theorists, such as Francis Fukuyama (see p. 17), proclaimed that liberal democracy had established itself as the final form of human government. Such a view, in effect, implies that liberal democracy is the 'default position' for human societies. The end of the Cold War also injected significantly greater impetus into the process of economic globalization. This made it possible, for the first time, to conceive of the world economy as a single, interlocking entity, built on liberal – or, more accurately, neoliberal – lines (economic liberalism is discussed at greater length later in the chapter).

> **State:** A political association that establishes sovereign jurisdiction over a defined territorial area, usually possessing a monopoly of coercive power.

KEY CONCEPT

GLOBALIZATION

Globalization is the emergence of a web of interconnectedness which means that our lives are shaped increasingly by events that occur, and decisions that are made, at a great distance from us, thus giving rise to 'supraterritorial' connections between people. However, globalization is a complex process that has a range of manifestations. Economic globalization is the process through which national economies have, to a greater or lesser extent, been absorbed into a single global economy. Cultural globalization is the process whereby information, commodities and images produced in one part of the world have entered into a global flow that tends to 'flatten out' cultural differences worldwide. Political globalization is the process through which policy-making responsibilities have been passed from national governments to international organizations.

However, the early decades of the twenty-first century have brought with them evidence of the retreat of liberalism. This has been particularly apparent in the fact that, since reaching its high-water mark in 2006–08, the spread of Western liberal democracy has been reversed, with authoritarian ideas and practices advancing across much of the world. For example, despite early expectations that the Arab Spring uprisings of 2011 would develop into the 'Arab world's 1989', bringing **democracy** to North Africa and parts of the Middle East, dictatorship was restored in most of the countries affected within months. A further challenge to liberalism has come in the form of a backlash against the advance of liberal values, especially affecting those sections of advanced industrial societies that have been 'left behind' due to the pace and direction of cultural change from the 1960s onwards. This 'silent counter-revolution' has seen a resurgence of conservative values, particularly in areas related to national identity – such as immigration and multiculturalism – and it has been expressed largely through the rise of right-wing populism. Finally, liberalism was damaged by the 2007–10 global financial crisis, which saw a series of major bank bailouts take place just as the world was falling into what was then the most serious recession since the Great Depression of the 1930s. This gave the impression that liberal political forces were more closely aligned to the interests of financial and corporate elites than they were to the interests of people. (See Chapter 8 for a fuller account of the relationship between populism and liberalism.)

CORE THEMES

Liberalism is the ideology of the industrialized West. So deeply have liberal ideas permeated political, economic and cultural life that their influence can become hard to discern, liberalism appearing to be indistinguishable from 'Western civilization' in general. Liberal thinkers in the eighteenth and nineteenth centuries, influenced by an Enlightenment belief in universal reason, tended to subscribe to an explicitly foundational form of liberalism, which sought to establish fundamental values and championed a particular vision of human flourishing or excellence, usually linked to personal autonomy. This form of liberalism was boldly universalist in that it implied that human history would be marked by the gradual but inevitable triumph of liberal principles and institutions. Progress, in short, was understood in strictly liberal terms.

During the twentieth century, however, it became fashionable to portray liberalism as morally neutral. This was reflected in the belief that liberalism gives priority to 'the right' over 'the good'. In other words, liberalism strives to establish the conditions in which people and groups can pursue the good life as each defines it, but it does not prescribe or try to promote any particular notion of what is good. From this perspective, liberalism is not simply an ideology but a 'meta-ideology'; that is, a body of rules that lays down the grounds on which political and ideological debate can take place. However, this does not mean that liberalism is simply a philosophy of 'do your own thing'. While liberalism undoubtedly favours openness, debate and self-determination, it is also characterized by a powerful moral thrust. The moral and ideological stance of liberalism is embodied in a commitment to a distinctive set of values and beliefs. The most important of these are:

- individualism
- freedom
- reason
- justice
- toleration.

Democracy: Rule by the people; democracy implies both popular participation in government and the public interest, and can take a wide variety of forms.

Individualism

In the modern world, the concept of the individual is so familiar that its political significance is often overlooked. In the feudal period, there was little idea of individuals having their own interests or possessing personal and unique identities. Rather, people were seen as members of the social groups to which they belonged: their family, village, local community or social class. Their lives and identities were largely determined by the character of these groups in a process that changed little from one generation to the next. However, as feudalism was displaced by increasingly market-orientated societies, individuals were confronted by a broader range of choices and social possibilities. They were encouraged, perhaps for the first time, to think *for* themselves, and to think *of* themselves in personal terms. A serf, for example, whose family might always have lived and worked on the same piece of land, became a 'free man' and acquired some ability to choose for whom to work, or perhaps the opportunity to leave the land altogether and look for work in the growing towns or cities.

As the certainties of feudal life broke down, a new intellectual climate emerged. Rational and scientific explanations gradually displaced traditional religious theories, and society was increasingly understood from the viewpoint of the human individual. Individuals were thought to possess personal and distinctive qualities: each was of special value. This was evident in the growth, in the seventeenth and eighteenth centuries, of natural rights theories, which are discussed later, in relation to classical liberalism. Immanuel Kant expressed a similar belief in the dignity and equal worth of human beings in his conception of individuals as 'ends in themselves' and not merely as means for the achievement of the ends of others. However, emphasizing the importance of the individual has two contrasting implications. First, it draws attention to the uniqueness of each human being: individuals are defined primarily by inner qualities and attributes specific to themselves. Second, they nevertheless each share the same status in that they are all, first and foremost, individuals, and so are equal. Many of the tensions within liberal ideology can, indeed, be traced back to these rival ideas of uniqueness and equality.

KEY FIGURE

Superstock

IMMANUEL KANT (1724–1804)

A German philosopher, Kant's 'critical' philosophy holds that knowledge is not merely an aggregate of sense impressions; it depends on the conceptual apparatus of human understanding. Kant's political thought was shaped by the central importance of morality. He believed that the law of reason dictates categorical imperatives, the most important of which is the obligation to treat others as 'ends', and never only as 'means'. Kant's most important works include *Critique of Pure Reason* (1781) and *Metaphysics of Morals* (1785).

A belief in the primacy of the individual is the characteristic theme of liberal ideology, but it has influenced liberal thought in different ways. It has led some liberals to view society as simply a collection of individuals, each seeking to satisfy his or her own needs and interests. Such a view has been equated with **atomism**; indeed, it can lead to the belief that 'society' itself does not exist, but is merely a collection of self-sufficient individuals. Such extreme individualism is based on the assumption that the individual is egoistical, essentially self-

Atomism: A belief that society is made up of a collection of self-interested and largely self-sufficient individuals, or atoms, rather than social groups.

KEY CONCEPT
INDIVIDUALISM

Individualism is the belief in the supreme importance of the individual over any social group or collective body. In the form of methodological individualism, this suggests that the individual is central to any political theory or social explanation – all statements about society should be made in terms of the individuals who compose it. Ethical individualism, on the other hand, implies that society should be constructed so as to benefit the individual, giving moral priority to individual rights, needs or interests. Classical liberals and the New Right subscribe to *egoistical* individualism, which places emphasis on self-interestedness and self-reliance. Modern liberals, in contrast, have advanced a *developmental* form of individualism that prioritizes human flourishing over the quest for interest satisfaction.

seeking, and largely self-reliant. C. B. Macpherson (1973) characterized early liberalism as 'possessive individualism', in that it regarded the individual as 'the proprietor of his own person or capacities, owing nothing to society for them'. In contrast, later liberals have held a more optimistic view of **human nature**, and have been more prepared to believe that **egoism** is tempered by a sense of social responsibility, especially a responsibility for those who are unable to look after themselves. Whether egoism is unrestrained or is qualified by a sense of social responsibility, liberals are united in their desire to create a society in which each person is capable of developing and flourishing to the fullness of his or her potential.

Freedom

A belief in the supreme importance of the individual leads naturally to a commitment to individual **freedom**. Individual liberty (liberty and freedom being interchangeable) is for liberals the supreme political value and, in many ways, the unifying principle within liberal ideology. For early liberals, liberty was a natural right, an essential requirement for leading a truly human existence. It also gave individuals the opportunity to pursue their own interests by exercising choice: the choice of where to live, for whom to work, what to buy and so on. Later liberals have seen liberty as the only condition in which people are able to develop their skills and talents and fulfil their potential.

Nevertheless, liberals do not accept that individuals have an absolute entitlement to freedom. If liberty is unlimited it can become 'licence', the right to abuse others. In *On Liberty* ([1859] 1972) John Stuart Mill argued that 'the only purpose for which power can be rightfully exercised over any member of a civilized community, against his will, is to prevent harm to others'. Mill's position is libertarian (see p. 61) in that it accepts only the most minimal restrictions on individual freedom, and then only in order to prevent 'harm to others'. He distinguished clearly between actions that are 'self-regarding', over which individuals should exercise absolute freedom, and those that are 'other-regarding', which can restrict the freedom of others or do them damage. Mill did not accept any restrictions on the individual that are designed to prevent a person from damaging himself or herself, either physically or morally. Such a view suggests, for example, that laws forcing car drivers to put on seat belts or motorcyclists to wear crash helmets are as unacceptable as any form of censorship that limits what an individual may read or listen to. Radical libertarians may defend the right of people to use addictive drugs, such as heroin and cocaine, on the same grounds. Although the individual may be sovereign over his or her body

Human nature: The essential and innate character of all human beings: what they owe to nature rather than to society.

Egoism: A concern for one's own welfare or interests, or the theory that the pursuit of self-interest is an ethical priority.

Freedom (or liberty): The ability to think or act as one wishes, a capacity that can be associated with the individual, a social group or a nation.

PERSPECTIVES ON . . . FREEDOM

LIBERALS give priority to freedom as the supreme individualist value. While classical liberals support negative freedom, understood as the absence of constraints – or freedom of choice – modern liberals advocate positive freedom in the sense of personal development and human flourishing.

CONSERVATIVES have traditionally endorsed a weak view of freedom as the willing recognition of duties and responsibilities, negative freedom posing a threat to the fabric of society. The New Right, however, endorses negative freedom in the economic sphere, freedom of choice in the marketplace.

SOCIALISTS have generally understood freedom in positive terms to refer to self-fulfilment achieved through either free creative labour or cooperative social interaction. Social democrats have drawn close to modern liberalism in treating freedom as the realization of individual potential.

ANARCHISTS regard freedom as an absolute value, believing it to be irreconcilable with any form of political authority. Freedom is understood to mean the achievement of personal autonomy, not merely being 'left alone' but being rationally self-willed and self-directed.

FASCISTS reject any form of individual liberty as a nonsense. 'True' freedom, in contrast, means unquestioning submission to the will of the leader and the absorption of the individual into the national community.

GREENS, particularly deep ecologists, treat freedom as the achievement of oneness, self-realization through the absorption of the personal ego into the ecosphere or universe. In contrast with political freedom, this is sometimes seen as 'inner' freedom, freedom as self-actualization.

FUNDAMENTALISTS see freedom as essentially an inner or spiritual quality. Freedom means conformity to the revealed will of God, spiritual fulfilment being associated with submission to religious authority.

and mind, each must respect the fact that every other individual enjoys an equal right to liberty. This has been expressed by John Rawls (see p. 39) in the principle that everyone is entitled to the widest possible liberty consistent with a like liberty for all.

KEY FIGURE

Historical/Corbis Historical/ Getty Images

JOHN STUART MILL (1806–73)

A British philosopher, economist and politician, Mill's varied and complex work straddles the divide between classical and modern forms of liberalism. His opposition to collectivist tendencies and traditions was firmly rooted in nineteenth-century principles, but his emphasis on the quality of individual life, reflected in a commitment to individuality, as well as his sympathy for causes such as female suffrage and workers' cooperatives, looked forward to later developments. Mill's major writings include *On Liberty* (1859), *Utilitarianism* (1861) and *Considerations on Representative Government* (1861).

While liberals agree about the value of liberty, they have not always agreed about what it means for an individual to be 'free'. In his 'Two Concepts of Liberty' ([1958] 1969), Isaiah Berlin (see p. 240) distinguished between a 'negative' theory of liberty and a 'positive' one. Early or classical liberals have believed in **negative freedom**, in that freedom consists in each person being

Negative freedom:
The absence of external restrictions or constraints on the individual, allowing freedom of choice.

left alone, free from interference and able to act in whatever way he or she may choose. This conception of freedom is 'negative' in that it is based on the absence of external restrictions or constraints on the individual. Modern liberals, on the other hand, have been attracted to a more 'positive' conception of liberty – **positive freedom** – defined by Berlin as the ability to be one's own master; to be autonomous. Self-mastery requires that the individual is able to develop skills and talents, broaden his or her understanding, and gain fulfilment. This led to an emphasis on the capacity of human beings to develop and ultimately achieve self-realization. These rival conceptions of liberty have not merely stimulated academic debate within liberalism, but have also encouraged liberals to hold very different views about the desirable relationship between the individual and the state.

Reason

The liberal case for freedom is closely linked to a faith in reason. Liberalism is, and remains, very much part of the Enlightenment project. The central theme of the Enlightenment was the desire to release humankind from its bondage to superstition and ignorance, and unleash an 'age of reason' (although early liberals were often willing to associate rationality only with men, and, not uncommonly, only with white men). Key Enlightenment thinkers included Jean-Jacques Rousseau (see p. 133), Immanuel Kant, Adam Smith (see p. 34) and Jeremy Bentham (see p. 33). Enlightenment rationalism influenced liberalism in a number of ways. In the first place, it strengthened its faith in both the individual and freedom. To the extent that human beings are rational, thinking creatures, they are capable of defining and pursuing their own best interests. By no means do liberals believe that individuals are infallible in this respect, but the belief in reason builds into liberalism a strong bias against **paternalism**. Not only does paternalism prevent individuals from making their own moral choices and, if necessary, from learning from their own mistakes, but it also creates the prospect that those invested with responsibility for others will abuse their position for their own ends.

> **Positive freedom:** Self-mastery or self-realization; the achievement of autonomy or the development of human capacities.
>
> **Paternalism:** Authority exercised from above for the guidance and support of those below, modelled on the relationship between fathers and children (see p. 70).

KEY CONCEPT
RATIONALISM

Rationalism is the belief that the world has a rational structure, and that this can be disclosed through the exercise of human reason and critical enquiry. As a philosophical theory, rationalism is the belief that knowledge flows from reason rather than experience, and thus contrasts with empiricism. As a general principle, however, rationalism places a heavy emphasis on the capacity of human beings to understand and explain their world, and to find solutions to problems. While rationalism does not dictate the ends of human conduct, it certainly suggests how these ends should be pursued. It is associated with an emphasis on principle and reason-governed behaviour, as opposed to a reliance on custom or tradition, or on non-rational drives and impulses.

A further legacy of rationalism is that liberals are inclined to view human history in terms of progress. Progress literally means advance, a movement forward. In the liberal view, the expansion of knowledge, particularly through the scientific revolution, enabled people not only to understand and explain their world but also to help shape it for the better. In short, the power of reason gives human beings the capacity to take charge of their own lives and fashion their own destinies. Reason emancipates humankind from the grip of the past and from the weight of custom and tradition. Each generation is thus able to advance beyond the last as the stock of human knowledge and understanding increases progressively. This also explains the characteristic liberal emphasis on education. People can better or improve themselves through the acquisition of knowledge and the abandonment of prejudice and superstition. Education, particularly in the modern liberal view, is therefore a good in itself. It is a vital means of promoting personal self-development and, if extended widely, of bringing about social advancement.

Reason, moreover, is significant in highlighting the importance of discussion, debate and argument. While liberals are generally optimistic about human nature, seeing people as reason-guided creatures, they have seldom subscribed to the utopian creed of human perfectibility because they recognize the power of self-interest and egoism. The inevitable result of this is rivalry and conflict. Individuals battle for scarce resources, businesses compete to increase profits, states struggle for security or strategic advantage, and so on. The liberal preference is clearly that such conflicts be settled through debate and negotiation. The great advantage of reason is that it provides a basis on which rival claims and demands can be evaluated – do they 'stand up' to analysis; are they 'reasonable'? Furthermore, it highlights the cost of not resolving disputes peacefully: namely, violence, bloodshed and death. Liberals therefore typically deplore the use of force and aggression; for example, war is invariably seen as an option of the very last resort. From the liberal perspective, the use of force is justified either on the grounds of self-defence or as a means of countering oppression, but always and only after reason and argument have been exhausted.

Justice

Justice denotes a particular kind of moral judgement, notably one about the distribution of rewards and punishment. In short, justice is about giving each person what he or she is 'due'. The narrower idea of social justice refers to the distribution of material rewards and benefits in society, such as wages, profits, housing, medical care, welfare benefits and so on. The liberal theory of justice is based on a belief in **equality** of various kinds. In the first place, individualism implies a commitment to foundational equality. Human beings are seen to be 'born' equal in the sense that each individual is of equal moral worth, an idea embodied in the notion of natural rights or **human rights**. As the norm of human rights transcends the norm of state sovereignty, liberals are inclined to believe in ideas such as global justice and decolonization.

Second, foundational equality implies a belief in formal equality or equal citizenship, the idea that individuals should enjoy the same formal status within society, particularly in terms of the distribution of rights and entitlements. Consequently, liberals fiercely disapprove of any social privileges or advantages that are enjoyed by some but denied to others on the basis of 'irrational' factors such as gender, race, colour, creed, religion or social background. Rights should not be reserved for any particular class of person, such as men, whites, Christians or the wealthy. This is the sense in which liberalism is 'difference blind'. The most important forms of formal equality are legal equality and political equality. The former emphasizes 'equality before the law' and insists that all non-legal factors be strictly irrelevant to the process of legal decision-making. The latter is embodied in the idea of 'one person, one vote; one vote, one value', and underpins the liberal commitment to democracy. Such thinking has provided fertile ground for the growth of feminist beliefs. Liberal feminism (discussed more fully in Chapter 9) has been articulated by thinkers ranging from Mary Wollstonecraft to Betty Friedan.

Justice: A moral standard of fairness and impartiality; social justice is the notion of a fair or justifiable distribution of wealth and rewards in society.

Equality: The principle that human beings are of identical worth or are entitled to be treated in the same way; equality can have widely differing applications.

Human rights: Rights to which people are entitled by virtue of being human; human rights are universal, fundamental and absolute.

KEY FIGURE

MARY WOLLSTONECRAFT (1759–97)

A British social theorist, Wollstonecraft was a pioneer feminist thinker, drawn into radical politics by the French Revolution. Her *A Vindication of the Rights of Woman* (1792) stressed the equal rights of women, especially in education, on the basis of the notion of 'personhood'. Wollstonecraft's work drew on an Enlightenment liberal belief in reason, but developed a more complex analysis of women as the objects and subjects of desire; it also presented the domestic sphere as a model of community and social order.

Photo 12/Universal Images Group/ Getty Images

Third, liberals subscribe to a belief in equality of opportunity. Each and every individual should have the same chance to rise or fall in society. The game of life, in that sense, must be played on a level playing field. This is not to say that there should be equality of outcome or reward, or that living conditions and social circumstances should be the same for all. Liberals believe social equality to be undesirable because people are not born the same. They possess different talents and skills, and some are prepared to work much harder than others. Liberals believe that it is right to reward merit (ability and the willingness to work); indeed, they think it is essential to do so if people are to have an incentive to realize their potential and develop the talents with which they were born. Equality, for a liberal, means that individuals should have an equal opportunity to develop their unequal skills and abilities.

KEY FIGURE

BETTY FRIEDAN (1921–2006)

A US political activist, Friedan is sometimes seen as the 'mother' of women's liberation. In *The Feminine Mystique* (1963) (often credited with having stimulated the emergence of second-wave feminism), Friedan attacked the cultural myths that sustained domesticity, highlighting the sense of frustration and despair that afflicted suburban American women confined to the roles of housewife and mother. In *The Second Stage* (1983), she nevertheless warned that the quest for 'personhood' should not encourage women to deny the importance of children, the home and the family.

Underwood Archives/Archive Photos/Getty Images

This leads to a belief in '**meritocracy**'. A meritocratic society is one in which, in principle, inequalities of wealth and social position solely reflect the unequal distribution of talent and application among human beings, or are based on factors beyond human control; for example, luck or chance (though some liberals believe that all aspects of luck, including natural ability, should be irrelevant to distributive justice, a position called 'luck egalitarianism' (Dworkin, 2000)). Such a society is supposedly just because individuals are judged not by their gender, the colour of their skin or their religion, but according to their talents and willingness to work, or what US Christian minister and activist Martin Luther King Jr called 'the content of their character'. By extension, social equality is thought to be unjust because

Meritocracy: Literally, rule by those with merit, merit being intelligence plus effort; a society in which social position is determined exclusively by ability and hard work.

it treats individuals alike despite their different qualities and capabilities. However, liberal thinkers have disagreed about how these broad principles of justice should be applied in practice. While classical liberals endorse strict meritocracy, both on the grounds that, being based on incentives, it promotes prosperity, and reflects individuals' just deserts, modern liberals have reservations about meritocracy on a number of grounds.

First, it endorses levels of material inequality which are difficult, and may be impossible, to defend. For example, in *A Theory of Justice* (1970), John Rawls argued that economic inequality is only justifiable if it works to the benefit of the poorest in society (an idea that is discussed in greater detail later in the chapter, in connection with social liberalism). Second, meritocracy is narrowly interested only in markets, economic efficiency and gross domestic product, and takes insufficient account of people's wider contribution to the public good. Third, the clearly implied link within meritocracy between poverty and a combination of laziness and a lack of talent damages the less well-off's sense of social esteem, breeding resentment and hostility towards the wealthy elite. This is what Michael Sandel (2020) dubbed the 'tyranny of merit'.

Toleration

The liberal social ethic is characterized very much by a willingness to accept and, in some cases, celebrate moral, cultural and political diversity. Indeed, an acceptance of **pluralism** can be said to be rooted in the principle of individualism, and the assumption that human beings are separate and unique creatures. However, the liberal preference for diversity has been associated more commonly with **toleration**. This commitment to toleration, attributed to the French writer Voltaire (1694–1778), is memorably expressed in the declaration that, 'I detest what you say but will defend to the death your right to say it.' Toleration and free speech are both an ethical ideal and a social principle. On the one hand, they represent the goal of personal **autonomy**; on the other, they establish a set of rules about how human beings should behave towards one another. The liberal case for toleration first emerged in the seventeenth century in the attempt by writers such as John Milton (1608–74) and John Locke to defend religious freedom. Locke argued that, since the proper function of government is to protect life, liberty and property, it has no right to meddle in 'the care of men's souls'. Toleration should be extended to all matters regarded as 'private', on the grounds that, like religion, they concern moral questions that should be left to the individual.

> **Pluralism:** A belief in diversity or choice, or the theory that political power is or should be widely and evenly dispersed (see p. 240).
>
> **Toleration:** Forbearance; a willingness to accept views or actions with which one is in disagreement.
>
> **Autonomy:** Literally, self-government; the ability to control one's own destiny by virtue of enjoying independence from external influences.

KEY FIGURE

Pictorial Press Ltd/Alamy Stock Photo

JOHN LOCKE (1632–1704)

Locke was a consistent opponent of absolutism and is often portrayed as the philosopher of the 1688 'Glorious Revolution' (which established a constitutional monarchy in England). Using social contract theory and accepting that, by nature, humans are free and equal, Locke upheld constitutionalism, limited government and the right of revolution, but the stress he placed on property rights prevented him from endorsing political equality or democracy in the modern sense. Locke's foremost political work is *Two Treatises of Government* (1690).

In *On Liberty* ([1859] 1972), J. S. Mill developed a wider justification for the toleration of other people's speech and actions that highlighted its importance to society as well as the individual. From the individual's point of view, toleration is primarily a guarantee of personal autonomy and is thus a condition for moral self-development. Nevertheless, toleration is also necessary to ensure the vigour and health of society as a whole. Only within a free market of ideas will 'truth' emerge, as good ideas displace bad ones and ignorance is progressively banished. Contest, debate and argument, the fruit of diversity or multiplicity, are therefore the motor of social progress. (For a discussion of liberal thinking regarding the limits of free speech in a plural society.) For Mill, this was particularly threatened by democracy and the spread of 'dull conformism', linked to the belief that the majority must always be right. Mill ([1859] 1972) was thus able to argue as follows:

> If all mankind minus one, were of one opinion, and only one person were of the contrary opinion, mankind would be no more justified in silencing that one person, than he, if he had the power, would be justified in silencing mankind.

POLITICAL IDEOLOGIES IN ACTION . . .

FREE SPEECH IN A PLURAL SOCIETY

EVENTS: In June 2020, J. K. Rowling, the author of the *Harry Potter* fantasy novels, published a blog post arguing that gender was determined by biology. It came after a tweet in which she took issue with an article referring to 'people who menstruate', rather than to women. She was swiftly condemned by transgender activists who claimed that her focus on biological sex was 'transphobic', a stance that was backed up by the beginning of a campaign to 'cancel', or boycott, her cultural output, with a view to subjecting her to financial pressure. In July 2020, some 152 academics and writers signed a letter on justice and open debate to the US magazine *Harper's* which defended the 'free exchange of information and ideas, the lifeblood of a liberal society'.

SIGNIFICANCE: A commitment to free speech is one of the core principles of liberal ideology. This does not, however, imply that liberals believe in unchecked free speech but, rather, that free speech should be constrained only when there is a strong likelihood that it will result in physical harm (for example, by threatening national security or, possibly, in the case of 'hate speech'). The liberal justification for free speech lies in scepticism, the doctrine that certain knowledge is impossible to achieve, in which case all truth-claims must be subject to doubt. In this view, the only way of advancing knowledge and ensuring social progress is by testing ideas and beliefs in open competition against rival ideas and

beliefs, a process that is more rigorous the wider the range of views considered. Even 'bad' or 'evil' ideas thus have a purpose, and so should not be silenced, either legally or through social pressure.

However, the emergence of plural societies, shaped by increased diversity in areas ranging from ethnicity and culture to gender and sexuality, has brought with it growing pressure to narrow the parameters of free speech. This trend reflects not so much a retreat from liberalism, as the sharpening of a philosophical divide within liberal culture. At the heart of the call for greater restraint over free speech is the argument that if different people are to occupy the same political space without conflict, they mutually have to limit the extent to which they subject each others' fundamental beliefs (beliefs that relate to their core identity) to criticism. In the case of marginalized or weak groups, this may extend to the creation of 'safe spaces', spaces where the discussion of topics which could cause offence is banned. According to such thinking, speech is only free when everyone is capable of enjoying its benefits equally.

Samir Hussein/WireImage

TYPES OF LIBERALISM

Liberalism comes in a variety of forms. These include the following:

- classical liberalism
- modern liberalism
- liberal democracy.

Classical liberalism

Classical liberalism was the earliest liberal tradition. Classical liberal ideas developed during the transition from feudalism to capitalism, and reached their high point during the early industrialization of the nineteenth century. As a result, classical liberalism has sometimes been called 'nineteenth-century liberalism'. The cradle of classical liberalism was the UK, where the capitalist and industrial revolutions were the most advanced. Its ideas have always been more deeply rooted in Anglo-Saxon countries, particularly the UK and the USA, than in other parts of the world. However, classical liberalism is not merely a nineteenth-century form of liberalism, whose ideas are now only of historical interest. Its principles and theories, in fact, have had growing appeal from the second half of the twentieth century onwards. Though what is called neoclassical liberalism, or neoliberalism (see p. 63), initially had the greatest impact in the UK and the USA, its influence has spread much more broadly, in large part fuelled by the advance of globalization (see p. 21).

Classical liberalism draws on a variety of doctrines and theories. The most important of these are:

- natural rights
- utilitarianism
- economic liberalism
- social Darwinism.

Natural rights

The **natural rights** theorists of the seventeenth and eighteenth centuries, such as John Locke and Thomas Jefferson (1743–1826), the US political philosopher and statesman, had a considerable influence on the development of liberal ideology. Modern political debate is littered with references to 'rights' and claims to possess 'rights'. A right, most simply, is an entitlement to act or be treated in a particular way. Such entitlements may be either moral or legal in character. For Locke and Jefferson, rights are 'natural' in that they are invested in human beings by nature or God. Natural rights are now more commonly called human rights. They are, in Jefferson's words, 'inalienable' because human beings are entitled to them by virtue of being human: they cannot, in that sense, be taken away. Natural rights are thus thought to establish the essential conditions for leading a truly human existence. For Locke, there were three such rights: 'life, liberty and property'. Jefferson did not accept that property was a natural or God-given right, but rather one that had developed for

Natural rights: God-given rights that are fundamental to human beings and are therefore inalienable (they cannot be taken away).

human convenience. In the American Declaration of Independence he therefore described inalienable rights as those of 'life, liberty and the pursuit of happiness'.

The idea of natural or human rights has affected liberal thought in a number of ways. For example, the weight given to such rights distinguishes authoritarian thinkers such as Thomas Hobbes from early liberals such as John Locke. As explained earlier, both Hobbes and Locke believed that government was formed through a '**social contract**'. However, Hobbes ([1651] 1968) argued that only a strong government, preferably a monarchy, would be able to establish order and security in society. He was prepared to invest the king with sovereign or absolute power, rather than risk a descent into a '**state of nature**'. The citizen should therefore accept *any* form of government because even repressive government is better than no government at all. Locke, on the other hand, argued against arbitrary or unlimited government. Government is established in order to protect natural rights. When these are protected by the state, citizens should respect government and obey the law. However, if government violates the rights of its citizens, they in turn have the right of rebellion. Locke thus approved of the English Revolution of the seventeenth century, and applauded the establishment of a constitutional monarchy in 1688.

For Locke, moreover, the contract between state and citizen is a specific and limited one: its purpose is to protect a set of defined natural rights. As a result, Locke believed in limited government. The legitimate role of government is limited to the protection of 'life, liberty and property'. Therefore, the realm of government should not extend beyond its three 'minimal' functions:

● maintaining public order and protecting property

● providing defence against external attack

● ensuring that contracts are enforced.

Other issues and responsibilities are properly the concern of private individuals. Jefferson expressed a similar sentiment a century later when he declared: 'That government is best which governs least.'

Utilitarianism

Social contract: A (hypothetical) agreement among individuals through which they form a state in order to escape from the disorder and chaos of the 'state of nature'.

State of nature: A pre-political society characterized by unrestrained freedom and the absence of established authority.

Utility: Use-value; in economics, utility describes the satisfaction that is gained from the consumption of material goods and services.

Natural rights theories were not the only basis of early liberalism. An alternative and highly influential theory of human nature was put forward in the early nineteenth century by utilitarian thinkers, notably Jeremy Bentham and James Mill. Bentham regarded the idea of rights as 'nonsense' and called natural rights 'nonsense on stilts'. In their place, he proposed what he believed to be the more scientific and objective idea that individuals are motivated by self-interest, and that these interests can be defined as the desire for pleasure, or happiness, and the wish to avoid pain, both calculated in terms of **utility**. The principle of utility is, furthermore, a moral principle in that it suggests that the 'rightness' of an action, policy or institution can be established by its tendency to promote happiness. Just as each individual can calculate what is morally good by the quantity of pleasure an action will produce, so the principle of 'the greatest happiness for the greatest number' can be used to establish which policies or institutions will benefit society at large.

KEY FIGURE

JEREMY BENTHAM (1748–1832)

A British philosopher, legal reformer and founder of utilitarianism, Bentham developed a moral and philosophical system based on the belief that human beings are rationally self-interested creatures, or utility maximizers. Using the principle of general utility – 'the greatest happiness for the greatest number' – he advanced a justification for *laissez-faire* economics, constitutional reform and, in later life, political democracy. Bentham's key works include *A Fragment on Government* (1776) and *An Introduction to the Principles of Morals and Legislation* (1789).

API/Gamma-Rapho/Getty Images

Utilitarian ideas have had a considerable impact on classical liberalism. In particular, they have provided a moral philosophy that explains how and why individuals act as they do. The utilitarian conception of human beings as rationally self-interested creatures was adopted by later generations of liberal thinkers. Moreover, each individual is thought to be able to perceive his or her own best interests. This cannot be done on their behalf by some paternal authority, such as the state. Bentham argued that individuals act so as to gain pleasure or happiness in whatever way they choose. No one else can judge the quality or degree of their happiness. If each individual is the sole judge of what will give him or her pleasure, then the individual alone can determine what is morally right.

On the other hand, utilitarian ideas can also have illiberal implications. Bentham held that the principle of utility could be applied to society at large and not merely to individual human behaviour. Institutions and legislation can be judged by the yardstick of 'the greatest happiness'. However, this formula has majoritarian implications, because it uses the happiness of 'the greatest number' as a standard of what is morally correct, and therefore allows that the interests of the majority outweigh those of the minority or the rights of the individual.

KEY CONCEPT

UTILITARIANISM

Utilitarianism is a moral philosophy that was developed by Jeremy Bentham and James Mill. It equates 'good' with pleasure or happiness, and 'evil' with pain or unhappiness. Individuals are therefore assumed to act so as to maximize pleasure and minimize pain, these being calculated in terms of utility or use-value, usually seen as satisfaction derived from material consumption. The 'greatest happiness' principle can be used to evaluate laws, institutions and even political systems. *Act* utilitarianism judges an act to be right if it produces at least as much pleasure-over-pain as any other act. *Rule* utilitarianism judges an act to be right if it conforms to a rule which, if generally followed, produces good consequences.

Economic liberalism

The late eighteenth and early nineteenth centuries witnessed the development of classical economic theory in the work of political economists such as Adam Smith and David Ricardo (1770–1823). Smith's *The Wealth of Nations* ([1776] 1976) was in many respects the first economics textbook. His ideas drew heavily on liberal and rationalist assumptions about human nature and made a powerful contribution to the debate about the desirable role of government within civil society. Smith wrote at a time of wide-ranging government restrictions on economic activity. **Mercantilism**, the dominant economic idea of the sixteenth and

Mercantilism: A school of economic thought that emphasizes the state's role in managing international trade and delivering prosperity.

seventeenth centuries, had encouraged governments to intervene in economic life in an attempt to encourage the export of goods and restrict imports. Smith's economic writings were designed to attack mercantilism, arguing instead for the principle that the economy works best when it is left alone by government.

KEY FIGURE

Hulton Archive/Hulton Archive/ Getty Images

ADAM SMITH (1723–90)

A Scottish economist and philosopher, Smith is usually seen as the founder of the 'dismal science'. In *The Theory of Moral Sentiments* (1759), he developed a theory of motivation that tried to reconcile human self-interestedness with unregulated social order. Smith's most famous work, *The Wealth of Nations* (1776), was the first systematic attempt to explain the workings of the economy in market terms. Although he is sometimes portrayed as a free-market theorist, Smith was nevertheless aware of the limitations of *laissez-faire*.

Smith thought of the economy as a **market**, indeed as a series of interrelated markets. He believed that the market operates according to the wishes and decisions of free individuals. Freedom within the market means freedom of choice: the ability of the businesses to choose what goods to make, the ability of workers to choose an employer, and the ability of consumers to choose what goods or services to buy. Relationships within such a market – between employers and employees, and between buyers and sellers – are therefore voluntary and contractual, made by self-interested individuals for whom pleasure is equated with the acquisition and consumption of wealth. Economic theory therefore drew on utilitarianism, in constructing the idea of 'economic man', the notion that human beings are essentially egoistical and bent on material acquisition.

Mercantilism: A school of economic thought that emphasizes the state's role in managing international trade and delivering prosperity.

Market: A system of commercial exchange between buyers and sellers, controlled by impersonal economic forces: 'market forces'.

Commercial liberalism: A form of liberalism that emphasizes the economic and international benefits of free trade, leading to mutual benefit and general prosperity, as well as peace among states.

Free trade: A system of trade between states not restricted by tariffs or other forms of protectionism.

The attraction of classical economics was that, while each individual is materially self-interested, the economy itself is thought to operate according to a set of impersonal pressures – market forces – that tend naturally to promote economic prosperity and well-being. For instance, no single producer can set the price of a commodity – prices are set by the market, by the number of goods offered for sale and the number of consumers who are willing to buy. These are the forces of supply and demand. The market is a self-regulating mechanism; it needs no guidance from outside. The market should be 'free' from government interference because it is managed by what Smith referred to as an 'invisible hand'. This idea of a self-regulating market reflects the liberal belief in a naturally existing harmony among the conflicting interests within society. Smith ([1776] 1976) expressed the economic version of this idea as:

It is not from the benevolence of the butcher, the brewer or the baker that we expect our dinner, but from their regard to their own interests.

Such thinking was further developed by David Ricardo and the so-called 'Manchester liberals', Richard Cobden (1804–65) and John Bright (1811–89). Their ideas are often referred to as **commercial liberalism**. The key theme within commercial liberalism is a belief in the virtues of **free trade**.

Free trade has economic benefits, as it allows each country to specialize in the production of goods and services that it is best suited to produce, the ones in which they have 'comparative advantage'. However, free trade is no less important in drawing states into a web of interdependence which means that the material costs of international conflict are so great that warfare becomes virtually unthinkable. Cobden and Bright argued that free trade would draw people of different races, creeds and languages together into what Cobden described as 'the bonds of eternal peace'.

Free market and free trade ideas became economic orthodoxy in the UK and the USA during the nineteenth century. The high point of free-market beliefs was reached with the doctrine of *laissez-faire*. This suggests that the state should have no economic role, but should simply leave the economy alone and allow businesspeople to act however they please. *Laissez-faire* ideas opposed all forms of factory legislation, including restrictions on the employment of children, limits to the number of hours worked, and any regulation of working conditions. Such economic individualism is usually based on a belief that the unrestrained pursuit of profit will ultimately lead to general benefit. *Laissez-faire* theories remained strong in the UK throughout much of the nineteenth century, and in the USA they were not seriously challenged until the 1930s.

However, since the late twentieth century, faith in the free market has been revived through the rise of neoliberalism. Neoliberalism was counter-revolutionary: it aimed to halt, and if possible reverse, the trend towards 'big' government that had dominated most Western countries, especially since 1945. Although it had its greatest initial impact in the two countries in which free-market economic principles had been most firmly established in the nineteenth century, the USA and the UK, from the 1980s onwards neoliberalism exerted a wider influence. At the heart of neoliberalism's assault on the 'dead hand' of government lies a belief in **market fundamentalism**. In that light, neoliberalism can be seen to go beyond classical economic theory. The matter is further complicated by the fact that in the case of both 'Reaganism' in the USA and 'Thatcherism' in the UK, neoliberalism formed part of a larger, New Right ideological project that sought to foster *laissez-faire* economics with an essentially conservative social philosophy. This project is examined in more detail in Chapter 3.

Social Darwinism

One of the distinctive features of classical liberalism is its attitude to poverty and social equality. An individualistic political creed will tend to explain social circumstances in terms of the talents and hard work of each individual human being. Individuals make what they want, and what they can, of their own lives. Those with ability and a willingness to work will prosper, while the incompetent or the lazy will not. This idea was memorably expressed in the title of Samuel Smiles' book *Self-Help* ([1859] 1986) which begins by reiterating the well-tried maxim that 'Heaven helps those who help themselves'. Such ideas of individual responsibility were widely employed by supporters of *laissez-faire* in the nineteenth century. For instance, Richard Cobden advocated an improvement of the conditions of the working classes, but argued that it should come about through 'their own efforts and self-reliance, rather than from law'. He advised them to 'look not to Parliament, look only to yourselves'.

Ideas of individual self-reliance reached their boldest expression in Herbert Spencer's *The Man versus the State* ([1884] 1940). Spencer (1820–1904), the

Free market: The principle or policy of unfettered market competition, free from government interference.

Laissez-faire: Literally, 'leave to do'; the doctrine that economic activity should be entirely free from government interference.

Market fundamentalism: An absolute faith in the market, reflecting the belief that the market mechanism offers solutions to all economic and social problems.

UK philosopher and social theorist, developed a vigorous defence of the doctrine of *laissez-faire*, drawing on ideas that the UK scientist Charles Darwin (1809–82) had developed in *The Origin of Species* ([1859] 1972). Darwin developed a theory of evolution that set out to explain the diversity of species found on Earth. He proposed that each species undergoes a series of random physical and mental changes, or mutations. Some of these changes enable a species to survive and prosper: they are pro-survival. Other mutations are less favourable and make survival more difficult or even impossible. A process of 'natural selection' therefore decides which species are fitted by nature to survive, and which are not. By the end of the nineteenth century, these ideas had extended beyond biology and were increasingly affecting social and political theory.

Spencer, for example, used the theory of natural selection to develop the social principle of 'the survival of the fittest'. People who are best suited by nature to survive rise to the top, while the less fit fall to the bottom. Inequalities of wealth, social position and political power are therefore natural and inevitable, and no attempt should be made by government to interfere with them. Spencer's US disciple, William Sumner (1840–1910), stated this principle boldly in 1884, when he asserted that 'the drunkard in the gutter is just where he ought to be'.

Modern liberalism

Modern liberalism is sometimes described as 'twentieth-century liberalism'. Just as the development of classical liberalism was closely linked to the emergence of industrial capitalism in the nineteenth century, so modern liberal ideas were related to the further development of industrialization. Industrialization had brought about a massive expansion of wealth for some, but was also accompanied by the spread of slums, poverty, ignorance and disease. Moreover, social inequality became more difficult to ignore as a growing industrial working class was seen to be disadvantaged by low pay, unemployment and degrading living and working conditions. These developments had an impact on UK liberalism from the late nineteenth century onwards, but in other countries they did not take effect until much later; for example, US liberalism was not affected until the depression of the 1930s. In these changing historical circumstances, liberals found it progressively more difficult to maintain the belief that the arrival of industrial capitalism had brought with it general prosperity and liberty for all. Consequently, many came to revise the early liberal expectation that the unrestrained pursuit of self-interest produced a socially just society. As the idea of economic individualism came increasingly under attack, liberals rethought their attitude towards the state. The minimal state of classical theory was quite incapable of rectifying the injustices and inequalities of civil society. Modern liberals were therefore prepared to advocate the development of an interventionist or enabling state.

The distinctive ideas of modern liberalism include:

- individuality
- positive freedom
- social liberalism
- economic management.

Individuality

John Stuart Mill's ideas have been described as the 'heart of liberalism'. This is because he provided a 'bridge' between classical and modern liberalism: his ideas look both back to the early nineteenth century and forward to the twentieth century and beyond. Mill's interests ranged from political economy to the campaign for female suffrage, but it was the ideas developed in *On Liberty* ([1859] 1972) that show Mill most clearly as a contributor to modern liberal thought. This work contains some of the boldest liberal statements in favour of individual freedom. Mill suggested that, 'Over himself, over his own body and mind, the individual is sovereign', a conception of liberty that is essentially negative as it portrays freedom in terms of the absence of restrictions on an individual's 'self-regarding' actions. Mill believed this to be a necessary condition for liberty, but not in itself a sufficient one. He thought that liberty was a positive and constructive force. It gave individuals the ability to take control of their own lives, to gain autonomy or achieve self-realization.

Mill was influenced strongly by European romanticism and found the notion of human beings as utility maximizers both shallow and unconvincing. He believed passionately in **individuality**. The value of liberty is that it enables individuals to develop, to gain talents, skills and knowledge and to refine their sensibilities. Mill disagreed with Bentham's utilitarianism insofar as Bentham believed that actions could only be distinguished by the quantity of pleasure or pain they generated. For Mill, there were 'higher' and 'lower' pleasures. Mill was concerned to promote those pleasures that develop an individual's intellectual, moral or aesthetic sensibilities. He was clearly not concerned with simple pleasure-seeking, but with personal self-development, declaring that he would rather be 'Socrates dissatisfied than a fool satisfied'. As such, he laid the foundations for a developmental model of individualism that placed emphasis on human flourishing rather than the crude satisfaction of interests.

Positive freedom

The clearest break with early liberal thought came in the late nineteenth century with the work of the UK philosopher and social theorist T. H. Green (1836–82), whose writing influenced a generation of so-called 'new liberals' such as L. T. Hobhouse (1864–1929) and J. A. Hobson (1854–1940). Green believed that the unrestrained pursuit of profit, as advocated by classical liberalism, had given rise to new forms of poverty and injustice. The economic liberty of the few had blighted the life chances of the many. Following J. S. Mill, he rejected the early liberal conception of human beings as essentially self-seeking utility maximizers, and suggested a more optimistic view of human nature. Individuals, according to Green, have sympathy for one another; their egoism is therefore constrained by some degree of **altruism**. The individual possesses social responsibilities and not merely individual responsibilities, and is therefore linked to other individuals by ties of caring and empathy. Such a conception of human nature was clearly influenced by socialist ideas that emphasized the sociable and cooperative nature of humankind. As a result, Green's ideas have been described as 'socialist liberalism'.

Green also challenged the classical liberal notion of freedom. Negative freedom merely removes external constraints on the individual, giving the individual freedom of choice. In the case of the businesses that wish

Individuality: Self-fulfilment achieved through the realization of an individual's distinctive or unique identity or qualities; what distinguishes one person from all others.

Altruism: Concern for the interests and welfare of others, based either on enlightened self-interest or a belief in a common humanity.

to maximize profits, negative freedom justifies their ability to hire the cheapest labour possible; for example, to employ children rather than adults, or women rather than men. Economic freedom can therefore lead to exploitation, even becoming the 'freedom to starve'. Freedom of choice in the marketplace is therefore an inadequate conception of individual freedom.

In the place of a simple belief in negative freedom, Green proposed that freedom should also be understood in positive terms. In this light, freedom is the ability of the individual to develop and attain individuality; it involves people's ability to realize their individual potential, attain skills and knowledge, and achieve fulfilment. Thus, whereas negative freedom acknowledges only legal and physical constraints on liberty, positive freedom recognizes that liberty may also be threatened by social disadvantage and inequality. This, in turn, implied a revised view of the state. By protecting individuals from the social evils that cripple their lives, the state can expand freedom, and not merely diminish it. In place of the minimal state of old, modern liberals therefore endorsed an enabling state, exercising an increasingly wide range of social and economic responsibilities.

While such ideas undoubtedly involved a revision of classical liberal theories, they did not amount to the abandonment of core liberal beliefs. Modern liberalism drew closer to socialism, but it did not place society before the individual. For Green, for example, freedom ultimately consisted in individuals acting morally. The state could not force people to be good; it could only provide the conditions in which they were able to make more responsible moral decisions. The central thrust of modern liberalism is therefore the desire to help individuals to help themselves.

Social liberalism

The twentieth century witnessed the growth of state intervention in most Western states and in many developing ones. Much of this intervention took the form of social welfare: attempts by government to provide welfare support for its citizens by overcoming poverty, disease and ignorance. If the minimal state was typical of the nineteenth century, during the twentieth century modern states became **welfare states**. This occurred as a consequence of a variety of historical and ideological factors. Governments, for example, sought to achieve national efficiency, healthier workforces and stronger armies. They also came under electoral pressure for social reform from newly enfranchised industrial workers and, in some cases, the peasantry. However, the political argument for welfarism has never been the prerogative of any single ideology. It has been put, in different ways, by socialists, liberals, conservatives, feminists and even at times by fascists. Within liberalism, the case for social welfare has been made by modern liberals, in marked contrast to classical liberals, who extol the virtues of self-help and individual responsibility.

Modern liberals defend welfarism on the basis of equality of opportunity. If particular individuals or groups are disadvantaged by their social circumstances, then the state possesses a social responsibility to reduce or remove these disadvantages to create equal,

Welfare state: A state that takes primary responsibility for the social welfare of its citizens, discharged through a range of social-security, health, education and other services.

or at least more equal, life chances. Citizens have thus acquired a range of welfare or social rights, such as the right to work, the right to education and the right to decent housing. Welfare rights are positive rights because they can only be satisfied by the positive actions of government, through the provision of state pensions, benefits and, perhaps, publicly funded health and education services. During the twentieth century, liberal parties and liberal governments were therefore converted to the cause of social welfare. For example, the expanded welfare state in the UK was based on the Beveridge Report (1942), which set out to attack the so-called 'five giants' – want, disease, ignorance, squalor and idleness. It memorably promised to protect citizens 'from the cradle to the grave'. In the USA, liberal welfarism developed in the 1930s during the administration of F. D. Roosevelt, but reached its height in the 1960s with the 'New Frontier' policies of John F. Kennedy, and Lyndon Johnson's 'Great Society' programme.

Social liberalism was further developed in the second half of the twentieth century, especially in the writings of John Rawls. In *A Theory of Justice* (1970), Rawls developed a defence of redistribution and welfare based on the idea of 'equality as fairness'. He argued that if people were unaware of their social position and circumstances (what Rawls called the 'original position'), they would view an egalitarian society as 'fairer' than an inegalitarian one, on the grounds that the desire to avoid poverty is greater than the attraction of riches. He therefore proposed the 'difference principle': that social and economic inequalities should be arranged so as to benefit the least well-off, accepting the need for some measure of inequality to provide an incentive to work. Nevertheless, in *Political Liberalism* (1993) Rawls advanced a somewhat modified version of' 'justice as fairness', in which egalitarianism is pushed into the background. This occurred through Rawls' recognition that principles of justice must enjoy not only strong philosophical justification but also strong citizen endorsement, something that is especially difficult to achieve in conditions of pluralism.

KEY FIGURE

JOHN RAWLS (1921–2002)

A US political philosopher, Rawls used a form of social contract theory to reconcile liberal individualism with the principles of redistribution and social justice. In his major work, *A Theory of Justice* (1970), he developed the notion of 'justice as fairness', based on the belief that behind a 'veil of ignorance' most people would accept that the liberty of each should be compatible with a like liberty for all, and that social inequality is only justified if it works to the benefit of the poorest in society.

Frederic Reglain/Getty

Economic management

In addition to providing social welfare, twentieth-century Western governments also sought to deliver prosperity by 'managing' their economies. This once again involved rejecting classical liberal thinking, in particular its belief in a self-regulating free market and the doctrine *of laissez-faire*. The abandonment of *laissez-faire* came about because of the increasing complexity of industrial capitalist economies and their apparent inability to guarantee general prosperity if left to their own devices. The Great Depression of the 1930s, sparked off by the Wall Street Crash of 1929, led to high levels of unemployment throughout the industrialized world and in much of the developing world. This was the most dramatic demonstration of the failure of the free market. After World War II, virtually all Western states adopted policies of economic intervention in an attempt to prevent a return to the pre-war levels of unemployment. To a large extent these interventionist policies were guided by the work of the UK economist John Maynard Keynes (1883–1946).

KEY CONCEPT
KEYNESIANISM

Keynesianism refers, narrowly, to the economic theories of J. M. Keynes (1883–1946) and, more broadly, to a range of economic policies that have been influenced by these theories. Keynesianism provides an alternative to neoclassical economics and, in particular, advances a critique of the 'economic anarchy' of *laissez-faire* capitalism. Keynes argued that growth and employment levels are largely determined by the level of 'aggregate demand' in the economy, and that government can regulate demand, primarily through adjustments to fiscal policy, so as to deliver full employment. Keynesianism came to be associated with a narrow obsession with 'tax and spend' policies, but this ignores the complexity and sophistication of Keynes' economic writings. Influenced by economic globalization, a form of neo-Keynesianism has emerged that rejects 'top-down' economic management but still acknowledges that markets are hampered by uncertainty, inequality and differential levels of knowledge.

In *The General Theory of Employment, Interest and Money* ([1936] 1963), Keynes challenged classical economic thinking and rejected its belief in a self-regulating market. Classical economists had argued that there was a 'market solution' to the problem of unemployment and, indeed, all other economic problems. Keynes argued, however, that the level of economic activity, and therefore of employment, is determined by the total amount of demand – aggregate demand – in the economy. He suggested that governments could 'manage' their economies by influencing the level of aggregate demand. Government spending is, in this sense, an 'injection' of demand into the economy. Taxation, on the other hand, is a 'withdrawal' from the economy: it reduces aggregate demand and dampens down economic activity. At times of high unemployment, Keynes recommended that governments should 'reflate' their economies by either increasing public spending or cutting taxes. Unemployment could therefore be solved, not by the invisible hand of capitalism, but by government intervention, in this case by running a budget deficit, meaning that the government literally 'overspends'.

TENSIONS WITHIN ... LIBERALISM ⟷

Classical liberalism	v.	Modern liberalism
economic liberalism	⟷	social liberalism
egoistical individualism	⟷	developmental individualism
maximize utility	⟷	personal growth
negative freedom	⟷	positive freedom
minimal state	⟷	enabling state
free-market economy	⟷	managed economy
rights-based justice	⟷	justice as fairness
strict meritocracy	⟷	concern for the poor
individual responsibility	⟷	social responsibility
safety-net welfare	⟷	cradle-to-grave welfare

Keynesian demand management thus promised to give governments the ability to manipulate employment and growth levels, and hence to secure general prosperity. As with the provision of social welfare, modern liberals have seen economic management as being constructive in promoting prosperity and harmony in civil society. Keynes was not opposed to capitalism; indeed, in many ways, he was its saviour. He simply argued that unrestrained private enterprise is unworkable within complex industrial societies. The first, if limited, attempt to apply Keynes' ideas was undertaken in the USA during Roosevelt's 'New Deal'. By the end of World War II, Keynesianism was widely established as an economic orthodoxy in the West, displacing the older belief in *laissez-faire*. Keynesian policies were credited with being the key to the 'long boom', the historically unprecedented economic growth of the 1950s and 1960s, which witnessed the achievement of widespread affluence, at least in Western countries. However, the re-emergence of economic difficulties in the 1970s generated renewed sympathy for the theories of classical political economy, and led to a shift away from Keynesian priorities. Nevertheless, the failure of the free-market revolution of the 1980s and 1990s to ensure sustained economic growth resulted in the emergence of the 'new' political economy, or neo-Keynesianism. Although this recognized the limitations of the 'crude' Keynesianism of the 1950s–1970s period, it nevertheless marked a renewed awareness of the link between unregulated capitalism and low investment, short-termism and social fragmentation.

Liberal democracy

Liberal democracy is the dominant political force in the developed world, and a significant force in the developing world (India, for example, is the world's largest liberal democracy). The greatest extent of liberal-democratic governance's spread came in the aftermath of the fall of communism, sparked by the East European Revolutions of 1989–90. Liberal democracy, nevertheless, has a hybrid nature. It combines a 'liberal' emphasis on limited and accountable government with a 'popular' stress on free, fair and competitive elections. It thus fuses two styles of rule:

- constitutional rule
- democratic rule.

Constitutional rule

Although liberals are convinced of the need for government, they are also acutely aware of the dangers that government embodies. In their view, all governments are potential tyrannies against the individual. On the one hand, this is based on the fact that government exercises sovereign power and so poses a constant threat to individual liberty. On the other hand, it reflects a distinctively liberal fear of power. As human beings are self-seeking creatures, if they have power – the ability to influence the behaviour of others – they will naturally use it for their own benefit and at the expense of others. Simply put, the liberal position is that egoism plus power equals corruption. This was expressed in Lord Acton's famous warning: 'Power tends to corrupt, and absolute power corrupts absolutely', and in his conclusion: 'Great men are almost always bad men' (1956). Liberals therefore fear arbitrary government and uphold the principle of limited government. Government can be limited, or 'tamed', through the establishment of constitutional constraints and, as discussed in the next section, by democracy.

A constitution is a set of rules that seeks to allocate duties, powers and functions among the various institutions of government. It therefore constitutes the rules that govern the government itself. As such, it both defines the extent of government power and limits its exercise. Support for constitutionalism can take two forms. In the first place, the powers of government bodies and politicians can be limited by the introduction of external and, usually, legal constraints. The most important of these is a so-called **written constitution**, which codifies the major powers and responsibilities of government institutions within a single document. The first such document was the US Constitution, but during the nineteenth and twentieth centuries written constitutions were adopted in all liberal democracies, with the exception of the UK, Israel and New Zealand. In many cases, **bills of rights** also exist, which entrench individual rights by providing a legal definition of the relationship between the individual and the state. The earliest example was the 'Declaration of the Rights of Man and the Citizen', which was passed by France's National Constituent Assembly in 1789. The principle of basic rights was enshrined in international law by the Universal Declaration of Human Rights. Where neither written constitutions nor entrenched bills of rights exist, as in the UK (the 1998 Human Rights Act being essentially a statute of rights), liberals have stressed the importance of statute law in checking government power through the principle of the **rule of law**.

Written constitution: A single authoritative document that defines the duties, powers and functions of government institutions and so constitutes 'higher' law.

Bill of rights: A constitutional document that specifies the rights and freedoms of the individual and so defines the relationship between the state and its citizens.

Rule of law: The principle that all conduct and behaviour, of private citizens and government officials, should conform to a framework of law.

Separation of powers: The principle that legislative, executive and judicial power should be separated through the construction of three independent branches of government.

Second, constitutionalism can be established by the introduction of internal constraints which disperse political power among a number of institutions and create a network of 'checks and balances'. As the French political philosopher Montesquieu (1689–1775) put it, 'power should be a check to power' (Montesquieu [1748] 1969). All liberal political systems exhibit some measure of internal fragmentation. This can be achieved by applying the doctrine of the **separation of powers**, proposed by Montesquieu himself. This seeks to prevent any individual or small group from gaining dictatorial power by controlling the legislative, executive and judicial functions of government. A particular emphasis is placed on the judiciary. As the judiciary interprets the meaning of law, both constitutional and statutory, and therefore reviews the powers of government itself, it must enjoy formal independence and political neutrality if it is to protect the individual from the state. Other devices for fragmenting government power include cabinet government (which checks the power of the prime minister), parliamentary government (which checks the power of the executive), bicameralism (which checks the power of each legislative chamber) and territorial divisions such as federalism (see p. 43), devolution and local government (each of which checks the power of central government).

KEY CONCEPT
CONSTITUTIONALISM

Constitutionalism, in a narrow sense, is the practice of limited government brought about by the existence of a constitution. Constitutionalism in this sense can be said to exist when government institutions and political processes are effectively constrained by constitutional rules. More broadly, constitutionalism refers to a set of political values and aspirations that reflect the desire to protect liberty through the establishment of internal and external checks on government power. It is typically expressed in support for constitutional provisions that establish this goal; notably, a codified constitution, a bill of rights, separation of powers, bicameralism and federalism (see p. 43) or decentralization. Constitutionalism is thus a species of political liberalism.

KEY CONCEPT
FEDERALISM

Federalism (from the Latin *foedus*, meaning 'pact' or 'covenant') usually refers to legal and political structures that distribute power between two distinct levels of government, neither of which is subordinate to the other. Its central feature is therefore the principle of shared sovereignty. 'Classical' federations are few in number: for example, the USA, Switzerland, Belgium, Canada and Australia. However, many more states have federal-type features. Most federal, or federal-type, states were formed by the coming together of a number of established political communities; they are often geographically large and may have culturally diverse populations. Federalism may nevertheless also have an international dimension, providing the basis, in particular, for regional integration, as in the case of 'European federalism'.

Democratic rule

Democracy literally means rule by the *demos* or people (although the Greeks originally used *demos* to mean 'the poor' or 'the many'). However, the simple notion of rule by the people is vague and has been subject to a bewildering variety of interpretations. Perhaps a more helpful starting point is Abraham Lincoln's Gettysburg Address, delivered in 1863, which extols the virtues of what he called government 'of the people, by the people, for the people'. Whereas all government is government 'of' the people, government 'by' and 'for' the people highlight core democratic principles while also suggesting contrasting models of democratic governance. Government *by* the people emphasizes the need, at some level, for the participation of citizens in the tasks of government. In the case of what are called direct, classical or radical democracy, popular participation is direct, unmediated and continuous, thus obliterating the distinction between the state and **civil society**. Government *for* the people, in contrast, implies that the essence of democracy is rule in the public interest. This notion is typically associated with the need for representatives to act on behalf of the people (using their allegedly superior knowledge and wisdom), with their right to rule deriving from success in a competitive struggle for the popular vote. This model of democracy is usually called **representative democracy**, and its most common form is liberal democracy.

The hybrid nature of liberal democracy reflects a basic ambivalence within liberalism towards democracy. In many ways, this is rooted in the competing implications of individualism, which both embodies a fear of collective power and leads to a belief in political equality. In the nineteenth century, liberals often saw democracy as threatening or dangerous. In this respect, they echoed the ideas of earlier political theorists, such as Plato and Aristotle, who viewed democracy as a system of rule by the masses at the expense of wisdom and property. The central liberal concern has been that democracy can become the enemy of individual liberty. This arises from the fact that 'the people' are not a single entity but rather a collection of individuals and groups, possessing different opinions and opposing interests. The 'democratic solution' to conflict is a recourse to numbers and the application of majority rule: the principle that the will of the majority or the greatest number should prevail over that of the minority. Democracy thus comes down to the rule of the 51 per cent, a prospect that the French politician and social commentator Alexis de Tocqueville (1805–59) famously described as 'the tyranny of the majority'. Individual liberty and minority rights can thus be crushed in the name of

Civil society: A realm of autonomous associations and groups, formed by private citizens and enjoying independence from the government; civil society includes businesses, clubs, families and so on.

Representative democracy: A limited and indirect form of democracy, in which people do not exercise power themselves, but merely select those who will rule on their behalf.

the people. James Madison articulated similar views at the Philadelphia Convention in 1787. Madison argued that the best defence against **majoritarianism** is a network of checks and balances that would make government responsive to competing minorities and safeguard the propertied few from the propertyless masses.

KEY FIGURE

Library of Congress Prints & Photographs Division/Unsplash

JAMES MADISON (1751–1836)

A US statesman and political theorist, Madison played a major role in writing the US Constitution and served as the fourth president of the USA (1809–17). Madison was a leading proponent of pluralism and divided government, urging the adoption of federalism, bicameralism and the separation of powers as the basis of US government. Madisonianism thus implies a strong emphasis on checks and balances as the principal means of resisting tyranny. His best-known political writings are his contributions to *The Federalist* (1787–8).

KEY CONCEPT
LIBERAL DEMOCRACY

A liberal democracy is a political regime in which a 'liberal' commitment to limited government is blended with a 'democratic' belief in popular rule. Its key features are: (1) the right to rule is gained through success in regular and competitive elections based on universal adult suffrage; (2) constraints on government imposed by a constitution, institutional checks and balances, and protections for individual rights; and (3) a vigorous civil society including a private enterprise economy, independent trade unions and a free press. While liberals view liberal democracy as being universally applicable, on the grounds that it allows for the expression of the widest possible range of views and beliefs, critics regard it as the political expression of either Western values or capitalist economic structures.

Liberals have expressed particular reservations about democracy, not merely because of the danger of majority rule, but also because of the make-up of the majority in modern, industrial societies. As far as J. S. Mill was concerned, for instance, political wisdom is unequally distributed and is largely related to education. The uneducated are more likely to act according to narrow class interests, whereas the educated are able to use their wisdom and experience for the good of others. He therefore insisted that elected politicians should speak for themselves rather than reflect the views of their electors, and he proposed a system of plural voting that would disenfranchise the illiterate and allocate one, two, three or four votes to people depending on their level of education or social position. Ortega y Gasset (1883–1955), the Spanish social thinker, expressed such fears more dramatically in *The Revolt of the Masses* ([1930] 1972). Gasset warned that the arrival of mass democracy had led to the overthrow of civilized society and the moral order, paving the way for authoritarian rulers to come to power by appealing to the basest instincts of the masses.

Majoritarianism: A belief in majority rule; majoritarianism implies either that the majority dominates the minority, or that the minority should defer to the judgement of the majority.

Consent: Assent or permission; in politics, usually an agreement to be governed or ruled.

By the twentieth century, however, a large proportion of liberals had come to see democracy as a virtue, though this was based on a number of arguments and doctrines. The earliest liberal justification for democracy was founded on **consent**, and the idea that citizens must have a means

PERSPECTIVES ON ... DEMOCRACY

LIBERALS understand democracy in individualist terms as consent expressed through the ballot box, democracy being equated with regular and competitive elections. While democracy constrains abuses of power, it must always be conducted within a constitutional framework to prevent majoritarian tyranny.

CONSERVATIVES endorse liberal-democratic rule but with qualifications about the need to protect property and traditional institutions from the untutored will of 'the many'. The New Right, however, has linked electoral democracy to the problems of over-government and economic stagnation.

SOCIALISTS traditionally endorsed a form of radical democracy based on popular participation and the desire to bring economic life under public control, dismissing liberal democracy as simply capitalist democracy. Nevertheless, modern social democrats are now firmly committed to liberal-democratic structures.

ANARCHISTS endorse direct democracy and call for continuous popular participation and radical decentralization. Electoral or representative democracy is merely a façade that attempts to conceal elite domination and reconcile the masses to their oppression.

FASCISTS embrace the ideas of totalitarian democracy, holding that a genuine democracy is an absolute dictatorship, as the leader monopolizes ideological wisdom and is alone able to articulate the 'true' interests of the people. Party and electoral competition are thus corrupt and degenerate.

POPULISTS have favoured an illiberal form of democracy. This involves a democratically elected government that routinely ignores constitutional limits on its power and deprives citizens of basic rights and freedoms, blurring the distinction between dictatorship and democracy.

ECOLOGISTS have often supported radical or participatory democracy. 'Dark' greens have developed a particular critique of electoral democracy that portrays it as a means of imposing the interests of the present generation of humans on (enfranchised) later generations, other species and nature as a whole.

of protecting themselves from the encroachment of government. In the seventeenth century, John Locke developed a theory of *protective* democracy by arguing that voting rights should be extended to the propertied, who could then defend their natural rights against government. If government, through taxation, possesses the power to expropriate property, citizens are entitled to protect themselves by controlling the composition of the tax-making body – the legislature. During the American Revolution, this idea was taken up in the slogan: 'No taxation without representation'. Utilitarian theorists such as Jeremy Bentham and James Mill developed the notion of democracy as a form of protection for the individual into a case for universal suffrage. Utilitarianism implies that individuals will vote to advance or defend their interests as they define them. Bentham came to believe that universal suffrage (conceived in his day as manhood suffrage) is the only way of promoting 'the greatest happiness for the greatest number'.

A more radical liberal endorsement of democracy is linked to the virtues of political participation. This has been associated with the ideas of J.-J. Rousseau, but received a liberal interpretation in the writings of J. S. Mill. In a sense, Mill encapsulates the ambivalence of the liberal attitude towards democracy. In its unrestrained form, democracy leads to tyranny, but, in the absence of democracy, ignorance and brutality will prevail. For Mill, the central virtue of democracy is that it promotes the 'highest and most harmonious' development of human capacities. By participating in political life, citizens enhance their understanding, strengthen their sensibilities and achieve a higher level of personal development. This form of *developmental* democracy holds democracy to be, primarily, an educational experience. As a result, while he rejected political equality, Mill believed that the franchise should be extended to all but those who are illiterate and, in the process, suggested (radically for his time) that suffrage should also be extended to women.

However, since the mid-twentieth century, liberal theories about democracy have tended to focus less on consent and participation and more on the need for **consensus** in society. This can be seen in the writings of pluralist theorists, who have argued that organized groups, not individuals, have become the primary political actors, and portrayed modern industrial societies as increasingly complex, characterized by competition between and among rival interests. From this point of view, the attraction of democracy is that it is the only system of rule capable of maintaining balance or equilibrium within complex and fluid modern societies. As *equilibrium* democracy gives competing groups a political voice, it binds them to the political system and so maintains political stability.

THE FUTURE OF LIBERALISM

Liberals have been ever optimistic about the future. Despite the recognition that the tides of change wax and wane, they believe that fundamental and irresistible forces draw history towards a determinant end-point, and that end-point is defined by the worldwide triumph of liberal values and structures. Liberalism, then, is not just another ideology; rather, it can be viewed as the end of ideology (as discussed in Chapter 1). Thus, although the claim that the fall of communism had precipitated the end of history in removing the final serious challenger to Western liberalism, this was quickly revealed as false; the mistake being that the declaration was not wrong-headed but simply premature. But where does the confidence that liberalism and history go hand in hand come from? In philosophical terms, it stems from **progressivism**, the belief that, step-by-step, the world always progresses, and this progress is inevitable. This process is driven, above all, by reason and the accumulation of knowledge, allowing each generation to progress beyond the last. In political terms, it reflects the assumption that liberalism brings benefits, particularly in relation to freedom and prosperity, which no other ideology can rival. While liberal democracy maximizes the sphere of civil liberty, protecting individuals both from the state and their fellow citizens, economic liberalism delivers remorseless growth and widening prosperity based on the use of the market to allocate scarce resources in the most efficient possible way.

Consensus: A broad agreement on fundamental principles that allows for disagreement on matters of emphasis or detail.

Progressivism: The belief that history is an inevitable march upwards into the light; a movement away from barbarism and towards civilization.

Yet the image of liberalism as an all-conquering force, its appeal increasingly extending beyond its Western homeland to become truly global, has also been challenged. Liberalism has been criticized from various directions. Marxists have argued that liberalism provides ideological protection for the capitalist mode of production, in both its national and global forms. By emphasizing the importance of foundational equality, liberalism serves to conceal, and thereby legitimize, a reality of unequal class power. Liberalism is thus the enemy of social justice. The principal target of criticism is nevertheless liberalism's defining value, individualism. Communitarians condemn liberalism for advancing a model of the self as asocial, atomized and 'unencumbered', which is not only grossly unrealistic but also fails to provide a moral basis for social order. Socialists claim that the emphasis within liberal individualism on self-interest and self-reliance weakens social responsibility and helps to perpetuate the myth that the distribution of wealth reflects the distribution of individual merit. Conservatives, especially traditional conservatives, argue that unrestrained individualism is destructive of the social fabric and produces a society of vulnerable and isolated individuals. Feminists, for their part, claim that individualism is invariably constructed on the basis of male norms which uphold gender inequality.

Finally, there are reasons for thinking that the future may belong not to liberalism but to **illiberalism**, especially as represented by authoritarianism. In a trend that dates back to the mid-1990s, authoritarian ideas and practices have advanced across much of the world. The most important and novel development underpinning this advance has been the ability of authoritarian regimes to compete with the economic performance of liberal democracies. Indeed, if current growth rates persist, by 2023 the share of global income held by countries that possess authoritarian political systems, such as China, Russia and Saudi Arabia, will surpass the share held by Western liberal democracies. Rising prosperity, in turn, has had profound implications for the political role of the middle class. Instead of acting as the traditional bastion of democracy, the educated middle class, benefiting from improved living standards, has often provided authoritarian regimes with crucial support. Thus, whereas the world's last two major encounters with illiberalism (associated, respectively, with fascism and communism) each ended with a resurgence of liberalism, the same may not happen in the case of 'new' authoritarianism.

Illiberalism: Opposition to or absence of liberalism; liberal democracies substitute authoritarian rule for constitutional rule.

QUESTIONS FOR DISCUSSION

- In what sense is liberalism linked to the Enlightenment project?
- Why do liberals reject unlimited freedom?
- How convincing is the liberal notion that human beings are reason-guided creatures?
- Which forms of equality do liberals support, and which do they reject?
- Why do liberals believe that power tends to corrupt, and how do they think it can be 'tamed'?
- How do classical liberals defend unregulated capitalism?

- How far are modern liberals willing to go in endorsing social and economic intervention?
- Do modern liberals have a coherent view of the state?
- To what extent is liberal constitutionalism compatible with democracy?
- Is liberal democracy the final solution to the problem of political organization?
- Is the decline of liberalism set to be an ongoing process?
- Are liberal principles universally valid?

◉ FURTHER READING

Charvet, J. *Liberalism: The Basics* (2018). An accessible introductory book with excellent discussions of what constitutes core liberal values and practices.

Fawcett, E. *Liberalism: The Life of an Idea*, 2nd edn (2018). A fluent and stimulating history of liberal thinking from the early nineteenth century to the present day.

Traub, J. *What Was Liberalism? The Past, Present, and Promise of a Noble Idea* (2019). An accessible overview of the history of liberalism as applied in politics, as well as a thought-provoking defence of its ongoing relevance to contemporary politics.

Wall, S. (ed.) *The Cambridge Companion to Liberalism* (2015). A compendium of leading scholars covering all aspects of liberalism including major variations and critiques.

Learn Liberty www.youtube.com/c/LearnLiberty. A YouTube channel that produces lectures and videos featuring leading scholars and thinkers speaking on a wide range of topics from a liberal perspective, particularly in relation to politics, philosophy and economics.

CHAPTER 3

CONSERVATISM

PREVIEW

In everyday language, the term 'conservative' has a variety of meanings. It can refer to moderate or cautious behaviour, a lifestyle that is conventional, even conformist, or a fear of, or refusal to accept, change, particularly denoted by the verb 'to conserve'. 'Conservatism' was first used in the early nineteenth century to describe a distinctive political position or ideology. In the USA, it implied a pessimistic view of public affairs. By the 1820s, the term was being used to denote opposition to the principles and spirit of the 1789 French Revolution, and the wider shift away from absolute monarchical rule. In the UK, the Tory faction in the House of Commons, and the principal opposition to the Whigs, gradually came to be known as 'Conservatives', the title being adopted as the party's official name in 1835.

As a political ideology, conservatism is defined by the desire to conserve, reflected in a resistance to, or at least a suspicion of, change. However, while the desire to resist change may be the recurrent theme within conservatism, what distinguishes conservatism from rival political creeds is the distinctive way in which this position is upheld, in particular through support for tradition, a belief in human imperfection, and the attempt to uphold the organic structure of society. Conservatism nevertheless encompasses a range of tendencies and inclinations. The chief distinction within conservatism is between what is called traditional conservatism and the New Right. Traditional conservatism defends established institutions and values on the ground that they safeguard the fragile 'fabric of society', giving security-seeking human beings a sense of stability and rootedness. The New Right is characterized by a belief in a strong but minimal state, combining economic libertarianism with social authoritarianism, as represented by neoliberalism and neoconservatism.

HISTORICAL OVERVIEW

Conservative ideas arose in reaction to the growing pace of political, social and economic change, which, in many ways, was symbolized by the French Revolution. One of the earliest, and perhaps the classic, statement of conservative principles is contained in Edmund Burke's *Reflections on the Revolution in France* ([1790] 1968), which deeply regretted the revolutionary challenge to the *ancien régime* that had occurred the previous year. During the nineteenth century, Western states were transformed by the pressures unleashed by industrialization and reflected in the growth of liberalism, socialism and nationalism. While these ideologies preached reform, and at times supported revolution, conservatism stood in defence of an increasingly embattled traditional social order.

KEY FIGURE

EDMUND BURKE (1729–97)

A Dublin-born British statesman and political theorist, Burke was the father of the Anglo-American conservative political tradition. In his major work, *Reflections on the Revolution in France* (1790), Burke deeply opposed the attempt to recast French politics in accordance with abstract principles such as 'the universal rights of man', arguing that wisdom resides largely in experience, tradition and history. Burke is associated with a pragmatic willingness to 'change in order to conserve', reflected, in his view, in the 'Glorious Revolution' of 1688.

Print Collector/Hulton Archive/Getty Images

Conservative thought varied considerably as it adapted itself to existing traditions and national cultures. UK conservatism, for instance, has drawn heavily on the ideas of Burke, who advocated not blind resistance to change, but rather a prudent willingness to 'change in order to conserve'. In the nineteenth century, UK conservatives defended a political and social order that had already undergone profound change, in particular the overthrow of the absolute monarchy, as a result of the English Revolution of the seventeenth century. Such pragmatic principles have also influenced the conservative parties established in other Commonwealth countries. For example, the Canadian Conservative Party used the title 'Progressive Conservative' between 1942 and 2003, precisely to distance itself from reactionary ideas. In continental Europe, where some autocratic monarchies persisted into the twentieth century, a very different and more authoritarian form of conservatism developed, one which defended monarchy and rigid autocratic values against the rising tide of reform. Only with the formation of **Christian democratic** parties after World War II did continental conservatives, notably in Germany and Italy, fully accept political democracy and social reform (see pp. 71–2 for further coverage of Christian democracy). The USA, on the other hand, was traditionally influenced relatively little by conservative ideas. The US system of government and its political culture reflect deeply established liberal and progressive values, and politicians of both major parties – the Republicans and the Democrats – have historically resented being labelled 'conservative'. It was only in 1964 that the USA was presented with an unequivocally conservative candidate for the presidency in the form of Barry Goldwater, who led a crusade against what his followers

Christian democracy: An ideological movement within European conservatism that is characterized by a commitment to the social market and qualified state intervention.

regarded as the establishment of the Republican Party's complicity with interventionist New Deal policies (Foley, 1991). The conservative takeover of the Republican Party was completed in the 1980s by Ronald Reagan, a protégé of Goldwater, and later consolidated by George W. Bush and Donald Trump, although Trump's conservatism was at best inconsistent, being more apparent on social issues such as abortion and immigration than on fiscal policy.

As conservative ideology arose in reaction to the French Revolution and the process of modernization in the West, it is less easy to identify political conservatism outside Europe and North America. In Africa, Asia and Latin America, political movements have developed that sought to resist change and preserve traditional ways of life, but they have seldom employed specifically conservative arguments and values. An exception to this is perhaps the Japanese Liberal Democratic Party (LDP), which has dominated politics in Japan since 1955. The LDP has close links with business interests and is committed to promoting a healthy private sector. At the same time, it has attempted to preserve traditional Japanese values and customs, and has therefore supported distinctively conservative principles such as loyalty, duty and **hierarchy**. Since the turn of the twenty-first century, forms of conservatism have emerged both within and beyond the West that have sought to blend the establishment of strong central authority under 'strongman' leaders with the mobilization of mass popular support on issues such as nationalism, economic progress and the defence of traditional values. Outside the West, examples of this have included Narendra Modi (see p. 262) in India, Recep Tayyip Erdogan in Turkey and Jair Bolsorano in Brazil. This form of conservative politics is associated with the wider phenomenon of right-wing populism, as discussed in Chapter 8.

Modern conservatism has undergone major changes since the 1970s, shaped by growing concerns about economic management and the welfare state. Particularly prominent in this respect were the Thatcher governments in the UK (1979–90) and the Reagan administration in the USA (1981–89), both of which practised an unusually radical and ideological brand of conservatism, commonly termed neoliberalism (see p. 63), which constituted one strain within what was once popularly called the New Right (see p. 62). Neoliberal ideas have drawn heavily on free-market economics and, in so doing, have exposed deep divisions within conservatism. Indeed, commentators argue that '**Thatcherism**' and 'Reaganism', and the neoliberal project in general, do not properly belong within conservative ideology at all, so deeply are they influenced by classical liberal economics. Neoliberals have challenged traditional conservative economic views, but they nevertheless remain part of conservative ideology. In the first place, they have not abandoned traditional conservative social principles such as a belief in order, authority and discipline, and in some respects they have strengthened them. Furthermore, neoliberal enthusiasm for the free market has exposed the extent to which conservatism had already been influenced by liberal ideas. From the late nineteenth century onwards, conservatism has been divided between paternalistic support for state intervention and a libertarian commitment to the free market. The significance of neoliberalism is that it sought to revive the electoral fortunes of conservatism by readjusting the balance between these traditions in favour of libertarianism (see p. 61).

Hierarchy: A pyramid-like ranked system of command and obedience, in which social position is unconnected with individual ability.

Thatcherism: The free-market/strong state ideological stance associated with Margaret Thatcher; the UK version of the New Right political project.

CORE THEMES

The character of conservative ideology has been the source of particular argument and debate. For example, it is often suggested that conservatives have a clearer understanding of what they oppose than of what they favour. In that sense, conservatism has been portrayed as a negative philosophy, its purpose being simply to preach resistance to, or at least suspicion of, change. However, if conservatism were to consist of no more than a knee-jerk defence of the *status quo*, it would be merely a political attitude rather than an ideology. In fact, many people or groups can be considered 'conservative', in the sense that they resist change, without in any way subscribing to a conservative political creed. For instance, socialists who campaign in defence of the welfare state or nationalized industries could be classified as conservative in terms of their actions, but certainly not in terms of their political principles. The desire to resist change may be the recurrent theme within conservatism, but what distinguishes conservatives from supporters of rival political creeds is the distinctive way they uphold this position.

A second problem is that to describe conservatism as an ideology is to risk irritating conservatives themselves. They have often preferred to describe their beliefs as an 'attitude of mind' or 'common sense', as opposed to an 'ism' or ideology. Others have argued that what is distinctive about conservatism is its emphasis on history and experience, and its distaste for rational thought. Conservatives have thus typically eschewed the 'politics of principle' (a reliance on ideals and abstract theory) and adopted instead a traditionalist political stance (see p. 7, for a discussion of the conservative view of ideology). Their opponents have also lighted upon this feature of conservatism, sometimes portraying it as little more than an unprincipled apology for the interests of a ruling class or elite. However, both conservatives and their critics ignore the weight and range of theories that underpin conservative 'common sense'. Conservatism is neither simple pragmatism (see p. 6) nor mere opportunism. It is founded on a particular set of political beliefs about human beings, the societies they live in, and the importance of a distinctive set of political values. As such, like liberalism and socialism, it should rightfully be described as an ideology. The most significant of its central beliefs are:

- tradition
- human imperfection
- society
- hierarchy and authority
- property.

Tradition

It is often argued that the 'desire to conserve' is the defining theme of conservative ideology, especially when it is linked to a defence of **tradition**. In its broadest sense, tradition encompasses anything that is passed down from the past to the present. Anything from long-standing customs and practices, to an institution, political or social system, or a value or set of beliefs, can therefore be regarded as a tradition. For some conservatives,

Tradition: Values, practices or institutions that have endured through time and, in particular, been passed down from one generation to the next.

the emphasis on tradition reflects their religious faith. If the world is thought to have been fashioned by God the Creator, traditional customs and practices in society will be regarded as 'God given'. Edmund Burke thus believed that society was shaped by 'the law of our Creator', or what he also called 'natural law'. If human beings tamper with the world, they are challenging the will of God, and as a result they are likely to make human affairs worse rather than better. Since the eighteenth century, however, it has become increasingly difficult to maintain that tradition reflects the will of God. As the pace of historical change accelerated, old traditions were replaced by new ones, and these new ones – for example, free elections and universal suffrage – were clearly seen to be man-made rather than in any sense 'God given'. Nevertheless, the religious objection to change has been kept alive by modern fundamentalists, particularly those who believe that God's wishes have been revealed to humankind through the literal truth of religious texts. Such ideas are discussed in Chapter 12.

Most conservatives, however, support tradition without needing to argue that it has divine origins. Burke, for example, described society as a partnership between 'those who are living, those who are dead and those who are to be born'. G. K. Chesterton (1874–1936), the UK novelist and essayist, expressed this idea as follows:

> Tradition means giving votes to the most obscure of all classes: our ancestors. It is a democracy of the dead. Tradition refuses to submit to the arrogant oligarchy of those who merely happen to be walking around. (Chesterton, 1908)

Tradition, in this sense, reflects the accumulated wisdom of the past. The institutions and practices of the past have been 'tested by time', and should therefore be preserved for the benefit of the living and for generations to come. This is the sense in which we should respect the actions – or 'votes' – of the dead, who will always outnumber the living. Such a notion of tradition reflects an almost Darwinian belief that those institutions and customs that have survived have only done so because they have worked and been found to be of value. They have been endorsed by a process of 'natural selection' and demonstrated their fitness to survive. Conservatives in the UK, for instance, argue that the institution of monarchy should be preserved because it embodies historical wisdom and experience. In particular, the crown has provided the UK with a focus of national loyalty and respect 'above' party politics; for conservatives, quite simply, it has worked.

Conservatives also venerate tradition because it generates a sense of identity for both society and the individual. Established customs and practices are ones that individuals can recognize; they are familiar and reassuring. Tradition thus provides people with a feeling of 'rootedness' and belonging, which is all the stronger because it is historically based. It generates social cohesion by linking people to the past and providing them with a collective sense of who they are. Change, on the other hand, is a journey into the unknown: it creates uncertainty and insecurity, and so endangers our happiness. Tradition therefore consists of rather more than political institutions that have stood the test of time. It encompasses all those customs and social practices that are familiar and generate security and belonging, ranging from the judiciary's insistence on wearing formal attire, and possibly traditional robes and wigs, to campaigns to preserve, for example, conventional styles of architecture.

Human imperfection

In many ways, conservatism is a 'philosophy of human imperfection' (O'Sullivan, 1976). Other ideologies assume that human beings are naturally 'good', or that they can be made 'good' if their social circumstances are improved. In their most extreme form, such beliefs are utopian and envisage the perfectibility of humankind in an ideal society. Conservatives dismiss these ideas as, at best, idealistic dreams, and argue instead that human beings are both imperfect and unperfectible.

Human imperfection is understood in several ways. In the first place, human beings are thought to be *psychologically* limited and dependent creatures. In the view of conservatives, people fear isolation and instability. They are drawn psychologically to the safe and the familiar, and, above all, seek the security of knowing 'their place'. Such a portrait of human nature is very different from the image of individuals as self-reliant, enterprising 'utility maximizers' proposed by early liberals. The belief that people desire security and belonging has led conservatives to emphasize the importance of social order, and to be suspicious of the attractions of liberty. Order ensures that human life is stable and predictable; it provides security in an uncertain world. Liberty, on the other hand, presents individuals with choices and can generate change and uncertainty. Conservatives have often echoed the views of Thomas Hobbes in being prepared to sacrifice liberty in the cause of social order.

Whereas other political philosophies trace the origins of immoral or criminal behaviour to society, conservatives believe it is rooted in the individual. Human beings are thought to be *morally* imperfect. Conservatives hold a pessimistic, even Hobbesian, view of human nature. Humankind is innately selfish and greedy, anything but perfectible; as Hobbes put it, the desire for 'power after power' is the primary human urge. Some conservatives explain this by reference to the Old Testament doctrine of 'original sin'. Crime is therefore not a product of inequality or social disadvantage, as socialists and modern liberals tend to believe; rather, it is a consequence of base human instincts and appetites. People can only be persuaded to behave in a civilized fashion if they are deterred from expressing their violent and anti-social impulses. And the only effective deterrent is law, backed up by the knowledge that it will be strictly enforced. This explains the conservative preference for strong government and for 'tough' criminal justice regimes, based, often, on long prison sentences and the use of corporal or even capital punishment. For conservatives, the role of law is not to uphold liberty, but to preserve order. The concepts of 'law' and 'order' are so closely related in the conservative mind that they have almost become a single, fused concept.

KEY FIGURE

THOMAS HOBBES (1588–1679)

An English political philosopher, Hobbes, in his classic work *Leviathan* (1651), used social contact theory to defend absolute government as the only alternative to anarchy and disorder, and proposed that citizens have an unqualified obligation towards their state. Though his view of human nature and his defence of authoritarian order have a conservative character, Hobbes' rationalist and individualist methodology prefigured early liberalism. His emphasis on power-seeking as the primary human urge has also been used to explain the behaviour of states in the international system.

Print Collector/Hulton Archive/Getty Images

Humankind's *intellectual* powers are also thought to be limited. Conservatives have traditionally believed that the world is simply too complicated for human reason to grasp fully. The political world, as Michael Oakeshott put it, is 'boundless and bottomless'. Conservatives are therefore suspicious of abstract ideas and systems of thought that claim to understand what is, they argue, simply incomprehensible. They prefer to ground their ideas in tradition, experience and history, adopting a cautious, moderate and above all pragmatic approach to the world, and avoiding, if at all possible, doctrinaire or dogmatic beliefs. High-sounding political principles such as the 'rights of man', 'equality' and 'social justice' are fraught with danger because they provide a blueprint for the reform or remodelling of the world. Reform and revolution, conservatives warn, often lead to greater suffering rather than less. For a conservative, to do nothing may be preferable to doing something, and a conservative will always wish to ensure, in Oakeshott's words, that 'the cure is not worse than the disease'. Nevertheless, conservative support for both traditionalism and pragmatism has weakened as a result of the rise of neoliberalism. In the first place, neoliberalism is radical, in that it has sought to advance free-market reforms by dismantling inherited welfarist and interventionist structures. Second, neoliberal radicalism is based on rationalism (see p. 26) and a commitment to abstract theories and principles, notably those associated with economic liberalism.

KEY FIGURE

History Collection 2016/Alamy Stock Photo

MICHAEL OAKESHOTT (1901–90)

A British political philosopher, Oakeshott advanced a powerful defence of a non-ideological style of politics that supported a cautious and piecemeal approach to change. Distrusting rationalism, he argued in favour of traditional values and established customs on the grounds that the conservative disposition is 'to prefer the familiar to the unknown, to prefer the tried to the untried, fact to mystery, the actual to the possible'. Oakeshott's best-known works include *Rationalism in Politics* (1962) and *On Human Conduct* (1975).

Organic society

Conservatives believe, as explained earlier, that human beings are dependent and security-seeking creatures. This implies that they do not, and cannot, exist outside society, but desperately need to belong, to have 'roots' in society. The individual cannot be separated from society, but is part of the social groups that nurture him or her: family, friends or peer group, workmates or colleagues, local community and even the nation. These groups provide individual life with security and meaning, a stance often called **social conservatism**. As a result, traditional conservatives are reluctant to understand freedom in 'negative' terms, in which the individual is 'left alone' and suffers, as the French sociologist Émile Durkheim (1856–1917) put it, from **anomie**. Freedom is, rather, a willing acceptance of social obligations and ties by individuals who recognize their value. Freedom involves 'doing one's duty'. When, for example, parents instruct children how to behave, they are not constraining their liberty, but providing guidance for their children's benefit. To act as a dutiful son

Social conservatism: The belief that society is fashioned out of a fragile network of relationships which need to be upheld through duty, traditional values and established institutions.

Anomie: A weakening of values and normative rules, associated with feelings of isolation, loneliness and meaninglessness.

PERSPECTIVES ON ... HUMAN NATURE

LIBERALS view human nature as a set of innate qualities intrinsic to the individual, placing little or no emphasis on social or historical conditioning. Humans are self-seeking and largely self-reliant creatures; but they are also governed by reason and are capable of personal development, particularly through education.

CONSERVATIVES believe that human beings are essentially limited and security-seeking creatures, drawn to the known, the familiar, the tried and tested. Human rationality is unreliable, and moral corruption is implicit in each human individual. Neoliberals nevertheless embrace a form of self-seeking individualism.

SOCIALISTS regard humans as essentially social creatures, their capacities and behaviour being shaped more by nurture than by nature, and particularly by creative labour. Their propensity for cooperation, sociability and rationality means that the prospects for personal growth and social development are considerable.

ANARCHISTS advance a complex theory of human nature in which rival potentialities co-exist within each person. While the human 'core' may be morally and intellectually enlightened, a capacity for corruption lurks within each and every individual.

FASCISTS believe that humans are ruled by the will and other non-rational drives, most particularly by a deep sense of social belonging focused on the nation or race. Although the masses are fitted only to serve and obey, elite members of the national community are capable of personal regeneration as 'new men' through dedication to the national or racial cause.

FEMINISTS usually hold that men and women share a common human nature, gender differences being culturally or socially imposed. Separatist feminists nevertheless argue that men are genetically disposed to domination and cruelty, while women are naturally sympathetic, creative and peaceful.

ECOLOGISTS, particularly deep ecologists, see human nature as part of the broader ecosystem, even as part of nature itself. Materialism, greed and egoism therefore reflect the extent to which humans have become alienated from the oneness of life and thus from their own true nature. Human fulfilment requires a return to nature.

or daughter and conform to parental wishes is to act freely, out of a recognition of one's obligations. Conservatives believe that a society in which individuals know only their rights, and do not acknowledge their duties, would be rootless and atomistic. Indeed, it is the bonds of duty and obligation that hold society together.

Such ideas are based on a very particular view of society, sometimes called **organicism**. Conservatives have traditionally thought of society as a living thing, an organism, whose parts work together just as the brain, heart, lungs and liver do within a human organism.

> **Organicism:** A belief that society operates like an organism or living entity, the whole being more than a collection of its individual parts.

Organisms differ from artefacts or machines in two important respects. First, unlike machines, organisms are not simply a collection of individual parts that can be arranged or rearranged at will. Within an organism, the whole is more than a collection of its individual parts; the whole is sustained by a fragile set of relationships between and among its parts, which, once damaged, can result in the organism's death. Thus, a human body cannot be stripped down and reassembled in the same way as, say, a bicycle. Second, organisms are shaped by 'natural' factors rather than human ingenuity. An organic society is fashioned, ultimately, by natural necessity. For example, the family has not been 'invented' by any social thinker or political theorist, but is a product of natural social impulses such as love, caring and responsibility. In no sense do children in a family agree to a 'contract' on joining the family – they simply grow up within it and are nurtured and guided by it. This inclination to see the family as an organic entity helps to explain, among other things, why many conservatives oppose same-sex marriage.

POLITICAL IDEOLOGIES IN ACTION . . .

SAME-SEX MARRIAGE

EVENTS: In 1989, Denmark became the first country in the world to legally recognize same-sex unions, after passing a bill legalizing 'registered partnerships'. Similar legislation recognizing 'civil unions' followed in Norway, Sweden, Iceland, the Netherlands, Belgium and France during the 1990s. In 2000, the Netherlands signed into law the first same-sex marriage law in the world. However, there was also a backlash against same-sex marriage, most particularly in the USA. In 2003, the Federal Marriage Amendment, which proposed to add language to the US Constitution stating that marriage should only occur between a man and a woman, was introduced to the House of Representatives, while 23 US states banned same-sex marriage between 2004 and 2006. By 2019, some 30 states and territories had enacted national laws allowing gays and lesbians to marry.

Hinterhaus Productions/Getty

SIGNIFICANCE: In a development that has been especially pronounced in the USA, same-sex marriage has been a prominent cultural 'wedge' issue, dividing liberals and conservatives, since the early 1990s. Conservatives have opposed same-sex marriage on a number of grounds. They have claimed, for example, that marriage is essentially a 'natural' – that is, biological – institution. As its defining purpose is to provide for the procreation of children, if procreation does not lie at its heart, marriage ceases to be virtuous and instead becomes selfish, even narcissistic. Furthermore, because conservatives take men and women to be 'equal but different', heterosexual unions are deemed to be more stable and 'balanced' than homosexual ones, husbands and wives, and fathers and mothers, tending to complement one

another. Finally, and most starkly, some religious conservatives declare that homosexuality is simply 'wrong' or 'evil', regardless of whether it takes place within the context of marriage.

However, the debate over same-sex marriage does not just take place between conservatives and liberals; it also divides conservatives themselves. Thus, although same-sex marriage was made legal in England and Wales in 2014 under a Conservative prime minister, David Cameron, many right-wing Conservative backbenchers were left feeling deeply aggrieved about this. At least three considerations have helped to reconcile conservatives to the idea of same-sex marriage. First, same-sex marriage has the advantage that it spreads the benefits of marriage – such as family cohesion and social stability – more widely across society. Second, if the objections to same-sex marriage are largely rooted in religious belief, this does not rule out secular marriages, or what are called 'civic unions' or 'domestic partnerships'. Third, neoliberal conservatives tend to view marriage as a contract made between two individuals, their gender being strictly irrelevant.

The use of the 'organic metaphor' for understanding society has some profoundly conservative implications. A mechanical view of society as adopted by liberals and most socialists, in which society is constructed by rational individuals for their own purposes, suggests that society can be tampered with and improved. This leads to a belief in progress, either in the shape of reform or revolution. If society is organic, its structures and institutions have been shaped by forces beyond human control and, possibly, human understanding. This implies that its delicate 'fabric' should be preserved and respected by the individuals who live within it. Organicism also shapes our attitude to particular institutions, society's 'parts'. These are viewed from a **functionalist** perspective: institutions develop and survive for a reason, and this reason is that they contribute to maintaining the larger social whole. In other words, by virtue of existing, institutions demonstrate they are worthwhile and desirable. Any attempt to reform or, worse, abolish an institution is thus fraught with dangers.

However, the rise of neoliberalism has weakened support within conservatism for organic ideas and theories. In line with the robust individualism (see p. 24) of classical liberalism, libertarian conservatives, including neoliberals, have held that society is a product of the actions of self-seeking and largely self-reliant individuals. This position was memorably expressed in Margaret Thatcher's assertion, paraphrasing Jeremy Bentham (see p. 33) that, 'There is no such thing as society, only individuals and their families'.

Hierarchy and authority

Conservatives have traditionally believed that society is naturally hierarchical, characterized by fixed or established social gradations. Social equality is therefore rejected as undesirable and unachievable; power, status and property are always unequally distributed. Conservatives agree with liberals in accepting natural inequality among individuals: some are born with talents and skills that are denied to others. For liberals, however, this leads to a belief in meritocracy, in which individuals rise or fall according to their abilities and willingness to work. Traditionally, conservatives have believed that inequality is more deep-rooted. Inequality is an inevitable feature of an organic society, not merely a consequence of individual differences. Pre-democratic conservatives such as Burke were, in this way, able to embrace the idea of a '**natural aristocracy**'. Just as the brain, the heart and the liver all perform very different functions within the body, the various classes and groups that make up society also have their own specific roles. There must be leaders and there must be followers; there must be managers and there must be workers; for that matter, there must be those who go out to work and those who stay at home and bring up children. Genuine social equality is therefore a myth; in reality, there is a natural inequality of wealth and social position, justified by a corresponding inequality of social responsibilities. The working class might not enjoy the same living standards and life chances as their employers, but, at the same time, they do not have the livelihoods and security of many other people resting on their shoulders. Hierarchy and organicism have thus invested in traditional conservatism a pronounced tendency towards paternalism (see p. 70).

The belief in hierarchy is strengthened by the emphasis conservatives place on **authority**. Conservatives do not accept the liberal belief that authority

Functionalism: The theory that social institutions and practices should be understood in terms of the functions they carry out in sustaining the larger social system.

Natural aristocracy: The idea that talent and leadership are innate or inbred qualities that cannot be acquired through effort or self-advancement.

Authority: The right to exert influence over others by virtue of an acknowledged obligation to obey.

PERSPECTIVES ON ... SOCIETY

LIBERALS regard society not as an entity in its own right but as a collection of individuals. To the extent that society exists, it is fashioned out of voluntary and contractual agreements made by self-interested human beings. Nevertheless, there is a general balance of interests in society that tends to promote harmony and equilibrium.

CONSERVATIVES believe that society should be viewed as an organism, a living entity. Society thus has an existence outside the individual, and in a sense is prior to the individual; it is held together by the bonds of tradition, authority and a common morality. Neoliberals nevertheless subscribe to a form of liberal atomism.

SOCIALISTS have traditionally understood society in terms of unequal class power, economic and property divisions being deeper and more genuine than any broader social bonds. Marxists believe that society is characterized by class struggle, and argue that the only stable and cohesive society is a classless one.

ANARCHISTS believe that society is characterized by unregulated and natural harmony, based on the natural human disposition towards cooperation and sociability. Social conflict and disharmony are thus clearly unnatural, a product of political rule and economic inequality.

NATIONALISTS view society in terms of cultural or ethnic distinctiveness. Society is thus characterized by shared values and beliefs, ultimately rooted in a common national identity. This implies that multinational or multicultural societies are inherently unstable.

FASCISTS regard society as a unified organic whole, implying that individual existence is meaningless unless it is dedicated to the common good rather than the private good. Nevertheless, membership of society is restricted on national or racial grounds.

FEMINISTS have understood society in terms of patriarchy and an artificial division between the 'public' and 'private' spheres of life. Society may therefore be seen as an organized hypocrisy designed to routinize and uphold a system of male power.

MULTICULTURALISTS view society as a mosaic of cultural groups, defined by their distinctive ethnic, religious or historical identities. The basis for wider social bonds, cutting across cultural distinctiveness, is thus restricted, perhaps, to civic allegiance.

arises out of contracts made by free individuals. In liberal theory, authority is thought to be established by individuals for their own benefit. In contrast, conservatives believe that authority, like society, develops naturally. In this case, it arises from the need to ensure that children are cared for, kept away from danger, have a healthy diet, go to bed at sensible times and so on. Such authority can only be imposed 'from above', quite simply because children do not know what is good for them. It does not and cannot arise 'from below': in no sense can children be said to have agreed to be governed. Authority is therefore rooted in the nature of society and all social institutions. In schools, authority should be exercised by the teacher; in the workplace, by the employer; and in society at large, by government. Conservatives believe that authority is necessary and beneficial as people need the guidance, support and security that comes from knowing 'where they stand' and what is expected of them. Authority thus counters rootlessness and anomie.

This has led conservatives to place special emphasis on leadership and discipline. Leadership is a vital ingredient in any society because it is the capacity to give direction and provide inspiration for others. Discipline is not just mindless obedience but a willing and healthy respect for authority. Authoritarian conservatives go further and portray authority as absolute and unquestionable. Most conservatives, however, believe that authority should be exercised within limits and that these limits are imposed not by an artificial contract but by the natural responsibilities that authority entails. Parents should have authority over their children, but this does not imply the right to treat them in any way they choose. The authority of a parent is intrinsically linked to the obligation to nurture, guide and, if necessary, punish their children. Thus it does not empower a parent to abuse a child or, for instance, sell the child into slavery.

Property

Property is an asset that possesses a deep and, at times, almost mystical significance for conservatives. Liberals believe that property reflects merit: those who work hard and possess talent will, and should, acquire wealth. Property, therefore, is 'earned'. This doctrine has an attraction for those conservatives who regard the ability to accumulate wealth as an important economic incentive. Nevertheless, conservatives also hold that property has a range of psychological and social advantages. For example, it provides security. In an uncertain and unpredictable world, property ownership gives people a sense of confidence and assurance, something to 'fall back on'. Property, whether the ownership of a house or savings in the bank, provides individuals with a source of protection. Conservatives therefore believe that thrift – caution in the management of money – is a virtue in itself and have sought to encourage private savings and investment in property. Property ownership also promotes a range of important social values. Those who possess and enjoy their own property are more likely to respect the property of others. They will also be aware that property must be safeguarded from disorder and lawlessness. Property owners therefore have a 'stake' in society; they have an interest, in particular, in maintaining law and order. In this sense, property ownership can promote what can be thought of as the 'conservative' values of respect for law, authority and social order.

However, a deeper and more personal reason why conservatives support property ownership is that it can be regarded as an extension of an individual's personality. People 'realize' themselves, even see themselves, in what they own. Possessions are not merely external objects, valued because they are useful – a house to keep us warm and dry, a car to provide transport and so on – but also reflect something of the owner's personality and character. This is why, conservatives point out, burglary is a particularly unpleasant crime: its victims suffer not only the loss of, or damage to, their possessions, but also the sense that they have been personally violated. A home is the most personal and intimate of possessions, it is decorated and organized according to the tastes and needs of its owner and therefore reflects his or her personality. The proposal of traditional socialists that property should be 'socialized', owned in common rather than by private individuals, thus strikes conservatives as particularly appalling because it threatens to create a soulless and depersonalized society.

Conservatives, however, have seldom been prepared to go as far as classical liberals in believing that individuals have an *absolute* right to use their property however they may choose. While libertarian conservatives, and therefore the neoliberals, support an essentially liberal view of property, conservatives have traditionally argued that all rights, including property rights, entail obligations. Property is not

Property: The ownership of physical goods or wealth, whether by private individuals, groups of people or the state.

an issue for the individual alone, but is also of importance to society. This can be seen, for example, in the social bonds that cut across generations. Property is not merely the creation of the present generation. Much of it – land, houses, works of art – has been passed down from earlier generations. The present generation is, in that sense, the custodian of the wealth of the nation and has a duty to preserve and protect it for the benefit of future generations. Harold Macmillan, the UK Conservative prime minister from 1957 to 1963, expressed just such a position in the 1980s when he objected to the Thatcher government's policy of **privatization**, describing it as 'selling off the family silver'.

TYPES OF CONSERVATISM

The chief sub-traditions within conservatism are as follows:

- libertarian conservatism
- authoritarian conservatism
- paternalistic conservatism
- Christian democracy.

Libertarian conservatism

Although conservatism draws heavily on pre-industrial ideas such as organicism, hierarchy and obligation, the ideology has also been much influenced by liberal ideas, especially classical liberal ideas. This is sometimes seen as a late twentieth-century development, neoliberals having in some way 'hijacked' conservatism in the interests of classical liberalism. Nevertheless, liberal doctrines, especially those concerning the free market, have been advanced by conservatives since the late eighteenth century, and can be said to constitute a rival tradition to conservative paternalism. These ideas are libertarian in that they advocate the greatest possible economic liberty and the least possible government regulation of social life. Libertarian conservatives have not simply converted to liberalism, but believe that liberal economics is compatible with a more traditional, conservative social philosophy, based on values such as authority and duty. This is evident in the work of Edmund Burke, in many ways the founder of traditional conservatism, but also a keen supporter of the **economic liberalism** of Adam Smith (see p. 34).

> **Privatization:** The transfer of state assets from the public to the private sector, reflecting a contraction of the state's responsibilities.
>
> **Economic liberalism:** A belief in the market as a self-regulating mechanism that tends naturally to deliver general prosperity and opportunities for all.

KEY CONCEPT

LIBERTARIANISM

Libertarianism refers to a range of theories that give strict priority to liberty (understood in negative terms) over other values, such as authority, tradition and equality. Libertarians thus seek to maximize the realm of individual freedom and minimize the scope of public authority, typically seeing the state as the principal threat to liberty. The two best-known libertarian traditions are rooted in the idea of individual rights (as with Robert Nozick, see p. 65) and in *laissez-faire* economic doctrines (as with Friedrich von Hayek, see p. 64), although socialists have also embraced libertarianism. Libertarianism is sometimes distinguished from liberalism on the grounds that the latter, even in its classical form, refuses to give priority to liberty over order. However, it differs from anarchism in that libertarians generally recognize the need for a minimal state, sometimes styling themselves as 'minarchists'.

Libertarian conservatives are not, however, consistent liberals. They believe in economic individualism and 'getting government off the back of business', but are less prepared to extend this principle of individual liberty to other aspects of social life. Conservatives, even libertarian conservatives, have a more pessimistic view of human nature. A strong state is required to maintain public order and ensure that authority is respected. Indeed, in some respects libertarian conservatives are attracted to free-market theories precisely because they promise to secure social order. Whereas liberals have believed that the market economy preserves individual liberty and freedom of choice, conservatives have at times been attracted to the market as an instrument of social discipline. Market forces regulate and control economic and social activity. For example, they may deter workers from pushing for wage increases by threatening them with unemployment. As such, the market can be seen as an instrument that maintains social stability and works alongside the more evident forces of coercion: the police and the courts. While some conservatives have feared that market capitalism will lead to endless innovation and restless competition, upsetting social cohesion, others have been attracted to it in the belief that it can establish a 'market order', sustained by impersonal 'natural laws' rather than the guiding hand of political authority. Nevertheless, the relationship between conservatism and economic libertarianism deepened further as a result of the emergence of neoliberalism.

Neoliberalism

During the early post-1945 period, pragmatic and paternalistic ideas dominated conservatism through much of the Western world. The remnants of authoritarian conservatism collapsed with the overthrow of the Portuguese and Spanish dictatorships in the 1970s. Just as conservatives had come to accept political democracy during the nineteenth century, after 1945 they came to accept a qualified form of social democracy. This tendency was confirmed by the rapid and sustained economic growth of the postwar years, the 'long boom', which appeared to bear out the success of 'managed capitalism'. During the 1970s, however, a set of more radical, market-based, ideas developed within conservatism, challenging directly the Keynesian-welfarist orthodoxy. These neoliberal or liberal New Right ideas had their greatest initial impact in the USA and the UK, but they also came to be influential in parts of continental Europe, Australia and New Zealand, and had an effect on Western states across the globe. (In the USA, this market-based set of economic ideas is commonly called 'neoconservatism', a term that has a quite different meaning elsewhere, as discussed later in the chapter.)

Neoliberal thinking is drawn from classical rather than modern liberalism. It amounts to a restatement of the case for a minimal state. This has been summed up as 'private, good;

KEY CONCEPT
NEW RIGHT

The New Right is a marriage between two apparently contrasting ideological traditions. The first of these is classical liberal economics, particularly the free-market theories that were revived in the second half of the twentieth century as a critique of 'big' government and economic and social intervention. This is called the liberal New Right, or neoliberalism. The second element in the New Right is traditional conservative – and notably pre-Disraelian – social theory, especially its defence of order, authority and discipline. This is called the conservative New Right, or neoconservatism (see p. 67). The ideological coherence within the New Right stems from its defence of a strong but minimal state: although it seeks to 'roll back' the state in the economic sphere, it aims to strengthen it in the social sphere.

public, bad'. Neoliberalism is anti-statist. The state is regarded as a realm of coercion and unfreedom: collectivism restricts individual initiative and saps self-respect. Government, however benignly disposed, invariably has a damaging effect on human affairs. Instead, faith is placed in the individual and the market. Individuals should be encouraged to be self-reliant and to make rational choices in their own interests. The market is respected as a mechanism through which the sum of individual choices will lead to progress and general benefit. As such, neoliberalism has attempted to establish the dominance of libertarian ideas over paternalistic ones within conservative ideology.

KEY CONCEPT

NEOLIBERALISM

Neoliberalism (sometimes called 'neoclassical liberalism') is widely seen as an updated version of classical liberalism, particularly classical political economy. Its central theme is that the economy works best when left alone by government, reflecting a belief in free market economics and atomistic individualism. While unregulated market capitalism delivers efficiency, growth and widespread prosperity, the 'dead hand' of the state saps initiative and discourages enterprise. In short, the neoliberal philosophy is: 'market: good; state: bad'. Key neoliberal policies include privatization, spending cuts (especially in social welfare), tax cuts (particularly corporate and direct taxes) and deregulation. Neoliberalism is often equated with a belief in market fundamentalism; that is, an absolute faith in the capacity of the market mechanism to solve all economic and social problems.

The dominant theme within this anti-statist doctrine is an ideological commitment to the free market, particularly as revived in the work of economists such as Ayn Rand, Friedrich von Hayek (see p. 64) and Milton Friedman (1912–2006). In her essays and popular novels, Rand advanced a moral justification for private enterprise, proclaiming herself to be a 'radical for capitalism'. Influenced in particular by Friedrich Nietzsche's (see p. 154) concept of the 'over-man' or superman, Rand was a vigorous defender of the virtues of selfishness, sometimes seen as 'ethical egoism', seeing the central purpose of life as a quest for excellence, achieved by the exercise of rational self-interest. While selfishness allows people to exist in order to advance their life's project by striving to be outstanding (wealth being the key measure of success in this respect), selflessness represents failure, a squandering of one's chances of excellence.

KEY FIGURE

Oscar White/Corbis
Historical/Getty Images

AYN RAND (1905–82)

A Russian-born writer and philosopher who emigrated to the USA when she was 21, Rand (Alice Rosenbaum) became a Hollywood screenwriter before developing a career as an essayist and novelist. Her philosophy of 'objectivism', which claimed to show people as they are (that is, as rationally self-interested creatures), rather than as we may like them to be, gave unabashed support to selfishness and condemned altruism. Rand defended pure, *laissez-faire* capitalism on the grounds that it both guarantees freedom and, by establishing untrammelled competition, provides for the emergence of the elites needed to govern society. Rand's most influential works were her best-selling novels, *The Fountainhead* ([1943] 2007) and *Atlas Shrugged* (1947), the latter being a portrait of a dystopian USA.

Neoliberal thinking nevertheless gained its greatest impetus from the revival of interest in free-market economic theories. Free-market ideas gained renewed credibility during the 1970s as governments experienced increasing difficulty in delivering economic stability and sustained growth. Doubts consequently developed about whether it was in the power of government at all to solve economic problems. Hayek and Friedman, for example, challenged the very idea of a 'managed' or 'planned' economy. They argued that the task of allocating resources in a complex, industrialized economy was simply too difficult for any set of state bureaucrats to achieve successfully. The virtue of the market, on the other hand, is that it acts as the central nervous system of the economy, reconciling the supply of goods and services with the demand for them. It allocates resources to their most profitable use and thereby ensures that consumer needs are satisfied. In the light of the re-emergence of unemployment and inflation in the 1970s, Hayek and Friedman argued that government was invariably the cause of economic problems, rather than the cure.

KEY FIGURE

Hulton Archive/Hulton Archive/
Getty Images

FRIEDRICH VON HAYEK (1899–1992)

An Austrian economist and political philosopher, Hayek was a firm believer in individualism and market order, and an implacable critic of socialism. His pioneering work, *The Road to Serfdom* (1944) developed a then deeply unfashionable defence of *laissez-faire* and attacked economic intervention as implicitly totalitarian. In later works, such as *The Constitution of Liberty* (1960) and *Law, Legislation and Liberty* (1979), Hayek supported a modified form of traditionalism and upheld an Anglo-American version of constitutionalism that emphasized limited government.

The ideas of Keynesianism were one of the chief targets of neoliberal criticism. Keynes had argued that capitalist economies were not self-regulating. He placed particular emphasis on the 'demand side' of the economy, believing that the levels of economic activity and employment were dictated by the level of 'aggregate demand' in the economy. Milton Friedman, on the other hand, argued that there is a 'natural rate of unemployment', which is beyond the ability of government to influence. He also argued that attempts to eradicate unemployment by applying Keynesian techniques merely cause other, more damaging, economic problems, notably **inflation**. Inflation, neoliberals believe, threatens the entire basis of a market economy because, in reducing faith in money, the means of exchange, it discourages people from undertaking commercial or economic activity. However, Keynesianism had, in effect, encouraged governments to 'print money', albeit in a well-meaning attempt to create jobs. The free-market solution to inflation is to control the supply of money by cutting public spending, a policy practised by both the Reagan and the Thatcher administrations during the 1980s. Both administrations also allowed unemployment to rise sharply, in the belief that only the market could solve the problem.

Neoliberalism is also opposed to the mixed economy and public ownership, and practises so-called 'supply-side economics'. Starting under Thatcher in the UK in the 1980s but later extending to many other Western states, and most aggressively pursued in postcommunist states in the 1990s, a policy of privatization has effectively dismantled both mixed and collectivized economies by transferring industries from public to private ownership. Nationalized industries were criticized for being inherently inefficient, because, unlike private firms and industries, they are not disciplined by the profit motive. Neoliberalism's emphasis

Inflation: A rise in the general price level, leading to a decline in the value of money.

on the supply side of the economy was reflected in the belief that governments should foster growth by providing conditions that encourage producers to produce, rather than consumers to consume. The main block to the creation of an entrepreneurial, supply-side culture is high taxes. Taxes, in this view, discourage enterprise and infringe property rights, a stance sometimes called '**fiscal conservatism**'.

Neoliberalism is not only anti-statist on the grounds of economic efficiency and responsiveness, but also because of its political principles, notably its commitment to individual liberty. Neoliberals claim to be defending freedom against 'creeping collectivism'. At the extreme, these ideas lead in the direction of anarcho-capitalism (discussed in Chapter 5) and the belief that all goods and services, including the courts and public order, should be delivered by the market. The freedom defended by neoliberals is negative freedom: the removal of external restrictions on the individual. As the collective power of government is seen as the principal threat to the individual, freedom can only be ensured by 'rolling back' the state. This, in particular, means rolling back social welfare. In addition to economic arguments against welfare – for example, that increased social expenditure pushes up taxes, and that public services are inherently inefficient – neoliberals object to welfare on moral grounds. In the first place, the welfare state is criticized for having created a 'culture of dependency': it saps initiative and enterprise, and robs people of dignity and self-respect. Welfare is thus the *cause* of disadvantage, not its cure. Such a theory resurrects the notion of the 'undeserving poor'. Charles Murray (1984) also argued that, as welfare relieves women of dependency on 'breadwinning' men, it is a major cause of family breakdown, creating an underclass largely composed of single mothers and fatherless children. A further neoliberal argument against welfare is based on a commitment to individual rights. Robert Nozick (1974) advanced this most forcefully in condemning all policies of welfare and redistribution as a violation of property rights. In this view, so long as property has been acquired justly, to transfer it, without consent, from one person to another amounts to 'legalized theft'. Underpinning this view is egoistical individualism, the idea that people owe nothing to society and are, in turn, owed nothing by society, a stance that calls the very notion of society into question.

> **Fiscal conservatism:** A political-economic stance that prioritizes the lowering of taxes, cuts in public spending and reduced government debt.

KEY FIGURE

ROBERT NOZICK (1938–2002)

A US political philosopher, Nozick developed a form of rights-based libertarianism in response to the ideas of John Rawls (see p. 39). Drawing on Locke (see p. 29) and nineteenth-century US individualists, he argued that property rights should be strictly upheld, provided that property was justly purchased or justly transferred from one person to another. His major work, *Anarchy, State and Utopia* (1974), rejects welfare and redistribution, and advances the case for minimal government and minimal taxation. In later life, Nozick modified his extreme libertarianism.

Martha Holmes/The LIFE Images Collection/Getty Images

Authoritarian conservatism

Whereas all conservatives would claim to respect the concept of authority, few modern conservatives would accept that their views are authoritarian. Nevertheless, while contemporary conservatives are keen to demonstrate their commitment to democratic, particularly liberal-democratic, principles, there is a tradition within conservatism that has favoured authoritarian rule, especially in continental Europe. At the time of the French Revolution, the principal defender of autocratic rule was the French political thinker Joseph de Maistre (1753–1821). De Maistre was a fierce critic of the French Revolution, but, in contrast to Burke, he wished to restore absolute power to the hereditary monarchy. He was a reactionary and was quite unprepared to accept any reform of the *ancien régime*, which had been overthrown in 1789. His political philosophy was based on willing and complete subordination to 'the master'. In *Du Pape* ([1817] 1971) de Maistre went further and argued that above the earthly monarchies a supreme spiritual power should rule in the person of the pope. His central concern was the preservation of order, which alone, he believed, could provide people with safety and security. Revolution, and even reform, would weaken the chains that bind people together and lead to a descent into chaos and oppression.

KEY CONCEPT

AUTHORITARIANISM

Authoritarianism is belief in or the practice of government 'from above', in which authority is exercised over a population with or without its consent. Authoritarianism thus differs from authority. The latter rests on legitimacy, and in that sense arises 'from below'. Authoritarian thinkers typically base their views on either a belief in the wisdom of established leaders or the idea that social order can only be maintained by unquestioning obedience. However, authoritarianism is usually distinguished from totalitarianism (see p. 159). The practice of government 'from above', which is associated with monarchical absolutism, traditional dictatorships and most forms of military rule, is concerned with the repression of opposition and political liberty, rather than the more radical goal of obliterating the distinction between the state and civil society.

Throughout the nineteenth century, conservatives in continental Europe remained faithful to the rigid and hierarchical values of autocratic rule, and stood unbending in the face of rising liberal, nationalist and socialist protest. Nowhere was authoritarianism more entrenched than in Russia, where Tsar Nicholas I (1825–55) proclaimed the principles of 'orthodoxy, autocracy and nationality', in contrast to the values that had inspired the French Revolution: 'liberty, equality and fraternity'. Nicholas' successors stubbornly refused to allow their power to be constrained by constitutions or the development of parliamentary institutions. In Germany, constitutional government did develop, but Otto von Bismarck, the imperial chancellor, 1871–90, ensured that it remained a sham. Elsewhere, authoritarianism remained particularly strong in Catholic countries. The papacy suffered not only the loss of its temporal authority with the achievement of Italian unification, which led Pope Pius IX to declare himself a 'prisoner of the Vatican', but also an assault on its doctrines with the rise of secular political ideologies. In 1864, Pius IX condemned all radical or progressive ideas, including those of nationalism, liberalism and socialism, as 'false doctrines of our most unhappy age', and when confronted with the loss of the papal states and Rome, he proclaimed in 1870 the edict of papal infallibility. The unwillingness of continental conservatives to come to terms with reform and democratic government extended well into the twentieth century. For instance, conservative elites in Italy and Germany helped to overthrow parliamentary democracy and bring Benito Mussolini (see p. 156) and Adolf Hitler (see p. 149) to power by providing support for, and giving respectability to, rising fascist movements. More recent manifestations of the link between social conservatism and authoritarianism have tended to be associated with neoconservatism.

Neoconservatism

Neoconservatism emerged in the USA in the 1970s as a backlash against the ideas and values of the 1960s. It was defined by a fear of social fragmentation or breakdown, which was seen as a product of liberal reform and the spread of '**permissiveness**'. In sharp contrast to neoliberalism, neoconservatives stress the primacy of politics and seek to strengthen leadership and authority in society. This emphasis on authority, allied to a heightened sensitivity to the fragility of society, demonstrates that neoconservatism has its roots in traditional or organic conservatism. However, it differs markedly from paternalistic conservatism, which also draws heavily on organic ideas. Whereas paternalistic conservatives believe, for instance, that community is best maintained by social reform and the reduction of poverty, neoconservatives look to strengthen community by restoring authority and imposing social discipline. Neoconservative authoritarianism is, to this extent, consistent with neoliberal libertarianism. Both of them accept the rolling back of the state's economic responsibilities.

Permissiveness: The willingness to allow people to make their own moral choices; permissiveness suggests that there are no authoritative values.

KEY CONCEPT

NEOCONSERVATISM

Neoconservatism refers to developments within conservative ideology that relate to both domestic policy and foreign policy. In domestic policy, neoconservatism is defined by support for a minimal but strong state, fusing themes associated with traditional or organic conservatism with an acceptance of economic individualism and qualified support for the free market. Neoconservatives have typically sought to restore public order, strengthen 'family' or 'religious' values, and bolster national identity. In foreign policy, neoconservatism was closely associated with the Bush administration in the USA in the years following 9/11. Its central aim was to preserve and reinforce what was seen as the USA's 'benevolent global hegemony' by building up US military power and pursuing a policy of worldwide 'democracy promotion'.

TENSIONS WITHIN ... CONSERVATISM (1) ⟷

Neoliberalism	v.	Neoconservatism
classical liberalism	⟷	traditional conservatism
atomism	⟷	organicism
radicalism	⟷	traditionalism
libertarianism	⟷	authoritarianism
economic dynamism	⟷	social order
self-interest/enterprise	⟷	traditional values
equality of opportunity	⟷	natural hierarchy
minimal state	⟷	strong state
internationalism	⟷	insular nationalism
pro-globalization	⟷	anti-globalization

Neoconservatives have developed distinctive views about both domestic policy and foreign policy. The two principal domestic concerns of neoconservatism have been with social order and public morality. Neoconservatives believe that rising crime, delinquency and anti-social behaviour are generally a consequence of a larger decline of authority that has affected most Western societies since the 1960s. They have therefore called for a strengthening of social disciplines and authority at every level. This can be seen in relation to the family. For neoconservatives, the family is an authority system: it is both naturally hierarchical – children should listen to, respect and obey their parents – and naturally patriarchal. The husband is the provider and the wife the home-maker. This social authoritarianism is matched by state authoritarianism, the desire for a strong state reflected in a 'tough' stance on law and order. This led, in the USA and the UK in particular, to a greater emphasis on custodial sentences and to longer prison sentences, reflecting the belief that 'prison works'.

Neoconservatism's concern about public morality is based on a desire to reassert the moral foundations of politics. A particular target of neoconservative criticism has been the 'permissive 1960s' and the growing culture of 'doing your own thing'. In the face of this, Thatcher in the UK proclaimed her support for 'Victorian values', and in the USA organizations such as the Moral Majority campaigned for a return to 'traditional' or 'family' values. Neoconservatives see two dangers in a permissive society. In the first place, the freedom to choose one's own morals or lifestyle could lead to the choice of immoral or 'evil' views. There is, for instance, a significant religious element in neoconservatism, especially in the USA. The second danger is not so much that people may adopt the *wrong* morals or lifestyles, but may simply choose *different* moral positions. In the neoconservative view, moral pluralism is threatening because it undermines the cohesion of society. A permissive society is a society that lacks ethical norms and unifying moral standards. It is a 'pathless desert', which provides neither guidance nor support for individuals and their families. If individuals merely do as they please, civilized standards of behaviour will be impossible to maintain.

The issue that links the domestic and foreign policy aspects of neoconservative thinking is a concern about the nation and the desire to strengthen national identity in the face of threats from within and without. The value of the nation, from the neoconservative perspective, is that it binds society together, giving it a common culture and civic identity, which is all the stronger for being rooted in history and tradition. National patriotism (see p. 125) thus strengthens people's political will. The most significant threat to the nation 'from within' is the growth of multiculturalism, which weakens the bonds of nationhood by threatening political community and creating the spectre of ethnic and racial conflict. Neoconservatives have therefore often been in the forefront of campaigns for stronger controls on immigration and, sometimes, for a privileged status to be granted to the 'host' community's culture. Such concerns have widened and deepened as a result of the advance of globalization. The threats to the nation 'from without' are many and various. In the UK, the main perceived threat came from the process of European integration. Indeed, in a process that commenced in the 1980s under Thatcher and culminated in withdrawal from the EU (Brexit) in 2020, UK conservatism was increasingly defined by '**Euroscepticism**'. Since the turn of the twenty-first century, however, neoconservatism has been associated more and more clearly with right-wing populism. (See Chapter 8 for a discussion of the rise and implications of right-wing populism.)

Euroscepticism: Hostility to European integration based on the belief that it is a threat to national sovereignty and/or national identity.

Paternalistic conservatism

While continental conservatives adopted an attitude of uncompromising resistance to change, a more flexible and ultimately more successful Anglo-American tradition can be traced back to Edmund Burke. The lesson that Burke drew from the French Revolution was that change can be natural and inevitable, in which case it should not be resisted. 'A state without the means of some change,' he suggested, 'is without the means of its conservation' (Burke [1790] 1968). The characteristic style of Burkean conservatism is cautious, modest and pragmatic; it reflects a suspicion of fixed principles, whether revolutionary or reactionary. As Ian Gilmour (1978) put it, 'the wise Conservative travels light'. The values that conservatives hold most dear – tradition, order, authority, property and so on – will be safe only if policy is developed in the light of practical circumstances and experience. Such a position will rarely justify dramatic or radical change, but accepts a prudent willingness to 'change in order to conserve'. Pragmatic conservatives support neither the individual nor the state in principle, but are prepared to support either, or, more frequently, recommend a balance between the two, depending on 'what works'. In practice, the reforming impulse in conservatism has also been associated closely with the survival into the modern period of neo-feudal paternalistic values, as represented in particular by One Nation conservatism.

One Nation conservatism

The Anglo-American paternalistic tradition is often traced back to Benjamin Disraeli (1804–81), UK prime minister in 1868 and again 1874–80. Disraeli developed his political philosophy in two novels, *Sybil* (1845) and *Coningsby* (1844), written before he assumed ministerial responsibilities. These novels emphasized the principle of social obligation, in stark contrast to the extreme individualism then dominant within the political establishment. Disraeli wrote against a background of growing industrialization, economic inequality and, in continental Europe at least, revolutionary upheaval. He tried to draw attention to the danger of Britain being divided into 'two nations: the Rich and the Poor'. In the best conservative tradition, Disraeli's argument was based on a combination of prudence and principle.

On the one hand, growing social inequality contains the seeds of revolution. A poor and oppressed working class, Disraeli feared, would not simply accept its misery. The revolutions that had broken out in Europe in 1830 and 1848 seemed to bear out this belief. Reform would therefore be sensible, because, in stemming the tide of revolution, it would ultimately be in the interests of the rich. On the other hand, Disraeli appealed to moral values. He suggested that wealth and privilege brought with them social obligations, in particular a responsibility for the poor or less well-off. In so doing, Disraeli drew on the organic conservative belief that society is held together by an acceptance of duty and obligations. He believed that society is naturally hierarchical, but also held that inequalities of wealth or social privilege give rise to an inequality of responsibilities. The wealthy and powerful must shoulder the burden of social responsibility, which, in effect, is the price of privilege.

These ideas were based on the feudal principle of *noblesse oblige*, the obligation of the aristocracy to be honourable and generous. For example, the landed nobility claimed to exercise a paternal responsibility for their peasants, as the king did in relation to the nation. Disraeli recommended that these obligations should not be abandoned, but should be expressed, in an increasingly industrialized world, in social reform. Such ideas came to be represented by the slogan 'One Nation'. In office, Disraeli was responsible both for the Second Reform Act of 1867, which for the first time extended the right to vote to the working class, and for the social reforms that improved housing conditions and hygiene.

Disraeli's ideas had a considerable impact on conservatism and contributed to a radical and reforming tradition that appeals both to the pragmatic instincts of conservatives and to their sense of social duty. In the UK, these ideas provide the basis of so-called 'One Nation conservatism', whose supporters sometimes style themselves as 'Tories' to denote their commitment to pre-industrial, hierarchic and paternal values. Disraeli's ideas were subsequently taken up in the late nineteenth century by Randolph Churchill in the form of 'Tory democracy'. In an age of widening political democracy, Churchill stressed the need for traditional institutions – for example, the monarchy, the House of Lords and the church – to enjoy a wider base of social support. This could be achieved by winning working-class votes for the Conservative Party by continuing Disraeli's policy of social reform. One Nation conservatism can thus be seen as a form of Tory welfarism.

KEY CONCEPT
PATERNALISM

Paternalism literally means to act in a fatherly fashion. As a political principle, it refers to power or authority being exercised over others with the intention of conferring benefit or preventing harm. Social welfare and laws such as the compulsory wearing of seat belts in cars are examples of paternalism. 'Soft' paternalism is characterized by broad consent on the part of those subject to paternalism. 'Hard' paternalism operates regardless of consent, and thus overlaps with authoritarianism. The basis for paternalism is that wisdom and experience are unequally distributed in society; and those in authority 'know best'. Opponents argue that authority is not to be trusted and that paternalism restricts liberty and contributes to the 'infantilization' of society.

TENSIONS WITHIN ... CONSERVATISM (2) ↔

Paternalistic conservatism	v.	Libertarian conservatism
pragmatism	↔	principle
traditionalism	↔	radicalism
social duty	↔	egoism
organic society	↔	atomistic individualism
hierarchy	↔	meritocracy
social responsibility	↔	individual responsibility
natural order	↔	market order
'middle way' economics	↔	laissez-faire economics
qualified welfarism	↔	anti-welfarism

The high point of the One Nation tradition was reached in the 1950s and 1960s, when conservative parties in the UK and elsewhere came into line with socialist and left-liberal parties in practising a version of Keynesian social democracy. This involved embracing economic management and the goal of full employment, as well as supporting enlarged welfare provision. This stance was based on the need for a non-ideological, 'middle way' between the extremes of *laissez-faire* liberalism and socialist state planning. Conservatism was therefore the way of moderation, and sought to draw a balance between rampant individualism and overbearing collectivism (see p. 80). In the UK, this idea was most clearly expressed in Harold Macmillan's *The Middle Way* ([1938] 1966). Macmillan, who was to be prime minister from 1957 to 1963, advocated what he called 'planned capitalism', which he described as 'a mixed system which combines state ownership, regulation or control of certain aspects of economic activity with the drive and initiative of private enterprise'.

Such ideas resurfaced more recently – in the USA under George W. Bush, in the UK under David Cameron and in New Zealand under John Key – in the notion of 'compassionate conservatism', even though it may, in practice, have served as little more than a rhetorical device. It is, nevertheless, important to remember that paternalist conservatism provides only a qualified basis for social and economic intervention. The purpose of One Nationism, for instance, is to consolidate hierarchy rather than to remove it, the wish to improve the conditions of the less well-off being motivated to a significant degree by the desire to ensure that the poor no longer pose a threat to the established order.

KEY CONCEPT

TORYISM

'Tory' was used in eighteenth-century Britain to refer to a parliamentary faction that (as opposed to the Whigs) supported monarchical power and the Church of England, and represented the landed gentry; in the USA, it implied loyalty to the British crown. Although in the mid-nineteenth century the British Conservative Party emerged out of the Tories, and in the UK 'Tory' is still widely (but unhelpfully) used as a synonym for Conservative, Toryism is best understood as a distinctive ideological stance within broader conservatism. Its characteristic features are a belief in hierarchy, tradition, duty and organicism. While 'high' Toryism articulates a neo-feudal belief in a ruling class and a pre-democratic faith in established institutions, the Tory tradition is also hospitable to welfarist and reformist ideas, provided these serve the cause of social continuity.

Christian democracy

Christian democracy is a political and ideological movement which has been prominent in Western and central Europe and, to a lesser extent, Latin America. Although it is often classified as a progressive, if doctrinally imprecise, form of conservatism, Christian democracy has also been portrayed as a species of liberal-conservatism and as an ideology in its own right. In the aftermath of World War II, Christian democratic parties emerged in Belgium, the Netherlands, Austria, Germany and Italy, the most significant ones being the Christian Democratic Union/Christian Social Union in then-West Germany and, until its effective collapse in 1993, the Christian Democratic Party in Italy. Christian democratic thinking has nevertheless had a wider impact, affecting centre-right parties in France, the Benelux countries, much of Scandinavia and parts of postcommunist Europe which are not 'confessional' parties or formally aligned to the Christian democratic movement. This certainly applies in the case of the European People's Party (EPP), the major centre-right group in the European Parliament and the Parliament's largest political group since 1999. In Latin America, significant Christian democratic parties have developed in countries such as Chile, Venezuela, Ecuador, Guatemala and El Salvador.

However, the ideological origins of Christian democracy can be traced back to well before 1945 and the break between continental European conservatism and authoritarianism in the early post-fascist period. Christian democratic thinking gradually took shape during the nineteenth century as the Catholic Church attempted to come to terms with the ramifications of industrialization and, in particular, the emergence of liberal capitalism. Indeed, in some respects, this process originated with the French Revolution and the explicit challenge that it posed to Church authority. The Catholic Church came, over time, to accept democratic political forms and to evince growing concern about the threats posed by unrestrained capitalism. The Centre party (*Zentrum*) in Germany, founded in 1870, was thus set up to defend the interests of the Catholic Church but also campaigned for a strengthening welfare provision. Pope Leo XIII's encyclical *Rerum Novarum* (1891) underlined the Vatican's openness to new thinking, in that it lamented the material suffering of the working class and emphasized the reciprocal duties of labour and capital.

Such developments are often seen to have been based on a distinctively Catholic social theory. In this view, as Protestantism is associated with the idea of spiritual salvation through individual effort, its social theory typically endorses individualism and extols the value of hard work, competition and personal responsibility. The 'Protestant ethic' has thus sometimes been treated as a form of capitalist ideology (Weber, [1904–5] 2011). Catholic social theory, by contrast, focuses on the social group rather than the individual, and has stressed balance or organic harmony rather than competition. In the writings of the French philosopher and political thinker Jacques Maritain (1884–1973), the leading figure in the attempt to develop an ideology of Christian democracy, this was expressed through the notion of 'integral humanism' (Maritain, [1936] 1996). Integral humanism underlines the role of cooperation in the achievement of shared practical goals, and thereby implies that unrestrained capitalism fails to serve the 'common good'.

The social market

Although Christian democracy is typically critical of *laissez-faire* capitalism, it certainly does not reject capitalism altogether. Rather, it advocates a 'third way' between market capitalism and socialism, often termed social capitalism. As such, clear parallels exist between Christian democracy and the neo-revisionist tradition within social democracy, examined in Chapter 4. The idea of social capitalism draws more heavily on the flexible and pragmatic ideas of economists such as Friedrich List (1789–1846) than on the strict market principles of classical political economy, as formulated by Adam Smith and David Ricardo (1772–1823). A leading advocate of the *Zollverein* (the German customs union), List emphasized the economic importance of politics and political power, arguing, for instance, that state intervention should be used to protect infant industries from the rigours of foreign competition. The central theme in this model is the idea of a **social market**; that is, an attempt to marry the disciplines of market competition with the need for social cohesion and solidarity. The market is thus viewed not as an end in itself but rather as a means of generating wealth in order to achieve broader social ends.

Social market: An economy that is structured by market principles and is relatively free from state interference, but which operates alongside comprehensive welfare provision and effective social services.

THE FUTURE OF CONSERVATISM

On the face of it, it is odd to discuss the future of an ideology that, through its wary scepticism of change and veneration of tradition, appears to be more closely associated with the past than the future. Surely one of the key implications of conservative traditionalism is that it means that conservative ideology is permanently outdated, its quest to remain relevant in the context of an ever-changing present being doomed to failure? Conservatism therefore seems to be trapped in an endless game of ideological catch-up. This can be seen in the difficulties that many conservative parties have encountered in coming to terms with issues such as gender equality, same-sex marriage, trans rights and minority rights, with the implication that they have sometimes struggled to attract support from voters who are young, female, gay, transgender or from ethnic minority backgrounds. And yet, it is abundantly clear that conservatism's attachment to the past has failed to consign it to the ideological fringe, still less threaten its survival. Indeed, a concern to ensure continuity with the past may be one of the sources of conservatism's remarkable ideological resilience. 'Traditional' values may be more compelling and enjoy greater substance than ones that, by contrast, appear merely fashionable, something that may be even more the case as the pace of change accelerates. For an ideology that is looking to secure its future, there may thus be many worse things to be than 'outdated'.

The claim that conservatism is destined to remain a major ideological force is most commonly linked to the relationship between conservatism and pragmatism. Unlike rationalist ideologies such as liberalism and socialism, conservatism is unwilling to be tied down to a fixed system of ideas. The most intellectually modest of political ideologies, conservatism enjoys an unusual degree of flexibility, allowing conservative thinking to adapt to new and challenging historical circumstances. This chameleon-like capacity for ideological reinvention has been demonstrated throughout its history. For instance, during the nineteenth century the UK Conservative Party (then the Tory Party), initially aligned to the interests of the landed gentry, responded to the pressures generated by industrialization by taking up the cause of social welfare, becoming more socially progressive than the Liberal Party of the day. Further examples include the swift conversion of the UK Conservative Party after 1945 to the central principles of social democracy, and its equally quick repudiation of postwar social democracy under Thatcher in the 1980s. However, this latter development arguably had wider implications for the future of UK conservatism. Not only did Thatcher's neoliberal revolution bring about a radical shift in economic priorities in the UK, but it also witnessed the switch to a markedly more ideological style of policy-making. In so doing, it may have entrenched free-market principles more deeply than ever before within the party, narrowing the scope for future pragmatic adjustments. This, nevertheless, did not stop the Conservative government under Boris Johnson from pushing up spending and borrowing in 2020 to levels that were unprecedented in the UK in peacetime, as it attempted to stimulate economic recovery in the context of the Covid-19 pandemic.

Although conservatism seems destined to remain a political ideology of major significance, it is less clear what form of conservatism will predominate in the future. In particular, it is possible to envisage two, sharply different conservative futures. In the first, conservatism is defined by its close alignment with 'accelerated' globalization. This form of conservatism is primarily concerned with economic issues and places a priority on the principles of individualism and market. Libertarian and anti-statist tendencies within conservatism therefore flourish at the expense of paternalistic ones. This neoliberal conservatism came to prominence in the final decades of the twentieth century. It gained impetus from the fact that conservative parties were often able to respond more quickly and more successfully to globalizing tendencies than their socialist and liberal counterparts, in part because they were less deeply wedded to Keynesian-welfarist orthodoxies. The second possible conservative future nevertheless emerged from the turn of the twenty-first century onwards, precipitated by the rise of right-wing populism and by the impact this often had on mainstream conservatism. Instead of operating hand in hand with globalism, this form of conservatism is decidedly anti-globalist in character. Defined by its alignment with illiberal nationalism, this form of conservatism places a particular emphasis on opposing immigration and rejecting multiculturalism, and, in some cases, introducing economic protectionism.

QUESTIONS FOR DISCUSSION

- Why, and to what extent, have conservatives supported tradition?
- Is conservatism a 'disposition' rather than a political ideology?
- Why has conservatism been described as a philosophy of imperfection?
- What are the implications of the belief that society is an organic entity?
- How does the conservative view of property differ from the liberal view?
- How far do conservatives go in endorsing authority?

- Is conservatism merely ruling class ideology?
- To what extent do conservatives favour pragmatism over principle?
- What are the similarities and differences between traditional conservatism and Christian democracy?
- How and why have neoliberals criticized welfare?
- To what extent are neoliberalism and neoconservatism compatible?
- What form of conservatism is most likely to predominate in the future?

FURTHER READING

Fawcett, E. *Conservatism: The Fight for a Tradition* (2020). A comprehensive history of conservative thought from the nineteenth century to the present.

Muller, J. (ed.) *Conservatism: An Anthology of Social and Political Thought from David Hume to the Present* (1997). The best general reader of traditional conservative political writings.

Scruton, R. *Conservatism: An Invitation to the Great Tradition* (2018). An erudite exploration of the development of conservative thought and an even-handed defence of traditional conservatism in the modern political discourse.

Sedgewick, M. *Key Thinkers of the Radical Right: Behind the New Threat to Liberal Democracy* (2019). A timely anthology exploring the intellectual foundations of far-right and alt-right conservative ideology that has gained increasing prominence in twenty-first-century politics.

The Hoover Institute www.hoover.org. The Hoover Institution is a leading conservative think tank, and is a prolific producer of media from a traditional conservative perspective. Especially notable is its interview series, Uncommon Knowledge, and its policy primer channel, PolicyEd.

CHAPTER 4

SOCIALISM

PREVIEW

The term 'socialist' derives from the Latin *sociare*, meaning to combine or to share. Its earliest known usage was in 1827 in the UK, in an issue of the *Co-operative Magazine*. By the early 1830s, the followers of Robert Owen in the UK and Henri de Saint-Simon in France had started to refer to their beliefs as 'socialism' and, by the 1840s, the term was familiar in a range of industrialized countries, notably France, Belgium and the German states.

Socialism, as an ideology, has traditionally been defined by its opposition to capitalism and the attempt to provide a more humane and socially worthwhile alternative. At the core of socialism is a vision of human beings as social creatures united by their common humanity. This highlights the degree to which individual identity is fashioned by social interaction and the membership of social groups and collective bodies. Socialists therefore prefer cooperation to competition. The central, and some would say defining, value of socialism is equality, especially social equality. Socialists believe that social equality is the essential guarantee of social stability and cohesion, and that it promotes freedom, in the sense that it satisfies material needs and provides the basis for personal development. Socialism, however, contains a bewildering variety of divisions and rival traditions. These divisions have been about both 'means' (how socialism should be achieved) and 'ends' (the nature of the future socialist society). For example, communists or Marxists traditionally supported revolution and sought to abolish capitalism through the creation of a classless society based on the common ownership of wealth. In contrast, social democrats have embraced gradualism and aimed to reform or 'humanize' the capitalist system through a narrowing of material inequalities and the abolition of poverty. During much of the twentieth century, the socialist movement was thus divided into two rival camps. Both forms of socialism, however, experienced crises in the late twentieth century, the most dramatic of which involved the collapse of orthodox communism.

HISTORICAL OVERVIEW

Although socialists have sometimes claimed an intellectual heritage that goes back to Plato's *Republic* or Thomas More's *Utopia* ([1516] 1965), as with liberalism and conservatism, the origins of socialism lie in the nineteenth century. Socialism arose as a reaction against the social and economic conditions generated in Europe by the growth of industrial capitalism (see p. 77). Socialist ideas were quickly linked to the development of a new but growing class of industrial workers, who suffered the poverty and degradation that are so often features of early industrialization. Although socialism and liberalism have common roots in the Enlightenment, and share a faith in principles such as reason and progress, socialism emerged as a critique of liberal market society and was defined by its attempt to offer an alternative to industrial capitalism.

The character of early socialism was influenced by the harsh and often inhuman conditions in which the industrial working class lived and worked. Wages were typically low, child and female labour were commonplace, the working day often lasted up to twelve hours and the threat of unemployment was ever present. In addition, the new working class was disorientated, being largely composed of first-generation urban dwellers, unfamiliar with the conditions of industrial life and work, and possessing few of the social institutions that could give their lives stability or meaning. As a result, early socialists often sought a radical, even revolutionary alternative to industrial capitalism. For instance, Charles Fourier (1772–1837) in France and Robert Owen (see p. 80) in the UK subscribed to **utopianism** in founding experimental communities based on sharing and cooperation. The Germans Karl Marx and Friedrich Engels (1820–95) developed more complex and systematic theories, which claimed to uncover the 'laws of history' and proclaimed that the revolutionary overthrow of capitalism was inevitable.

KEY FIGURE

Bettmann/Getty Images

KARL MARX (1818–83)

A German philosopher, economist and life-long revolutionary, Marx is usually portrayed as the father of twentieth-century communism. The centrepiece of Marx's thought is a 'scientific' critique of capitalism that highlights, in keeping with previous class society, systemic inequality and therefore fundamental instability. Marx's materialist theory of history holds that social development will inevitably culminate in the establishment of a classless communist society. His vast works include the *Communist Manifesto* (1848) (written with Friedrich Engels (1820–95)) and the three-volume *Capital* (1867, 1885 and 1894).

In the late nineteenth century, the character of socialism was transformed by a gradual improvement in working-class living conditions and the advance of political democracy. The growth of trade unions, working-class political parties and sports and social clubs served to provide greater economic security and to integrate the working class into industrial society. In the advanced industrial societies of Western Europe, it became increasingly difficult to continue to see the working class as a revolutionary force. Socialist political parties progressively adopted legal and constitutional tactics, encouraged by the gradual extension of the vote to working-class men. By World War I, the socialist world was clearly divided between those socialist parties that had sought power through the ballot box and preached reform, and those that proclaimed a continuing need for revolution. The Russian Revolution of

Utopianism: A belief in the unlimited possibilities of human development, typically embodied in the vision of a perfect or ideal society, a utopia (see p. 110).

1917 entrenched this split: revolutionary socialists, following the example of V. I. Lenin (see p. 91) and the Bolsheviks, usually adopted the term '**communism**', while reformist socialists described their ideas as either 'socialism' or '**social democracy**'.

KEY CONCEPT
CAPITALISM

Capitalism is an economic system as well as a form of property ownership. It has a number of key features. First, it is based on generalized commodity production, a 'commodity' being a good or service produced for exchange – it has market value rather than use value. Second, productive wealth in a capitalist economy is predominantly held in private hands. Third, economic life is organized according to impersonal market forces, in particular the forces of demand (what consumers are willing and able to consume) and supply (what producers are willing and able to produce). Fourth, in a capitalist economy, material self-interest and maximization provide the main motivations for enterprise and hard work. Some degree of state regulation is nevertheless found in all capitalist systems.

The twentieth century witnessed the spread of socialism across Eastern Europe and into parts of Africa, Asia and Latin America. Eastern Europe was incorporated into the Soviet bloc through the westward expansion of the Red Army in the final phase of World War II, a process that was consolidated by the formation of the Warsaw Pact in 1949. Socialism in African, Asian and Latin American countries often developed out of the post-1945 anticolonial struggle, rather than a class struggle. The idea of class exploitation was replaced by that of colonial oppression, creating a potent fusion of socialism and nationalism, which is examined more fully in Chapter 5. The Chinese Communist Party, under the leadership of Mao Zedong, seized power in 1949 through the Chinese Communist Revolution, with communism subsequently spreading to North Korea, Vietnam, Cambodia and elsewhere. More moderate forms of socialism were practised elsewhere in the developing world; for example, by the Congress Party in India. Distinctive forms of African and Arab socialism also developed, being influenced respectively by the communal values of traditional tribal life and the moral principles of Islam. In Latin America in the 1960s and 1970s, socialist revolutionaries waged war against military dictatorships, often seen to be operating in the interests of US imperialism.

Communism: The principle of the common ownership of wealth, or a system of comprehensive collectivization; communism is often viewed as 'Marxism in practice' (see p. 87).

Social democracy: A moderate or reformist brand of socialism that favours a balance between the market and the state, rather than the abolition of capitalism (see p. 95).

KEY FIGURE

Bettmann/Getty Images

MAO ZEDONG (MAO TSE-TUNG) (1893–1976)

A Chinese Marxist theorist and leader of the People's Republic of China, 1949–76. Mao helped to found the Chinese Communist Party and, in 1935, became its leader. As a political theorist, Mao adapted Marxism-Leninism to the needs of an overwhelmingly agricultural and still traditional society. His legacy is often associated with the Cultural Revolution (1966–70), a radical egalitarian movement that denounced elitism and 'capitalist roaders' (those inclined to bow to pressure from bourgeois forces), and that resulted in widespread social disruption, repression and death.

During the late twentieth century, socialism suffered a number of major setbacks. The most dramatic of these was the collapse of communism in Eastern Europe through a series of largely peaceful revolutions that culminated in the fall of the Berlin Wall in November

1989. By the end of 1991, the Soviet Union had collapsed and elsewhere, notably in China, a process of economic reform had been initiated. Significant developments also took place within Western social democracy. Confronted by both the end of the post-1945 economic boom, which had helped to sustain the politics of redistribution, and the shrinking size of the working class, socialist parties in many parts of the world went into ideological retreat during the 1980s and 1990s. In countries such as the UK, Germany, Netherlands, Australia and New Zealand, this meant reaching an accommodation with globalization and accepting a wider role for the market in economic affairs.

Nevertheless, the early twenty-first century brought indications of a revival of socialism. This was evident in, among other things, Jeremy Corbyn's surprise victory in the UK Labour Party's 2015 leadership election, the impact of Bernie Sanders on the race to become the Democratic Party nominee in the 2016 and 2020 US presidential elections, and the emergence of left-wing populist movements such as Syriza in Greece and Podemos in Spain. Two explanations have been advanced for these developments. In the first, they have been a backlash against the politics of **austerity**, which was widely adopted as economies fell into recession and tax revenues plummeted in the aftermath of the 2007–09 global financial crisis. In the second, far-left parties and movements have tapped in to a growing mood of anti-establishment radicalism, sometimes called 'anti-politics' (see p. 171), that stems, in part, from a narrowing of the ideological divide between left- and right-wing parties.

CORE THEMES

One of the difficulties of analysing socialism is that the term has been understood in at least three distinctive ways. From one point of view, socialism is seen as an economic model, usually linked to some form of collectivization and planning. Socialism, in this sense, stands as an alternative to capitalism, the choice between these two qualitatively different productive systems traditionally being seen as the most crucial of all economic questions. However, the choice between 'pure' socialism and 'pure' capitalism was always an illusion, as all economic forms have, in different ways, blended features of both systems. Indeed, modern socialists tend to view socialism not so much as an alternative to capitalism, but as a means of harnessing capitalism to broader social ends. The second approach treats socialism as an instrument of the labour movement. Socialism, in this view, represents the interests of the working class and offers a programme through which the workers can acquire political or economic power. Socialism is thus really a form of **'labourism'**, a vehicle for advancing the interest of organized labour. From this perspective, the significance of socialism fluctuates with the fortunes of the working-class movement worldwide. Nevertheless, though the historical link between socialism and organized labour cannot be doubted, socialist ideas have also been associated with artisans, the peasantry and, for that matter, with political and bureaucratic elites. That is why, in this book, socialism is understood in a third and broader sense as a political creed or ideology, characterized by a particular cluster of ideas, values and theories. The most significant of these are:

Austerity: Sternness or severity; as an economic strategy, austerity refers to public spending cuts designed to eradicate a budget deficit, underpinned by faith in market forces.

Labourism: A tendency exhibited by socialist parties to serve the interests of the organized labour movement rather than pursue broader ideological goals.

- community

- cooperation

- equality
- class politics
- common ownership.

Community

At its heart, socialism offers a unifying vision of human beings as social creatures, capable of overcoming social and economic problems by drawing on the power of the community rather than simply individual effort. This is a collectivist vision because it stresses the capacity of human beings for collective action, their willingness and ability to pursue goals by working together, as opposed to striving for personal self-interest. Most socialists, for instance, would be prepared to echo the words of the English metaphysical poet, John Donne (1571–1631):

> No man is an Island entire of itself;
> every man is a piece of the Continent, a part of the main...
> any man's death diminishes me, because I am involved in Mankind; and therefore
> never send to know for whom the bell tolls;
> it tolls for thee.

Human beings are therefore 'comrades', 'brothers' or 'sisters', tied to one another by the bonds of a common humanity. This is expressed in the principle of **fraternity**.

Socialists are far less willing than either liberals or conservatives to assume that human nature is unchanging and fixed at birth. Rather, they believe that human nature is malleable or 'plastic', shaped by the experiences and circumstances of social life. In the long-standing philosophical debate about whether 'nurture' or 'nature' determines human behaviour, socialists side resolutely with nurture. From birth – perhaps even while in the womb – each individual is subjected to experiences that mould and condition his or her personality. All human skills and attributes are learned from society, from the fact that we stand upright to the language we speak. Whereas liberals draw a clear distinction between the 'individual' and 'society', socialists believe that the individual is inseparable from society. Human beings are neither self-sufficient nor self-contained; to think of them as separate or atomized 'individuals' is absurd. Individuals can only be understood, and understand themselves, through the social groups to which they belong. The behaviour of human beings therefore tells us more about the society in which they live and have been brought up, than it does about any abiding or immutable human nature.

The radical edge of socialism derives not from its concern with what people are like, but with what they have the capacity to become. This has led socialists to develop utopian visions of a better society, in which human beings can achieve genuine emancipation and fulfilment as members of a community. African and Asian socialists have often stressed that their traditional, pre-industrial societies already emphasize the importance of social life and the value of community. In these circumstances, socialism has sought to preserve traditional social values in the face of the challenge from Western individualism (see p. 24). As Julius Nyerere, president of Tanzania 1964–85, pointed out, 'We, in Africa, have no more real need to be "converted" to socialism, than we have of being "taught" democracy.' He therefore described his own views as 'tribal socialism'.

Fraternity: Literally, brotherhood; bonds of sympathy and comradeship between and among human beings.

KEY CONCEPT

COLLECTIVISM

Collectivism is, broadly, the belief that collective human endeavour is of greater practical and moral value than individual self-striving. It thus reflects the idea that human nature has a social core, and implies that social groups, whether 'classes', 'nations', 'races' or whatever, are meaningful political entities. However, the term is used with little consistency.

Mikhail Bakunin (see p. 111) and other anarchists used collectivism to refer to self-governing associations of free individuals. Others have treated collectivism as strictly the opposite of individualism (see p. 24), holding that it implies that collective interests should prevail over individual ones. It is also sometimes linked to the state as the mechanism through which collective interests are upheld, suggesting that the growth of state responsibilities marks the advance of collectivism.

In the West, however, the social dimension of life has had to be 'reclaimed' after generations of industrial capitalism. This was the goal of nineteenth-century utopian socialists such as Charles Fourier and Robert Owen, who organized experiments in communal living. Fourier encouraged the founding of model communities, each containing about 1,800 members, which he called 'phalansteries'. Owen also set up a number of experimental communities, the best known being New Harmony in Indiana, 1824–9. The most enduring communitarian experiment has been the *kibbutz* system in Israel, which consists of a system of cooperative, usually rural, settlements that are collectively owned and run by their members. However, the communitarian emphasis of the *kibbutz* system has been substantially diluted since the 1960s by, for instance, the abandonment of collective child rearing.

KEY FIGURE

ROBERT OWEN (1771–1858)

A British socialist, industrialist and pioneer of the cooperative movement, Owen's *A New View of Society* (1816) envisaged a transformation in human nature consequent on a change in its environment, suggesting that progress requires the construction of a 'rational system of society'. Owen advanced a moral indictment of market capitalism, which he proposed should be replaced with a society based on small-scale cooperative communities in which property would be communally owned and essential goods freely distributed.

Photo 12/Universal Images Group/Getty Images

Cooperation

If human beings are social animals, socialists believe that the natural relationship among them is one of **cooperation** rather than competition. Socialists believe that competition pits one individual against another, encouraging each of them to deny or ignore their social nature rather than embrace it. As a result, competition fosters only a limited range of social attributes and, instead, promotes selfishness and aggression. Cooperation, on the other hand, makes moral and economic sense. Individuals who work together rather than against each other develop bonds of sympathy, caring and affection. Furthermore, the energies of the community rather than those of the single individual can be harnessed. Peter Kropotkin (see p. 113),

Cooperation: Working together; collective effort intended to achieve mutual benefit.

for example, suggested that the principal reason why the human species had survived and prospered was because of its capacity for 'mutual aid'.

Socialists believe that human beings can be motivated by moral incentives, and not merely by material incentives. In theory, capitalism rewards individuals for the work they do: the harder they work, or the more abundant their skills, the greater their rewards will be. The moral incentive to work hard, however, is the desire to contribute to the common good, which develops out of a sympathy, or sense of responsibility, for fellow human beings, especially those in need. While few modern social democrats would contemplate the outright abolition of material incentives, they nevertheless insist on the need for a balance of some kind between material and moral incentives. For instance, socialists would argue that an important incentive for achieving economic growth is that it helps to finance the provision of welfare support for the poorest and most vulnerable elements in society.

The socialist commitment to cooperation has stimulated the growth of cooperative enterprises, designed to replace the competitive and hierarchic businesses that have proliferated under capitalism. Both producers' and consumers' cooperatives have attempted to harness the energies of groups of people working for mutual benefit. In the UK, cooperative societies sprang up in the early nineteenth century. These societies bought goods in bulk and sold them cheaply to their working-class members. The 'Rochdale Pioneers' set up a grocery shop in 1844 and their example was soon taken up throughout industrial England and Scotland. Producer cooperatives, owned and run by their workforce, are common in parts of northern Spain and the former Yugoslavia, where industry is organized according to the principle of workers' self-management. Collective farms in the Soviet Union were also designed to be cooperative and self-managing, though in practice they operated within a rigid planning system and were usually controlled by local party bosses.

Equality

A commitment to equality is in many respects the defining feature of socialist ideology, equality being the political value that most clearly distinguishes socialism from its rivals, notably liberalism and conservatism. Socialist **egalitarianism** is characterized by a belief in social equality, or equality of outcome. Socialists have advanced at least three arguments in favour of this form of equality. First, social equality upholds *justice* or fairness. Socialists are reluctant to explain the inequality of wealth simply in terms of innate differences of ability among individuals. Socialists believe that just as capitalism has fostered competitive and selfish behaviour, human inequality very largely reflects the unequal structure of society. They do not hold the naive belief that all people are born identical, possessing precisely the same capacities and skills. An egalitarian society would not, for instance, be one in which all students gained the same mark in their mathematics examinations. Nevertheless, socialists believe that the most significant forms of human inequality are a result of unequal treatment by society, rather than unequal endowment by nature. Justice, from a socialist perspective, therefore demands that people are treated equally (or at least more equally) by society in terms of their rewards and material circumstances. Formal equality, in its legal and political senses, is clearly inadequate in itself because it disregards the structural inequalities of the capitalist system. Equality of opportunity, for its part, legitimizes inequality by perpetuating the myth of innate inequality.

Egalitarianism: A theory or practice based on the desire to promote equality; egalitarianism is sometimes seen as the belief that equality is the primary political value.

PERSPECTIVES ON . . . EQUALITY

LIBERALS believe that people are 'born' equal in the sense that they are of equal moral worth. This implies formal equality, notably legal and political equality, as well as equality of opportunity; but social equality is likely to threaten freedom and penalize talent. Whereas classical liberals emphasize the need for strict meritocracy and economic incentives, modern liberals argue that genuine equal opportunities require relative social equality.

CONSERVATIVES have traditionally viewed society as naturally hierarchical and have thus dismissed equality as an abstract and unachievable goal. Nevertheless, the New Right evinces a strongly individualist belief in equality of opportunity while emphasizing the economic benefits of material inequality.

SOCIALISTS regard equality as a fundamental value and, in particular, endorse social equality. Despite shifts within social democracy towards a liberal belief in equality of opportunity, social equality, whether in its relative (social democratic) or absolute (communist) sense, has been seen as essential to ensuring social cohesion and fraternity, establishing justice or equity, and enlarging freedom in a positive sense.

ANARCHISTS place a particular stress on political equality, understood as an equal and absolute right to personal autonomy, implying that all forms of political inequality amount to oppression. Anarcho-communists believe in absolute social equality achieved through the collective ownership of productive wealth.

FASCISTS believe that humankind is marked by radical inequality, both between leaders and followers and between the various nations or races of the world. Nevertheless, the emphasis on the nation or race implies that all members are equal, at least in terms of their core social identity.

FEMINISTS take equality to mean sexual equality, in the sense of equal rights and equal opportunities (liberal feminism) or equal social or economic power (socialist feminism) irrespective of gender. However, some radical feminists have argued that the demand for equality may simply lead to women being 'male-identified'.

ECOLOGISTS advance the notion of biocentric equality, which emphasizes that all life forms have an equal right to 'live and blossom'. Conventional notions of equality are therefore seen as anthropocentric, in that they exclude the interests of all organisms and entities other than humankind.

Second, social equality underpins *community* and cooperation. If people live in equal social circumstances, they will be more likely to identify with one another and work together for common benefit. Equal outcomes therefore strengthen social **solidarity**. Social inequality, by the same token, leads to conflict and instability. This also explains why socialists have criticized equality of opportunity for breeding a 'survival of the fittest' mentality. For example, the British and social philosopher and historian R. H. Tawney (1880–1962), dismissed the idea of equal opportunities as a 'tadpole philosophy', emphasizing the tiny proportion of tadpoles that develop into frogs.

Third, socialists support social equality because they hold that *need-satisfaction* is the basis for human fulfilment and self-realization. A 'need' is a necessity: it *demands* satisfaction; it is not simply a frivolous wish or a passing fancy. Basic needs, such as the need for food, water, shelter, companionship and so on, are fundamental to the human condition, which means that, for socialists,

Solidarity: A unity based on shared interests or common standards.

their satisfaction is the very stuff of freedom. Marx expressed this in his communist theory of distribution: 'From each according to his ability, to each according to his needs.' Since all people have broadly similar needs, distributing wealth on the basis of need-satisfaction clearly has egalitarian implications. Nevertheless, need-satisfaction can also have inegalitarian implications, as in the case of so-called 'special' needs, arising, for instance, from physical or mental disability.

While socialists agree about the virtue of social and economic equality, they disagree about the extent to which this can and should be brought about. Marxists and communists believe in *absolute* social equality, brought about by the abolition of private property and **collectivization** of productive wealth. Perhaps the most famous experiment in such radical egalitarianism took place in China under the 'Cultural Revolution', 1966–76. Social democrats, however, believe in *relative* social equality, usually achieved by the redistribution of wealth through the welfare state and a system of **progressive taxation**, although other mechanisms have also been proposed, such as universal basic income (see p. 84). The social-democratic desire to tame capitalism rather than abolish it reflects an acceptance of a continuing role for material incentives, and the fact that the significance of need-satisfaction is largely confined to the eradication of poverty. This, in turn, blurs the distinction between social equality and equality of opportunity.

Class politics

Socialists have traditionally viewed **social class** as the deepest and most politically significant of social divisions. Socialist class politics have been expressed in two ways, however. In the first, social class is an analytical tool. In pre-socialist societies at least, socialists have believed that human beings tend to think and act together with others with whom they share a common economic position or interest. In other words, social classes, rather than individuals, are the principal actors in history and therefore provide the key to understanding social and political change. This is demonstrated most clearly in the Marxist belief that historical change is the product of class conflict. The second form of socialist class politics focuses specifically on the working class, and is concerned with political struggle and emancipation. Socialism has often been viewed as an expression of the interests of the working class, and the working class has been seen as the vehicle through which socialism will be achieved. Nevertheless, social class has not been accepted as a necessary or permanent feature of society: socialist societies have either been seen as classless or as societies in which class inequalities have been substantially reduced. In emancipating itself from capitalist exploitation, the working class thus also emancipates itself from its own class identity, becoming, in the process, fully developed human beings.

Socialists have nevertheless been divided about the nature and importance of social class. In the Marxist tradition, class is linked to economic power, as defined by the individual's relationship to the means of production. From this perspective, class divisions are divisions between 'capital' and 'labour'; that is, between the owners of productive wealth (the **bourgeoisie**) and those who live off the sale of their labour power (the **proletariat**). This Marxist two-class model is characterized by irreconcilable conflict between

Collectivization: The abolition of private property and the establishment of a comprehensive system of common or public ownership, usually through the mechanisms of the state.

Progressive taxation: A system of taxation in which the rich pay a higher proportion of their income in tax than the poor.

Social class: A social division based on economic or social factors; a social class is a group of people who share a similar socio-economic position.

Bourgeoisie: A Marxist term denoting the ruling class of a capitalist society, the owners of productive wealth.

Proletariat: A Marxist term denoting a class that subsists through the sale of its labour power; strictly speaking, the proletariat is not equivalent to the manual working class.

POLITICAL IDEOLOGIES IN ACTION . . .

UNIVERSAL BASIC INCOME

EVENTS: In 1981, the Alaska Permanent Fund was launched. It has since become the world's only enduring attempt to put the idea of universal basic income (UBI) into practice. The Permanent Fund, financed by Alaska's oil and gas resources, pays all adults and children a dividend each year – in 2019, it was $1,606 – the only condition for which is they must be full-time Alaskan residents. In effect, this is 'free money'. However, unlike most versions of UBI, Permanent Fund dividends are not fixed, guaranteed amounts and they are not high enough to cover basic expenses. Among other prominent experiments with UBI is the scheme in Finland, under which 2,000 people, randomly chosen from the ranks of the unemployed, were given a monthly sum of €560, from January 2017 to December 2018, no strings attached.

SIGNIFICANCE: Public debate about UBI has grown as socialists and leftists, in particular, have seen it as a possible solution to both growing inequality and economic insecurity in an age of neoliberal globalization, and the increasing effect of automation on jobs and income. The key argument in favour of UBI is that, as payments are made at a flat rate, it promotes social justice (monthly stipends have a greater relative impact on the poor than on the rich) and reduces – or (if payments are generous enough) eradicates – poverty. Such thinking is underpinned by the belief that, in boosting spending power, UBI stimulates economic growth, so helping to pay for itself through increased tax revenues. Moreover, UBI may redress the relationship between employers

martaposemuckel/Pixabay

and workers to the benefit of the latter, whose greater economic freedom serves to alleviate wage slavery.

UBI, nevertheless, also attracts criticism. First, it may serve ideological purposes quite opposed to those of socialist egalitarianism. For example, the US free-market economist, Milton Friedman, defended the related idea of a negative income tax (in which the state pays citizens, rather than the other way round) on the grounds that it would allow for the dismantlement of the welfare state while, at the same time, strengthening self-sufficiency. Second, even if its purpose is to reduce inequality, UBI may be an ineffective tool. Among the reasons for this is that it threatens to draw funding away from public services like health and education that may be more reliable in meeting the needs of the less well-off. Finally, not only may UBI undermine the incentive to work – and, in the process, turn people into passive consumers – but there is also no guarantee that income from UBI schemes is used wisely.

the bourgeoisie and the proletariat, leading, inevitably, to the overthrow of capitalism through a proletarian revolution. Social democrats, on the other hand, have tended to define social class in terms of income and status differences between 'white collar' or non-manual workers (the middle class) and 'blue collar' or manual workers (the working class). From this perspective, the advance of socialism is associated with the *narrowing* of divisions between the middle class and the working class brought about through economic and social intervention. Social democrats have therefore believed in social amelioration and class harmony rather than social polarization and class war.

However, the link between socialism and class politics has declined significantly since the mid-twentieth century. This has largely been a consequence of declining levels of class solidarity and, in particular, the shrinkage of the traditional working class or urban proletariat. The waning in class politics is a consequence of de-industrialization, reflected in the decline of traditional labour-intensive industries such as coal, steel, shipbuilding and so on. Not only has this forced traditional socialist parties to revise their policies in order to appeal to middle-class voters, but it has also encouraged them to define their radicalism less in terms of class emancipation and more in relation to issues such as gender equality, ecological sustainability, or peace and international development.

Common ownership

Socialists have often traced the origins of competition and inequality to the institution of private property, by which they usually mean productive wealth or 'capital', rather than personal belongings such as clothes, furniture or houses. This attitude to property sets socialism apart from liberalism and conservatism, which both regard property ownership as natural and proper. Socialists criticize private property for a number of reasons:

- Property is *unjust*: wealth is produced by the collective effort of human labour and should therefore be owned by the community, not by private individuals.

- It breeds acquisitiveness and so is *morally corrupting*. Private property encourages people to be materialistic, to believe that human happiness or fulfilment can be gained through the pursuit of wealth. Those who own property wish to accumulate more, while those who have little or no wealth long to acquire it.

PERSPECTIVES ON . . . THE ECONOMY

LIBERALS see the economy as a vital part of civil society and have a strong preference for a market or capitalist economic order based on property, competition and material incentives. However, while classical liberals favour *laissez-faire* capitalism, modern liberals recognize the limitations of the market and accept limited economic management.

CONSERVATIVES show clear support for private enterprise but have traditionally favoured pragmatic, if limited, intervention, fearing the free-for-all of *laissez-faire* and the attendant risks of social instability. Neoliberal conservatives nevertheless endorse unregulated capitalism.

SOCIALISTS in the Marxist tradition have expressed a preference for common ownership and absolute social equality, which in orthodox communism was expressed in state collectivization and central planning. Social democrats, though, support welfare or regulated capitalism, believing that the market is a good servant but a bad master.

ANARCHISTS reject any form of economic control or management. However, while anarcho-communists endorse common ownership and small-scale self-management, anarcho-capitalists advocate an entirely unregulated market economy.

FASCISTS have sought to find an alternative to both capitalism and communism, often linked to corporatism and its supposed ability to draw labour and capital together into an organic whole. Planning and nationalization are supported as attempts to subordinate profit to the (alleged) needs of the nation or race.

ECOLOGISTS condemn both market capitalism and state collectivism for being growth-obsessed and environmentally unsustainable. Economics must therefore be subordinate to ecology, and the drive for profit at any cost must be replaced by a concern with long-term sustainability and harmony between humankind and nature.

● It is *divisive*. It fosters conflict in society; for example, between owners and workers, employers and employees, or simply the rich and the poor.

Socialists have therefore proposed that the institution of private property either be abolished and replaced by the common ownership of productive wealth, or, more modestly, that the right to property be balanced against the interests of the community. **Fundamentalist socialists**, such as Marx and Engels, envisaged the abolition of private property, and hence the creation of a classless, communist society in place of capitalism. Their clear preference was that property be owned collectively and used for the benefit of humanity. However, they said little about how this goal could be achieved in practice. When Lenin and the Bolsheviks seized power in Russia in 1917, they believed that socialism could be built through **nationalization**. This process was not completed until the 1930s, when Stalin's 'second revolution' witnessed the construction of a centrally planned economy, a system of state collectivization.

'Common ownership' came to mean 'state ownership', or what the Soviet constitution described as 'socialist state property'. The Soviet Union thus developed a form of **state socialism.**

Social democrats have also been attracted to the state as an instrument through which wealth can be collectively owned and the economy rationally planned. However, in the West, nationalization has been applied more selectively, its objective being not full state collectivization but the construction of a **mixed economy**. In the UK, for example, the Attlee Labour government (1945–51) nationalized what it called the 'commanding heights' of the economy: major industries such as coal, steel, electricity and gas. Through these industries, the government hoped to regulate the entire economy without the need for comprehensive collectivization. However, since the 1950s, parliamentary socialist parties have gradually distanced themselves from the 'politics of ownership', preferring to define socialism in terms of the pursuit of equality and social justice rather than the advance of public ownership. Nevertheless, in the aftermath of the 2007–09 global financial crisis, there was evidence of a reappraisal of the importance of capital in socialist thought, as, for example, in the writings of Thomas Piketty.

Fundamentalist socialism: A form of socialism that seeks to abolish capitalism and replace it with a qualitatively different kind of society.

Nationalization: The extension of state or public ownership over private assets or industries, either individual enterprises or the entire economy (often called collectivization).

State socialism: A form of socialism in which the state controls and directs economic life, acting, in theory, in the interests of the people.

Mixed economy: An economy in which there is a mixture of publicly owned and privately owned industries.

KEY FIGURE

Eric Piermont/AFP/Getty Images

THOMAS PIKETTY (BORN 1971)

A French economist, Piketty's work focuses primarily on the issues of wealth and income distribution. In his best-selling *Capital in the Twenty-First Century* (2014), Piketty advanced the central theory that the return on capital grows more quickly than the economy, meaning that inequality will widen remorselessly unless bold action is taken to cut the rich down to size. In this light, he proposed a 'progressive, global tax on wealth'. Such thinking was further developed in *Capital and Ideology* (2020), which analysed the history of what Piketty called the 'inequality regime', and urged the introduction of a 'triptych' of progressive taxes – income tax, an annual property tax and inheritance tax – each having a maximum rate of 90 per cent.

TYPES OF SOCIALISM

The two major sub-traditions of socialism are as follows:

● communism

● social democracy.

Communism

The communist tradition within socialism is defined by a rejection of private property and a clear preference for common or collective ownership. It is a tradition that has a variety of manifestations, even overlapping with anarchism, as in the case of anarcho-communism (discussed in Chapter 5). However, historically its most significant association has undoubtedly been with Marxism. Strictly speaking, 'Marxism' as a codified body of thought only came into existence after Marx's death in 1883. It was the product of the attempt, notably by Marx's lifelong collaborator, Friedrich Engels, the SPD leader Karl Kautsky (1854–1938) and the Russian theoretician Georgi Plekhanov (1857–1918), to condense Marx's ideas and theories into a systematic and comprehensive world-view that suited the needs of the growing socialist movement. This 'orthodox' Marxism later formed the basis of Soviet communism. Some see Marx as an economic determinist, while others proclaim him to be a humanist socialist. Moreover, distinctions have also been drawn between his early and later writings, sometimes presented as the distinction between the 'young Marx' and the 'mature Marx'. It is nevertheless clear that Marx himself believed he had developed a new brand of socialism that was scientific, in the sense that it was primarily concerned with disclosing the nature of social and historical development, rather than with advancing an essentially ethical critique of capitalism.

KEY CONCEPT

COMMUNISM

Communism, in its simplest sense, refers to the communal organization of social existence, especially through the collective ownership of property. For Marxists, communism is a theoretical ideal. In this sense, communism is characterized by classlessness (wealth is owned in common), rational economic organization (production-for-use replaces production-for-exchange) and statelessness (in the absence of class conflict, the state 'withers away'). 'Orthodox' communism refers to the societies founded in the twentieth century supposedly on the basis of Marxist principles. In such societies: (1) Marxism-Leninism was used as an 'official' ideology; (2) the communist party had a monopoly of power, based on its 'leading and guiding' role in society; and (3) economic life was collectivized and organized through a system of central planning.

At least three forms of Marxism can be identified. These are:

● classical Marxism

● orthodox communism

● neo-Marxism.

Classical Marxism

Philosophy

The core of classical Marxism – the Marxism of Marx – is a philosophy of history that outlines why capitalism is doomed and why socialism is destined to replace it, based on supposedly scientific analysis. But in what sense did Marx believe his work to be scientific? Marx criticized earlier socialist thinkers such as the French social reformer Saint-Simon (1760–1825), Fourier and Owen as 'utopians' on the basis that their socialism was grounded in a desire for total social transformation unconnected with the necessity of class struggle and revolution. Marx, in contrast, undertook a laborious empirical analysis of history and society, hoping thereby to gain insight into the nature of future developments. However, whether with Marx's help or not, Marxism as the attempt to gain historical understanding through the application of scientific methods, later developed into Marxism as a body of scientific truths, gaining a status more akin to that of a religion. Engels' declaration that Marx had uncovered the 'laws' of historical and social development was a clear indication of this transition.

What made Marx's approach different from that of other socialist thinkers was that he subscribed to what Engels called the 'materialist conception of history', or **historical materialism** (see Figure 4.1). Rejecting the idealism of the German philosopher G. W. F. Hegel (1770–1831), who believed that history amounted to the unfolding of the so-called

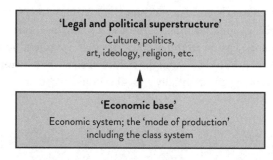

Figure 4.1   Historical materialism

'world spirit', Marx held material circumstances to be fundamental to all forms of social and historical development. This reflected the belief that the production of the means of subsistence is the most crucial of all human activities. Since humans cannot survive without food, water, shelter and so on, the way in which these are produced conditions all other aspects of life; in short, 'social being determines consciousness'. In the preface to *A Contribution to the Critique of Political Economy*, written in 1859, Marx gave this theory its most succinct expression, by suggesting that social consciousness and the 'legal and political superstructure' arise from the 'economic base', the real foundation of society. This 'base' consists essentially of the 'mode of production' or economic system – feudalism, capitalism, socialism and so on. This led Marx to conclude that political, legal, cultural, religious, artistic and other aspects of life could be explained primarily by reference to economic factors (see pp. 3–5 for an account of how this applies to Marx's theory of ideology).

While in other respects a critic of Hegel, Marx nevertheless embraced his belief that the driving force of historical change was the **dialectic**. In

Historical materialism: A Marxist theory that holds that material or economic conditions ultimately structure law, politics, culture and other aspects of social existence.

Dialectic: A process of development in which interaction between two opposing forces (thesis and antithesis) leads to a further or higher stage (synthesis); historical change resulting from internal contradictions within a society.

effect, progress is the consequence of internal conflict. For Hegel, this explained the movement of the 'world spirit' towards self-realization through conflict between a thesis and its opposing force, an antithesis, producing a higher level, a synthesis, which in turn constitutes a new thesis. Marx, as Engels put it, 'turned Hegel on his head', by investing this Hegelian dialectic with a materialistic interpretation. Marx thus explained historical change by reference to internal contradictions within each mode of production, arising from the existence of private property. Capitalism is thus doomed because it embodies its own antithesis, the proletariat, seen by Marx as the 'grave digger of capitalism'. Conflict between capitalism and the proletariat will therefore lead to a higher stage of development in the establishment of a socialist, and eventually a communist, society.

Marx's theory of history is therefore teleological, in the sense that it invests history with meaning or a purpose, reflected in its goal: classless communism. This goal would nevertheless only be achieved once history had developed through a series of stages or epochs, each characterized by its own economic structure and class system. In *The German Ideology* ([1846] 1970) Marx identified four such stages:

- primitive communism or tribal society, in which material scarcity provided the principal source of conflict

- slavery, covering classical or ancient societies and characterized by conflict between masters and slaves

- feudalism, marked by antagonism between land owners and serfs

- capitalism, dominated by the struggle between the bourgeoisie and the proletariat.

Human history has therefore been a long struggle between the oppressed and the oppressor, the exploited and the exploiter. However, following Hegel, Marx envisaged an end of history, which would occur when a society was constructed that embodied no internal contradictions or antagonisms. This, for Marx, meant communism, a classless society based on the common ownership of productive wealth. With the establishment of communism, what Marx called the 'pre-history of mankind' would come to an end.

Economics

In Marx's early writings much of his critique of capitalism rests on the notion of **alienation**, which applies in four senses. Since capitalism is a system of production for exchange, it alienates humans from the *product* of their labour: they work to produce not what they need or what is useful, but 'commodities' to be sold for profit. They are also alienated from the *process* of labour, because most are forced to work under the supervision of foremen or managers. In addition, work is not social: individuals are encouraged to be self-interested and are therefore alienated from *fellow workers*. Finally, workers are alienated from *themselves*. Labour itself is reduced to a mere commodity and work becomes a depersonalized activity instead of a creative and fulfilling one.

However, in his later work, Marx analysed capitalism more in terms of class conflict and exploitation. Marx defined class in terms of economic power, specifically where people stand in relation to the ownership of the 'means of production', or productive wealth. He believed that capitalist society was being divided increasingly into 'two great classes facing one another: Bourgeoisie and Proletariat'. For Marx and later Marxists, the analysis of the class system provides the key to historical understanding and enables

Alienation: To be separated from one's genuine or essential nature; used by Marxists to describe the process whereby, under capitalism, labour is reduced to being a mere commodity.

predictions to be made about the future development of capitalism: in the words of the *Communist Manifesto* ([1848] 1967), 'The history of all hitherto existing societies is the history of class struggle.' Classes, rather than individuals, parties or other movements, are the chief agents of historical change.

Crucially, Marx believed that the relationship between classes is one of irreconcilable antagonism, the subordinate class being necessarily and systematically exploited by the **'ruling class'**. This he explained by reference to the idea of **'surplus value'**. Capitalism's quest for profit can only be satisfied through the extraction of surplus value from its workers, by paying them less than the value their labour generates. Economic exploitation is therefore an essential feature of the capitalist mode of production, and it operates regardless of the meanness or generosity of particular employers. Marx was concerned not only to highlight the inherent instability of capitalism, based on irreconcilable class conflict, but also to analyse the nature of capitalist development. In particular, he drew attention to its tendency to experience deepening economic crises. These stemmed, in the main, from cyclical crises of overproduction, plunging the economy into stagnation and bringing unemployment and immiseration to the working class. Each crisis would be more severe than the last, because, Marx calculated, in the long term the rate of profit would fall. This would eventually, and inevitably, produce conditions in which the proletariat, the vast majority of society, would rise up in revolution.

Politics

Marx's most important prediction was that capitalism was destined to be overthrown by a proletarian revolution. This would be not merely a political revolution that would remove the governing elite or overthrow the state machine, but a **social revolution** that would establish a new mode of production and culminate in the achievement of full communism. Such a revolution, he anticipated, would occur in the most mature capitalist countries – for example, Germany, Belgium, France or the UK – where the forces of production had expanded to their limit within the constraints of the capitalist system. Nevertheless, revolution would not simply be determined by objective conditions alone. The subjective element would be supplied by a 'class-conscious' proletariat, meaning that revolution would occur when both objective and subjective conditions were 'ripe'. As class antagonisms intensified, the proletariat would recognize the fact of its own exploitation and become a revolutionary force: a class for-itself and not merely a class in-itself. In this sense, revolution would be a spontaneous act, carried out by a proletarian class that would, in effect, lead or guide itself.

The initial target of this revolution was to be the bourgeois state. The state, in this view, is an instrument of oppression wielded by the economically dominant class. However, Marx recognized that there could be no immediate transition from capitalism to communism. A transitional 'socialist' stage of development would last as long as class antagonisms persisted. This would be characterized by what Marx called the **dictatorship of the proletariat**. The purpose of this proletarian state was to safeguard the gains of the revolution by preventing counter-revolution carried out by the dispossessed bourgeoisie. However, as class antagonisms began to fade

Ruling class: A Marxist term denoting the class that owns the means of production, and so wields economic and political power.

Surplus value: A Marxist term denoting the value that is extracted from the labour of the proletariat by the mechanism of capitalist exploitation.

Social revolution: A qualitative change in the structure of society; for Marxists a social revolution involves a change in the mode of production and the system of ownership.

Dictatorship of the proletariat: A Marxist term denoting the transitional phase between the collapse of capitalism and the establishment of full communism, characterized by the establishment of a proletarian state.

with the emergence of full communism, the state would 'wither away' – once the class system had been abolished, the state would lose its reason for existence. The resulting communist society would therefore be stateless as well as classless, and would allow a system of commodity production to give way to one geared to the satisfaction of human needs.

Orthodox communism

The Russian Revolution and its consequences dominated the image of communism in the twentieth century. The Bolshevik party, led by V. I. Lenin, seized power in a *coup d'état* in October 1917, and the following year adopted the name 'Communist Party'. As the first successful communist revolutionaries, the Bolshevik leaders enjoyed unquestionable authority within the communist world, at least until the 1950s. Communist parties set up elsewhere accepted the ideological leadership of Moscow and joined the Communist International, or 'Comintern', founded in 1919. The communist regimes established in eastern Europe after 1945, in China in 1949, in Cuba in 1959 and elsewhere, were consciously modelled on the structure of the Soviet Union. Thus, Soviet communism became the dominant model of communist rule, and the ideas of Marxism-Leninism became the ruling ideology of the communist world.

However, twentieth-century communism differed significantly from the ideas and expectations of Marx and Engels. In the first place, although the communist parties that developed in the twentieth century were founded on the theories of classical Marxism, they were forced to adapt these to the tasks of winning and retaining political power. Twentieth-century communist leaders had, in particular, to give greater attention to issues such as leadership, political organization and economic management than Marx had done. Second, the communist regimes were shaped by the historical circumstances in which they developed. Communist parties did not achieve power, as Marx had anticipated, in the developed capitalist states of Western Europe, but in backward, largely rural countries such as Russia and China. In consequence, the urban proletariat was invariably small and unsophisticated, quite incapable of carrying out a genuine class revolution. Communist rule thus became the rule of a communist elite, and of communist leaders. Soviet communism, furthermore, was crucially shaped by the decisive personal contribution of the first two Bolshevik leaders, V. I. Lenin and Joseph Stalin (1879–1953).

KEY FIGURE

Hulton Deutsch/Corbis Historical/ Getty Images

VLADIMIR ILICH LENIN (1870–1924)

A Russian Marxist revolutionary and theorist, Lenin was the first leader of the Soviet state (1917–21). In *What Is to Be Done?* (1902), he emphasized the central importance of a tightly organized 'vanguard' party to lead and guide the proletarian class. In *Imperialism, the Highest Stage of Capitalism* (1916), he developed an economic analysis of colonialism, highlighting the possibility of turning world war into class war. *The State and Revolution* (1917) outlined Lenin's firm commitment to the 'insurrectionary road' and rejected 'bourgeois parliamentarianism'.

Lenin's theoretical contributions to Marxism were shaped by his overriding concern with the problems of winning power and establishing communist rule. The central feature of **Leninism** was a belief in the need for a new kind of political party, a revolutionary party or **vanguard party**. Unlike Marx, Lenin did not believe that the proletariat would spontaneously develop revolutionary **class consciousness**, as the working class was deluded by bourgeois ideas and beliefs. He suggested that only a 'revolutionary party' could lead the working class from 'trade union consciousness' to revolutionary class consciousness. Such a party should be composed of professional and dedicated revolutionaries. Its claim to leadership would lie in its ideological wisdom, specifically its understanding of Marxist theory. This party could therefore act as the 'vanguard of the proletariat' because, armed with Marxism, it would perceive the genuine interests of the proletariat and would act to awaken the proletarian class to its revolutionary potential. Lenin further proposed that the vanguard party should be organized according to the principles of **democratic centralism**. Lenin's theory of the party nevertheless attracted criticism from fellow Marxists. In particular, Rosa Luxemburg associated the notion of the vanguard party with the problem of 'substitutionism', in which a ruling party would substitute itself for the proletariat and, eventually, a supreme leader would substitute himself for the party.

Leninism: Lenin's theoretical contributions to Marxism, notably his belief in the need for a revolutionary or 'vanguard' party to raise the proletariat to class consciousness.

Vanguard party: A Leninist term denoting a party whose purpose is to lead and guide the proletariat to the achievement of revolutionary class consciousness.

KEY FIGURE

ullstein bild/Getty

ROSA LUXEMBURG (1871–1919)

A Polish-born socialist and exponent of revolutionary Marxism, Luxemburg advanced the first Marxist critique of the Bolshevik tradition from the point of view of democracy. Emphasizing the benefits of a broadly based democratic organization, she condemned Lenin's conception of a tightly centralized vanguard party as an attempt to exert political control over the working class. By associating vanguardism with the rise of despotism, she predicted the subsequent course of Russian communism. In also condemning the revisionism of Bernstein and others, Luxemburg steered a course between the two major traditions of twentieth-century socialism: orthodox communism and social democracy. With Karl Liebknecht, she formed the Spartacus League, which later became the German Communist Party. Luxemburg was arrested and murdered during the Spartacist uprising in Berlin.

Class consciousness: A Marxist term denoting ideas and theories that serve the interests of the bourgeoisie by disguising the contradictions of capitalist society.

Democratic centralism: The Leninist principle of party organization, based on a supposed balance between freedom of discussion and strict unity of action.

When the Bolsheviks seized power in 1917 they did so as a vanguard party, and therefore in the name of the proletariat. If the Bolshevik Party was acting in the interests of the working class, it followed that opposition parties must represent the interests of classes hostile to the proletariat, in particular the bourgeoisie. The dictatorship of the proletariat required that the revolution be protected against its class enemies, which effectively meant the suppression of all parties other than the Communist Party. By 1920, Russia had become a one-party state. Leninist theory therefore implied the existence of a monopolistic party, which enjoys sole responsibility for articulating the interests of the proletariat and guiding the revolution toward its ultimate goal, that of 'building communism'.

Soviet communism was no less deeply influenced by the rule of Joseph Stalin, 1924–53, than that of Lenin. Indeed more so, as the Soviet Union was affected more profoundly by Stalin's 'second revolution' in the 1930s than it had been by the October Revolution. Stalin's most important ideological shift was to embrace the doctrine of 'Socialism in One Country', initially developed by Nikolai Bukharin. Announced in 1924, this proclaimed that the Soviet Union could succeed in 'building socialism' without the need for international revolution. After consolidating himself in power, however, Stalin oversaw a dramatic economic and political upheaval, beginning with the announcement of the first Five Year Plan in 1928. Stalin's Five Year Plans brought about rapid industrialization as well as the swift and total eradication of private enterprise. From 1929, agriculture was collectivized, and Soviet peasants were forced at the cost of literally millions of lives to give up their land and join state or collective farms. Economic **Stalinism** therefore took the form of state collectivization or 'state socialism'. The capitalist market was entirely removed and replaced by a system of central planning, dominated by the State Planning Committee, 'Gosplan', and administered by a collection of powerful economic ministries based in Moscow.

Major political changes accompanied this 'second revolution'. During the 1930s, Stalin used his power to brutal effect, removing anyone suspected of disloyalty or criticism in an increasingly violent series of purges carried out by the secret police, the NKVD. The membership of the Communist Party was almost halved, over a million people lost their lives, including all the surviving members of Lenin's Politburo, and many millions were imprisoned in labour camps, or gulags. Political Stalinism was therefore a form of totalitarian dictatorship, operating through a monolithic ruling party, in which all forms of debate or criticism were eradicated by terror in what amounted to a civil war conducted against the party itself.

Neo-Marxism

While Marxism – or, more usually, Marxism-Leninism – was turned into a secular religion by the orthodox communist regimes of Eastern Europe and elsewhere, a more subtle and complex form of Marxism developed in Western Europe. Referred to as modern Marxism, Western Marxism or **neo-Marxism**, this amounted to an attempt to revise or recast the classical ideas of Marx while remaining faithful to certain Marxist principles or aspects of Marxist methodology.

Two principal factors shaped the character of neo-Marxism. First, when Marx's prediction about the imminent collapse of capitalism failed to materialize, neo-Marxists were forced to re-examine conventional class analysis. In particular, they took a greater interest in Hegelian ideas and in the stress on 'Man the creator' found in Marx's early writings. Neo-Marxists were thus able to break free from the rigid 'base/superstructure' straitjacket. In short, the class struggle was no longer treated as the beginning and end of social analysis. Second, neo-Marxists were usually at odds with, and sometimes profoundly repelled by, the Bolshevik model of orthodox communism.

The Hungarian Marxist Georg Lukács (1885–1971) was one of the first to present Marxism as a humanistic philosophy, emphasizing the process of 'reification', through which capitalism dehumanizes workers by reducing them to passive objects or marketable commodities. Antonio Gramsci

Stalinism: A centrally planned economy supported by systematic and brutal political oppression, based on the structures of Stalin's Russia.

Neo-Marxism: An updated and revised form of Marxism that rejects determinism, the primacy of economics and the privileged status of the proletariat.

drew attention to the degree to which the class system is upheld not simply by unequal economic and political power, but also by bourgeois 'hegemony', the spiritual and cultural supremacy of the ruling class, brought about through the spread of bourgeois values and beliefs via civil society – the media, churches, youth movements, trade unions and so on. A more overtly Hegelian brand of Marxism was developed by the so-called Frankfurt School, whose leading early figures were Theodor Adorno (1903–69), Max Horkheimer (1895–1973) and Herbert Marcuse. Frankfurt theorists developed what was called 'critical theory', a blend of Marxist political economy, Hegelian philosophy and Freudian psychology, that came to have a considerable impact on the so-called 'New Left'. The leading exponent of the 'second generation' of the Frankfurt School is the German philosopher and social theorist Jürgen Habermas (born 1929). His wide-ranging work includes an analysis of 'crisis tendencies' in capitalist society that arise from tensions between capital accumulation and democracy.

KEY FIGURE

ullstein bild Dtl./ullstein bild/
Getty Images

HERBERT MARCUSE (1898–1979)

A German political philosopher and social theorist, Marcuse portrayed advanced industrial society as an all-encompassing system of repression that subdues argument and debate, and absorbs all forms of opposition. Drawing on Marxist, Hegelian and Freudian ideas, Marcuse held up the unashamedly utopian prospect of personal and sexual liberation, looking not to the conventional working class as a revolutionary force but to groups such as students, ethnic minorities, women and workers in the developing world. His key works include *Eros and Civilization* (1958) and *One-Dimensional Man* (1964).

KEY CONCEPT

NEW LEFT

The New Left comprises thinkers and intellectual movements that emerged in the 1960s and early 1970s, seeking to revitalize socialist thought by developing a radical critique of advanced industrial society. The New Left rejected both 'old' left alternatives: Soviet-style state socialism and de-radicalized Western social democracy. Influenced by the humanist writings of the 'young' Marx, and by anarchism and radical forms of phenomenology and existentialism, New Left theories are often diffuse. Common themes nevertheless include a fundamental rejection of conventional society ('the system') as oppressive, a commitment to personal autonomy and self-fulfilment in the form of 'liberation', disillusionment with the role of the working class as the revolutionary agent, sympathy for identity politics (see p. 232), and a preference for decentralization and participatory democracy.

Social democracy

As an ideological stance, social democracy took shape around the mid-twentieth century, resulting from the tendency among Western socialist parties not only to adopt parliamentary strategies, but also to revise their socialist goals. In particular, they abandoned the goal of abolishing capitalism and sought instead to reform or 'humanize' it. Social democracy therefore came to stand for a broad balance between the market economy, on the one hand, and state intervention on the other.

Social democracy was most fully developed in the early post-1945 period, during which enthusiasm for social-democratic ideas and theories extended well beyond its socialist homeland, creating, in many Western states, a social-democratic consensus. However, since the 1970s and 1980s, social democracy has struggled to retain its electoral and political relevance in the face of the advance of neoliberalism (see p. 63) and changed economic and social circumstances. The final decades of the twentieth century therefore witnessed a process of ideological retreat on the part of reformist socialist parties across the globe.

KEY CONCEPT
SOCIAL DEMOCRACY

Social democracy is an ideological stance that supports a broad balance between market capitalism, on the one hand, and state intervention on the other. Being based on a compromise between the market and the state, social democracy lacks a systematic underlying theory and is, arguably, inherently vague. It is nevertheless associated with the following views: (1) capitalism is the only reliable means of generating wealth, but it is a morally defective means of distributing wealth because of its tendency towards poverty and inequality; (2) the defects of the capitalist system can be rectified through economic and social intervention, the state being the custodian of the public interest; (3) social change can and should be brought about peacefully and constitutionally.

Ethical socialism

The theoretical basis for social democracy has been provided more by moral or religious beliefs than by scientific analysis. Social democrats have not accepted the materialist and highly systematic ideas of Marx and Engels, but rather advanced an essentially moral critique of capitalism. In short, socialism is portrayed as morally superior to capitalism because human beings are ethical creatures, bound to one another by the ties of love, sympathy and compassion. The moral vision that underlies ethical socialism has been based on both humanistic and religious principles. Socialism in France, the UK and other Commonwealth countries has been influenced more strongly by the humanist ideas of Fourier, Owen and William Morris (1854–96) than by the 'scientific' creed of Karl Marx. However, ethical socialism has also drawn heavily on Christianity. For example, there is a long-established tradition of Christian socialism in the UK, reflected in the twentieth century in the works of R. H. Tawney. The Christian ethic that has inspired UK socialism is that of universal brotherhood, the respect that should be accorded to all individuals as creations of God, a principle embodied in the commandment 'Thou shalt love thy neighbour as thyself'. In *The Acquisitive Society* (1921), Tawney condemned unregulated capitalism because it is driven by the 'sin of avarice' rather than faith in a 'common humanity'.

In abandoning scientific analysis in favour of moral or religious principles, however, social democracy weakened the theoretical basis of socialism. Social democracy has been concerned primarily with the notion of a just or fair distribution of wealth in society. This is embodied in the overriding principle of social democracy: **social justice**. Social democracy consequently came to stand for a broad range of views, extending from a left-wing commitment to extending equality and expanding the collective ownership of wealth, to a more right-wing acceptance of the need for market efficiency and individual self-reliance that may be difficult to distinguish from certain forms of liberalism or conservatism. Attempts have nevertheless been made to give social democracy a theoretical basis, usually involving re-examining capitalism itself and redefining the goal of socialism.

Social justice: A morally justifiable distribution of wealth, usually implying a commitment to greater equality.

Reformist socialism

The original, fundamentalist goal of socialism was that productive wealth should be owned in common by all, and therefore used for the collective benefit. This required the abolition of private property and the transition from a capitalist mode of production to a socialist one, usually through a process of revolutionary change. Capitalism, in this view, is unredeemable: it is a system of class exploitation and oppression that deserves to be abolished altogether, not merely reformed. However, influenced by both the steady integration of the working class into society and the gradual advance of political democracy, from the late nineteenth century onwards a growing number of socialist groups and parties embraced **reformism**. At the heart of this was the goal of 'taming' capitalism rather than abolishing it. A major influence on this process in the UK was the Fabian Society, formed in 1884. Led by Beatrice Webb (1858–1943) and Sidney Webb (1859–1947), and including noted intellectuals such as George Bernard Shaw and H. G. Wells, the Fabians took their name from the Roman General Fabius Maxim who was noted for the patient and defensive tactics he had employed in defeating Hannibal's invading armies. In their view, socialism would develop naturally and peacefully out of liberal capitalism via a very similar process. Placing their faith in the belief that the spread of democracy guarantees the ultimate victory of socialism, the Fabians embrace the idea of 'the inevitability of **gradualism**'.

Fabian ideas also had an impact on the German Social Democratic Party (SPD), formed in 1875. While committed in theory to a Marxist strategy, in practice SPD adopted a reformist approach, influenced by the ideas of Ferdinand Lassalle (1825–64). Lassalle had argued that the extension of political democracy could enable the state to respond to working-class interests, and he envisaged socialism being established through a gradual

Reformism: The advocacy of improvement through reform, as opposed to fundamental revolutionary change.

Gradualism: Progress brought about by gradual, piecemeal improvements, rather than dramatic upheaval; change through legal and peaceful reform.

Revisionism: The revision or reworking of a political theory that departs from earlier interpretations in an attempt to present a 'corrected' view.

process of social reform, introduced by a benign state. Such ideas were developed more thoroughly by Eduard Bernstein, whose *Evolutionary Socialism* ([1898] 1962) was the first major work of Marxist **revisionism**. Bernstein suggested that capitalism was becoming increasingly complex and differentiated. In particular, the ownership of wealth had widened as a result of the introduction of joint stock companies, owned by a number of shareholders, instead of a single powerful industrialist. The ranks of the middle classes had also been swollen by the growing number of salaried employees, technicians, government officials and professional workers, who were neither capitalists nor proletarians. In Bernstein's view, this meant that capitalism could be reformed by the nationalization of major industries and the extension of legal protection and welfare benefits to the working class, a process that could be achieved peacefully and democratically.

KEY FIGURE

ullstein bild/Getty

EDUARD BERNSTEIN (1850–1932)

A German socialist politician and theorist, Bernstein attempted to revise and modernize orthodox Marxism in the light of changing circumstances. In *Evolutionary Socialism* (1898), Bernstein argued that economic crises were becoming less, not more, acute, and drew attention to the 'steady advance of the working class'. On this basis, he drew attention to the possibility of a gradual and peaceful transition to socialism, and questioned the distinction between liberalism and socialism, later abandoning all semblance of Marxism.

Western socialist parties have been reformist in practice, if not always in theory. In some cases they long retained a formal commitment to fundamentalist goals, as in the UK Labour Party's belief in 'the common ownership of the means of production, distribution and exchange', expressed in clause IV of its 1918 constitution. Nevertheless, as the twentieth century progressed, social democrats dropped their commitment to planning as they recognized the efficiency and vigour of the capitalist market. The Swedish Social Democratic Labour Party formally abandoned planning in the 1930s, as did the West German Social Democrats at the Bad Godesberg Congress of 1959, which accepted the principle of 'competition when possible; planning when necessary'. In the UK, a similar bid to embrace revisionism formally in the late 1950s ended in failure when the Labour Party conference rejected the then leader Hugh Gaitskell's attempt to abolish clause IV. Nevertheless, when in power, the Labour Party never revealed an appetite for wholesale nationalization.

TENSIONS WITHIN ... SOCIALISM (1)

Communism	v.	Social democracy
scientific socialism	←→	ethical socialism
fundamentalism	←→	revisionism
utopianism	←→	reformism
revolution	←→	evolution/gradualism
abolish capitalism	←→	'humanize' capitalism
common ownership	←→	redistribution
classless society	←→	ameliorate class conflict
absolute equality	←→	relative equality
state collectivization	←→	mixed economy
central planning	←→	economic management
vanguard party	←→	parliamentary party
dictatorship of proletariat	←→	political pluralism
proletarian/people's state	←→	liberal-democratic state

The abandonment of planning and comprehensive nationalization left social democracy with three more modest objectives. Social democrats support:

● The *mixed economy*, a blend of public and private ownership that stands between free-market capitalism and state collectivism. Nationalization, when advocated by social democrats, is invariably selective and reserved for the 'commanding heights' of the economy, or industries that are thought to be 'natural monopolies'. The 1945–51 Attlee Labour government, for instance, nationalized the major utilities – electricity, gas, coal, steel, the railways and so on – but left most of UK industry in private hands.

- *Economic management*, seeing the need for capitalism to be regulated in order to deliver sustainable growth. After 1945, most social democratic parties were converted to Keynesianism (see p. 40) as a device for controlling the economy and delivering full employment.

- The *welfare state*, viewing it as the principal means of reforming or humanizing capitalism. Its attraction is that it acts as a redistributive mechanism that helps to promote social equality and eradicate poverty. Capitalism no longer needs to be abolished, only modified through the establishment of reformed or welfare capitalism.

An attempt to give theoretical substance to these developments, and in effect update Bernstein, was made by Anthony Crosland (1918–77) in *The Future of Socialism* (1956). He subscribed to **managerialism**, in believing that modern capitalism bore little resemblance to the nineteenth-century model that Marx had had in mind. Crosland suggested that a new class of managers, experts and technocrats had supplanted the old capitalist class and come to dominate all advanced industrial societies, both capitalist and communist.

The ownership of wealth had therefore become divorced from its control. Whereas shareholders, who own businesses, were principally concerned with profit, salaried managers, who make day-to-day business decisions, have a broader range of goals, including maintaining industrial harmony and upholding the public image of the company.

Such developments implied that Marxism had become irrelevant: if capitalism could no longer be viewed as a system of class exploitation, the fundamentalist goals of nationalization and planning were simply outdated. Crosland thus recast socialism in terms of politics of social justice, rather than the politics of ownership. Wealth need not be owned in common, because it could be redistributed through a welfare state that is financed by progressive taxation. However, Crosland recognized that economic growth plays a crucial role in the achievement of socialism. A growing economy is essential to generate the tax revenues needed to finance more generous social expenditure, and the prosperous will only be prepared to finance the needy if their own living standards are underwritten by economic growth.

The crisis of social democracy

During the early post-1945 period, Keynesian social democracy – or traditional social democracy – appeared to have triumphed. Its strength was that it harnessed the dynamism of the market without succumbing to the levels of inequality and instability that Marx believed would doom capitalism. Nevertheless, Keynesian social democracy was based on an (arguably) inherently unstable compromise. On the one hand, there was a pragmatic acceptance of the market as the only reliable means of generating wealth. This reluctant conversion to the market meant that social democrats accepted that there was no viable socialist alternative to the market, meaning that the socialist project was reborn as an attempt to reform, not replace, capitalism. On the other hand, the socialist ethic survived in the form of a commitment to social justice. This, in turn, was linked to a weak notion of equality: distributive equality, the idea

Managerialism: The theory that a governing class of managers, technocrats and state officials – those who possess technical and administrative skills – dominates both capitalist and communist societies.

that poverty should be reduced and inequality narrowed through the redistribution of wealth from rich to poor.

At the heart of Keynesian social democracy there lay a conflict between its commitment to both economic efficiency and egalitarianism. During the 'long boom' of the post-1945 period, social democrats were not forced to confront this conflict because sustained growth, low unemployment and low inflation improved the living standards of all social groups and helped to finance more generous welfare provision. However, as Crosland had anticipated, recession in the 1970s and 1980s created strains within social democracy, polarizing socialist thought into more clearly defined left-wing and right-wing positions. Recession precipitated a 'fiscal crisis of the welfare state', simultaneously increasing demand for welfare support as unemployment re-emerged, and squeezing the tax revenues that financed welfare spending (because fewer people were at work and businesses were less profitable). A difficult question had to be answered: should social democrats attempt to restore efficiency to the market economy, which might mean cutting inflation and possibly taxes, or should they defend the poor and the lower paid by maintaining or even expanding welfare provision?

This crisis of social democracy was intensified in the 1980s and 1990s by a combination of political, social and international factors. In the first place, the electoral viability of social democracy was undermined by de-industrialization and the shrinkage of the traditional working class, the social base of Keynesian social democracy. Whereas in the early post-1945 period the tide of democracy had flowed with progressive politics, since the 1980s it has been orientated increasingly around the interests of what J. K. Galbraith (1992) called the 'contented majority'. Social democratic parties paid a high price for these social and electoral shifts. For instance, the UK Labour Party lost four successive general elections between 1979 and 1992; the SPD in Germany was out of power between 1982 and 1998; and the French Socialist Party suffered crushing defeats, notably in 1993 and 2002. Furthermore, the intellectual credibility of social democracy was badly damaged by the collapse of communism. Not only did this create a world without any significant non-capitalist economic forms, but it also undermined faith in what Anthony Giddens (see p. 15) called the 'cybernetic model' of socialism, in which the state, acting as the brain within society, serves as the principal agent of economic and social reform. In this light, Keynesian social democracy could be viewed as only a more modest version of the 'top-down' state socialism that had been discarded so abruptly in the revolutions of 1989–91.

From the 1980s onwards, reformist socialist parties across the globe, but particularly in countries such as the UK, the Netherlands, Germany, Italy, Australia and New Zealand, underwent a further bout of revisionism, sometimes termed neo-revisionism. In so doing, they distanced themselves, to a greater or lesser extent, from the principles and commitments of traditional social democracy. The resulting ideological stance has been described in various ways, including 'new' social democracy, the **'third way'**, the 'radical centre', the 'active centre' and the '*Neue Mitte*' (new middle). However, the ideological significance of neo-revisionism, and its relationship to traditional social democracy in particular and to socialism in general, have been shrouded in debate and confusion. Its central thrust is nevertheless encapsulated in the notion of the third way, highlighting the idea of an alternative, in a broad sense, to capitalism and socialism. In its modern form, the third way represents, more specifically, an alternative to old-style social democracy and neoliberalism.

Third way: The notion of an alternative form of economics to both state socialism and free-market capitalism, sought at different times by conservatives, socialists and fascists.

Social democracy	v.	Third way
TENSIONS WITHIN ... SOCIALISM (2) ↔		
ideological	↔	pragmatic
nation-state	↔	globalization
industrial society	↔	information society
class politics	↔	community
mixed economy	↔	market economy
full employment	↔	full employability
concern for underdog	↔	meritocracy
social justice	↔	opportunity for all
eradicate poverty	↔	promote inclusion
social rights	↔	rights and responsibilities
cradle-to-grave welfare	↔	welfare-to-work
social-reformist state	↔	competition/market state

THE FUTURE OF SOCIALISM

For much of the twentieth century, it was widely accepted – by its enemies as well as its friends – that socialism and history marched hand in hand. The expansion of the franchise to include, over time, working-class voters gave a powerful impetus to the growth of democratic socialism. The 1917 Russian Revolution demonstrated the potency of revolutionary socialism, by leading to the creation of the world's first socialist state. Socialism's influence spread yet more widely in the aftermath of World War II. As orthodox communism spread throughout Eastern Europe and into China, Cuba and beyond, democratic socialist parties practising Keynesian social democracy often dominated the policy agenda, even, sometimes, converting liberal and conservative parties to 'socialist-style' thinking. However, the advance of socialism was reversed in the final decades of the twentieth century, most dramatically by the fall of communism but also by the retreat of social democratic parties in many parts of the world from traditional values. Since then, debate about the future of socialism has been dominated by the assumption that socialism is a spent force, a dead ideology.

Those who argue that the difficult times socialism has experienced since the late twentieth century signal the end of socialism as a meaningful ideological force usually claim that its demise simply reflects the manifest superiority of capitalism over socialism as an economic model. In this view, capitalism is a uniquely effective means of generating wealth, and thereby delivering prosperity. This is because it is based on a market mechanism that ensures unrivalled efficiency by drawing resources to their most profitable use. In this light, socialism's key flaw is that, by relying on the state to manage economic life, whether through a system of comprehensive planning or a mixed economy, it constrains the workings of the market. Any group of planners or officials, however dedicated and well-trained, are certain to be overwhelmed by the sheer complexity of a modern economy. These drawbacks have always been the case, but they became particularly apparent with the advent of globalization from the 1980s onwards. Time, in a sense, had caught up with socialism. Globalization widened the gulf between capitalism and socialism. While capitalism benefited from freer trade, new investment opportunities and sharpened competition in a globalized economy, socialism suffered from the fact that globalization further restricted the scope for economic management at a national level.

Socialism's prospects may not be so gloomy, however. Hopes for the survival of socialism rest largely on the enduring, and perhaps intrinsic, imperfections of the capitalist system. As Ralph Miliband (1995) put it, 'the notion that capitalism has been thoroughly transformed and represents the best that humankind can ever hope to achieve is a dreadful slur on the human race'. In that sense, socialism is destined to survive, if only because it serves as a reminder that human development extends beyond market individualism. Moreover, globalization may bring opportunities for socialism as well as challenges. Just as capitalism has been transformed by the growing significance of the supranational dimension of economic life, socialism may be in the process of being transformed into a critique of global exploitation and inequality. Lastly, urgency has been injected into the revival of socialism by the steady growth, over at least four decades, of within-country inequality. Unless this trend can be effectively challenged, it creates the prospect of deepening social divisions and increasingly acute political dysfunction.

◎ QUESTIONS FOR DISCUSSION

- What is distinctive about the socialist view of equality?
- Why do socialists favour collectivism, and how have they tried to promote it?
- Is class politics an essential feature of socialism?
- What are the implications of trying to achieve socialism through revolutionary means?
- How persuasive is the socialist critique of private property?
- What are the implications of trying to achieve socialism through democratic means?

- On what grounds have Marxists predicted the inevitable collapse of capitalism?
- How closely did orthodox communism reflect the classical idea of Marx?
- To what extent is socialism defined by a rejection of capitalism?
- Is social democracy really a form of socialism?
- Is the social-democratic 'compromise' inherently unstable?
- Can there be a 'third way' between capitalism and socialism?

◉ FURTHER READING

Honneth, A. *The Idea of Socialism: Towards a Renewal* (2016). An ambitious but important work that attempts to reconcile socialist thought with modern post-industrial societies.

Lamb, P. *Socialism* (2019). A clear and concise introduction to socialism, both as a philosophical and as an ideological and political platform.

McLellan, D. *Marxism after Marx* (2007). An authoritative and comprehensive account of twentieth-century Marxism and more recent developments that also contains useful biographical information.

Moschonas, G. *In the Name of Social Democracy – The Great Transformation: 1945 to the Present* (2002). An impressive and thorough account of the nature, history and impact of social democracy that focuses on the emergence of 'new social democracy'.

Socialist Appeal www.socialist.net. A long-running British Marxist newspaper that has an extensive archive (and YouTube channel) of videos, writing and guides designed to explain all aspects of socialist and Marxist theory.

CHAPTER 5

ANARCHISM

PREVIEW

The word 'anarchy' comes from the Greek *anarkhos* and literally means 'without rule'. The term 'anarchism' has been in use since the French Revolution, and was initially employed in a critical or negative sense to imply a breakdown of civilized or predictable order. In everyday language, anarchy implies chaos and disorder. Needless to say, anarchists themselves fiercely reject such associations. It was not until Pierre-Joseph Proudhon proudly declared in *What Is Property?* ([1840] 1970), 'I am an anarchist', that the word was clearly associated with a positive and systematic set of political ideas.

Anarchist ideology is defined by the central belief that political authority in all its forms, and especially in the form of the state, is both evil and unnecessary. Anarchists therefore look to the creation of a stateless society through the abolition of law and government. In their view, the state is evil because, as a repository of sovereign, compulsory and coercive authority, it is an offence against the principles of freedom and equality. Anarchism is thus characterized by principled opposition to certain forms of social hierarchy. Anarchists believe that the state is unnecessary because order and social harmony do not have to be imposed 'from above' through government. Central to anarchism is the belief that people can manage their affairs through voluntary agreement, without the need for top-down hierarchies or a system of rewards and punishments. However, anarchism draws from two quite different ideological traditions: liberalism and socialism. This has resulted in rival individualist and collectivist forms of anarchism. While both accept the goal of statelessness, they advance very different models of the future anarchist society.

HISTORICAL OVERVIEW

Anarchist ideas have sometimes been traced back to Taoist or Buddhist ideas, to the Stoics and Cynics of Ancient Greece, or to the Diggers of the English Civil War. However, the first, and in a sense classic, statement of anarchist principles was produced by William Godwin (see p. 117) in his *Enquiry Concerning Political Justice* ([1793] 1971), although Godwin never described himself as an anarchist. During the nineteenth century, anarchism was a significant component of a broad but growing socialist movement. In 1864, Pierre-Joseph Proudhon's (see p. 115) followers joined with Karl Marx's (see p. 76) to set up the International Workingmen's Association, or First International. The International collapsed in 1871 because of growing antagonism between Marxists and anarchists, led by Mikhail Bakunin (see p. 111). In the late nineteenth century, anarchists sought mass support among the landless peasants of Russia and southern Europe and, more successfully, through anarcho-syndicalism, among the industrial working classes.

Syndicalism was popular in France, Italy and Spain, and helped to make anarchism a genuine mass movement in the early twentieth century. The powerful CGT union in France was dominated by anarchists before 1914, as was the CNT in Spain, which claimed a membership of over two million during the Spanish Civil War (1936–9). Anarcho-syndicalist movements also emerged in Latin America in the early twentieth century, especially in Argentina and Uruguay, and syndicalist ideas influenced the Mexican Revolution, led by Emiliano Zapata. However, the spread of authoritarianism and political repression gradually undermined anarchism in both Europe and Latin America. The victory of General Franco in the Spanish Civil War brought an end to anarchism as a mass movement. The CNT was suppressed, and anarchists, along with left-wingers in general, were persecuted. The influence of anarchism was also undermined by the success of Lenin and the Bolsheviks in 1917, and thus by the growing prestige of communism within the socialist and revolutionary movements.

Syndicalism: A form of revolutionary trade unionism that focuses on labour syndicates as free associations of workers and emphasizes the use of direct action and the general strike.

Social anarchism: A form of anarchism that combines socialist collectivism and anti-statism, its central theme being social solidarity.

Direct action: Political action taken outside the constitutional and legal framework; direct action may range from passive resistance to terrorism.

Anarcho-capitalism: A form of anarchism that seeks to replace government with a system of unregulated market competition.

Despite these setbacks, anarchism has stubbornly refused to die. Early signs of an anarchist revival came with the emergence in the 1960s and 1970s, respectively, of the New Left (see p. 94) and the New Right (see p. 62). Encompassing neo-Marxists, radical democrats, **social anarchists** and others, the New Left endorsed an activist style of politics based on popular protest and **direct action**. The New Right revived interest in free-market economics, most radically through **anarcho-capitalism**. Anarchism subsequently gained greater prominence due to the upsurge in anti-capitalist protest from the late 1990s onwards. The clearest manifestation of this 'new' anarchism has been the activist-based theatrical politics that was first employed during the so-called 'Battle of Seattle' in 1999 (when some 50,000 activists forced the cancellation of the opening ceremony of a World Trade Organization meeting) and has been used in most subsequent anti-capitalist protests, including those organized by the Occupy movement. Finally, it has also been argued that widening anarchist influence is linked to the growth of cyberspace and the upsurge in the use of digital technologies generally (see p. 106).

CORE THEMES

The defining feature of anarchism is its opposition to hierarchy and domination, with the state often being seen as the paradigmatic form of hierarchy and domination. Anarchists have a preference for a stateless society in which free individuals manage their affairs by voluntary agreement, without compulsion or coercion. However, anarchism has been bedevilled by misleading stereotypes and distortions of various kinds. The most common of these is the idea that anarchism rests on little more than a faith in natural 'goodness', the belief that human beings are, at heart, moral creatures. Anarchists certainly believe that people are capable of leading productive and peaceful lives without the need for rulers or leaders, but this view is rarely sustained simply by optimistic assumptions about human nature (Marshall, 2007). In the first place, anarchists do not share a common view of human nature. For example, despite sharing common individualist assumptions, Godwin stressed rational benevolence, while Max Stirner (see p. 118) emphasized conscious egoism. Second, rather than seeing human nature as fixed or determined, the majority of anarchists believe that human beings are products of their environment, even though they are also capable of changing it. In that sense, anarchists believe that human nature develops through creative and voluntary interaction with others. Third, to the extent that anarchists have a theory of human nature, it can be said to be viewed as realistic, even pessimistic. This is because anarchists are profoundly aware of the corruption inherent in the exercise of power. Indeed, if human nature were naturally good, it is difficult to see how hierarchy and domination, and for that matter the state, could have emerged in the first place.

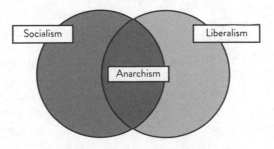

Figure 5.1   **The nature of anarchism**

POLITICAL IDEOLOGIES IN ACTION . . .

ANARCHISM AND CYBERSPACE

EVENTS: The period between 1969 and 1989 witnessed the birth of the digital revolution in information and communication technologies (also known as the third industrial revolution) through, among other things the invention of the Internet and the rise of home computers. This marked the beginning of the 'information age'. In 1991, the earliest version of the World Wide Web (often simply called WWW or the Web) became publicly available as a global information medium, popularly termed 'cyberspace', through which users can read and write via computers connected to the Internet. Other products of the digital revolution include smartphones, satellite and cable television, websites and blogs, and social media. By 2020, 67 per cent of the world's population were connected to other people via digital technologies.

SIGNIFICANCE: Cyberspace has widely been viewed as an experiment in anarchy, with digital technology promising to make many anarchists' dreams a reality. This certainly reflects the expectations and high optimism of many of the Internet's early exponents, especially those influenced by the hacker-punk culture that reigned in Silicon Valley in the 1990s. Practising what has been called cyber-libertarianism (or techno-libertarianism), they were inspired by the goal of reallocating concentrations of power away from states and institutions and transferring them to individuals on an equal basis. Cyberspace is therefore characterized by absolute freedom of expression, made possible, above all, by the absence of government interference. Libertarian dreams have, moreover, been given practical expression through so-called 'crypto-anarchism'. This is a form of anarchism that operates through market arrangements sustained by computer networks, while also preserving confidentiality and security. Examples of crypto-anarchism include Bitcoin and other cryptocurrencies and online marketplace companies such as Uber and Airbnb.

However, the notion of an intrinsic link between hyperspace and anarchism has become increasingly

Source: Dean Mitchell/Getty

difficult to uphold. For one thing, Big Tech, which has come about through the emergence of 'tech giants' such as Amazon, Apple, Google, Facebook and Microsoft, has meant that cyberspace came to be dominated by a few large companies. Among the consequences of this is that Internet technologies and platforms routinely suppress competition and abuse their market influence by sharing sensitive information about users' relationships, tastes and preferences, and, in the process, stoking demands for government regulation and frameworks accountability. For another thing, rather than operating beyond the control of the state and public authorities, cyberspace has in many cases become an instrument of state power. This is evident not only in the growth of Internet-based systems of state security but also in the rising phenomenon of 'cyberwars', in which digital technologies are used to disrupt the activities of other states for strategic or military purposes.

An additional feature of anarchism is that it is less a unified and coherent ideology in its own right, and more a point of overlap between two rival ideologies – liberalism and socialism – the point at which both ideologies reach anti-statist conclusions. This is illustrated in Figure 5.1. Anarchism thus has a dual character: it can be interpreted as either a form of 'ultra-liberalism', which resembles extreme liberal individualism (see p. 24), or as a form of 'ultra-socialism', which resembles extreme socialist collectivism (see p. 80). Nevertheless, anarchism is justified in being treated as a separate ideology, in that its supporters, despite drawing on very different political traditions, are united by a series of broader principles and positions. The most significant of these are:

- anti-statism

- natural order

- anti-clericalism

- economic freedom.

Anti-statism

Sébastien Faure, in his four-volume *Encyclopédie anarchiste* (published between 1925 and 1934), defined anarchism as 'the negation of the principle of Authority'. The anarchist case against authority is simple and clear: authority is an offence against the principles of freedom and equality. Authority, based as it is on political inequality and the alleged right of one person to influence the behaviour of others, enslaves, oppresses and limits human life. It damages and corrupts both those who are subject to authority and those who are in authority. Since human beings are free and autonomous creatures, to be subject to authority means to be diminished, to have one's essential nature suppressed and thereby succumb to debilitating dependency. To be in authority is to acquire an appetite for prestige, control and eventually domination. Authority therefore gives rise to a 'psychology of power', based on a pattern of 'dominance and submission', a society in which, according to the US anarchist and social critic Paul Goodman (1911–72), 'many are ruthless and most live in fear' (1977).

PERSPECTIVES ON . . . STATE

LIBERALS see the state as a neutral arbiter among the competing interests and groups in society, a vital guarantee of social order. While classical liberals treat the state as a necessary evil and extol the virtues of a minimal or nightwatchman state, modern liberals recognize the state's positive role in widening freedom and promoting equal opportunities.

CONSERVATIVES link the state to the need to provide authority and discipline and to protect society from chaos and disorder, hence their traditional preference for a strong state. However, whereas traditional conservatives support a pragmatic balance between the state and civil society, neoliberals have called for the state to be 'rolled back', as it threatens economic prosperity and is driven, essentially, by bureaucratic self-interest.

SOCIALISTS have adopted contrasting views of the state. Marxists have stressed the link between the state and the class system, seeing it as either an instrument of class rule or as a means of ameliorating class tensions. Other socialists, however, regard the state as an embodiment of the common good, and thus approve of interventionism in either its social-democratic or state-collectivist form.

ANARCHISTS reject the state outright, believing it to be an unnecessary evil. The sovereign, compulsory and coercive authority of the state is seen as nothing less than legalized oppression operating in the interests of the powerful, propertied and privileged. As the state is inherently evil and oppressive, all states have the same essential character.

FASCISTS particularly in the Italian tradition, see the state as a supreme ethical ideal, reflecting the undifferentiated interests of the national community, hence their belief in totalitarianism. The Nazis, however, saw the state more as a vessel that contains, or tool that serves, the race or nation.

FEMINISTS have viewed the state as an instrument of male power, the patriarchal state serving to exclude women from, or subordinate them within, the public or 'political' sphere of life. Liberal feminists nevertheless regard the state as an instrument of reform that is susceptible to electoral and other pressures.

FUNDAMENTALISTS view the state as an instrument of social and political regeneration, carried out in line with religious principles. For example, the Islamic state is a means of 'purifying' Islam, by both returning it to its supposed original values and practices, and countering Western influence generally.

In practice, the anarchist critique of authority usually focuses on *political* authority, especially when it is backed up by the machinery of the modern state. Anarchism is defined by its radical rejection of state power, a stance that sets anarchism apart from all other political ideologies (with the exception of Marxism). The flavour of this anarchist critique of law and government is conveyed by one of Pierre-Joseph Proudhon's ([1851] 1923) famous diatribes:

> To be governed is to be watched over, inspected, spied on, directed, legislated, regimented, closed in, indoctrinated, preached at, controlled, assessed, evaluated, censored, commanded; all by creatures that have neither the right, nor the wisdom, nor the virtue.

The state is a *sovereign* body that exercises supreme authority over all individuals and associations living within a defined geographical area. Anarchists emphasize that the authority of the state is absolute and unlimited: law can restrict public behaviour, limit political activity, regulate economic life, interfere with private morality and thinking, and so on. The authority of the state is also *compulsory*. Anarchists reject the liberal notion that political authority arises from voluntary agreement, through some form of 'social contract', and argue instead that individuals become subject to state authority either by being born in a particular country or through conquest. Furthermore, the state is a *coercive* body, whose laws must be obeyed because they are backed up by the threat of punishment. For Emma Goldman (see p. 109), government was symbolized by 'the club, the gun, the handcuff, or the prison' (Goldman, 1969). The state can deprive individuals of their property, their liberty and ultimately, through capital punishment, their lives. The state is also *exploitative*, in that it robs individuals of their property through a system of taxation, once again backed up by the force of law and the possibility of punishment. Anarchists often argue that the state acts in alliance with the wealthy and privileged, and therefore serves to oppress the poor and weak. Finally, the state is *destructive*. 'War', as the US anarchist Randolph Bourne (1886–1918) suggested, 'is the health of the State' (1977). Individuals are required to fight, kill and die in wars that are invariably precipitated by a quest for territorial expansion, plunder or national glory by one state at the expense of others.

KEY FIGURE

Photo 12/Universal Images Group/Getty Images

EMMA GOLDMAN (1869–1940)

A Russian-born propagandist, political agitator and revolutionary, Goldman was a prominent figure in US anarchist circles between 1890 and her deportation to the Soviet Union in 1919. She defined anarchism as 'the theory that all forms of government rest on violence, and are therefore wrong and harmful, as well as unnecessary'. Goldman developed an iconoclastic anarchist vision that drew from both the communist anarchism of Kropotkin (see p. 113) and the individualism of Stirner (see p. 118). She was also one of the first thinkers to blend anarchism with feminism. Seeing political and economic freedom as incomplete without sexual and social freedom, she not only attacked the state as immoral and intrinsically corrupting but also condemned the patriarchal family as the source of female dependency and gender inequality.

The basis of this critique of the state lies in the anarchist thinking about human nature. While anarchists emphasize that humanity has a strong libertarian potential, they are also deeply pessimistic about the corrupting influence of political authority and economic inequality. Human beings can be either 'good' or 'evil' depending on the political and social circumstances in which they live. People who would otherwise be cooperative, sympathetic and sociable, become nothing less than oppressive tyrants when raised up above others by power, privilege or wealth. In other words, anarchists replace the liberal warning that 'power tends to corrupt and absolute power corrupts absolutely' (Acton, 1956) with the more radical and alarming warning that power in any shape or form will corrupt absolutely. The state, as a repository of sovereign, compulsory and coercive authority, is therefore nothing less than a concentrated form of evil. The anarchist theory of the state has nevertheless also attracted criticism. Quite apart from concerns about the theory of human nature on which it is based, the assumption that state oppression stems from the corruption of individuals by their political and social circumstances is circular, in that it is unable to explain how political authority arose in the first place.

Natural order

Anarchists regard the state not only as evil, but also as unnecessary. William Godwin sought to demonstrate this by, in effect, turning the most celebrated justification for the state – social contract theory – on its head. The social contract arguments of Thomas Hobbes (see p. 54) and John Locke (see p. 29) suggest that a stateless society, the 'state of nature', amounts to a civil war of each against all, making orderly and stable life impossible. The source of such strife lies in human nature, which according to Hobbes and Locke is essentially selfish, greedy and potentially aggressive. Only a sovereign state can restrain such impulses and guarantee social order. In short, order is impossible without law. Godwin, in contrast, suggested that human beings are essentially rational creatures, inclined by education and enlightened judgement to live in accordance with truth and universal moral laws. He thus believed that people have a natural propensity to organize their own lives in a harmonious and peaceful fashion. Indeed, in his view it is the corrupting influence of government and unnatural laws, rather than any 'original sin' in human beings, that creates injustice, greed and aggression. Government, in other words, is not the solution to the problem of order, but its cause. Anarchists have often sympathized with the famous opening words of Jean-Jacques Rousseau's (see p. 133) *Social Contract* ([1762] 1913): 'Man was born free, yet everywhere he is in chains'.

At the heart of anarchism lies a distinctive tendency towards utopianism, at least in the sense that utopian thought has the imagination to visualize a society quite different from our own. As pointed out earlier, anarchists believe that human beings are capable of living together peacefully without the need for imposed order. Anarchist thought has thus sought to explain how social order can arise and be sustained in the absence of the machinery of 'law and order'. This has been done in two contrasting but usually interlocking ways. The first way in which anarchists have upheld the idea of natural, as opposed to political, order is through an analysis of human nature, or, more accurately, an analysis of the potentialities that reside in human nature. For example, collectivist anarchists have highlighted the human capacity for sociable and cooperative behaviour, while individualist anarchists have drawn attention to the importance of enlightened human reason.

KEY CONCEPT

UTOPIANISM

A utopia (from the Greek outopia, meaning 'nowhere', or eutopia, meaning 'good place') is usually taken to be perfect, or at least qualitatively better, society. Though utopias of various kinds can be envisaged, most are characterized by the abolition of want, the absence of conflict and the avoidance of oppression and violence.

Utopianism is a style of political theorizing that develops a critique of the existing order by constructing a model of an ideal or perfect alternative. Good examples are anarchism and Marxism. Utopian theories are usually based on assumptions about the unlimited possibilities of human self-development. However, utopianism is often used as a pejorative term to imply deluded or fanciful thinking, a belief in an unrealistic and unachievable goal.

For some anarchists, this potential for spontaneous harmony within human nature is linked to the belief that nature itself, and indeed the universe, is biased in favour of natural order. Anarchists have therefore sometimes been drawn to the ideas of Eastern religions such as Buddhism and Daoism, which emphasize interdependence and oneness. An alternative basis for natural order can be found in the notion of ecology, particularly the 'social ecology' of thinkers such as Murray Bookchin (see p. 120). (Social ecology is discussed in Chapter 10 in relation to eco-anarchism.) However, anarchism does not merely stress positive human potentialities. Anarchist theories of human nature are often complex, and acknowledge that rival potentialities reside within the human soul. For instance, in their different ways, Proudhon, Bakunin and Kropotkin (see p. 113) accepted that human beings could be selfish and competitive as well as sociable and cooperative (Morland, 1997). While the human 'core' may be morally and intellectually enlightened, a capacity for corruption lurks within each and every individual.

The second way in which anarchists have supported the idea of natural order is through a stress on the social institutions that foster positive human potential. In this view, human nature is 'plastic', in the sense that it is shaped by the social, political and economic

KEY FIGURE

MIKHAIL BAKUNIN (1814–76)

A Russian political agitator and revolutionary, Bakunin was one of the key proponents of collectivist anarchism and a leading figure within the nineteenth-century anarchist movement. Arguing that political power is intrinsically oppressive and placing his faith in human sociability, Bakunin proposed that freedom could only be achieved through 'collectivism', by which he meant self-governing communities based on voluntary cooperation, the absence of private property, and with rewards reflecting contributions. Bakunin extolled the 'sacred instinct of revolt' and was ferociously anti-theological.

Heritage Images/Hulton
Archive/Getty Images

circumstances within which people live. Just as law, government and the state breed a domination/subordination complex, other social institutions nurture respect, cooperation and harmony. Collectivist anarchists thus endorse common ownership or mutualist institutions, while individualist anarchists have supported the market mechanism. Nevertheless, the belief in a stable and peaceful yet stateless society has often been viewed as the weakest and most contentious aspect of anarchist theory. Opponents of anarchism have argued that, however socially enlightened institutions may be, if selfish or negative impulses are basic to human nature and not merely evidence of corruption, the prospect of natural order is simply a delusion. This is why utopianism is most pronounced within the collectivist tradition of anarchism and least pronounced within the individualist tradition, with some anarcho-capitalists rejecting utopianism altogether (Friedman, 1973).

Anti-clericalism

Although the state has been the principal target of anarchist hostility, the same criticisms apply to any other form of compulsory authority. Indeed, anarchists have sometimes expressed as much bitterness towards the church as they have towards the state, particularly in the nineteenth century. This perhaps explains why anarchism has prospered in countries with strong religious traditions, such as Catholic Spain, France, Italy and the countries of Latin America, where it has helped to articulate anti-clerical sentiments.

Anarchist objections to organized religion serve to highlight broader criticisms of authority in general. Religion, for example, has often been seen as the source of authority itself. The idea of God represents the notion of a 'supreme being' who commands ultimate and unquestionable authority. For anarchists such as Proudhon and Bakunin, an anarchist political philosophy had to be based on the rejection of Christianity, because only then could human beings be regarded as free and independent. Moreover, anarchists have suspected that religious and political authority usually work hand in hand. Bakunin proclaimed that '[t]he abolition of the Church and the State must be the first and indispensable condition of the true liberation of society'. Anarchists view religion as one of the pillars of the state: it propagates an ideology of obedience and submission to both spiritual leaders and earthly rulers. As the Bible says, 'give unto Caesar that which is Caesar's'. Earthly rulers have often looked to religion to legitimize their power, most obviously in the doctrine of the divine right of kings.

Finally, religion seeks to impose a set of moral principles on the individual, and to establish a code of acceptable behaviour. Religious belief requires conformity to standards of 'good' and 'evil', which are defined and policed by figures of religious authority such as priests, imams or rabbis. The individual is thus robbed of moral autonomy and the capacity to make ethical judgements. Nevertheless, anarchists do not reject the religious impulse altogether. There is a clear mystical strain within anarchism. Anarchists can be said to hold an essentially spiritual conception of human nature, a utopian belief in the virtually unlimited possibilities of human self-development and in the bonds that unite humanity, and indeed all living things. Early anarchists were sometimes influenced by **millenarianism**; indeed, anarchism has often been portrayed as a form of political millenarianism. Modern anarchists have often been attracted to religions such as Daoism and Zen Buddhism, which offer the prospect of personal insight and preach the values of toleration, respect and natural harmony (Christoyannopoulos, 2011).

Economic freedom

Anarchists have rarely seen the overthrow of the state as an end in itself, but have also been interested in challenging the structures of social and economic life. Bakunin (1973) argued that 'political power and wealth are inseparable'. In the nineteenth century, anarchists usually worked within the working-class movement and subscribed to a broadly socialist philosophy. Capitalism (see p. 77) was understood in class terms: a 'ruling class' exploits and oppresses 'the masses'. However, this 'ruling class' was not, in line with Marxism, interpreted in narrow economic terms, but was seen to encompass all those who command wealth, power or privilege in society. It therefore included kings and princes, politicians and state officials, judges and police officers, and bishops and priests, as well as industrialists and bankers. Bakunin thus argued that, in every developed society, three social groups can be identified: a vast majority who are exploited; a minority who are exploited but also exploit others in equal measure; and 'the supreme governing estate', a small minority of 'exploiters and oppressors pure and simple'. Hence, nineteenth-century anarchists identified themselves with the poor and oppressed and sought to carry out a social revolution in the name of the 'exploited masses', in which both capitalism and the state would be swept away.

However, it is the economic structure of life that most keenly exposes tensions within anarchism. While many anarchists acknowledge a kinship with socialism, based on a common distaste for property and inequality, others have defended property rights and even revered competitive capitalism. This highlights the distinction between the two major anarchist traditions, one of which is collectivist and the other individualist. Collectivist anarchists advocate an economy based on cooperation and collective ownership, while individualist anarchists support the market and private property.

Despite such fundamental differences, anarchists nevertheless agree about their distaste for the economic systems that dominated much of the twentieth century. All anarchists oppose the 'managed capitalism' that flourished in Western countries in the aftermath of World War II. Collectivist anarchists argue that state intervention merely props up a system of class exploitation and gives capitalism a human face. Individualist anarchists suggest that intervention distorts the competitive market and creates economies dominated by both public and private monopolies. Anarchists have been even more united in their disapproval of Soviet-style 'state socialism'. Individualist anarchists object to the violation of property rights and individual freedom that, they argue, occurs in a planned economy. Collectivist anarchists argue that 'state socialism' is a contradiction in terms,

Millenarianism: A belief in a thousand-year period of divine rule; political millenarianism offers the prospect of a sudden and complete emancipation from misery and oppression.

in that the state merely replaces the capitalist class as the main source of exploitation. Anarchists of all kinds have a preference for an economy in which free individuals manage their own affairs without the need for state ownership or regulation. However, this has allowed them to endorse a number of quite different economic systems, ranging from anarcho-communism to anarcho-capitalism.

TYPES OF ANARCHISM

Collectivist anarchism

The philosophical roots of collectivist anarchism (sometimes called anarcho-collectivism or social anarchism) lie in socialism rather than liberalism. Anarchist conclusions can be reached by pushing socialist collectivism to its limits. Collectivism is, in essence, the belief that human beings are social animals, better suited to working together for the common good than striving for individual self-interest. Collectivist anarchism stresses the human capacity for social solidarity, or what Kropotkin termed 'mutual aid'. As pointed out earlier, this does not amount to a naive belief in 'natural goodness', but rather highlights the potential for goodness that resides within all human beings. Human beings are, at heart, sociable, gregarious and cooperative creatures. In this light, the natural and proper relationship between and among people is one of sympathy, affection and harmony. When people are linked together by the recognition of a common humanity, they have no need to be regulated or controlled by government: as Bakunin (1973) proclaimed, 'Social solidarity is the first human law; freedom is the second law'. Not only is government unnecessary but, in replacing freedom with oppression, it also makes social solidarity impossible.

KEY FIGURE

PETER KROPOTKIN (1842–1921)

A Russian geographer and anarchist theorist, Kropotkin's work was imbued with a scientific spirit, based on a theory of evolution that he proposed as an alternative to Darwin's. By seeing 'mutual aid' as the principal means of human and animal development, he claimed to provide an empirical basis for both anarchism and communism, looking to reconstruct society on the basis of self-management and decentralization. Kropotkin's major works include *Mutual Aid* (1902), *The Conquest of Bread* (1892) and *Fields, Factories and Workshops* (1898).

Hulton Archive/Hulton Royals Collection/Getty Images

Philosophical and ideological overlaps between anarchism and socialism, particularly Marxist socialism, are evident in the fact that anarchists have often worked within a broad revolutionary socialist movement. For example, the First International, 1864–72, was set up by supporters of Proudhon and Marx. A number of clear theoretical parallels can be identified between collectivist anarchism and Marxism. Both:

● fundamentally reject capitalism, regarding it as a system of class exploitation and structural injustice

● have endorsed revolution as the preferred means of bringing about political change

● exhibit a preference for the collective ownership of wealth and the communal organization of social life

- believe that a fully communist society would be anarchic, expressed by Marx in the theory of the 'withering away' of the state

- agree that human beings have the ultimate capacity to order their affairs without the need for political authority.

Nevertheless, anarchism and socialism diverge at a number of points. This occurs most clearly in relation to parliamentary socialism. Anarchists dismiss parliamentary socialism as a contradiction in terms. Not only is it impossible to reform or 'humanize' capitalism through the corrupt and corrupting mechanisms of government, but also any expansion in the role and responsibilities of the state can only serve to entrench oppression, albeit in the name of equality and social justice. The bitterest disagreement between collectivist anarchists and Marxists centres on their rival conceptions of the transition from capitalism to communism. Marxists have called for a revolutionary 'dictatorship of the proletariat'. They nevertheless argue that this proletarian state will 'wither away' as capitalist class antagonisms abate. In this view, state power is nothing but a reflection of the class system, the state being, in essence, an instrument of class oppression. Anarchists, on the other hand, regard the state as evil and oppressive in its own right: it is, by its very nature, a corrupt and corrupting body. They therefore draw no distinction between bourgeois states and proletarian states. Genuine revolution, for an anarchist, requires not only the overthrow of capitalism but also the immediate and final overthrow of state power. The state cannot be allowed to 'wither away'; it must be abolished. Nevertheless, anarcho-collectivism has taken a variety of forms. The most significant of these are:

- mutualism

- anarcho-syndicalism

- anarcho-communism.

Mutualism

The anarchist belief in social solidarity has been used to justify various forms of cooperative behaviour. At one extreme, it has led to a belief in pure communism, but it has also generated the more modest ideas of **mutualism**, associated with Pierre-Joseph Proudhon. In a sense, Proudhon stood between the individualist and collectivist traditions of anarchism, Proudhon's ideas sharing much in common with those of US individualists such as Josiah Warren (1798–1874). In *What Is Property?* ([1840] 1970), Proudhon came up with the famous statement that 'Property is theft', and condemned a system of economic exploitation based on the accumulation of capital.

Nevertheless, unlike Marx, Proudhon was not opposed to all forms of private property, distinguishing between property and what he called 'possessions'. In particular, he admired the independence and initiative of small communities of peasants, craftsmen and artisans, especially the watchmakers of Switzerland, who had traditionally managed their affairs on the basis of mutual cooperation. Proudhon therefore sought, through mutualism, to establish a system of property ownership that would avoid exploitation and promote social

Mutualism: A system of fair and equitable exchange, in which individuals or groups bargain with one another, trading goods and services without profiteering or exploitation.

harmony. Social interaction in such a system would be voluntary, mutually beneficial and harmonious, thus requiring no regulation or interference by government. Proudhon's followers tried to put these ideas into practice by setting up mutual credit banks in France and Switzerland, which provided cheap loans for investors and charged a rate of interest only high enough to cover the cost of running the bank, but not so high that it made a profit.

KEY FIGURE

PIERRE-JOSEPH PROUDHON (1809–65)

A French social theorist, political activist and largely self-educated printer, Proudhon's writings influenced many nineteenth-century anarchists, socialists and communists. His best-known work, *What Is Property?* (1840), attacked both traditional property rights and collective ownership, and argued instead for mutualism, a cooperative productive system geared towards need rather than profit and organized within self-governing communities. In *The Federal Principle* (1863), Proudhon proposed that such communities should interact on the basis of 'federal' compacts, although this federal state would have minimal functions.

adoc-photos/Corbis Historical/
Getty Images

Anarcho-syndicalism

Although mutualism and anarcho-communism exerted significant influence within the broader socialist movement in the late nineteenth and early twentieth centuries, anarchism only developed into a mass movement in its own right in the form of anarcho-syndicalism. Syndicalism is a form of revolutionary trade unionism, drawing its name from the French word *syndicat*, meaning union or group. Syndicalism emerged first in France, and was embraced by the powerful CGT union in the period before 1914. Syndicalist ideas spread to Italy, Latin America, the USA and, most significantly, Spain, where the country's largest union, the CNT, supported them.

Syndicalism draws on socialist ideas and advances a theory of stark class war. Workers and peasants are seen to constitute an oppressed class, and industrialists, landlords, politicians, judges and the police are portrayed as exploiters. Workers defend themselves by organizing syndicates or unions, based on particular crafts, industries or professions. In the short term, these syndicates act as conventional trade unions, raising wages, shortening hours and improving working conditions.

However, syndicalists are also revolutionaries, who look forward to the overthrow of capitalism and the seizure of power by the workers. In *Reflections on Violence* ([1908] 1950), Georges Sorel (1847–1922), the influential French syndicalist theorist, argued that such a revolution would come about through a general strike, a 'revolution of empty hands'. Sorel believed that the general strike was a '**political myth**', a symbol of working-class power, capable of inspiring popular revolt.

While syndicalist theory was at times unsystematic and confused, it nevertheless exerted a strong attraction for anarchists who wished to spread their ideas among the masses. As anarchists entered the syndicalist movement, they developed the distinctive ideas of anarcho-syndicalism. Two features of syndicalism inspired particular anarchist enthusiasm. First, syndicalists rejected conventional politics as corrupting and pointless. Working-class power, they believed, should be exerted through direct action, boycotts, sabotage and strikes, and ultimately a general strike. Second, anarchists saw the syndicate as a model for the decentralized, non-hierarchic society of the future. Syndicates typically exhibited a high degree of grassroots democracy and formed federations with other syndicates, either in the same area or in the same industry.

Although anarcho-syndicalism enjoyed genuine mass support, at least until the Spanish Civil War, it failed to achieve its revolutionary objectives.

> **Political myth:** A belief that has the capacity to provoke political action by virtue of its emotional power rather than through an appeal to reason.

Beyond the rather vague idea of the general strike, anarcho-syndicalism did not develop a clear political strategy or a theory of revolution. Other anarchists have criticized syndicalism for concentrating too narrowly on short-term trade union goals, and therefore for leading anarchism away from revolution and towards reformism.

Anarcho-communism

In its most radical form, a belief in social solidarity leads in the direction of collectivism and full communism. Sociable and gregarious human beings should lead a shared and communal existence. For example, labour is a social experience, people work in common with fellow human beings and the wealth they produce should therefore be owned in common by the community, rather than by any single individual. In this sense, *all* forms of private property are theft: they represent the exploitation of workers, who alone create wealth, by employers who merely own it. Furthermore, private property encourages selfishness and, particularly offensive to the anarchist, promotes conflict and social disharmony. Inequality in the ownership of wealth fosters greed, envy and resentment, and therefore breeds crime and disorder.

Anarcho-communism stresses the human potential for cooperation, expressed most famously by Peter Kropotkin's theory of 'mutual aid'. Kropotkin attempted to provide a biological foundation for social solidarity via a re-examination of Darwin's theory of evolution. Whereas theorists such as the UK social thinker Herbert Spencer (1820–1903) had used Darwinism to support the idea that humankind is naturally competitive and aggressive, Kropotkin argued that species are successful precisely because they manage to harness collective energies through cooperation. The process of evolution thus strengthens sociability and favours cooperation over competition. Successful species, such as the human species, must, Kropotkin concluded, have a strong propensity for mutual aid. Kropotkin argued that while mutual aid had flourished in, for example, the city-states of Ancient Greece and medieval Europe, it had been subverted by competitive capitalism, threatening the further evolution of the human species.

Although Proudhon had warned that communism could only be brought about by an authoritarian state, anarcho-communists such as Kropotkin and Errico Malatesta (1853–1932) argued that true communism requires the abolition of the state. Anarcho-communists admire small, self-managing communities along the lines of the medieval city-state or the peasant commune. Kropotkin envisaged that an anarchic society would consist of a collection of largely self-sufficient communes, each owning its wealth in common.

From the anarcho-communist perspective, the communal organization of social and economic life has three key advantages. First, as communes are based on the principles of sharing and collective endeavour, they strengthen the bonds of compassion and solidarity, and help to keep greed and selfishness at bay. Second, within communes, decisions are made through a process of participatory or **direct democracy**, which guarantees a high level of popular participation and political equality. Popular self-government is the only form of government that would be acceptable to anarchists. Third, communes are small-scale or 'human-scale' communities, which allow people to manage their own affairs through face-to-face interaction. In the anarchist view, centralization is always associated with depersonalized and bureaucratic social processes.

Direct democracy: Popular self-government, characterized by the direct and continuous participation of citizens in the tasks of government.

Individualist anarchism

The philosophical basis of individualist anarchism (sometimes called anarcho-individualism) lies in the liberal idea of the sovereign individual. In many ways, anarchist conclusions are reached by pushing liberal individualism to its logical extreme. For example, William Godwin's anarchism amounts to a form of extreme classical liberalism. At the heart of liberalism is a belief in the primacy of the individual and the central importance of individual freedom. In the classical liberal view, freedom is negative: it consists in the absence of external constraints on the individual. When individualism is taken to its extreme, it therefore implies individual sovereignty: the idea that absolute and unlimited authority resides within each human being. From this perspective, any constraint on the individual is evil; but when this constraint is imposed by the state, by definition a sovereign, compulsory and coercive body, it amounts to an absolute evil. Quite simply, the individual cannot be sovereign in a society ruled by law and government. Individualism and the state are thus irreconcilable principles. As Wolff (1998) put it, 'The autonomous man, insofar as he is autonomous, is not subject to the will of another'.

KEY FIGURE

WILLIAM GODWIN (1756–1836)

A British philosopher and novelist, Godwin developed a thorough-going critique of authoritarianism that amounted to the first full exposition of anarchist beliefs. Adopting an optimism based on the Enlightenment view of human nature as rational and perfectible, based on education and social conditioning, Godwin argued that humanity would become increasingly capable of self-government, meaning that the need for government (and, with it, war, poverty, crime and violence) would disappear. Godwin's chief political work is *Enquiry Concerning Political Justice* (1793).

Culture Club/Hulton Archive/ Getty Images

Although these arguments are liberal in inspiration, significant differences exist between liberalism and individualist anarchism. First, while liberals accept the importance of individual liberty, they do not believe this can be guaranteed in a stateless society. Classical liberals argue that a minimal or 'nightwatchman' state is necessary to prevent self-seeking individuals from abusing one another by theft, intimidation, violence or even murder. Law therefore exists to protect freedom, rather than constrain it. Modern liberals take this argument further, and defend state intervention on the grounds that it enlarges positive freedom. Anarchists, in contrast, believe that individuals can conduct themselves peacefully, harmoniously and prosperously without the need for government to 'police' society and protect them from their fellow human beings. Anarchists differ from liberals because they believe that free individuals can live and work together constructively because they are rational and moral creatures. Reason and morality dictate that where conflict exists it should be resolved by arbitration or debate, and not by violence.

Second, liberals believe that government power can be 'tamed' or controlled by the development of constitutional and representative institutions. Constitutions claim to protect the individual by limiting the power of government and creating checks and balances among its various institutions. Regular elections are designed to force government to be accountable to the general public, or at least a majority of the electorate. Anarchists dismiss the idea of limited, constitutional or representative government. All laws infringe individual liberty, whether the government that enacts them is constitutional or arbitrary, democratic or dictatorial. In other words, all states are an offence against individual liberty. However, anarcho-individualism has taken a number of forms. The most important of these are:

- egoism
- libertarianism
- anarcho-capitalism.

Egoism

The boldest statement of anarchist convictions built on the idea of the sovereign individual is found in Max Stirner's *The Ego and His Own* ([1845] 1971). Like Marx, Stirner was deeply influenced by the ideas of the German philosopher G. W. F. Hegel (1770–1831), but the two arrived at fundamentally different conclusions. Stirner's theories represent an extreme form of individualism. The term 'egoism' can have two meanings. It can suggest that individuals are essentially concerned about their ego or 'self', that they are self-interested or self-seeking, an assumption that would be accepted by thinkers such as Hobbes or Locke. Self-interestedness, however, can generate conflict among individuals and justify the existence of a state, which would be needed to restrain each individual from harming or abusing others.

KEY FIGURE

MAX STIRNER (1806–56)

A German philosopher, Stirner developed an extreme form of individualism, based on egoism, which condemned all checks on personal autonomy. In contrast to other anarchists' stress on moral principles such as justice, reason and community, Stirner emphasized solely the 'ownness' of the human individual, thereby placing the individual self at the centre of the moral universe. Such thinking influenced Nietzsche (see p. 154) and later provided a basis for existentialism. Stirner's most important political work is *The Ego and His Own* (1845).

INTERFOTO/Alamy Stock Photo

In Stirner's view, egoism is a philosophy that places the individual self at the centre of the moral universe. The individual, from this perspective, should simply act as he or she chooses, without any consideration for laws, social conventions, religious or moral principles. This is a position that clearly points in the direction of both atheism and an extreme form of individualist anarchism. However, as Stirner's anarchism also dramatically turned its back on the principles of the Enlightenment and contained few proposals about how order could be maintained in a stateless society, it had relatively little impact on the emerging anarchist movement. His ideas nevertheless influenced Friedrich Nietzsche (see p. 154) and twentieth-century existentialism.

Libertarianism

The individualist argument was more fully developed in the USA by libertarian thinkers such as Henry David Thoreau (see p. 119), Lysander Spooner (1808–87), Benjamin Tucker (1854–1939) and Josiah Warren (1798–1874). Thoreau's quest for spiritual truth and self-reliance led him to flee from civilized life and live for several years in virtual solitude, close to nature, an experience described in *Walden* ([1854] 1983). In his most political work, 'Civil Disobedience' ([1849] 1983), Thoreau approved of Jefferson's liberal motto, 'That government is best which governs least', but adapted it to conform with his own anarchist sentiment: 'That government is best which governs not at all'. For Thoreau, individualism leads in the direction of civil disobedience: the individual has to be faithful to his or her conscience and do only what each believes to be right, regardless of the demands of society or the laws made by government. Thoreau's anarchism places individual conscience above the demands of political obligation. In Thoreau's case, this led him to disobey a US government he thought was acting immorally, both in upholding slavery and in waging war against other countries.

KEY FIGURE

HENRY DAVID THOREAU (1817–62)

A US author, poet and philosopher, Thoreau's writings had a significant impact on individualist anarchism and, later, on the environmental movement. A follower of transcendentalism, Thoreau's major work, *Walden* (1854), described his two-year 'experiment' in simple living, which emphasized the virtues of self-reliance, contemplation and a closeness to nature. In 'Civil Disobedience' (1849), he defended the validity of conscientious objection to unjust laws, emphasizing that government should never conflict with individual conscience, but he stopped short of explicitly advocating anarchy.

Hulton Archive/Hulton Archive/ Getty Images

Benjamin Tucker took libertarianism (see p. 61) further by considering how autonomous individuals could live and work with one another without the danger of conflict or disorder. Two possible solutions to this problem are available to the individualist. The first emphasizes human rationality, and suggests that when conflicts or disagreements develop they can be resolved by reasoned discussion. This, for example, was the position adopted by Godwin, who believed that truth will always tend to displace falsehood. The second solution is to find some sort of mechanism through which the independent actions of free individuals could be brought into harmony with one another. Extreme individualists such as Warren and Tucker believed that this could be achieved through a system of market exchange. Warren thought that individuals have a sovereign right to the property they themselves produce, but are also forced by economic logic to work with others in order to gain the advantages of the division of labour. He suggested that this could be achieved by a system of 'labour-for-labour' exchange, and set up 'time stores' through which one person's labour could be exchanged for a promise to return labour in kind. Tucker argued that 'Genuine anarchism is consistent Manchesterism', referring to the nineteenth-century free-trade, free-market principles of Richard Cobden and John Bright (Nozick, 1974).

Anarcho-capitalism

The revival of interest in free-market economics in the late twentieth century led to increasingly radical political conclusions. New Right conservatives, attracted to classical economics, wished to 'get government off the back of business' and allow the economy to be disciplined by market forces, rather than managed by an interventionist state. Right-wing libertarians such as Robert Nozick (see p. 65) revived the idea of a minimal state, whose principal function is to protect individual rights. Other thinkers, for instance Ayn Rand (see p. 63), Murray Rothbard and David Friedman (1973), have pushed free-market ideas to their limit and developed a form of anarcho-capitalism. They have argued that government can be abolished and be replaced by unregulated market competition. Property should be owned by sovereign individuals, who may choose, if they wish, to enter into voluntary contracts with others in the pursuit of self-interest. The individual thus remains free and the market, beyond the control of any single individual or group, regulates all social interaction.

KEY FIGURE

MURRAY ROTHBARD (1926–95)

A US economist and libertarian thinker, Rothbard advocated 'anarcho-capitalism' based on combining an extreme form of Lockean liberalism with Austrian School free-market economics. Taking the right of total self-ownership to be a 'universal ethic', he argued that economic freedom is incompatible with the power of government and became a fierce enemy of the 'welfare-warfare' state, championing non-intervention in both domestic and foreign affairs. Rothbard's key writings include *Man, Economy and State* (1962), *For a New Liberty* (1978) and *The Ethics of Liberty* (1982).

Bettmann/Getty Images

TENSIONS WITHIN... ANARCHISM

Individualist anarchism	v.	Collectivist anarchism
Ultra-liberalism	⬌	Ultra-socialism
Extreme individualism	⬌	Extreme collectivism
Sovereign individual	⬌	Social solidarity
Civil disobedience	⬌	Social revolution
Atomism	⬌	Organicism
Egoism	⬌	Communalism
Market relations	⬌	Social obligations
Private property	⬌	Common ownership
Anarcho-capitalism	⬌	Anarcho-communism

Anarcho-capitalists go well beyond the ideas of free-market liberalism. Liberals believe that the market is an effective and efficient mechanism for delivering most goods, but argue that it also has its limits. Some services, such as the maintenance of domestic order, the enforcement of contracts and protection against external attack, are 'public goods', which must be provided by the state because they cannot be supplied through market competition. Anarcho-capitalists, however, believe that the market can satisfy all human wants. For example, Rothbard (1978) recognized that in an anarchist society individuals will seek protection from one another, but argued that such protection can be delivered competitively by privately owned 'protection associations' and 'private courts', without the need for a police force or a state court system.

Indeed, according to anarcho-capitalists, profit-making protection agencies would offer a better service than the present police force because competition would provide consumers with a choice, ensuring that agencies are cheap, efficient and responsive to consumer needs. Similarly, private courts would be forced to develop a reputation for fairness in order to attract custom from individuals wishing to resolve a conflict. Most important, unlike the authority of public bodies, the contracts thus made with private agencies would be entirely voluntary, regulated only by impersonal market forces. Radical though such proposals may sound, the policy of privatization has already made substantial advances in many Western countries. In the USA, several states already use private prisons, and experiments with private courts and arbitration services are well established. In the UK, private prisons and the use of private protection agencies have become commonplace, and schemes such as 'Neighbourhood Watch' have helped to transfer responsibility for public order from the police to the community.

THE FUTURE OF ANARCHISM

The future prospects for anarchism are widely considered to be strictly limited. The fact that experiments in anarchism have been rare and always short-lived – examples include Makhnovia in 1918–21 (during the Ukrainian Civil War) and Catalonia in 1936 (at the outbreak of the Spanish Civil War) – has encouraged many to treat anarchism as an ideology of less significance than, say, liberalism, socialism, conservatism or fascism. In this light, anarchism is destined to be confined to the political fringe. It has the capacity, at times, to disrupt conventional patterns of politics, or to challenge (and possibly fertilize) other ideological traditions, but never to win power, at least at the national level. For critics of anarchism, this reflects two key flaws in the ideology. The first and most serious of these is that the goal of anarchism – the overthrow of the state and dismantling of all forms of political authority – is simply unworkable, an impossible dream. This claim is often associated with a naive belief in natural goodness that misrepresents the complexity of most anarchists' theories of human nature. But it also highlights major doubts about how far social harmony can be upheld in the absence of political order, except in non-hierarchic and egalitarian traditional societies, such as the Nuer people centred around South Sudan in Africa, who live in a cluster of autonomous sections and clans.

The second obstacle to the future influence of anarchism relates more to the means available to anarchists rather than the ends they seek to achieve. If the state is evil and oppressive, any attempt to win government power or even influence government must be corrupting and unhealthy. For example, electoral politics is based on a model of representative democracy, which anarchists firmly reject. Political power is always oppressive, regardless of whether it is acquired through the ballot box or at the point of a gun. Similarly, anarchists are disenchanted by political parties, both parliamentary and revolutionary, because they are bureaucratic and hierarchic organizations. The idea of an anarchist government, an anarchist party or an anarchist politician would therefore appear to be contradictions in terms. To make matters worse, denied the option of using conventional means of political activism, anarchists have sometimes employed terrorist tactics, creating a damaging link in the popular consciousness between anarchism and violence. Anarchist violence was prominent in two periods in particular – in the late nineteenth century, reaching its peak in the 1890s; and again in the 1970s – but, on each occasion, it left the state stronger not weaker, its repressive machinery significantly expanded.

Nevertheless, not only does anarchism stubbornly refuse to die, but it may also be set to remain a significant ideological force for years to come. One reason for this is that, because of its uncompromising attitude to authority and political activism, anarchism has an enduring and often strong, moral appeal, especially to the young. By its very existence, anarchism thus keeps alive the idea that, in the words of the anti-capitalist slogan, a 'better world is possible'. Furthermore, using anarchism's failure to achieve power and reshape societies as evidence of its limited influence may be to miss the point of anarchism itself. By seeking to radically disperse and decentralize political power – rather than to *seize* power in the conventional sense – anarchism exerts a socio-cultural influence that extends over a broader range of concerns than many other ideologies. Thus, not only does anarchism currently operate within a highly diverse and sometimes fragmented anti-anti-globalization movement, but the anarchist element within this movement is itself highly eclectic. Among other things, anarchists give priority to addressing the climate crisis, uphold animal rights, oppose **consumerism**, condemn global inequality, and support new thinking in areas ranging from transport and urban development to drugs policy and gender politics. However, while this span of political concerns may be impressive, particularly in demonstrating anarchism's capacity to stimulate innovative and wider reflection, it may also underline the disparate nature of anarchist ideology, calling its coherence into question.

Consumerism: A psychic and social phenomenon whereby personal happiness is equated with the consumption of material possessions.

QUESTIONS FOR DISCUSSION

- Why do anarchists view the state as evil and oppressive?
- How and why is anarchism linked to utopianism?
- How, and how effectively, have anarchists sustained the idea of natural order?
- Is collectivist anarchism simply an extreme form of socialism?
- How do anarcho-communists and Marxists agree, and over what do they disagree?
- To what extent are anarchism and syndicalism compatible?

- How do individualist anarchists reconcile egoism with statelessness?
- Is anarcho-individualism merely free-market liberalism taken to its logical conclusion?
- To what extent do anarchists disagree about the nature of the future anarchist society?
- How can the political success of anarchism best be judged?
- Why have anarchist ideas been attractive to modern social movements?
- Do anarchists demand the impossible?

⦿ FURTHER READING

Huemer, M. *The Problem of Political Authority* (2013). A thoroughly argued volume on anarchist philosophy and politics, and specifically anarcho-capitalism, which is less covered elsewhere.

Kinna, R. (ed.) *The Bloomsbury Companion to Anarchism* (2014). The most comprehensive handbook on anarchist scholarship and research, particularly from non-Western perspectives.

Kinna, R. *The Government of No One: The Theory and Practice of Anarchism* (2020). A sympathetic general introduction to anarchism, providing a general overview of its key principles, traditions, and practices.

Marshall, P. *Demanding the Impossible: A History of Anarchism* (2009). A very comprehensive, authoritative and enthusiastic account of the full range of anarchist theories and beliefs.

An Anarchist FAQ https://theanarchistlibrary.org/. Collectively produced and freely licensed since 1995, the Anarchist FAQ is an enormous wealth of information on various anarchist branches, movements and history across the world, continuously updated.

CHAPTER 6

NATIONALISM

PREVIEW

The word 'nation' has been used since the thirteenth century and derives from the Latin *nasci*, meaning to be born. In the form of *natio*, it referred to a group of people united by birth or birthplace. In its original usage, nation thus implied a breed of people or a racial group, but possessed no political significance. It was not until the late eighteenth century that the term acquired political overtones, as individuals and groups started to be classified as 'nationalists'. The term 'nationalism' was first used in print in 1789 by the anti-Jacobin French priest Augustin Barruel. By the mid-nineteenth century, nationalism was widely recognized as a political doctrine or movement; for example, as a major ingredient of the revolutions that swept across Europe in 1848.

Nationalism can be defined broadly as the belief that the nation is the central principle of political organization. As such, it is based on two core assumptions. First, humankind is naturally divided into distinct nations and, second, the nation is the most appropriate, and perhaps only legitimate, unit of political rule. Classical political nationalism therefore set out to bring the borders of the state into line with the boundaries of the nation. Within so-called nation-states, nationality and citizenship would therefore coincide. However, nationalism is a complex and highly diverse ideological phenomenon. Not only are there distinctive political, cultural and ethnic forms of nationalism, but the political implications of nationalism have also been wide-ranging and sometimes contradictory. Although nationalism has been associated with a principled belief in national self-determination, based on the assumption that all nations are equal, it has also been used to defend traditional institutions and the established social order, as well as to fuel programmes of war, conquest and imperialism. Nationalism, moreover, has been linked to widely contrasting ideological traditions, ranging from liberalism to fascism.

HISTORICAL OVERVIEW

The idea of nationalism was born during the French Revolution. Previously, countries had been thought of as 'realms', 'principalities' or 'kingdoms'. The inhabitants of a country were 'subjects', their political identity being formed by an allegiance to a ruler or ruling dynasty, rather than any sense of national identity or patriotism. However, the revolutionaries in France who rose up against Louis XVI in 1789 did so in the name of the people, and understood the people to be the 'French nation'. Their ideas were influenced by the writings of Jean-Jacques Rousseau (see p. 133) and the new doctrine of popular self-government. Nationalism was therefore a revolutionary and democratic creed, reflecting the idea that 'subjects of the crown' should become 'citizens of France'. The **nation** should be its own master, or, as the French rationalist scholar Ernest Renan (1823–92) put it, the nation is a 'daily plebiscite'. However, such ideas were not the exclusive property of the French. During the Revolutionary and Napoleonic Wars (1792–1815), much of continental Europe was invaded by France, giving rise to both resentment against France and a desire for **independence**. In Italy and Germany, long divided into a collection of states, the experience of conquest helped to forge, for the first time, a consciousness of national unity, expressed in a new language of nationalism, inherited from France. Nationalist ideas also spread to Latin America in the early nineteenth century, where Simon Bolivar (1783–1830), 'the Liberator', led revolutions against Spanish rule in what was then New Grenada, now the countries of Colombia, Venezuela and Ecuador, as well as in Peru and Bolivia.

In many respects, nationalism developed into the most successful and compelling of political creeds, helping to shape and reshape history in many parts of the world for over two hundred years. The rising tide of nationalism re-drew the map of Europe in the nineteenth century as the autocratic and multinational empires of Turkey, Austria and Russia started to crumble in the face of liberal and nationalist pressure. In 1848, nationalist uprisings broke out in the Italian states, among the Czechs and the Hungarians, and in Germany, where the desire for national unity was expressed in the creation of the short-lived Frankfurt parliament. The nineteenth century was a period of nation building. Italy, once dismissed by the Austrian Chancellor Metternich as a 'mere geographical expression', became a united state in 1861, the process of **unification** being completed with the acquisition of Rome in 1870. Germany, formerly a collection of 39 states, was unified in 1871, following the Franco-Prussian War.

Nation: A collection of people bound together by shared values and traditions, a common language, religion and history, and usually occupying the same geographical area (see p. 131).

Independence: The process through which a nation is liberated from foreign rule, usually involving the establishment of sovereign statehood.

Unification: The process through which a collection of separate political entities, usually sharing cultural characteristics, are integrated into a single state.

KEY CONCEPT

PATRIOTISM

Patriotism (from the Latin *patria*, meaning 'fatherland') is a sentiment, a psychological attachment to one's nation, literally a 'love of one's country'. The terms nationalism and patriotism are often confused. Nationalism has a doctrinal character and embodies the belief that the nation is in some way the central principle of political organization. Patriotism provides the affective basis for that belief, and thus underpins all forms of nationalism. It is difficult to conceive of a national group demanding, say, political independence without possessing at least a measure of patriotic loyalty or national consciousness. However, not all patriots are nationalists. Not all of those who identify with, or even love, their nation, see it as a means through which political demands can be articulated.

Nevertheless, it would be a mistake to assume that nationalism was either an irresistible or a genuinely popular movement during this period. Enthusiasm for nationalism was largely restricted to the rising middle classes, who were attracted to the ideas of national unity and constitutional government. Although middle-class nationalist movements kept the dream of national unity or independence alive, they were nowhere strong enough to accomplish the process of nation building on their own. Where nationalist goals were realized, as in Italy and Germany, it was because nationalism coincided with the ambition of rising states such as Piedmont and Prussia. For example, German unification owed more to the Prussian army (which defeated Denmark in 1864, Austria in 1866 and France in 1870–71) than it did to the liberal nationalist movement.

However, by the end of the nineteenth century nationalism had become a truly popular movement, with the spread of flags, national anthems, patriotic poetry and literature, public ceremonies and national holidays. Nationalism became the language of mass politics, made possible by the growth of primary education, mass literacy and the spread of popular newspapers. The character of nationalism also changed. Nationalism had previously been associated with liberal and progressive movements, but was taken up increasingly by conservative and reactionary politicians. Nationalism came to stand for social cohesion, order and stability, particularly in the face of the growing challenge of socialism, which embodied the ideas of social revolution and international working-class solidarity. Nationalism sought to integrate the increasingly powerful working class into the nation, and so to preserve the established social structure. Patriotic fervour was no longer aroused by the prospect of political liberty or democracy, but by the commemoration of past national glories and military victories. Such nationalism became increasingly **chauvinistic** and **xenophobic**. Each nation claimed its own unique or superior qualities, while other nations were regarded as alien, untrustworthy, even menacing. This new climate of popular nationalism helped to fuel policies of imperialism that intensified dramatically in the 1870s and 1880s and, by the end of the century, had brought most of the world's population under European control. It also contributed to a mood of international rivalry and suspicion, which led to the outbreak of World War I in 1914.

Chauvinism: Uncritical and unreasoned dedication to a cause or group, typically based on a belief in its superiority, as in 'national chauvinism' or 'male chauvinism'.

Xenophobia: A fear or hatred of foreigners; pathological ethnocentrism.

The end of World War I in 1918 saw the completion of the process of nation building in Central and Eastern Europe. At the Paris Peace Conference, Woodrow Wilson (see p. 138) advocated the principle of national self-determination. The German, Austro-Hungarian and Russian empires were broken up and eight new states created, including Finland, Hungary,

KEY CONCEPT
IMPERIALISM

Imperialism is, broadly, the policy of extending the power or rule of the state beyond its boundaries, typically through the establishment of an empire. In its earliest usage, imperialism was an ideology that supported military expansion and imperial acquisition, usually by drawing on nationalist and racialist doctrines. In its traditional form, imperialism involves the establishment of formal political domination or colonialism and reflects the expansion of state power through a process of conquest and (possibly) settlement. Neo-imperialism (sometimes called neocolonialism) is characterized less by political control and more by economic and ideological domination; it is often seen as a product of structural imbalances in the international economy and/or biases that operate within the institutions of global economic governance.

Czechoslovakia, Poland and Yugoslavia. These new countries were designed to be **nation-states** that conformed to the geography of existing national or ethnic groups. However, World War I failed to resolve the serious national tensions that had precipitated conflict in the first place. Indeed, the experience of defeat and disappointment with the terms of the peace treaties left an inheritance of frustrated ambition and bitterness. This was most evident in Germany, Italy and Japan, where fascist or authoritarian movements came to power in the interwar period by promising to restore national pride through policies of expansion and **empire**. Nationalism was therefore a powerful factor leading to war in both 1914 and 1939.

During the twentieth century the doctrine of nationalism, which had been born in Europe, spread throughout the globe as the peoples of Asia and Africa rose in opposition to colonial rule. The process of colonialism had involved not only the establishment of political control and economic dominance, but also the importation of Western ideas, including nationalism, which began to be used against the colonial masters themselves. Nationalist uprisings took place in Egypt in 1919 and quickly spread throughout the Middle East. The Anglo-Afghan war also broke out in 1919, and rebellions took place in India, the Dutch East Indies and Indochina. After 1945, the maps of Africa and Asia were redrawn as the British, French, Dutch and Portuguese empires each disintegrated in the face of nationalist movements that either succeeded in negotiating independence or winning wars of 'national liberation'. The collapse of the world's last major empire, the Soviet empire, which took place against the backdrop of the fall of communism during 1989–91, encouraged many to believe that the task of nationalism had been substantially completed: the world had become a world of nation-states.

However, the early decades of the twenty-first century have been marked by a resurgence of nationalism. This has happened in at least two ways. First, nationalism has returned as a reaction against globalization (see p. 21) and the deep economic, cultural and political changes it brings in its wake. This became more apparent in the aftermath of the 2007–09 global financial crisis, as national populist parties made progress across much of Europe, and beyond, and the UK voted in a referendum in 2016 to leave the European Union ('Brexit'). Opposition to immigration and cultural mixing played a major part in this process, as discussed in Chapter 8. Second, nationalism has grown in prominence due to intensifying rivalries between great powers since the end of the Cold War. For example, China's remarkable economic revival has been accompanied by rising nationalism, in forms including the increased prominence of Confucianism and the firm and sometimes forcible response to independence movements in Tibet and Xinjiang. Similar tendencies can be identified in Russia under Vladimir Putin, perhaps most clearly demonstrated by the annexation of Crimea from Ukraine in 2014. As far as the USA is concerned, the election of Donald Trump in 2016 was followed by a wave of **economic nationalism** under the banner of 'America First', which especially aimed at reordering the USA's trading relationship with China. These great-power rivalries were further intensified by the outbreak of the Covid-19 pandemic (see p. 128).

Nation-state: A sovereign political association within which citizenship and nationality overlap; one nation within a single state.

Empire: A structure of domination in which diverse cultural, ethnic or nation groups are subjected to a single source of authority.

Economic nationalism: An economic policy that seeks to bolster the domestic economy through protectionism, involving the use of tariffs and so-called non-tariff barriers.

POLITICAL IDEOLOGIES IN ACTION . . .

NATIONALISM AND THE PANDEMIC

EVENTS: Towards the end of December 2019, reports started to emerge of a cluster of pneumonia cases of unknown origin in the Chinese city of Wuhan and surrounding Hubei province. In late January 2020, the cause of this outbreak was identified as a new strain of coronavirus, Covid-19. Although Covid-19 turned out to be less deadly than some earlier viruses, it spread at devastating speed. In part, this was because the disease can be transmitted without people having symptoms and so without them knowing that they are ill. Declared a pandemic by the World Health Organization on 11 March 2020, the areas worst hit by the disease shifted first from East Asia to Europe, and from there to the USA, South America, India and Africa. The worldwide death rate from the Covid-19 pandemic passed 2 million in January 2021.

Greg Baker/Getty

SIGNIFICANCE: One of the major consequences of the Covid-19 pandemic has been a general strengthening of nationalism, reinforcing a pre-existing trend for nations to turn inward. This was demonstrated most clearly by the fact that during the pandemic national governments were the chief decision-making bodies, international institutions playing little or no role. Policy responses to the mounting crisis also tended to be isolationist and exclusionary in character: borders were closed, international travel was restricted and controls were imposed on exports such as protective medical equipment. This drift towards nationalism was bolstered by heightened great-power rivalry, especially a further deterioration in Sino–US relations. Thus, while the USA focused on Chinese responsibility for the pandemic and the virus (the 'Chinese' virus, as President Trump sometimes put it), China used its success in speedily bringing the disease under control as a means of demonstrating the superiority of its system of rule.

Furthermore, it has been claimed that national populist leaders and regimes responded to the intensifying public health crisis in broadly similar ways. After all, the leaders of the three countries that, in July 2020, had the highest death toll from Covid-19 each, in his own way, cultivated a populist 'strongman' image – the USA's Donald Trump, Brazil's Jai Bolsonaro and the UK's Boris Johnson. It has been argued that while some national populist leaders used the severity of the outbreak to enhance their own power and silence their critics, others treated the threat as bogus or at least seriously exaggerated. Bolsonaro (to use but one example) consistently downplayed the crisis and defied his health minister's advice on social distancing by going into the streets to eat doughnuts and mingle with his supporters.

CORE THEMES

To treat nationalism as an ideology in its own right is to encounter at least three problems. The first is that nationalism is sometimes classified as a political doctrine rather than a fully-fledged ideology. Whereas, for instance, liberalism, conservatism and socialism constitute complex sets of interrelated ideas and values, nationalism, the argument goes, is at heart the simple belief that the nation is the natural and proper unit of government. The drawback of this view is that it focuses only on what might be regarded as 'classical' **political nationalism,** and ignores the many other, and in some respects no less

Political nationalism: A form of nationalism that regards the nation as a natural political community, usually expressed through the idea of national self-determination.

significant, manifestations of nationalism, such as **cultural nationalism** and **ethnic nationalism**. The core feature of nationalism is therefore not its narrow association with self-government and the nation-state, but its broader link to movements and ideas that in whatever way acknowledge the central importance to political life of the nation.

Second, nationalism is sometimes portrayed as an essentially psychological phenomenon – usually as loyalty towards one's nation or dislike of other nations – instead of as a theoretical construct. Undoubtedly, one of the key features of nationalism is the potency of its affective or emotional appeal, but to understand it in these terms alone is to mistake the ideology of nationalism for the sentiment of patriotism.

Third, nationalism has a schizophrenic political character. At different times, nationalism has been progressive and reactionary, democratic and authoritarian, rational and irrational, and left-wing and right-wing. It has also been associated with almost all the major ideological traditions. In their different ways, liberals, conservatives, socialists, fascists and even communists have been attracted to nationalism; perhaps only anarchism, by virtue of its outright rejection of the state, is fundamentally at odds with nationalism. Nevertheless, although nationalist doctrines have been used by a bewildering variety of political movements and associated with sometimes diametrically opposed political causes, a bedrock of nationalist ideas and theories can be identified. The most important of these are:

- the nation

- organic community

- self-determination

- culturalism.

The nation

The basic belief of nationalism is that the nation is, or should be, the central principle of political organization. However, much confusion surrounds what nations are and how they can be defined. In everyday language, words such as 'nation', 'state', 'country' and even 'race' are often confused or used as if they are interchangeable. Many political disputes, moreover, are really disputes about whether a particular group of people should be regarded as a nation, and should therefore enjoy the rights and status associated with nationhood. This applies, for instance, to the Tibetans, the Kurds, the Palestinians, the Basques, the Tamils, and so on.

On the most basic level, nations are cultural entities, collections of people bound together by shared values and traditions, in particular a common language, religion and history, and usually occupying the same geographical area. From this point of view, the nation can be defined by 'objective' factors: people who satisfy a requisite set of cultural criteria can be said to belong to a nation; those who do not can be classified as non-nationals or members of foreign nations. However, to define a nation simply as a group of people bound together by a common culture and traditions raises some very difficult questions. Although particular cultural features are commonly associated with nationhood, notably language, religion, **ethnicity**, history and tradition, there is no blueprint nor any objective criteria that can establish where and when a nation exists.

Cultural nationalism: A form of nationalism that places primary emphasis on the regeneration of the nation as a distinctive civilization rather than on self-government.

Ethnic nationalism: A form of nationalism that is fuelled primarily by a keen sense of ethnic distinctiveness and the desire to preserve it.

Ethnicity: The quality of belonging to a particular population, cultural group or territorial area; bonds that are cultural rather than racial.

Language is often taken to be the clearest symbol of nationhood. A language embodies distinctive attitudes, values and forms of expression that produce a sense of familiarity and belonging. German nationalism, for instance, has traditionally been founded on a sense of cultural unity, reflected in the purity and survival of the German language. Nevertheless, at the same time, there are peoples who share the same language without having any conception of a common national identity: Americans, Australians and New Zealanders may speak English as a first language, but certainly do not think of themselves as members of an 'English nation'. Other nations have enjoyed a substantial measure of national unity without possessing a national language, as is the case in Switzerland where, in the absence of a Swiss language, three major languages are spoken: French, German and Italian.

Religion is another major component of nationhood. Religion expresses common moral values and spiritual beliefs. In Northern Ireland, people who speak the same language have traditionally been divided along religious lines: most Protestants regarding themselves as Unionists and wishing to preserve their links with the UK, while many in the Catholic community have favoured a united Ireland. Islam has been a major factor in forming national consciousness in much of North Africa and the Middle East. On the other hand, religious beliefs do not always coincide with a sense of nationhood. Divisions between Catholics and Protestants in mainland UK do not inspire rival nationalisms, nor has the remarkable religious diversity found in the USA threatened to divide the country into a collection of distinct nations. At the same time, countries such as Poland, Italy, Brazil and the Philippines share a common Catholic faith but do not feel that they belong to a unified 'Catholic nation'.

Nations have also been based on a sense of *ethnic* or, in certain circumstances, *racial* unity. This was particularly evident in Germany during the Nazi period. However, nationalism usually has a cultural rather than a biological basis; it reflects an ethnic unity that may be based on race, but more usually draws on shared values and common cultural beliefs. The nationalism of US blacks, for example, is based less on colour than on their distinctive history and culture. Nations thus usually share a common *history* and *traditions*. Not uncommonly, national identity is preserved by recalling past glories, national independence, the birthdays of national leaders or important military victories. The USA celebrates Independence Day and Thanksgiving; Bastille Day is commemorated in France; in the UK, ceremonies continue to mark Armistice Day. However, nationalist feelings may be based more on future expectations than on shared memories or a common past. This applies in the case of immigrants who have been 'naturalized', and is most evident in the USA, a 'land of immigrants'. The journey of the Mayflower and the War of Independence have no direct relevance for most Americans, whose families arrived centuries after these events occurred.

The cultural unity that supposedly expresses itself in nationhood is therefore very difficult to pin down. It reflects a varying combination of cultural factors, rather than any precise formula. Ultimately, therefore, nations can only be defined 'subjectively', by their members, not by any set of external factors. In this sense, the nation is a psycho-political entity, a group of people who regard themselves as a natural political community and are distinguished by shared loyalty or affection in the form of patriotism. Objective difficulties such as the absence of land, a small population or lack of economic resources are of little significance if a group of people insists on demanding what it sees as 'national rights'. Latvia, for example, became an independent nation in 1991 despite having a population of only 2.6 million (barely half of whom were ethnic Lats), no source of fuel and very few natural resources. Likewise, the Kurdish peoples of the Middle East have nationalist aspirations, even though the Kurds have never enjoyed formal political unity and are at present spread over parts of Turkey, Iraq, Iran and Syria.

PERSPECTIVES ON... NATION

LIBERALS subscribe to a 'civic' view of the nation that places as much emphasis on political allegiance as on cultural unity. Nations are moral entities in the sense that they are endowed with rights, notably an equal right to self-determination.

CONSERVATIVES regard the nation as primarily an 'organic' entity, bound together by a common ethnic identity and a shared history. As the source of social cohesion and collective identity, the nation is perhaps the most politically significant of social groups.

SOCIALISTS tend to view the nation as an artificial division of humankind whose purpose is to disguise social injustice and prop up the established order. Political movements and allegiances should therefore have an international, not a national, character.

ANARCHISTS have generally held that the nation is tainted by its association with the state, and therefore with oppression. The nation is thus seen as a myth, designed to promote obedience and subjugation in the interests of the ruling elite.

FASCISTS view the nation as an organically unified social whole, often defined by race, which gives purpose and meaning to individual existence. However, nations are pitted against one another in a struggle for survival in which some are fitted to succeed and others to go to the wall.

POPULISTS who subscribe to national populism define the people in ethnic terms, meaning that the people are equivalent to the nation. Above all, they look to safeguard 'native' people from the alleged threats of immigration and internationalism.

The fact that nations are formed through a combination of objective and subjective factors has given rise to rival concepts of the nation. While all nationalists agree that nations are a blend of cultural and psycho-political factors, they disagree strongly about where the balance between the two lies. On the one hand, 'exclusive' concepts of the nation stress the importance of ethnic unity and a shared history. By viewing national identity as 'given', unchanging and indeed unchangeable, this implies that nations are characterized by common descent and so blurs the distinction between nations and races. Nations are thus held together by '**primordial** bonds', powerful and seemingly innate emotional attachments to a language, religion, traditional way of life and a homeland. To different degrees, conservatives and fascists adopt such a view of the nation. On the other hand, 'inclusive' concepts of the nation, as found in **civic nationalism**, highlight the importance of civic consciousness and patriotic loyalty. From this perspective, nations may be multi-racial, multi-ethnic, multi-religious and so forth. This, in turn, tends to blur the distinction between the nation and the state, and thus between nationality and citizenship. Liberals and socialists tend to adopt an inclusive view of the nation. These different approaches to the nation are illustrated in Figure 6.1.

Primordialism: The belief that nations are ancient and deep-rooted, fashioned variously out of psychology, culture and biology.

Civic nationalism: A form of nationalism that emphasizes political allegiance based on a vision of a community of equal citizens, allowing for significant levels of ethnic and cultural diversity.

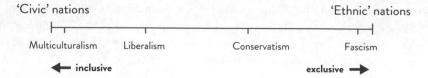

Figure 6.1 Views of the nation

Organic community

Although nationalists may disagree about the defining features of the nation, they are unified by their belief that nations are organic communities. Humankind, in other words, is naturally divided into a collection of nations, each possessing a distinctive character and separate identity. This, nationalists argue, is why a 'higher' loyalty and deeper political significance attaches to the nation than to any other social group or collective body. Whereas, for instance, class, gender, religion and language may be important in particular societies, or may come to prominence in particular circumstances, the bonds of nationhood are more fundamental. National ties and loyalties are found in all societies, they endure over time, and they operate at an instinctual, even primordial, level. Nevertheless, different explanations have been provided for this, the most significant being based on the ideas of primordialism, modernism and constructivism.

Primordialist approaches to nationalism portray national identity as historically embedded: nations are rooted in a common cultural heritage and language that may long pre-date statehood or the quest for independence, and are characterized by deep emotional attachments that resemble kinship ties. All nationalists, in that sense, are primordialists. Anthony Smith (1986) highlighted the importance of primordialism by stressing the continuity between modern nations and pre-modern ethnic communities, which he called 'ethnies'. This implies that there is little difference between ethnicity and nationality, modern nations essentially being updated versions of long-established ethnic communities, although Smith rejected the idea that these proto-nations have existed from time immemorial.

In contrast, *modernist* approaches to nationalism suggest that national identity is forged in response to changing situations and historical challenges. Ernest Gellner (1983) thus emphasized the degree to which nationalism is linked to modernization, and in particular to the process of industrialization. He stressed that, while pre-modern or 'agro-literate' societies were structured by a network of feudal bonds and loyalties, emerging industrial societies promoted social mobility, self-striving and competition, and so required a new source of cultural cohesion. This was provided by nationalism. Although Gellner's theory suggests that nations coalesced in response to particular social conditions and circumstances, it also implies that the national community is deep-rooted and enduring, as a return to pre-modern loyalties and identities is unthinkable. Benedict Anderson (1983) also portrayed modern nations as a product of socio-economic change, in his case stressing the combined impact of the emergence of capitalism and the advent of modern mass communications, which he dubbed 'print-capitalism'. In his view, the nation is an 'imagined community', in that, within nations, individuals only ever meet a tiny proportion of those with whom they supposedly share a national identity.

The idea that nations are 'imagined', not organic, communities has nevertheless been seized on by critics of nationalism. *Constructivist* approaches to nationalism regard national identity as very largely an ideological construct, usually serving the interests of powerful groups. The Marxist historian Eric Hobsbawm (1983), for example, highlighted the extent to which nations are based on 'invented traditions'. Hobsbawm argued that a belief in historical continuity and cultural purity is invariably a myth, and, what is more, a myth created by nationalism itself. **Constructivism** suggests that nationalism creates nations, not the other way round. In the case of Marxism, nationalism has been viewed as a device through which the ruling class counters the threat of social revolution by ensuring that national loyalty is stronger than class solidarity, thereby binding the working class to the existing power structure.

Self-determination

Nationalism as a political ideology only emerged when the idea of national community encountered the doctrine of popular **sovereignty**. This occurred during the French Revolution and was influenced by the writings of Jean-Jacques Rousseau, sometimes seen as the 'father' of modern nationalism. Although Rousseau did not specifically address the question of the nation, or discuss the phenomenon of nationalism, his stress on popular sovereignty, expressed in the idea of the '**general will**', was the seed from which nationalist doctrines sprang. As a result of the Polish struggle for independence from Russia, he came to believe that this is vested in a culturally unified people. Rousseau argued that government should be based not on the absolute power of a monarch, but on the indivisible collective will of the entire community. During the French Revolution, these beliefs were reflected in the assertion that the French people were 'citizens' possessed of inalienable rights and duties, no longer merely 'subjects' of the crown. Sovereign power thus resided with the 'French nation'. The form of nationalism that emerged from the French Revolution was therefore based on the vision of a people or nation governing itself. In other words, the nation is not merely a natural community: it is a natural *political* community.

Constructivism: The theory that meaning is imposed on the external world by the beliefs and assumptions we hold; reality is a social construct.

Sovereignty: The principle of absolute or unrestricted power expressed either as unchallengeable legal authority or unquestionable political power.

General will: The genuine interests of a collective body, equivalent to the common good; the will of all, provided each person acts selflessly.

KEY FIGURE

JEAN-JACQUES ROUSSEAU (1712–78)

A Geneva-born French moral and political philosopher, Rousseau is commonly viewed as the architect of political nationalism, but also influenced liberal, socialist, anarchist and, some claim, fascist thought. In *The Social Contract* (1762), Rousseau argued that 'natural man' could only throw off the corruption, exploitation and domination imposed by society and regain the capacity for moral choice through a radical form of democracy, based on the 'general will'. This subordinates the individual to the collective and promises political liberty and equality for all.

Superstock

In this tradition of nationalism, nationhood and statehood are intrinsically linked. The litmus test of national identity is the desire to attain or maintain political independence, usually expressed in the principle of national self-determination. The goal of nationalism is therefore the founding of a 'nation-state'. To date, this has been achieved in one of two ways. First, it may involve a process of unification. German history, for instance, has repeatedly witnessed unification. This occurred in medieval times under Charlemagne through the Holy Roman Empire; in the nineteenth century under Otto von Bismarck; and when the 'two Germanies' (East Germany and West Germany) were reunited in 1990. Second, nation-states can be created through the achievement of independence. For example, much of Polish history has witnessed successive attempts to achieve independence from the control of various foreign powers. Poland ceased to exist in 1793 when the Poles were partitioned by Austria, Russia and Prussia. Recognized by the Treaty of Versailles of 1919, Poland was proclaimed in 1918 and became an independent republic. However, in accordance with the Nazi–Soviet Pact of 1939, Poland was invaded by Germany and repartitioned, this time between Germany and the Soviet Union. Although Poland achieved formal independence in 1945, for much of the postwar period it remained firmly under Soviet control. The election of a non-communist government in 1989 therefore marked a further liberation of the country from foreign control.

For nationalists, the nation-state is the highest and most desirable form of political organization. The great strength of the nation-state is that it offers the prospect of both cultural cohesion and political unity. When a people who share a common cultural or ethnic identity gain the right to self-government, nationality and citizenship coincide. Moreover, nationalism legitimizes the authority of government. Political sovereignty in a nation-state resides with the people or the nation itself. Consequently, nationalism represents the notion of popular self-government, the idea that government is carried out either by the people or for the people, in accordance with their 'national interest'. This is why nationalists believe that the forces that have created a world of independent nation-states are natural and irresistible, and that no other social group could constitute a meaningful political community. The nation-state, in short, is the only viable political unit.

However, it would be misleading to suggest that nationalism is always associated with the nation-state or is necessarily linked to the idea of self-determination. Some nations, for instance, may be satisfied with a measure of political autonomy that stops short of statehood and full independence. This can be seen in the case of Welsh nationalism in the UK, and Breton and Basque nationalism in France. Nationalism is thus not always associated with **separatism**, but may instead be expressed through federalism (see p. 43) or **devolution**. Nevertheless, it is unclear whether devolution, or even federalism, establishes a sufficient measure of self-government to satisfy nationalist demands.

Culturalism

Although 'classical' nationalism is associated with political goals – most commonly the pursuit, or defence, of independent statehood – other forms of nationalism are related more closely to ethnocultural aspirations and demands. This applies particularly in the case of cultural nationalism and ethnic nationalism. Cultural nationalism is a form of nationalism that emphasizes the strengthening or defence of cultural identity over overt political demands. Its principal stress is on the regeneration of the nation as a distinctive civilization, with the state being viewed as a peripheral, if not as an alien, entity. Whereas political nationalism is 'rational' and may be principled, cultural nationalism tends to be 'mystical', in that it is based on a romantic belief in the nation as a unique historical and organic whole. Typically, cultural nationalism is a 'bottom-up' form of nationalism that draws more on popular rituals,

Separatism: The quest to secede from a larger political formation with a view to establishing an independent state.

Devolution: The transfer of power from central government to regional institutions, without relinquishing sovereignty.

traditions and legends than on elite or 'higher' culture. Although it usually has an anti-modern character, cultural nationalism may also serve as an agent of modernization, providing a people with a means of 'recreating' itself.

Whereas Rousseau is commonly seen as the 'father' of political nationalism, Johann Herder is usually viewed as the architect of cultural nationalism. Herder, together with writers such as Johann Fichte (1762–1814) and Friedrich Jahn (1778–1852), highlighted what they believed to be the uniqueness and superiority of German culture, in contrast to the ideas of the French Revolution. Herder believed that each nation possesses a *Volksgeist* which reveals itself in songs, myths and legends, and provides a nation with its source of creativity. Herder's nationalism therefore amounts to a form of **culturalism**. In this light, the role of nationalism is to develop an awareness and appreciation of national traditions and collective memories rather than to provide the basis for an overtly political quest for statehood. The tendency for nationalism to be expressed through cultural regeneration was particularly marked in nineteenth-century Germany, where it was reflected in the revival of folk traditions and the rediscovery of German myths and legends. The Brothers Grimm, for example, collected and published German folk tales, and the composer Richard Wagner (1813–83) based many of his operas on ancient myths.

KEY FIGURE

clu/iStock

JOHANN GOTTFRIED HERDER (1744–1803)

A German poet, critic and philosopher, Herder is often portrayed as the 'father' of cultural nationalism. A leading intellectual opponent of the Enlightenment, Herder's emphasis on the nation as an organic group characterized by a distinctive language, culture and 'spirit' helped both to found cultural history and to give rise to a form of nationalism that emphasizes the intrinsic value of the national culture. Herder's major work was *Reflections on the Philosophy of the History of Mankind* (1784–91).

Although cultural nationalism has often emerged within a European context, with early German nationalism sometimes being viewed as its archetypal form, cultural nationalism has been found in many parts of the world. It was, for instance, evident in black nationalism in the USA, as articulated by figures such as Marcus Garvey (see p. 136) and by groups such as the Black Panthers and the Black Muslims (later the Nation of Islam). Similarly, it has been apparent in India, in forms of nationalism that have been based on the image of India as a distinctively Hindu civilization, as advanced by the Bharatiya Janata Party, which has been in power since 2014 under the leadership of Narendra Modi (see p. 262). It is also evident in modern China in the increasing prominence given by party and state officials to the idea of 'Chineseness', expressed, among other things, in a revival of traditional cultural practices and an emphasis on 'Chinese' principles and moral values.

However, there has been disagreement about the implications of viewing nations primarily as cultural communities rather than political communities. On the one hand, cultural forms of nationalism have been viewed as being tolerant and consistent with progressive political goals, in which case they clearly differ from ethnic nationalism, even though the terms culture and ethnicity overlap. Ethnicity refers to a common consciousness of shared

Volksgeist: (German) Literally, the spirit of the people; the organic identity of a people reflected in their culture and particularly in their language.

Culturalism: The belief that human beings are culturally defined creatures, culture being the universal basis for personal and social identity.

KEY FIGURE

MARCUS GARVEY (1887–1940)

A Jamaican political thinker and activist, and founder of the Universal Negro Improvement Association, Garvey was an early advocate of black nationalism. Placing a particular emphasis on establishing black pride, Garvey's vision of Africa as a 'homeland' provided the basis for a pan-African philosophy and an associated political movement. Although his call for a return to Africa to 'redeem' it from European colonialism was largely ignored, his views provided the basis for the later Black Power movement and helped to inspire Rastafarianism.

World History Archive/Alamy
Stock Photo

origins and traditions. The term is complex because it has both racial and cultural overtones. Members of ethnic groups are often seen, correctly or incorrectly, to have descended from common ancestors, suggesting that ethnic groups are extended kinship groups, united by blood. A further indication of ethnic belonging is a link with an ancient or historic territory, a 'homeland', as in the case of Zionism (see p. 263).

As it is not possible to 'join' an ethnic group (except perhaps through intermarriage), ethnic nationalism has a clearly exclusive character and tends to overlap with racism (see p. 162). On the other hand, cultural and ethnic forms of nationalism have been viewed as closely related, even as part of the same phenomenon, commonly termed 'ethnocultural nationalism'. In this view, a distinction is drawn between inclusive or 'open' political nationalism and exclusive or 'closed' cultural nationalism. Cultural nationalism, from this perspective, is often taken to be, either implicitly or explicitly, chauvinistic or hostile towards other nations or minority groups, being fuelled by a mixture of pride and fear. To the extent that cultural nationalism is associated with demands for assimilation and cultural 'purity', it becomes incompatible with multiculturalism (the relationship between multiculturalism and nationalism is examined in greater depth in Chapter 11).

TENSIONS WITHIN ... NATIONALISM (1)

Civic nationalism	v.	Ethnocultural nationalism
political nation	↔	cultural/historical nation
inclusive	↔	exclusive
universalism	↔	particularism
equal nations	↔	unique nations
rational/principled	↔	mystical/emotion
national sovereignty	↔	national 'spirit'
voluntaristic	↔	organic
based on citizenship	↔	based on descent
civic loyalty	↔	ethnic allegiance
cultural diversity	↔	cultural unity

TYPES OF NATIONALISM

Political nationalism is a highly complex phenomenon, being characterized more by ambiguity and contradictions than by a single set of values and goals. For example, nationalism has been both liberating and oppressive: it has brought about self-government and freedom, and it has led to conquest and subjugation. Nationalism has been both progressive and regressive: it has looked to a future of national independence or national greatness, and it has celebrated past national glories and entrenched established identities. Nationalism has also been both rational and irrational: it has appealed to principled beliefs, such as national self-determination, and it has bred from non-rational drives and emotions, including ancient fears and hatreds. This ideological shapelessness is a product of a number of factors. Nationalism has emerged in very different historical contexts, been shaped by contrasting cultural inheritances, and it has been used to advance a wide variety of political causes and aspirations. However, it also reflects the capacity of nationalism to fuse with and absorb other political doctrines and ideas, thereby creating a series of rival nationalist traditions. The most significant of these traditions are:

- liberal nationalism
- conservative nationalism
- expansionist nationalism
- anti-colonial and postcolonial nationalism.

Liberal nationalism

Liberal nationalism is the oldest form of nationalism, dating back to the French Revolution and embodying many of its values. Its ideas spread quickly through much of Europe and were expressed most clearly by Giuseppe Mazzini, often thought of as the 'prophet' of Italian unification. They also influenced the remarkable exploits of Simon Bolivar, who led the Latin American independence movement in the early nineteenth century and expelled the Spanish from much of Hispanic America. US President Woodrow Wilson's 'Fourteen Points', proposed as the basis for the reconstruction of Europe after World War I, were also based on liberal nationalist principles. Moreover, many twentieth-century anti-colonial leaders were inspired by liberal ideas, as in the case of Sun Yat-Sen (1866–1925), one of the leaders of China's 1911 Revolution, and Jawaharlal Nehru (1889–1964), the first prime minister of India.

KEY FIGURE

GUISEPPE MAZZINI (1805–72)

bauhaus1000/iStock

An Italian nationalist, often portrayed as the 'prophet' of Italian unification. Mazzini practised a form of liberal nationalism that fused a belief in the nation as a distinctive language and cultural community with the principles of liberal republicanism. In this view, nations are effectively sublimated individuals endowed with the right to self-government, a right to which all nations are equally entitled. Mazzini was also one of the earliest thinkers to link nationalism to the prospect of perpetual peace.

The ideas of liberal nationalism were clearly shaped by J.-J. Rousseau's defence of popular sovereignty, expressed in particular in the notion of the 'general will'. As the nineteenth century progressed, the aspiration for popular self-government was fused progressively with liberal principles. This fusion was brought about by the fact that the multinational empires against which nationalists fought were also autocratic and oppressive. Mazzini, for example, wished the Italian states to unite, but this also entailed throwing off the influence of autocratic Austria. For many European revolutionaries in the mid-nineteenth century, liberalism and nationalism were virtually indistinguishable. Indeed, their nationalist creed was largely forged by applying liberal ideas, initially developed in relation to the individual, to the nation and to international politics.

Liberalism was founded on a defence of individual freedom, traditionally expressed in the language of rights. Nationalists believed nations to be sovereign entities, entitled to liberty, and also possessing rights, the most important being the right of self-determination. Liberal nationalism is therefore a liberating force in two senses. First, it opposes all forms of foreign domination and oppression, whether by multinational empires or colonial powers. Second, it stands for the ideal of self-government, reflected in practice in a belief in constitutionalism (see p. 42) and representation. Woodrow Wilson, for example, argued in favour of a Europe composed not only of nation-states, but also one in which political democracy rather than autocracy ruled. For him, only a democratic republic, on the US model, could be a genuine nation-state.

KEY FIGURE

WOODROW WILSON (1856–1924)

A US historian and political scientist and later politician, Wilson was the 28th president of the USA (1913–21). His 'Fourteen Points', laid down in 1918 as the basis for peace after World War I, proposed to reconstruct Europe according to the principle of national self-determination, and to ban secret diplomacy, expand trade and achieve security through a 'general association of nations'. Wilsonian liberalism is usually associated with the idea that constructing a world of democratic nation-states (modelled on the USA) is the surest way of preventing war.

Library of Congress Prints & Photographs Division/Unsplash

Furthermore, liberal nationalists believe that nations, like individuals, are equal, at least in the sense that they are equally entitled to the right of self-determination. The ultimate goal of liberal nationalism is, therefore, the construction of a world of independent nation-states, not merely the unification or independence of a particular nation. John Stuart Mill (see p. 25) expressed this as the principle that 'the boundaries of government should coincide in the main with those of nationality'. Mazzini formed the clandestine organization 'Young Italy' to promote the idea of a united Italy, but he also founded 'Young Europe' in the hope of spreading nationalist ideas throughout the continent. At the Paris Peace Conference, Woodrow Wilson advanced the principle of self-determination not simply because the break-up of the European empire served US national interests, but because he believed that the Poles, Czechs, Hungarians and so on all had the same right to political independence that Americans already enjoyed.

Liberals also believe that the principle of balance or natural harmony applies to the nations of the world, not just to individuals within society. The achievement of national self-determination is a means of establishing a peaceful and stable international order. Wilson believed that World War I had been caused by an 'old order', dominated by autocratic and militaristic empires. Democratic nation-states, on the other hand, would respect the national sovereignty of their neighbours and have no incentive to wage war or subjugate others. For a liberal, nationalism does not divide nations from one another, promoting distrust, rivalry and possibly war. Rather, it is a force that is capable of promoting both unity within each nation and brotherhood among all nations on the basis of mutual respect for national rights and characteristics. At heart, liberalism looks beyond the nation to the ideas of internationalism and cosmopolitanism.

KEY CONCEPT
INTERNATIONALISM

Internationalism is the theory or practice of politics based on transnational or global cooperation. It is rooted in universalist assumptions about human nature that put it at odds with political nationalism, the latter emphasizing the degree to which political identity is shaped by nationality. However, internationalism is compatible with nationalism in the sense that it calls for cooperation or solidarity between or among pre-existing nations, rather than for the removal or abandonment of national identities altogether. Internationalism thus differs from cosmopolitanism, the latter implying the displacement of national allegiances by global allegiances. 'Weak' forms of internationalism can be seen in doctrines such as feminism, racism and religious fundamentalism, which hold that national ties are secondary to other political bonds. 'Strong' forms of internationalism have usually drawn on the universalist ideas of either liberalism or socialism.

Liberal internationalism is grounded in a fear of an international 'state of nature'. Liberals have long accepted that national self-determination is a mixed blessing. While it preserves self-government and forbids foreign control, it also creates a world of sovereign nation-states in which each nation has the freedom to pursue its own interests, possibly at the expense of other nations. Liberal nationalists have certainly accepted that constitutionalism and democracy reduce the tendency towards militarism and war, but when sovereign nations operate within conditions of 'international anarchy', self-restraint alone may not be sufficient to ensure what Kant (see p. 23) called 'perpetual peace'. Liberals have generally proposed two means of preventing a recourse to conquest and plunder. The first is national interdependence, aimed at promoting mutual understanding and cooperation. This is why liberals have traditionally supported the policy of **free trade**: economic interdependence means that the material costs of international conflict are so great that warfare becomes virtually unthinkable.

Free trade: A system of trading between states that is unrestricted by tariffs or other forms of protectionism.

KEY CONCEPT
COSMOPOLITANISM

Cosmopolitanism literally means a belief in a *cosmopolis* or 'world state'. *Moral* cosmopolitanism is the belief that the world constitutes a single moral community, in that people have obligations (potentially) towards all other people in the world, regardless of nationality, religion, ethnicity and so on. All forms of moral cosmopolitanism are based on a belief that every individual is of equal moral worth, most commonly linked to the doctrine of human rights (see p. 58). *Political* cosmopolitanism (sometimes called 'legal' or 'institutional' cosmopolitanism) is the belief that there should be global political institutions, and possibly a world government. However, most modern political cosmopolitans favour a system in which authority is divided between global, national and local levels.

Second, Liberals have proposed that national ambition should be checked by the construction of international organizations capable of bringing order to an otherwise lawless international scene. This explains Woodrow Wilson's support for the first, if flawed, experiment in world government, the League of Nations, set up in 1919, and far wider support for its successor, the United Nations, founded by the San Francisco Conference of 1945. Liberals have looked to these bodies to establish a law-governed state system to make possible the peaceful resolution of international conflicts.

Conservative nationalism

In the early nineteenth century, conservatives regarded nationalism as a radical, if not revolutionary, force, a threat to order and political stability. However, as the century progressed, conservative statesmen such as Disraeli, Bismarck and even Tsar Alexander III became increasingly sympathetic towards nationalism, seeing it as a natural ally in maintaining social order and defending traditional institutions. In the modern period, nationalism has become an article of faith for most conservatives in most parts of the world.

Conservative nationalism tends to develop in established nation-states, rather than in those that are in the process of nation building. Conservatives care less for the principled nationalism of universal self-determination and more about the promise of social cohesion and public order embodied in the sentiment of national patriotism. For conservatives, society is organic: they believe that nations emerge naturally from the desire of human beings to live with others who possess the same views, habits and appearance as themselves. Human beings are thought to be limited and imperfect creatures, who seek meaning and security within the national community. Therefore, the principal goal of conservative nationalism is to maintain national unity by fostering patriotic loyalty and 'pride in one's country', especially in the face of the divisive idea of class solidarity preached by socialists. Indeed, by incorporating the working class into the nation, conservatives have often seen nationalism as the antidote to social revolution. Charles de Gaulle, French president 1959–69, harnessed nationalism to the conservative cause in France with particular skill. De Gaulle appealed to national pride by pursuing an independent, even anti-American, defence and foreign policy, and by attempting to restore order and authority to social life and build up a powerful state. In some respects, Thatcherism in the UK amounted to a British form of Gaullism, in that it fused an appeal based on nationalism, or at least national independence within Europe, with the promise of strong government and firm leadership.

The conservative character of nationalism is maintained by an appeal to tradition and history; nationalism thereby becomes a defence for traditional institutions and a traditional way of life. Conservative nationalism is essentially nostalgic and backward-looking, reflecting on a past age of national glory or triumph. This is evident in the widespread tendency to use ritual and commemoration to present past military victories as defining moments in a nation's history. It is also apparent in the use of traditional institutions as symbols of national identity. This occurs in the case of British, or, more accurately, English nationalism, which is closely linked to the institution of monarchy. Britain (plus Northern Ireland) is the United Kingdom, its national anthem is 'God Save the Queen', and the royal family plays a prominent role in national celebrations such as Armistice Day, and on state occasions such as the opening of Parliament.

Conservative nationalism is particularly prominent when the sense of national identity is felt to be threatened or in danger of being lost. The issues of immigration and **supranationalism** have therefore helped to keep this form of nationalism alive in many modern states. Conservative reservations about immigration stem from the belief that cultural diversity leads to instability and conflict. As stable and successful societies must be based on shared values and a common culture, immigration, particularly from societies with different religious and other traditions, should either be firmly restricted or minority ethnic groups should be encouraged to assimilate into the culture of the 'host' society. This puts conservative nationalism particularly at odds with multiculturalism.

Conservative nationalists are also concerned about the threat that supranational bodies, such as the EU, pose to national identity and so to the cultural bonds of society. This is expressed in the UK in the form of 'Euroscepticism', particularly strong within the Conservative Party, with similar views being expressed in continental Europe by a variety of right-wing populist groups such as the French National Rally (formerly the National Front). Eurosceptics not only defend sovereign national institutions and a distinctive national currency on the grounds that they are vital symbols of national identity, but also warn that the 'European project' is fatally misconceived because a stable political union cannot be forged out of such national, language and cultural diversity. In the UK, the growing strength of such sentiments contributed to the decision to hold an in/out referendum on EU membership in 2016. The 'Leave' victory in the referendum set the UK on course to exit the organization, which formally happened in 2020.

Expansionist nationalism

In many countries the dominant image of nationalism is one of aggression and **militarism**, quite the opposite of a principled belief in national self-determination. The aggressive face of nationalism became apparent in the late nineteenth century as European powers indulged in a 'scramble for Africa' in the name of national glory and their 'place in the sun'. The imperialism of the late nineteenth century differed from earlier periods of colonial expansion in that it was supported by a climate of popular nationalism: national prestige was linked increasingly to the possession of an empire and each colonial victory was greeted by demonstrations of public approval. In the UK, a new word, **jingoism**, was coined to describe this mood of popular nationalism. In the early twentieth century, the growing rivalry of the European powers divided the continent into two armed camps, the Triple Entente, comprising the UK, France and Russia, and the Triple Alliance, containing Germany, Austria and Italy. When world war eventually broke out in August 1914, after a prolonged arms race and a succession of international crises, it provoked public rejoicing in all the major cities of Europe. Aggressive and expansionist nationalism reached its high point in the interwar period when the authoritarian or fascist regimes of Japan, Italy and Germany embarked on policies of imperial expansion and world domination, eventually leading to war in 1939.

What distinguished this form of nationalism from earlier liberal nationalism was its chauvinism, a term derived from the name of Nicolas Chauvin, a French soldier who had been fanatically devoted to Napoleon I. Nations are not thought to be equal in their right to self-determination; rather, some nations are believed to possess characteristics or qualities that make them superior to others. Such ideas were clearly evident in European imperialism, which was justified by an ideology of racial and

Supranationalism: The ability of bodies with transnational or global jurisdictions to impose their will on nation-states.

Militarism: The achievement of ends by military means, or the extension of military ideas, values and practices to civilian society.

Jingoism: A mood of nationalist enthusiasm and public celebration provoked by military expansion or imperial conquest.

cultural superiority. In nineteenth-century Europe it was widely believed that the 'white' peoples of Europe and America were intellectually and morally superior to the 'black', 'brown' and 'yellow' peoples of Africa and Asia. Indeed, Europeans portrayed imperialism as a moral duty: colonial peoples were the 'white man's burden'. Imperialism supposedly brought the benefits of civilization, and in particular Christianity, to the less fortunate and less sophisticated peoples of the world.

More particular varieties of national chauvinism have developed in the form of **pan-nationalism**. In Russia this took the form of pan-Slavism, sometimes called Slavophile nationalism, which was particularly strong in the late nineteenth and early twentieth centuries. The Russians are Slavs, and enjoy linguistic and cultural links with other Slavic peoples in eastern and south-eastern Europe. Pan-Slavism was defined by the goal of Slavic unity, which many Russian nationalists believed to be their country's historic mission. The chauvinistic character of pan-Slavism derived from the belief that the Russians are the natural leaders of the Slavic people, and that the Slavs are culturally and spiritually superior to the peoples of central or western Europe. Pan-Slavism is therefore both anti-Western and anti-liberal in orientation. Forms of pan-Slavism have been re-awakened since 1991 and the collapse of communist rule in Russia. This has been most apparent in the adoption of a more assertive and sometimes expansionist foreign policy under Vladimir Putin, including the annexation of Crimea in 2014.

Pan-nationalism: A style of nationalism that is dedicated to unifying a disparate people either through expansionism or political solidarity ('pan' means 'all' or 'every').

TENSIONS WITHIN ... NATIONALISM (2)

Liberal nationalism	v.	Expansionist nationalism
national self-determination	↔	national chauvinism
inclusive	↔	exclusive
voluntaristic	↔	organic
progressive	↔	reactionary
rational/principled	↔	emotional/instinctive
human rights	↔	national interest
equal nations	↔	hierarchy of nations
constitutionalism	↔	authoritarianism
ethnic/cultural pluralism	↔	ethnic cultural purity
cosmopolitanism	↔	imperialism/militarism
collective security	↔	power politics
supranationalism	↔	international anarchy

Traditional German nationalism also exhibited a marked chauvinism, which was born out of defeat in the Napoleonic Wars. Writers such as Fichte and Jahn reacted strongly against France and the ideals of its revolution, emphasizing instead the uniqueness of German culture and its language, and the racial purity of its people. After unification in 1871, German nationalism developed a pronounced chauvinistic character with the emergence of pressure groups such as the Pan-German League and the Navy League, which campaigned for closer ties with German-speaking Austria and for a German empire, Germany's 'place in the sun'. German chauvinism found its highest expression in the racialist and anti-Semitic doctrines developed by the Nazis. The Nazis adopted the expansionist goals of pan-Germanism with enthusiasm, but justified them in the language of biology rather than politics. This is examined more fully in Chapter 7, in connection with racism.

National chauvinism breeds from a feeling of intense, even hysterical nationalist enthusiasm. The individual as a separate, rational being is swept away on a tide of patriotic emotion, expressed in the desire for aggression, expansion and war. Charles Maurras called such intense patriotism 'integral nationalism': individuals and independent groups lose their identity within an all-powerful 'nation', which has an existence and meaning beyond the life of any single individual. Such militant nationalism is often accompanied by militarism.

Military glory and conquest are the ultimate evidence of national greatness and have been capable of generating intense feelings of nationalist commitment. The civilian population is, in effect, militarized: it is infected by the martial values of absolute loyalty, complete dedication and willing self-sacrifice. When the honour or integrity of the nation is in question, the lives of ordinary citizens become unimportant. Such emotional intensity was amply demonstrated in August 1914, and perhaps also underlies the emotional power of *jihad* (crudely defined as 'holy war') from the viewpoint of militant Islamist groups.

KEY FIGURE

CHARLES MAURRAS (1868–1952)

A French political thinker and leading figure within the political movement *Action Française*, Maurras was a key exponent of right-wing nationalism and an influence on fascism. His idea of 'integral nationalism' emphasized the organic unity of the nation, fusing a clearly illiberal rejection of individualism with a stress on hierarchy and traditional institutions (in his case, the French monarchy and the Roman Catholic Church). His insular and exclusionary nationalism articulated hostility towards, among others, Protestants, Jews, Freemasons and foreigners in general.

ullstein bild Dtl./ullstein bild/ Getty Images

Anti-colonial and postcolonial nationalism

Nationalism may have been born in Europe, but it became a worldwide phenomenon thanks to imperialism. The experience of colonial rule helped to forge a sense of nationhood and a desire for 'national liberation' among the peoples of Asia and Africa, and gave rise to a specifically anti-colonial form of nationalism. During the twentieth century, the political geography of much of the world was transformed by anti-colonialism. Although the Treaty of Versailles applied the principle of self-determination to Europe, it was conveniently ignored in other parts of the world, where German colonies were simply transferred to UK and French control. However, during the interwar period, independence movements increasingly threatened the overstretched empires of the UK and France. The final collapse of the European empires came after World War II. In some cases, a combination of mounting nationalist pressure and declining domestic economic performance persuaded colonial powers to depart relatively peacefully, as occurred in India and Pakistan in 1947 and in Malaysia in 1957. However, decolonization in the post-1945 period was often characterized by revolution, and sometimes periods of armed struggle. This occurred, for instance, in the case of China, 1937–45 (against Japan), Algeria, 1954–62 (against France), and Vietnam, 1946–54 (against France) and 1964–75 (against USA).

In a sense, the colonizing Europeans had taken with them the seed of their own destruction: the doctrine of nationalism. For example, it is notable that many of the leaders of independence or liberation movements were Western educated. It is therefore not surprising that anti-colonial movements sometimes articulated their goals in the language of liberal nationalism, reminiscent of Mazzini or Woodrow Wilson. However, emergent African and Asian nations were in a very different position from the newly created European states of the nineteenth and early twentieth centuries. For these African and Asian nations, the quest for political independence was closely related to their awareness of economic under-development and their subordination to the industrialized states of Europe and North America. Anti-colonialism thus came to express the desire for national liberation in both political and economic terms, and this has left its mark on the form of nationalism practised in the developing world.

Some forms of anti-colonial nationalism nevertheless distanced themselves more clearly from Western political traditions by constructing non-European models of national liberation. This had a range of implications, however. For example, Mahatma Gandhi advanced a political philosophy that fused Indian nationalism with an ethic of non-violence and self-sacrifice that was ultimately rooted in Hinduism. 'Home rule' for India was thus a spiritual condition, and not merely a political one, a stance underpinned by Gandhi's anti-industrialism, famously embodied in his wearing of home-spun clothes. In contrast, Frantz Fanon (see p. 145) emphasized links between the anti-colonial struggle and violence. His theory of imperialism stressed the psychological dimension of colonial subjugation. For Fanon (1965), colonization was not simply a political process, but also one through which a new 'species' of human is created. He argued that only the cathartic experience of violence is powerful enough to bring about this psycho-political regeneration.

KEY FIGURE

MOHANDAS KARAMCHAND GANDHI (1869–1948)

An Indian spiritual and political leader (called *Mahatma*, 'Great Soul'), Gandhi campaigned tirelessly for Indian independence, which was finally achieved in 1947. His ethic of non-violent resistance, *satyagraha*, reinforced by his ascetic lifestyle, gave the movement for Indian independence enormous moral authority. Derived from Hinduism, Gandhi's political philosophy was based on the assumption that the universe is regulated by the primacy of truth, or *satya*, and that humankind is 'ultimately one'. Gandhi was a trenchant opponent of both Hindu and Muslim sectarianism.

Everett Collection Historical/ Alamy Stock Photo

However, most of the leaders of Asian and African anti-colonial movements were attracted to some form of socialism, ranging from the moderate and peaceful ideas represented by Gandhi and Nehru in India, to the revolutionary Marxism espoused by Mao Zedong (see p. 77) in China, Ho Chi Minh in Vietnam and Fidel Castro in Cuba. On the surface, socialism is more clearly related to internationalism than to nationalism. This reflects the stress within socialism, first, on social class, class loyalties having an intrinsically transnational character, and, at a deeper level, on the idea of a common humanity. Karl Marx (see p. 76) thus declared in the *Communist Manifesto* that 'working men have no country'.

KEY FIGURE

FRANTZ FANON (1925–61)

A Martinique-born French revolutionary theorist, Fanon is best known for his views on the anti-colonial struggle. In his classic work on decolonization, *The Wretched of the Earth* (1965), he drew on psychiatry, politics, sociology and the existentialism of Jean-Paul Sartre in arguing that only total revolution and absolute violence can help black or colonized people to liberate themselves from the social and psychological scars of imperialism. Fanon's other works include *Black Skin, White Masks* (1952) and *Towards the African Revolution* (1964).

Everett Collection Historical/Alamy

Socialist ideas nevertheless appealed powerfully to nationalists in the developing world. This was partly because socialism embodies values such as community and cooperation that are deeply entrenched in traditional, preindustrial societies. More important, socialism, and in particular Marxism, provided an analysis of inequality and exploitation through which the colonial experience could be understood and colonial rule challenged. During the 1960s and 1970s, in particular, developing-world nationalists were drawn to revolutionary Marxism, influenced by the belief that colonialism is in practice an extended form of class oppression. V. I. Lenin (see p. 91) had earlier provided the basis for such a view by portraying imperialism as essentially an economic phenomenon, a quest for profit by capitalist countries seeking investment opportunities, cheap labour and raw materials, and secure markets (Lenin, [1916] 1970). The class struggle thus became a struggle against colonial exploitation and oppression. As a result, the overthrow of colonial rule implied not only political independence, but also a social revolution which would bring about economic as well as political emancipation.

In some cases, developing-world regimes have openly embraced Marxist-Leninist principles. On achieving independence, China, North Korea, Vietnam and Cambodia moved swiftly to seize foreign assets and nationalize economic resources. They founded one-party states and centrally planned economies, closely following the Soviet model. In other cases, states in Africa and the Middle East have developed a less ideological form of nationalistic socialism, as has been evident in Algeria, Libya, Zambia, Iraq and South Yemen. The 'socialism' proclaimed in such countries usually took the form of an appeal to a unifying national cause or interest, in most cases economic or social development, as in the case of so-called 'African socialism', embraced, for instance, by Tanzania, Zimbabwe and Angola.

The postcolonial period has thrown up quite different forms of nationalism, however. With the authority of socialism and especially the attraction of Marxism-Leninism, declining significantly since the 1970s, nation building in the postcolonial period has been shaped increasingly by the rejection of Western ideas and culture more than by the attempt to reapply them. If the West is regarded as the source of oppression and exploitation, postcolonial nationalism must seek an anti-Western voice. In part, this has been a reaction against the dominance of Western, and particularly US, culture and economic power in much of the developing world. A significant vehicle for expressing such views has been fundamentalism, especially religious fundamentalism (as discussed in Chapter 12).

THE FUTURE OF NATIONALISM

Probably no political ideology has featured in the obituary columns of academic journals as frequently as nationalism. It is no surprise, therefore, that nationalism has often been portrayed as a beleaguered ideology, beset by both internal pressures and external threats. Internally, modern nations are subject to centrifugal pressures, generated by an upsurge in ethnic, regional and multicultural politics. This heightened concern with ethnicity and culture may, indeed, reflect the fact that, in the context of economic and cultural globalization, nations are no longer able to provide a collective identity or sense of social belonging. Given that all modern nations embody a measure of cultural diversity, the politics of ethnic assertiveness cannot but challenge the principle of the nation. Especially in the closing decades of twentieth century, this led some to suggest that nationalism was in the process of being replaced by multiculturalism. Unlike nations, ethnic, regional and cultural groups are not viable political entities in their own right, and have thus sometimes looked to forms of federal governance to provide an alternative to political nationalism.

External threats to nationalism take a variety of forms. First, advances in the technology of warfare, and especially the advent of the nuclear age, have brought about demands that world peace be policed by intergovernmental and supranational bodies. This led to the creation of the League of Nations and, later, the United Nations. Second, economic life has been progressively globalized. Markets are now world markets, businesses have increasingly become transnational corporations, and capital moves around the globe in the blink of an eye. Is there a future for nationalism in a world in which no national government controls its economic destiny? Third, the nation may be the enemy of the natural environment and a threat to the global ecological balance. Nations are primarily concerned with their own strategic and economic interests, and pay little attention to the ecological consequences of their actions. The folly of this was demonstrated in the Ukraine in 1986 by the Chernobyl nuclear accident, which released a wave of nuclear radiation across Northern Europe that will cause an estimated 4,000 cancer-related deaths over 50 years in Europe.

And yet, nationalism has consistently defied its obituary notices. Each pronouncement that politics has effectively evolved beyond nationalism is quickly followed by evidence of its revival. One of the sources of nationalism's resilience is surely its chameleon-like capacity to assume whatever ideological identity is needed in any set of circumstances. Nationalism has thus been used, for example, to establish democratic rule and to bolster dictatorial rule, to spark national liberation and to promote expansionism and war, to counter, as well as forge alliances with, globalization, and to consolidate liberalism and to fuel populism. Nevertheless, nationalism has – and is likely to continue to have – a strong and particular appeal to the isolated and powerless, for whom it offers the prospect of security, self-respect and pride. Not only does nationalism create a heightened sense of socio-cultural belonging but, in breeding from a clear distinction between 'us' and 'them', it provides simple (and therefore seductive) solutions to complex problems. There has to be a 'them' to fear or hate in order to forge a sense of 'us', sometimes understood in populist terms as conflict between the elite and the people. However, perhaps the firmest basis for confidence about the continuing importance of nationalism in world politics stems from the alleged lessons of social psychology. These suggest that, especially in circumstances of disruption, uncertainty and anxiety, people are inclined to divide the world into an 'in group' and an 'out group', with the 'out group' serving as a scapegoat for the misfortunes and frustrations suffered by the 'in group'.

◎ QUESTIONS FOR DISCUSSION

- Do nations develop 'naturally', or are they, in some sense, invented?
- Why have nations and states often been confused?
- Is any group of people entitled to define itself as a 'nation'?
- How does nationalism differ from racism?
- To what extent is nationalism compatible with ethnic and cultural diversity?
- In what sense is liberal nationalism principled?

- Why have liberals viewed nationalism as the antidote to war?
- Are all conservatives nationalists? If so, why?
- Why has nationalism so often been associated with expansionism, conquest and war?
- To what extent is nationalism a backward-looking ideology?
- Why and how has developing-world nationalism differed from nationalism in the developed world?
- What is the relationship between nationalism and globalization?

◎ FURTHER READING

Bruilly, J. *The Oxford Handbook of the History of Nationalism* (2013). Leading scholars in a variety of fields present the latest research on nationalism across a broad array of areas.

Coakley, J. *Nationalism, Ethnicity and the State* (2012). A broad and comprehensive overview of nationalism, and its expression across many spheres of public and political life.

Greenfeld, L. *Nationalism: A Short History* (2019). A concise overview of the evolution of nationalism and its ongoing presence in a globalized world.

Jones, C. & Vernon, R. *Patriotism* (2018). Explores the concept and phenomenon of patriotism, its central role in nationalism, and its broader social and moral implications.

Özkirimli, U. *Theories of Nationalism*, 3rd edn (2017). A clear and genuinely international account of classical and modern contributions to debates about nationalism.

CHAPTER 7

FASCISM

PREVIEW

The term 'fascism' derives from the Italian word *fasces*, meaning a bundle of rods with an axe-blade protruding that signified the authority of magistrates in Imperial Rome. By the 1890s, the word *fascia* was being used in Italy to refer to a political group or band, usually of revolutionary socialists. It was not until Mussolini employed the term to describe the paramilitary armed squads he formed during and after World War I that *fascismo* acquired a clearly ideological meaning.

The defining theme of fascism is the idea of an organically unified national community, embodied in a belief in 'strength through unity'. The individual, in a literal sense, is nothing; individual identity must be entirely absorbed into the community or social group. The fascist ideal is that of the 'new man', a hero, motivated by duty, honour and self-sacrifice, prepared to dedicate his life to the glory of his nation or race, and to give unquestioning obedience to a supreme leader. In many ways, fascism constitutes a revolt against the ideas and values that dominated Western political thought from the French Revolution onwards; in the words of the Italian fascists' slogan: '1789 is Dead'. Values such as rationalism, progress, freedom and equality were thus overturned in the name of struggle, leadership, power, heroism and war. Fascism therefore has a strong 'anti-character': it is anti-rational, anti-liberal, anti-conservative, anti-capitalist, anti-bourgeois, anti-communist and so on.

Fascism has nevertheless been a complex historical phenomenon, encompassing, many argue, two distinct traditions. Italian fascism was essentially an extreme form of statism that was based on absolute loyalty towards a 'totalitarian' state. In contrast, German fascism, or Nazism, was founded on racial theories, which portrayed the Aryan people as a 'master race' and advanced a virulent form of anti-Semitism. Although these traditions are most clearly associated with the interwar period, they have sometimes re-emerged since 1945 in the form of neo-fascism and neo-Nazism.

HISTORICAL OVERVIEW

Whereas liberalism, conservatism and socialism are nineteenth-century ideologies, fascism is a child of the twentieth century, some would say specifically of the period between the two world wars. Indeed, fascism emerged very much as a revolt against modernity, against the ideas and values of the Enlightenment and the political creeds that it spawned. The Nazis in Germany, for instance, proclaimed that '1789 is Abolished'. In Fascist Italy, slogans such as 'Believe, Obey, Fight' and 'Order, Authority, Justice' replaced the more familiar principles of the French Revolution, 'Liberty, Equality and Fraternity'. Fascism came not only as a 'bolt from the blue', as O'Sullivan (1983) put it, but also attempted to make the political world anew, quite literally to root out and destroy the inheritance of conventional political thought.

Although the major ideas and doctrines of fascism can be traced back to the nineteenth century, they were fused together and shaped by World War I and its aftermath, in particular by a potent mixture of war and revolution. Fascism emerged most dramatically in Italy and Germany. In Italy, a Fascist Party was formed in 1919, its leader, Benito Mussolini (see p. 156), was appointed prime minister in 1922 against the backdrop of the March on Rome, and by 1926 a one-party fascist state had been established. The National Socialist German Workers' Party, known as the Nazis, was also formed in 1919 and, under the leadership of Adolf Hitler, it consciously adopted the style of Mussolini's Fascists. Hitler was appointed German chancellor in 1933 and in little over a year had turned Germany into a Nazi dictatorship. During the same period, democracy collapsed or was overthrown in much of Europe, often being supplanted by right-wing, authoritarian or openly fascist regimes, especially in Eastern Europe. Regimes that bear some relationship to fascism have also developed outside Europe, notably in the 1930s in Imperial Japan and in Argentina under Juan Domingo Perón (see p. 171). These developments had dramatic implications for world affairs. Starting with the occupation of the Rhineland in 1936, Nazi Germany pursued a policy of relentless military expansion, which led to the outbreak of World War II in 1939. Germany fought this war together with Fascist Italy and Imperial Japan, as members of the Axis opposing the Allies.

KEY FIGURE

ADOLF HITLER (1889–1945)

An Austrian-born German politician, Hitler became leader of the Nazi Party (German National Socialist Workers' Party) in 1921 and was the German leader from 1933 to 1945. Largely expressed in *Mein Kampf* [*My Struggle*] (1925), Hitler's world-view drew expansionist German nationalism, racial anti-Semitism and a belief in relentless struggle together in a theory of history that highlighted the endless battle between the Germans and the Jews. Under Hitler, the Nazis sought German world domination and, after 1941, the wholesale extermination of the Jewish people.

Bettmann/Getty Images

The defeat of the Axis powers in 1945 largely discredited fascism as an ideological project, in Europe and elsewhere. Nevertheless, fascist-inspired or fascist-like movements have since emerged, albeit without anywhere coming close to rivalling the impact of interwar fascism. For want of a better term, these movements have been classified as '**neo-fascist**', although they have also been portrayed, variously, as the 'radical right', the 'far right' and the 'extreme right'. While certain, usually underground, groups have continued to endorse a militant

Neo-fascism: A form of fascism that has been shaped by the political, economic and social changes that have taken place since 1945.

or revolutionary fascism that harks back to Hitler and Mussolini, most neo-fascist parties have either broken ideologically with the past, at least formally, or denied that they are or ever have been fascist. Neo-fascism and 'classical' fascism differ in a number of substantive ways. These include the neo-fascist tendency to scapegoat non-European immigrants in particular, as opposed to communists, liberals and Jews; its greatly reduced emphasis on expansionism and war; and the accommodation it has reached with democracy (although this is an area of significant debate). Examples of parties commonly viewed as neo-fascist include the Italian Social Movement (MSI), which was superseded in 1995 by the self-styled 'post-fascist' National Alliance (AN); the French National Front (now known as the National Rally), especially under the leadership, until 2011, of Jean-Marie Le Pen; the Liberal-Democratic Party in Russia, led, from 1991, by Vladimir Zhirinovsky; and Greece's Golden Dawn (see p. 151). (For more on the far-right, see p. 181.)

CORE THEMES

Fascism is a difficult ideology to analyse, for at least two reasons. First, it is sometimes doubted if fascism can be regarded, in any meaningful sense, as an ideology. Lacking a rational and coherent core, fascism appears to be, as Hugh Trevor-Roper put it, 'an ill-assorted hodge-podge of ideas' (Woolf, 1981). Hitler, for instance, preferred to describe his ideas as a *Weltanschauung*, rather than a systematic ideology. In this sense, a world-view is a complete, almost religious, set of attitudes that demand commitment and faith, rather than invite reasoned analysis and debate. Fascists were drawn to ideas and theories less because they helped to make sense of the world, in rational terms, but more because they had the capacity to stimulate political activism. Fascism may thus be better described as a political movement or even a political religion, rather than an ideology.

Second, so complex has fascism been as a historical phenomenon that it has been difficult to identify its core principles or a 'fascist minimum', sometimes seen as generic fascism. Where does fascism begin and where does it end? Which movements and regimes can be classified as genuinely fascist? Among the attempts to define the ideological core of fascism have been Ernst Nolte's (1965) theory that it is a 'resistance to transcendence', A. J. Gregor's (1969) belief that it looks to construct 'the total charismatic community', Roger Griffin's (1993) assertion that it constitutes 'palingenetic ultranationalism' (palingenesis meaning rebirth) and Roger Eatwell's (2003) assertion that it is a 'holistic-national radical Third Way'. While each of these undoubtedly highlights an important feature of fascism, it is difficult to accept that any single-sentence formula can sum up a phenomenon as resolutely shapeless as fascist ideology. Perhaps the best we can hope to do is to identify a collection of themes that, when taken together, constitute fascism's structural core. The most significant of these include:

Weltanschauung: (German) Literally, a 'world-view'; a distinctive, even unique, set of presuppositions that structure how a people understands and engages emotionally with the world.

- anti-rationalism

- struggle

- leadership and elitism

- socialism

- ultranationalism.

POLITICAL IDEOLOGIES IN ACTION . . .

GREECE'S GOLDEN DAWN

EVENTS: Golden Dawn had its origins in the movement for the restoration in Greece of military dictatorship. Assuming its name from the title of a magazine launched in 1980 by Nikolaos Michaloliakos and a group of supporters, Golden Dawn was registered as a political party in 1993, Michalioliakos becoming its leader. Golden Dawn made its electoral breakthrough in May 2012 when it won 21 seats and 7 per cent of the vote. The party emerged from the January 2015 election as the third strongest political force in Greece, despite winning only 17 seats However, Golden Dawn collapsed electorally in 2019, its share of the vote having fallen to less than 3 per cent, under the level needed to gain seats in the Greek parliament.

SIGNIFICANCE: Golden Dawn made its electoral breakthrough in the context of the 2007–09 global financial crisis, which seriously destabilized the economies of many countries in the south of the eurozone, Greece included. For example, Greek unemployment hit 28 per cent in 2013, with youth unemployment soaring to almost 60 per cent. Swingeing austerity measures were also imposed as a condition of EU/IMF bailouts for Greece in 2010 and in 2012. Nevertheless, similarly grievous economic conditions developed in countries such as Spain and Portugal without a comparable spike in support for the far-right. This shows that parties like Golden Dawn flourish not just in conditions of poverty and economic dislocation, but when an economic crisis is accompanied by a crisis of democratic representation. In Greece, nevertheless, such circumstances were unable to overcome a widespread revulsion at the use

NurPhoto/Getty

of violence, an association with violence having dogged Golden Dawn throughout its existence and contributed to its 2019 defeat.

But how should Golden Dawn be classified ideologically? Despise the party's past use of Nazi symbols and paraphernalia, Golden Dawn has always rejected fascist and Nazi labels, preferring instead to call themselves 'Greek nationalists'. Nevertheless, unlike most other far-right and national populist parties in Europe, Golden Dawn espouses all core fascist, and more specifically Nazi, principles, so justifying its categorization as neo-Nazi. The central theme of Golden Dawn's ideology is thus a belief in the continuation of the 'Greek race' from antiquity to the modern day. Myths from ancient Greece, especially ones that stress heroism, are used to keep alive the prospect of a national revival in which all political divisions will be eliminated and Greece's moral and cultural decay reversed. This process of 'catharsis' will supposedly see the cleansing of the Greek nation from the pollution imposed by political dissidents (particularly communists) and 'outsiders'.

Anti-rationalism

Although fascist political movements were born out of the upheavals that accompanied World War I, they drew on ideas and theories that had been circulating since the late nineteenth century. Among the most significant of these were anti-rationalism and the growth of counter-Enlightenment thinking generally. The Enlightenment, based on the ideas of universal reason, natural goodness and inevitable progress, was committed to liberating humankind from the darkness of irrationalism and superstition. In the late nineteenth century, however, thinkers had started to highlight the limits of human reason and draw attention to other, perhaps more powerful, drives and impulses.

For instance, Friedrich Nietzsche (see p. 154) proposed that human beings are motivated by powerful emotions, their 'will' rather than the rational mind, and in particular by what he called the 'will to power'. In *Reflections on Violence* ([1908] 1950), the French syndicalist Georges Sorel (1847–1922) highlighted the importance of 'political myths', and especially the 'myth of the general strike', which are not passive descriptions of political reality but 'expressions of the will' that engaged the emotions and provoked action. Henri Bergson (1859–1941), the French philosopher, advanced the theory of **vitalism**. This suggests that the purpose of human existence is to give expression to the life force, rather than to allow it to be confined or corrupted by the tyranny of cold reason or soulless calculation.

Although anti-rationalism does not necessarily have a right-wing or proto-fascist character, fascism gave political expression to the most radical and extreme forms of counter-Enlightenment thinking. Anti-rationalism has influenced fascism in a number of ways. In the first place, it gave fascism a marked anti-intellectualism, reflected in a tendency to despise abstract thinking and revere action. For example, Mussolini's favourite slogans included 'Action not Talk' and 'Inactivity Is Death'. Intellectual life was devalued, even despised: it is cold, dry and lifeless. Fascism, instead, addresses the soul, the emotions, the instincts. Its ideas possess little coherence or rigour, but seek to exert a mythic appeal. Its major ideologists, in particular Hitler and Mussolini, were essentially propagandists, interested in ideas and theories largely because of their power to elicit an emotional response and spur the masses to action. Fascism thus practises the 'politics of the will'.

Second, the rejection of the Enlightenment gave fascism a predominantly negative or destructive character. Fascists, in other words, have often been clearer about what they oppose than what they support. Fascism thus appears to be an 'anti-philosophy': it is anti-rational, anti-liberal, anti-conservative, anti-capitalist, anti-bourgeois, anti-communist and so on. In this light, some have portrayed fascism as an example of **nihilism**. Nazism, in particular, has been described as a 'revolution of nihilism'. However, fascism is not merely the negation of established beliefs and principles. Rather, it is an attempt to reverse the heritage of the Enlightenment. It represents the darker underside of the Western political tradition, the central and enduring values of which were not abandoned but rather transformed or turned upside-down. For example, in fascism, 'freedom' came to mean unquestioning submission, 'democracy' was equated with absolute dictatorship, and 'progress' implied constant struggle and war. Moreover, despite an undoubted inclination towards nihilism, war and even death, fascism saw itself as a creative force, a means of constructing a new civilization through 'creative destruction'. Indeed, this conjunction of birth and death, creation and destruction, can be seen as one of the characteristic features of the fascist world-view.

Third, by abandoning the standard of universal reason, fascism has placed its faith entirely in history, culture and the idea of organic community. Such a community is shaped not by the calculations and interests of rational individuals but by innate loyalties and emotional bonds forged by a common past. In fascism, this idea of organic unity is taken to its extreme. The national community, or as the Nazis called it, the *Volksgemeinschaft*, was viewed as an indivisible whole, all rivalries and conflicts being subordinated to a higher, collective purpose. The strength of the nation or **race** is therefore a reflection of its moral and cultural unity. This prospect of unqualified social cohesion was expressed in the Nazi slogan, 'Strength through Unity'. The revolution that fascists sought was thus 'revolution of

Vitalism: The theory that living organisms derive their characteristic properties from a universal 'life-force'; vitalism implies an emphasis upon instinct and impulse rather than intellect and reason.

Nihilism: Literally a belief in nothing; a rejection of all moral and political principles.

Race: A collection of people who supposedly share a common genetic inheritance and are thus, it is claimed, distinguished from others by biological factors.

the spirit', aimed at creating a new type of human being (always understood in male terms). This was the 'new man' or 'fascist man', a hero, motivated by duty, honour and self-sacrifice, and prepared to dissolve his personality in that of the social whole.

Struggle

The ideas that the UK biologist Charles Darwin (1809–82) developed in *On the Origin of Species* ([1859] 1972), popularly known as the theory of '**natural selection**', had a profound effect not only on the natural sciences, but also, by the end of the nineteenth century, on social and political thought. This was most clearly demonstrated through the influence of Herbert Spencer (1820–1904), an advocate of extreme liberal individualism and the earliest exponent of social Darwinism (see Chapter 2). The notion that human existence is based on biologically impelled competition or struggle was particularly attractive in the period of intensifying international rivalry that eventually led to war in 1914. Social Darwinism also had a considerable impact on emerging fascism. In the first place, fascists regarded struggle as the natural and inevitable condition of both social and international life. Only competition and conflict guarantee human progress and ensure that the fittest and strongest will prosper. As Hitler told German officer cadets in 1944, 'Victory is to the strong and the weak must go to the wall.' If the testing ground of human existence is competition and struggle, then the ultimate test is war, which Hitler described as 'an unalterable law of the whole of life'. Fascism is perhaps unique among political ideologies in regarding war as good in itself, a view reflected in Mussolini's belief that 'War is to men what maternity is to women'.

Darwinian thought also invested fascism with a distinctive set of political values, which equate 'goodness' with strength, and 'evil' with weakness. In contrast to traditional humanist or religious values, such as caring, sympathy and compassion, fascists respect a very different set of martial values: loyalty, duty, obedience and self-sacrifice. When the victory of the strong is glorified, power and strength are worshipped for their own sake. Similarly, weakness is despised and the elimination of the weak and inadequate is positively welcomed: they must be sacrificed for the common good, just as the survival of a species is more important than the life of any single member of that species. Weakness and disability must therefore not be tolerated; they should be removed. This was illustrated most graphically by the programme of **eugenics**, introduced by the Nazis in Germany, whereby mentally and physically handicapped people were first forcibly sterilized and then, between 1939 and 1941, systematically murdered. The attempt by the Nazis to exterminate European Jewry from 1941 onwards was, in this sense, an example of racial eugenics.

Finally, fascism's conception of life as an 'unending struggle' gave it a restless and expansionist character. National qualities can only be cultivated through conflict and demonstrated by conquest and victory. This was clearly reflected in Hitler's foreign policy goals, as outlined in *Mein Kampf* ([1925] 1969): '*Lebensraum* [living space] in the East', and the ultimate prospect of world domination. Once in power in 1933, Hitler embarked on a programme of rearmament in preparation for expansion in the late 1930s. Austria was annexed in the *Anschluss* of 1938; Czechoslovakia was dismembered in the spring of 1939; and Poland invaded in September 1939, provoking war with the UK and France. In 1941, Hitler launched Operation Barbarossa, the invasion of the Soviet Union. Even when facing imminent defeat in 1945, Hitler did not abandon social Darwinism, but

Natural selection: The theory that species go through a process of random mutations that fits some to survive (and possibly thrive) while others become extinct.

Eugenics: The theory or practice of selective breeding, achieved either by promoting procreation among 'fit' members of a species or by preventing procreation by the 'unfit'.

declared that the German nation had failed him and gave orders, never fully carried out, for a fight to the death and, in effect, the annihilation of Germany.

Leadership and elitism

Fascism also stands apart from conventional political thought in its radical rejection of equality. Fascism is deeply elitist and fiercely patriarchal; its ideas were founded on the belief that absolute leadership and elitism (see p. 174) are natural and desirable. Human beings are born with radically different abilities and attributes, a fact that emerges as those with the rare quality of leadership rise, through struggle, above those capable only of following. Fascists believe that society is composed, broadly, of three kinds of people. First, and most important, there is a supreme, all-seeing leader who possesses unrivalled authority. Second, there is a 'warrior' elite, exclusively male and distinguished, unlike traditional elites, by its heroism, vision and the capacity for self-sacrifice. In Germany, this role was ascribed to the SS, which originated as a bodyguard but developed during Nazi rule into a state within a state. Third, there are the masses, who are weak, inert and ignorant, and whose destiny is unquestioning obedience.

Such a pessimistic view of the capabilities of ordinary people puts fascism starkly at odds with the ideas of liberal democracy (see p. 44). Nevertheless, the idea of supreme leadership was also associated with a distinctively fascist, if inverted, notion of democratic rule. The fascist approach to leadership, especially in Nazi Germany, was crucially influenced by Friedrich Nietzsche's idea of the *Übermensch*, the 'over-man' or 'superman', a supremely gifted or powerful individual. Most fully developed in *Thus Spoke Zarathustra* ([1884] 1961), Nietzsche portrayed the 'superman' as an individual who rises above the 'herd instinct' of conventional morality and lives according to his own will and desires. Fascists, however, turned the superman ideal into a theory of supreme and unquestionable political leadership. Fascist leaders styled themselves simply as 'the Leader' – Mussolini proclaimed himself to be *Il Duce*, while Hitler adopted the title *Der Führer* – precisely in order to emancipate themselves from any constitutionally defined notion of leadership. In this way, leadership became exclusively an expression of **charismatic** authority emanating from the leader himself. While constitutional or, in Max Weber's term, legal-rational authority operates

Charisma: Charm or personal power; the ability to inspire loyalty, emotional dependence or even devotion in others.

within a framework of laws or rules, charismatic authority is potentially unlimited. As the leader was viewed as a uniquely gifted individual, his authority was absolute. At the Nuremburg Rallies, the Nazi faithful thus chanted 'Adolf Hitler is Germany, Germany is Adolf Hitler.' In Italy, the principle that 'Mussolini is always right' became the core of fascist dogma.

KEY FIGURE

FRIEDRICH NIETZSCHE (1844–1900)

A German philosopher, Nietzsche's complex and ambitious work stressed the importance of will, especially the 'will to power', and influenced anarchism and feminism, as well as fascism. Anticipating modern existentialism, he emphasized that people create their own world and make their own values, expressed in the idea that 'God is dead'. In *Thus Spoke Zarathustra* ([1884] 1961), Neitzche emphasized the role of the *Übermensch*, crudely translated as the 'supermen', who alone are unrestrained by conventional morality. His other works include *Beyond Good and Evil* (1886).

WikiImages/Pixabay

The 'leader principle' (in German, the *Führerprinzip*), the principle that all authority emanates from the leader personally, thus became the guiding principle of the fascist state. Intermediate institutions such as elections, parliaments and parties were either abolished or weakened to prevent them from challenging or distorting the leader's will. This principle of absolute leadership was underpinned by the belief that the leader possesses a monopoly of ideological wisdom: the leader, and the leader alone, defines the destiny of his people, their 'real' will, their 'general will'. A Nietzschean theory of leadership thus coincided with a Rousseauian belief in a single, indivisible public interest. In this light, a genuine democracy is an absolute dictatorship, absolutism and popular sovereignty being fused into a form of **'totalitarian democracy'** (Talmon, 1952). The role of the leader is to awaken the people to their destiny, to transform an inert mass into a powerful and irresistible force. Fascist regimes therefore exhibited populist-mobilizing features that set them clearly apart from traditional dictatorships. Whereas traditional dictatorships aimed to exclude the masses from politics, totalitarian dictatorships set out to recruit them into the values and goals of the regime through constant propaganda and political agitation. In the case of fascist regimes, this was reflected in the widespread use of plebiscites, rallies and popular demonstrations.

PERSPECTIVES ON ... AUTHORITY

LIBERALS believe that authority arises 'from below' through the consent of the governed. Though a requirement of orderly existence, authority is rational, purposeful and limited, a view reflected in a preference for legal-rational authority and public accountability.

CONSERVATIVES see authority as arising from natural necessity, being exercised 'from above' by virtue of the unequal distribution of experience, social position and wisdom. Authority is beneficial as well as necessary, in that it fosters respect and loyalty, and promotes social cohesion.

SOCIALISTS, typically, are suspicious of authority, which is regarded as implicitly oppressive and generally linked to the interests of the powerful and privileged. Socialist societies have nevertheless endorsed the authority of the collective body, however expressed, as a means of checking individualism and greed.

ANARCHISTS view all forms of authority as unnecessary and destructive, equating authority with oppression and exploitation. Since there is no distinction between authority and naked power, all checks on authority and all forms of accountability are entirely bogus.

FASCISTS regard authority as a manifestation of personal leadership or charisma, a quality possessed by unusually gifted (if not unique) individuals. Such charismatic authority is, and should be, absolute and unquestionable, and is thus implicitly, and possibly explicitly, totalitarian in character.

Socialism

At times, both Mussolini and Hitler portrayed their ideas as forms of 'socialism' (although the notion of a link between socialism and fascism is deeply controversial, and rejected by virtually all socialists). Mussolini had previously been an influential member of the Italian Socialist Party and editor of its newspaper, *Avanti*, while the Nazi Party espoused a

Totalitarian democracy: An absolute dictatorship that masquerades as a democracy, typically based on the leader's claim to a monopoly of ideological wisdom.

philosophy it called 'national socialism'. To some extent, undoubtedly, this represented a cynical attempt to elicit support from urban workers. Nevertheless, despite obvious ideological rivalry between fascism and socialism, fascists did have an affinity for certain socialist ideas and positions. In the first place, lower-middle-class fascist activists had a profound distaste for large-scale capitalism, reflected in a resentment towards big business and financial institutions. For instance, small shopkeepers were under threat from the growth of department stores, the smallholding peasantry was losing out to large-scale farming, and small businesses were increasingly in hock to the banks. Socialist or 'leftist' ideas were therefore prominent in German grassroots organizations such as the SA, or Brownshirts, which recruited significantly from among the lower middle classes. Second, fascism, like socialism, subscribes to collectivism (see p. 80), putting it at odds with the 'bourgeois' values of capitalism. Fascism places the community above the individual; Nazi coins, for example, bore the inscription 'Common Good before Private Good'. Capitalism, in contrast, is based on the pursuit of self-interest and therefore threatens to undermine the cohesion of the nation or race. Fascists also despise the materialism that capitalism fosters: the desire for wealth or profit runs counter to the idealistic vision of national regeneration or world conquest that inspires fascists.

KEY FIGURE

BENITO MUSSOLINI (1883–1945)

An Italian politician, Mussolini founded the Fascist Party in 1919 and was the leader of Italy from 1922 to 1943. Claiming to be the founder of fascism, Mussolini's political philosophy drew on the work of Plato, Sorel, Nietzsche and Vilfredo Pareto, and stressed that human existence is only meaningful if it is sustained and determined by the community. This required the construction of a 'totalitarian' state, based on the principle that no human or spiritual values exist or have meaning outside the state.

Archive Photos/Getty Images

Third, fascist regimes often practised socialist-style economic policies designed to regulate or control capitalism. Capitalism was thus subordinated to the ideological objectives of the fascist state. As Oswald Mosley (1896–1980), leader of the British Union of Fascists, put it, 'Capitalism is a system by which capital uses the nation for its own purposes. Fascism is a system by which the nation uses capital for its own purposes.' Both the Italian and German regimes tried to bend big business to their political ends through policies of nationalization and state regulation. For example, after 1939, German capitalism was reorganized under Hermann Göring's Four Year Plan, deliberately modelled on the Soviet idea of Five Year Plans.

However, the notion of fascist socialism has severe limitations. For instance, 'leftist' elements within fascist movements, such as the SA in Germany and Sorelian revolutionary syndicalists in Italy, were quickly marginalized once fascist parties gained power, in the hope of cultivating the support of big business. This occurred most dramatically in Nazi Germany, through the purge of the SA and the murder of its leader, Ernst Rohm, in the 'Night of the Long Knives' in 1934. Marxists have thus argued that the purpose of fascism was to salvage capitalism rather than to subvert it. Moreover, fascist ideas about the organization of economic life were, at best, vague and sometimes inconsistent; pragmatism (see p. 6), not ideology, determined fascist economic policy. Finally, anti-communism was more prominent within fascism than anti-capitalism. A core objective of fascism was to seduce the working class away from Marxism and Bolshevism, which preached the insidious, even traitorous, idea of international working-class solidarity and upheld the misguided values of cooperation and equality. Fascists were dedicated to national unity and integration, and so wanted the allegiances of race and nation to be stronger than those of social class.

Ultranationalism

Fascism embraced an extreme version of chauvinistic and expansionist nationalism. This tradition regarded nations not as equal and interdependent entities, but as rivals in a struggle for dominance. Fascist nationalism did not preach respect for distinctive cultures or national traditions, but asserted the superiority of one nation over all others. In the explicitly racial nationalism of Nazism this was reflected in the ideas of **Aryanism**. Between the wars, such militant nationalism was fuelled by an inheritance of bitterness and frustration, which resulted from World War I and its aftermath.

Fascism seeks to promote more than mere patriotism (see p. 125); it wishes to establish an intense and militant sense of national identity, which the right-wing French nationalist Charles Maurras (1868–1952) called '**integral nationalism**'. Fascism embodies a sense of messianic or fanatical mission: the prospect of national regeneration and the rebirth of national pride. Indeed, the popular appeal that fascism has exerted has largely been based on the promise of national greatness. According to Griffin (1993), the mythic core of generic fascism is the conjunction of the ideas of 'palingenesis', or recurrent rebirth, and 'populist ultranationalism'. All fascist movements therefore highlight the moral bankruptcy and cultural decadence of modern society, but proclaim the possibility of rejuvenation, offering the image of the nation 'rising phoenix-like from the ashes'. Fascism thus fuses myths about a glorious past with the image of a future characterized by renewal and reawakening, hence the idea of the 'new' man. In Italy, this was reflected in attempts to recapture the glories of Imperial Rome; in Germany, the Nazi regime was portrayed as the 'Third Reich', in succession to Charlemagne's 'First Reich' and Bismarck's 'Second Reich'.

However, in practice, national regeneration invariably meant the assertion of power over other nations through expansionism, war and conquest. Influenced by social Darwinism and a belief in national and sometimes racial superiority, fascist nationalism became inextricably linked to militarism and imperialism. Nazi Germany looked to construct a 'Greater Germany' and build an empire stretching into the Soviet Union – '*Lebensraum* (living space) in the East'. Fascist Italy sought to found an African empire through the invasion of Abyssinia in 1934. Imperial Japan occupied Manchuria in 1931 in order to found a 'co-prosperity' sphere in a new Japanese-led Asia. These empires were to be **autarkic**, based on strict self-sufficiency. In the fascist view, economic strength is based on the capacity of the nation to rely solely on resources and energies it directly controls. Conquest and expansionism are therefore a means of gaining economic security as well as national greatness. National regeneration and economic progress are therefore intimately tied up with military power.

Aryanism: The belief that the Aryans, or German people, are a 'master race', destined for world domination.

Integral nationalism: An intense, even hysterical, form of nationalist enthusiasm, in which individual identity is absorbed within the national community.

Autarky: Economic self-sufficiency, brought about either through expansionism aimed at securing markets and sources of raw materials, or by withdrawal from the international economy.

TYPES OF FASCISM

Although it is possible to identify a common set of fascist values and principles, Fascist Italy and Nazi Germany nevertheless represented different versions of fascism and were inspired by distinctive and sometimes rival beliefs, with, for example, Franco's Spain being closer to the former. Fascist regimes and movements have therefore corresponded to one of two major traditions, as illustrated in Figure 7.1. These are:

● extreme statism

● extreme racism.

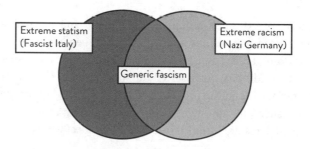

Figure 7.1   Types of fascism

Extreme statism

The totalitarian ideal

Totalitarianism (see p. 159) is a controversial concept. The height of its popularity came during the Cold War period, when it was used to draw attention to parallels between fascist and communist regimes, highlighting the brutal features of both. As such, it became a vehicle for expressing anticommunist views and, in particular, hostility towards the Soviet Union. Nevertheless, totalitarianism remains a useful concept for the analysis of fascism. Generic fascism tends towards totalitarianism in at least three respects. First, the extreme collectivism that lies at the heart of fascist ideology, the goal of the creation of 'fascist man' – loyal, dedicated and utterly obedient – effectively obliterates the distinction between 'public' and 'private' existence. The good of the collective body, the nation or the race, is placed firmly before the good of the individual: collective egoism consumes individual egoism. Second, as the fascist leader principle invests the leader with unlimited authority, it violates the liberal idea of a distinction between the state and civil society. An unmediated relationship between the leader and his people implies active participation and total commitment on the part of citizens; in effect, the politicization of the masses. Third, the **monistic** belief in a single value system, and a single source of truth, places fascism firmly at odds with the notions of pluralism (see p. 240) and civil liberty. However, the idea of an all-powerful state has particular significance for Italian fascism, hence the notion of extreme **statism**.

Monism: A belief in only one theory or value; monism is reflected politically in enforced obedience to a unitary power and is thus implicitly totalitarian.

Statism: The belief that the state is the most appropriate means of resolving problems and of guaranteeing economic and social development.

The essence of Italian fascism was a form of state worship. In a formula regularly repeated by Mussolini, Giovanni Gentile (see p. 159) proclaimed: 'Everything for the state; nothing against the state; nothing outside the state.' The individual's political obligations are thus absolute and all-encompassing. Nothing less than unquestioning obedience and constant devotion are required of the citizen. This fascist theory of the state has sometimes been associated with the ideas of the German philosopher G. W. F. Hegel (1770–1831). Hegel portrayed the state as an ethical idea, reflecting the altruism and mutual sympathy of its members. In this view, the state is capable of motivating and inspiring individuals to act in the common interest, and Hegel thus believed that higher levels of civilization would only be achieved as the state itself developed and expanded. Hegel's political philosophy therefore amounted to an uncritical reverence for the state, expressed in practice in firm admiration for the autocratic Prussian state of his day.

KEY FIGURE

GIOVANNI GENTILE (1875–1944)

An Italian idealist philosopher, Gentile was a leading figure in the Fascist government, 1922–9, and is sometimes called the 'philosopher of fascism'. Strongly influenced by the ideas of Hegel, Gentile advanced a radical critique of individualism, based on an 'internal' dialectic in which distinctions between subject and object, and between theory and practice, are transcended. In political terms, this implied the establishment of an all-encompassing state that would abolish the division between public and private life once and for all.

VTR/Alamy Stock Photo

KEY CONCEPT

TOTALITARIANISM

Totalitarianism is an all-encompassing system of political rule that is typically established by pervasive ideological manipulation and open terror and brutality. It differs from autocracy, authoritarianism and traditional dictatorship in that it seeks 'total power' through the politicization of every aspect of social and personal existence. Totalitarianism thus implies the outright abolition of civil society: the abolition of 'the private'. Fascism and communism have sometimes been seen as left- and right-wing forms of totalitarianism, based on their rejection of toleration, pluralism and the open society. However, radical thinkers such as Marcuse (see p. 76) have claimed that liberal democracies also exhibit totalitarian features.

In contrast, the Nazis did not venerate the state as such, but viewed it as a means to an end. Hitler, for instance, described the state as a mere 'vessel', implying that creative power derives not from the state but from the race, the German people. Alfred Rosenberg (see p. 160) dismissed the idea of the 'total state', describing the state instead as an 'instrument of the National Socialist *Weltanschauung*'. However, there is little doubt that the Hitler regime came closer to realizing the totalitarian ideal in practice than did the Mussolini regime. Although it seethed with institutional and personal rivalries, the Nazi state was brutally effective in suppressing political opposition, and succeeded in extending political control over the media, art and culture, education and youth organizations. By comparison, despite its formal commitment to totalitarianism, the Italian state operated, in some ways, like a traditional or personalized dictatorship rather than a totalitarian dictatorship. For example, the Italian monarchy survived throughout the fascist period; many local political leaders, especially in the south, continued in power; and the Catholic Church retained its privileges and independence throughout the fascist period.

ALFRED ROSENBERG (1895–1946)

A German politician and wartime Nazi leader, Rosenberg was a major intellectual influence on Hitler and the Nazi Party. In *The Myth of the Twentieth Century* (1930), Rosenberg developed the idea of the 'race-soul', arguing that race is the key to a people's destiny. His hierarchy of racial attributes allowed him to justify both Nazi expansionism (by emphasizing the superiority of the 'Aryan' race) and Hitler's genocidal policies (by portraying Jews as fundamentally 'degenerate', along with 'sub-human' Slavs, Poles and Czechs).

ullstein bild Dtl./ullstein bild/ Getty Images

Corporatism

Although Italian fascists revered the state, this did not extend to an attempt to collectivize economic life. Fascist economic thought was seldom systematic, reflecting the fact that fascists sought to transform human consciousness rather than social structures. Its distinguishing feature was the idea of corporatism, which Mussolini portrayed as the 'third way', an alternative to both capitalism and socialism. This was a common theme in fascist thought, also embraced by Mosley in the UK and Perón in Argentina. Corporatism opposes both the free market and central planning: the former leads to the unrestrained pursuit of profit by individuals, while the latter is linked to the divisive idea of class war. In contrast, corporatism is based on the belief that business and labour are bound together in an organic and spiritually unified whole. This holistic vision was based on the assumption that social classes do not conflict with one another, but can work in harmony for the common good or national interest. Such a view was influenced by traditional Catholic social thought, which, in contrast to the Protestant stress on the value of individual hard work, emphasizes that social classes are bound together by duty and mutual obligations.

KEY CONCEPT

CORPORATISM

Corporatism, in its broadest sense, is a means of incorporating organized interests into the processes of government. There are two faces of corporatism. *Authoritarian* corporatism (closely associated with Fascist Italy) is an ideology and an economic form. As an ideology, it offers an alternative to capitalism and socialism based on holism and group integration. As an economic form, it is characterized by the extension of direct political control over industry and organized labour. Liberal corporatism ('neo-corporatism' or 'societal' corporatism) refers to a tendency found in mature liberal democracies for organized interests to be granted privileged and institutional access to policy formulation. In contrast to its authoritarian variant, liberal corporatism strengthens groups rather than the government.

Social harmony between business and labour offers the prospect of both moral and economic regeneration. However, class relations have to be mediated by the state, which is responsible for ensuring that the national interest takes precedence over narrow sectional interests. Twenty-two corporations were set up in Italy in 1927, each representing employers, workers and the government. These corporations were charged with overseeing the development of all the major industries in Italy. The 'corporate state' reached its peak in 1939, when a Chamber of Fasces and Corporations was created to replace the Italian parliament. Nevertheless, there was a clear divide between corporatist theory and the reality of economic policy in Fascist Italy. The 'corporate state' was little more than an ideological slogan, corporatism in practice amounting, effectively, to an instrument through which the fascist state controlled major economic interests. Working-class organizations were smashed and private businesses were intimidated.

Modernization

The state also exerted a powerful attraction for Mussolini and Italian fascists because they saw it as an agent of modernization. Italy was less industrialized than many of its European neighbours, notably the UK, France and Germany, and many fascists equated national revival with economic modernization. All forms of fascism tend to be backward-looking, highlighting the glories of a lost era of national greatness; in Mussolini's case, Imperial Rome. However, Italian fascism was also distinctively forward-looking, extolling the virtues of modern technology and industrial life, and looking to construct an advanced industrial society. This tendency within Italian fascism is often linked to the influence of **futurism**, led by Filippo Marinetti (1876–1944). After 1922, Marinetti and other leading futurists were absorbed into fascism, bringing with them a belief in dynamism, a cult of the machine and a rejection of the past. For Mussolini, the attraction of an all-powerful state was, in part, that it would help Italy break with backwardness and tradition, and become a future-orientated industrialized country.

Extreme racism

Not all forms of fascism involve overt racism (see p. 162), and not all racists are necessarily fascists. Italian fascism, for example, was based primarily on the supremacy of the fascist state over the individual, and on submission to the will of Mussolini. It was therefore a **voluntaristic** form of fascism, in that, at least in theory, it could embrace all people regardless of race, colour or, indeed, country of birth. When Mussolini passed anti-Semitic laws after 1937, he did so largely to placate Hitler and the Germans, rather than for any ideological purpose. Nevertheless, fascism has often coincided with, and bred from, racist ideas. Indeed, some argue that its emphasis on militant nationalism means that all forms of fascism are either hospitable to racism or harbour implicit or explicit racist doctrines (Griffin, 1993). Nowhere has this link between race and fascism been so evident as in Nazi Germany, where official ideology at times amounted to little more than hysterical, pseudo-scientific anti-Semitism (see p. 164).

The politics of race

The term 'race' implies that there are meaningful biological or genetic differences among human beings. While it may be possible to drop one national identity and assume another by a process of 'naturalization', it is impossible to change one's race, determined as it is at birth, indeed before birth, by the racial identity of one's parents. The symbols of race – skin tone, hair colour, physiognomy and blood – are thus fixed and unchangeable. The use of racial terms and categories became commonplace in the West during the nineteenth century as imperialism brought the predominantly 'white' European races into increasingly close contact with the 'black', 'brown' and 'yellow' races of Africa and Asia.

Futurism: An early twentieth-century movement in the arts that glorified factories, machinery and industrial life generally.

Voluntarism: A theory that emphasizes free will and personal commitment, rather than any form of determinism.

However, racial categories largely reflect cultural stereotypes and enjoy little, if any, scientific foundation. The broadest racial classifications – for example those based on skin colour – white, brown, yellow and so on – are at best misleading and at worst simply arbitrary. More detailed and ambitious racial theories, such as those of the Nazis, simply produced anomalies, one of the most glaring being that Adolf Hitler himself certainly did not fit the racial stereotype of the tall, broad-shouldered, blond-haired, blue-eyed Aryan commonly described in Nazi literature.

KEY CONCEPT

RACISM

Racism ('racism' and 'racialism' are now generally treated as synonymous) is, broadly, the belief that political or social conclusions can be drawn from the idea that humankind is divided into biologically distinct races. Racist theories are thus based on two assumptions. The first is that there are fundamental genetic, or species-type, differences among the peoples of the world – racial differences matter. The second is that these genetic divisions are reflected in cultural, intellectual and/or moral differences, making them politically or socially significant. Political racism is manifest in calls for racial segregation (for example, apartheid) and in doctrines of 'blood' superiority or inferiority (for example, Aryanism or anti-Semitism). 'Institutionalized' racism operates through the norms and values of an institution.

The core assumption of racism is that political and social conclusions can be drawn from the idea that there are innate or fundamental differences between the races of the world. At heart, genetics determines politics: racist political theories can be traced back to biological assumptions, as illustrated in Figure 7.2. A form of implicit racism has been associated with conservative nationalism. This is based on the belief that stable and successful societies must be bound together by a common culture and shared values. For example, Enoch Powell in the UK in the 1960s and Jean-Marie Le Pen in France since the 1980s have argued against 'non-white' immigration into their countries on the grounds that the distinctive traditions and culture of the 'white' host community would be threatened.

However, more systematic and developed forms of racism are based on explicit assumptions about the nature, capacities and destinies of different racial groups. In many cases, these assumptions have had a religious basis. For example, nineteenth-century European imperialism was justified, in part, by the alleged superiority of the Christian peoples of Europe over the 'heathen' peoples of Africa and Asia.

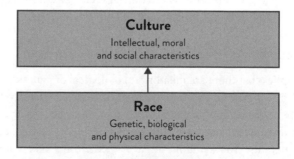

Figure 7.2   The nature of racism

Apartheid: (Afrikaans) Literally, 'apartness'; a system of racial segregation practised in South Africa after 1948.

Biblical justification was also offered for doctrines of racial segregation preached by the Ku Klux Klan, formed in the USA after the American Civil War, and by the founders of the **apartheid** system, which operated in South Africa from 1948 until 1993. In Nazi Germany, however, racism was rooted in biological, and therefore quasi-scientific, assumptions. Biologically based racial theories, as opposed to those that are linked to culture or religion, are particularly militant and radical because they make claims about the essential and inescapable nature of a people that are supposedly backed up by the certainty and objectivity of scientific belief.

Nazi race theories

Nazi ideology was fashioned out of a combination of racial anti-Semitism and social Darwinism. Anti-Semitism had been a force in European politics, especially in Eastern Europe, since the dawn of the Christian era. Its origins were largely theological: the Jews were responsible for the death of Christ, and in refusing to convert to Christianity they were both denying the divinity of Jesus and endangering their own immortal souls. The association between the Jews and evil was therefore not a creation of the Nazis, but dated back to the Christian Middle Ages, a period when the Jews were first confined in ghettoes and excluded from respectable society. However, anti-Semitism intensified in the late nineteenth century. As nationalism and imperialism spread throughout Europe, Jews were subjected to increasing persecution in many countries. In France, this led to the celebrated Dreyfus affair, 1894–1906 (in which the Jewish army officer, Alfred Dreyfus, was falsely charged with delivering defence secrets to the Germans) and, in Russia, it was reflected in a series of pogroms carried out against the Jews by the government of Alexander III.

The character of anti-Semitism also changed during the nineteenth century. The growth of a 'science of race', which applied pseudo-scientific ideas to social and political issues, led to Jewish people being thought of as a race rather than a religious, economic or cultural group. Thereafter, they were defined inescapably by biological factors such as hair colour, facial characteristics and blood. Anti-Semitism was therefore elaborated into a racial theory, which assigned to the Jewish people a pernicious and degrading racial stereotype. The first attempt to develop a scientific theory of racism was undertaken by Joseph-Arthur Gobineau. Gobineau argued that there is a hierarchy of races, with very different qualities and characteristics. The most developed and creative race is the 'white peoples', whose highest element Gobineau referred to as the 'Aryans'. Jewish people, on the other hand, were thought to be fundamentally uncreative. Unlike the Nazis, however, Gobineau was a pessimistic racist, believing that, by his day, intermarriage had progressed so far that the glorious civilization built by the Aryans had already been corrupted beyond repair.

KEY FIGURE

JOSEPH ARTHUR GOBINEAU (1816–82)

A French social theorist, Gobineau is widely viewed as the architect of modern racial theory. In his major work, *Essay on the Inequality of the Human Races* ([1853–55] 1970), Gobineau advanced a 'science of history' in which the strength of civilizations was seen to be determined by their racial composition. In this, 'white' people – and particularly the 'Aryans' (the Germanic peoples) – were superior to 'black', 'brown' and 'yellow' people, and miscegenation (racial mixing) was viewed as a source of corruption and civilizational decline.

Sueddeutsche Zeitung Photo/Alamy Stock Photo

KEY CONCEPT
ANTI-SEMITISM

By tradition, Semites are descendants of Shem, son of Noah, and include most of the peoples of the Middle East. Anti-Semitism refers specifically to prejudice against or hatred towards the Jews. In its earliest systematic form, anti-Semitism had a religious character, reflecting the hostility of Christians towards the Jews, based on their complicity in the murder of Jesus and their refusal to acknowledge him as the Son of God. Economic anti-Semitism developed from the Middle Ages onwards, expressing a distaste for the Jews as moneylenders and traders. The nineteenth century saw the birth of racial anti-Semitism in the works of Richard Wagner and H. S. Chamberlain, who condemned the Jewish peoples as fundamentally evil and destructive. Such ideas provided the ideological basis for German Nazism and found their most grotesque expression in the Holocaust.

The doctrine of racial anti-Semitism entered Germany through Gobineau's writing and took the form of Aryanism, a belief in the biological superiority of the Aryan peoples. These ideas were taken up by the composer Richard Wagner and his UK-born son-in-law, H. S. Chamberlain, whose writings had an enormous impact on Hitler and the Nazis. Chamberlain defined the highest race more narrowly as the 'Teutons', clearly understood to mean the German peoples. All cultural development was ascribed to the German way of life, while Jewish people were described as 'physically, spiritually and morally degenerate'. Chamberlain presented history as a confrontation between the Teutons and the Jews, and therefore prepared the ground for Nazi race theory, which portrayed Jewish people as a universal scapegoat for all of Germany's misfortunes. The Nazis blamed the Jews for Germany's defeat in 1918; they were responsible for its humiliation at Versailles; they were behind the financial power of the banks and big business that enslaved the lower middle classes; and their influence was exerted through the working-class movement and the threat of social revolution. In Hitler's view, the Jews were responsible for an international conspiracy of capitalists and communists, whose prime objective was to weaken and overthrow the German nation.

KEY FIGURE

HOUSTON STEWART CHAMBERLAIN (1855–1929)

A British-born German writer, Chamberlain played a major role in popularizing racial theories, having a major impact on Hitler and the Nazis. In *Foundations of the Nineteenth Century* ([1899] 1913), largely based on the writings of Gobineau, Chamberlain used the term 'Aryan race' to describe almost all the peoples of Europe, but portrayed the 'Nordic' or 'Teutonic' peoples (by which he meant the Germans) as its supreme element, with the Jewish people being their implacable enemy.

ullstein bild Dtl./ullstein bild/Getty Images

Nazism, or national socialism, portrayed the world in pseudo-religious, pseudo-scientific terms as a struggle for dominance between the Germans and the Jews, representing, respectively, the forces of 'good' and 'evil'. Hitler himself divided the races of the world into three categories:

● The first, the Aryans, were the *Herrenvolk*, the 'master race'; Hitler described the Aryans as the 'founders of culture' and literally believed them to be responsible for all creativity, whether in art, music, literature, philosophy or political thought.

● Second, there were the 'bearers of culture', peoples who were able to utilize the ideas and inventions of the German people, but were themselves incapable of creativity.

● At the bottom were the Jews, who Hitler described as the 'destroyers of culture', pitted in an unending struggle against the noble and creative Aryans.

Hitler's **Manichaean** world-view was therefore dominated by the idea of conflict between good and evil, reflected in a racial struggle between the Germans and the Jews, a conflict that could only end in either Aryan world domination (and the elimination of the Jews) or the final victory of the Jews (and the destruction of Germany).

This ideology took Hitler and the Nazis in appalling and tragic directions. In the first place, Aryanism, the conviction that the Aryans are a uniquely creative 'master race', dictated a policy of expansionism and war. If the Germans are racially superior, other races are biologically relegated to an inferior and subservient position. Nazi ideology therefore dictated an aggressive foreign policy in pursuit of a racial empire and, ultimately, world domination. Second, the Nazis believed that Germany could never be secure so long as its arch-enemies, the Jews, continued to exist. The Jews had to be persecuted, indeed they deserved to be persecuted, because they represented evil. The Nuremburg Laws, passed in 1935, prohibited both marriage and sexual relations between Germans and Jews. After *Kristallnacht* ('The Night of Broken Glass') in 1938, Jewish people were effectively excluded from the economy. However, Nazi race theories drove Hitler from a policy of persecution to one of terror and, eventually, **genocide** and racial extermination. In 1941, with a world war still to be won, the Nazi regime embarked on what it called the 'final solution', an attempt to exterminate the Jewish population of Europe in an unparalleled process of mass murder, which led to the death of some six million Jewish people.

Peasant ideology

A further difference between the Italian and German brands of fascism is that the latter advanced a distinctively anti-modern philosophy. While Italian fascism was eager to portray itself as a modernizing force and to embrace the benefits of industry and technology, Nazism reviled much of modern civilization as decadent and corrupt. This applied particularly in the case of urbanization and industrialization. In the Nazi view, the Germans are in truth a peasant people, ideally suited to a simple existence lived close to the land and ennobled by physical labour. However, life in overcrowded, stultifying and unhealthy cities had undermined the German spirit and threatened to weaken the racial stock. Such fears were expressed in the 'Blood and Soil' ideas of the Nazi Peasant Leader Walter Darré, which blended Nordic racism with rural romanticism to create a peasant philosophy that prefigured many of the ideas of ecologism (discussed in Chapter 10). They also explain why the Nazis extolled the virtues of *Kultur*, which embodied the folk traditions and craft skills of the German peoples, over the essentially empty products of Western civilization. This peasant or rural ideology had important implications for foreign policy. In particular, it helped to fuel expansionist tendencies by strengthening the attraction of *Lebensraum*. Only through territorial expansion could overcrowded Germany acquire the space to allow its people to resume their proper, peasant existence.

Manichaeanism: A third-century Persian religion that presented the world in terms of conflict between light and darkness, and good and evil.

Genocide: The attempt to destroy, in whole or in part, a national, ethnic, racial or religious group.

TENSIONS WITHIN . . . FASCISM		
Fascism	**v.**	**Nazism**
state worship	↔	state as vessel
chauvinist nationalism	↔	extreme racism
voluntarism	↔	essentialism
national greatness	↔	biological superiority
organic unity	↔	racial purity/eugenics
pragmatic anti-Semitism	↔	genocidal anti-Semitism
futurism/modernism	↔	peasant ideology
corporatism	↔	war economy
colonial expansion	↔	world domination

This policy was based on a deep contradiction, however. War and military expansion, even when justified by reference to a peasant ideology, cannot but be pursued through the techniques and processes of a modern industrial society. The central ideological goals of the Nazi regime were conquest and empire, and these dictated the expansion of the industrial base and the development of the technology of warfare. Far from returning the German people to the land, the Hitler period witnessed rapid industrialization and the growth of the large towns and cities so despised by the Nazis. Peasant ideology thus proved to be little more than rhetoric. Militarism also brought about significant cultural shifts. While Nazi art remained fixated with simplistic images of small-town and rural life, propaganda constantly bombarded the German people with images of modern technology, from the Stuka dive-bomber and Panzer tank to the V1 and V2 rockets.

THE FUTURE OF FASCISM

One view of fascism is that it was the product of a unique, and dramatically combustible, combination of circumstances that surfaced during the interwar period (Nolte, 1965). These circumstances included the following. First, democratic government had only recently been established in many parts of Europe, and democratic political values had not replaced older, autocratic ones. Second, European society had been disrupted by the experience of industrialization, which had particularly threatened a lower middle class of shopkeepers, small businessmen, farmers and craftsmen, who were squeezed between the growing might of big business, on the one hand, and the rising power of organized labour, on the other. Third, the period after World War I was deeply affected by the 1917 Russian Revolution and the fear among the propertied classes that social revolution was about to spread throughout Europe. Fourth, World War I had failed to resolve international conflicts and rivalries, leaving a bitter inheritance of frustrated nationalism and the desire for revenge. Finally, the Great Depression of the 1930s led to rising unemployment and economic failure, creating an atmosphere of crisis and deep pessimism which could be exploited by political extremists and demagogues.

The implication of this analysis is that, as this nexus of circumstances would never be replicated, the spectre of fascism no longer hung over Europe or the wider world. In other words, fascism is an ideology without a future; in effect, it died in 1945, with the defeat of the Axis powers. Others, nevertheless, regard fascism as an ever-present threat, seeing its roots in human psychology, or as Erich Fromm (1984) called it, 'the fear of freedom'. From this perspective, modern civilization has produced greater individual freedom but, with it, the danger of isolation and insecurity. At times of crisis, individuals may therefore flee from freedom, seeking security in submission to an all-powerful leader or a totalitarian state. This suggests that fascism could revive whenever conditions of crisis, uncertainty and disorder arise, and not just when a particular set of circumstances coincide. For example, the end of communist rule in Eastern Europe allowed long-suppressed national rivalries and racial hatreds to re-emerge, giving rise, particularly in the former Yugoslavia, to forms of extreme nationalism that sometimes exhibited fascist-type features. Similarly, figures such as Viktor Orban (see p. 181) in Hungary and Jai Bolsorano in Brazil have emerged who, while not fascists, have used rhetoric that sometimes resembles fascism.

Another possibility is that a form of fascism could emerge that, while being faithful to certain core fascist beliefs and values, is more in line with the expectations and practices that prevail in the wider political system. In short, the future of fascism is neo-fascism, in some form or guise. In some respects, neo-fascism may be well positioned to prosper in the future. For one thing, in reaching an accommodation (of sorts) with liberal democracy, neo-fascists appear to no longer be burdened by the barbarism of the Hitler and Mussolini period. For another, neo-fascists still possess the ability to advance a politics of organic unity and social cohesion in the event of future economic crises or bouts of political instability. But is 'democratic fascism' – that is, fascism divorced from principles such as absolute leadership, totalitarianism and overt racism – ideologically viable? For critics of neo-fascism, democratic fascism is simply a contradiction in terms. On the one hand, in accepting political pluralism and electoral democracy, neo-fascism ceases to be fascist in any meaningful sense. On the other hand, the neo-fascist 'conversion' to democracy may merely be a tactical ruse, in which case democracy will be used to destroy democracy. This is what happened when Hitler and the Nazis were elected to power in 1933, only, subsequently, to abolish elections.

QUESTIONS FOR DISCUSSION

- Was fascism merely a product of the specific historical circumstances of the interwar period?
- Is there such a thing as a 'fascist minimum', and if so, what are its features?
- How has anti-rationalism shaped fascist ideology?
- Why do fascists value struggle and war?
- How can the fascist leader principle be viewed as a form of democracy?
- Is fascism simply an extreme form of nationalism?

- In what sense is fascism a revolutionary creed?
- To what extent can fascism be viewed as a blend of nationalism and socialism?
- Why and how is fascism linked to totalitarianism?
- Are all fascists racists, or only some of them?
- Why and how have some fascists objected to capitalism?
- To what extent is modern 'neo-fascism' a genuine form of fascism?

FURTHER READING

Bosworth, R. *The Oxford Handbook of Fascism* (2012). A comprehensive collection of writings and research on fascism, and its ideological practice across many contexts.

Griffin, R. *Fascism* (2018). A compact introduction to the concept of fascism and its development, with an emphasis on its relevance in contemporary global politics.

Griffin, R. (ed.), *International Fascism: Theories, Causes and the New Consensus* (1998). A collection of essays that examine contrasting interpretations of fascism and a diversity of fascist movements from an international perspective.

Kallis, A. *The Fascism Reader* (2003). An excellent collection of writings from leading scholars of fascism on a broad range of topics.

Mann, M. *Fascists* (2004). An extensive survey of the six regimes where fascism became the dominant ideology, and their political, intellectual, and sociological traits.

POPULISM

PREVIEW

Derived from the Latin *populus*, meaning people, the term 'populism' was originally used to refer to the ideas and beliefs of the US People's Party (also known as the Populist Party), which was founded in 1892. The term later acquired a range of pejorative associations, being used to imply, for example, mass manipulation or political irresponsibility. Few politicians therefore identify themselves as populists. These difficulties are compounded by a lack of scholarly agreement about both the nature of populism as a political phenomenon – is it an ideology, a movement, a political style or whatever? – and its defining features.

It is nevertheless widely accepted that, as an ideology, populism is shaped by two key stances: adulation of 'the people' and outright condemnation of the elite or establishment. The central image of populism is therefore of a society divided into two homogeneous and antagonistic groups: the 'pure' people and the 'corrupt' elite. From the populist perspective, the people – typically conceived selectively as the 'real people' or the 'true people' – constitute the only source of moral worth in politics, their wishes and instincts providing the sole legitimate guide to political action. Populists thus embrace a monist stance that is firmly opposed to pluralism, and puts it at odds with liberalism in general and liberal democracy in particular. However, in contrast to other forms of pro-people illiberalism (notably fascism and communism), populism is essentially reformist rather than revolutionary.

It is nevertheless important to note that there are ideological tensions within populism, in particular between left-wing and right-wing populism. Left-wing populists typically define the people in class terms, and tend to prioritize socio-economic concerns such as poverty, inequality and job insecurity. This form of populism overlaps with socialist thinking of one kind or another. By comparison, right-wing populists view the people in narrower and often ethnically restricted terms. Focusing primarily on socio-cultural concerns such as immigration, crime and corruption, this form of populism overlaps with social conservatism.

HISTORICAL OVERVIEW

The origins of populism are sometimes traced back to the latter stages of the French Revolution and the attempt by Robespierre and the Jacobins to put the radical democratic thinking of Jean-Jacques Rousseau (see p. 133) into practice. (The contested relationship between populism and democracy is discussed later in the chapter.) More commonly, however, populism is seen to have emerged during the final decades of the nineteenth century as a movement for the protection of peasants' or farmers' interests in the context of rising industrialization. This so-called agrarian populism was particularly evident in Russia and the USA. In Russia, it was associated with the growth of the *narodniki* (a term that comes from the phrase 'going to the people') in the early 1870s. The *narodniki* were young people from mostly privileged, well-educated and urban backgrounds, who, inspired by the belief that the hope for political and social change in Russia lay with an awakened peasantry, went into the countryside to proselytize this political doctrine. Confronted by often baffled peasants, who, not uncommonly, handed them in to the police, the movement became more conspiratorial over time and some of its offshoots turned to terrorism.

In the USA, populism surfaced through the founding of the People's Party in 1892. Espousing a left-wing agenda, the party drew support from farmers and agricultural labourers in the American West and South, who had become disenchanted with the economic and social policies imposed on them by the more industrialized East. However, after the People's Party's high point of success in 1892, when its candidate in the 1892 presidential election, James B. Weaver, won over one million votes, divisions within the party deepened, particularly over the extent to which it should collaborate with the Democratic Party. By the turn of the century the People's Party had effectively disappeared as a political force separate from the Democrats.

A further wave of populism emerged during the 1930s and 1940s, initially drawing its impetus from the intensified hardships imposed by the Great Depression. This was especially apparent in Latin America. Although Latin American populism has had diverse manifestations, its two most common themes have been a primary concern with socio-economic issues (usually related to the attempt to strengthen the role of the state in the economy) and a pronounced tendency towards charismatic leadership, with Juan Perón's (see p. 171) rule in Argentina widely being seen as the paradigmatic example. Following a period dominated by military **dictatorships**, Latin America has experienced a resurgence in populism since the late 1980s. This revived populism has nevertheless had two contrasting manifestations. The first, exemplified by figures such as Carlos Menem in Argentina, Fernando Collor de Mello in Brazil and Alberto Fujimori in Peru, was characterized by the adoption of free-market economic strategies, encouraged by the International Monetary Fund. (Some, nevertheless, question whether populism can be properly associated with pro-market, anti-state economics.) The second manifestation was linked to the so-called 'pink tide', which saw

Dictatorship: A system of rule in which a single individual or group acts beyond the law and constitutional constraints.

a succession of left-wing presidents sweep to power. Claiming to represent the poor and disadvantaged, and committed to reversing the drift towards neoliberalism (see p. 63), prominent examples of such figures have included Hugo Chavez (see p. 183) and Nicolas Maduro in Venezuela, Evo Morales in Bolivia and Rafael Correa in Ecuador.

KEY FIGURE

Central Press/Hulton Archive/Getty Images

JUAN DOMINGO PERÓN (1895–1974)

An Argentine soldier and politician, Perón took a leading part in an army coup in 1943, giving him his first taste of political office. In 1946, he was elected to the presidency, being re-elected in 1951. Peron derived immense popularity by cultivating the support of the urban working and middle classes in Buenos Aires through a programme of sweeping nationalization and expanded government spending, aided by the charismatic oratory of his wife, 'Evita' Peron (1919–52). Basing his power on the multi-class appeal of the Justicialista (Peronist) Party, Perón embraced ideas that ranged across the political spectrum, from the far-left to the far-right. Deposed and exiled following a military coup in 1955, Perón returned triumphantly to Argentina and the presidency in 1973, before dying the following year.

The period since the turn of the twenty-first century has witnessed a major resurgence of populism, encouraging some to dub the contemporary period the 'age of populism'. Affecting most dramatically Europe and North America (although its influence has extended from Australia and Brazil to Thailand and India), this process gained momentum from the so-called Great Recession that came in the wake of the 2007–09 global financial crisis. Manifestations of this particular form of 'anti-politics' have been many and various. These have included the increased prominence of right-wing nationalist parties (such as the French National Rally, the Sweden Democrats, Alternative for Germany (AfD) and Austria's Freedom Party); the emergence of new political groups and movements (such as Syriza (Coalition for the Radical Left) in Greece, Podemos (We Can) in Spain and the Five Star Movement in Italy); and the rise of 'strongman' leaders (such as Viktor Orban (see p. 181) in Hungary, Recep Tayyip Erdogan in Turkey and Jair Bolsonaro in Brazil). The clearest evidence that politics had entered a turbulent new age came in 2016, when Donald Trump, first, won the Republican presidential nomination and then defeated Hillary Clinton in the race to become the US president, and the UK voted in a referendum in favour of leaving the European Union, the world's largest trading bloc. In both cases, the events were crucially influenced by a populist revolt against **mainstream politics** ('politics as normal'), whose strength defied the predictions of almost all pundits.

> **Mainstream politics:**
> Political activities, processes and structures that are regarded as conventional; the dominant trend in politics.

KEY CONCEPT

ANTI-POLITICS

'Anti-politics' is a rejection of, or alienation from, conventional politicians and political processes, especially mainstream political parties and established representative mechanisms. One manifestation of anti-politics is a decline in civic engagement, as citizens turn away from politics and retreat into private existence. This is reflected most clearly in a fall in voter turnout and declining levels of party membership and political activism. However, anti-politics has also spawned new forms of politics, which, in various ways, articulate resentment or hostility towards political structures and offer more 'authentic' alternatives. These include the rise of 'fringe' or anti-political parties and the emergence of populist leaders. The attraction of such parties and leaders is substantially linked to their image as political 'outsiders', which is often maintained even if they win power.

CORE THEMES

Much disagreement surrounds the nature of populism as a political phenomenon. Not only has populism often assumed different forms in different parts of world – leading some to question whether populism in Latin America has the same underlying character as populism in, say, Europe – but populism has also been treated, variously, as a movement, a syndrome, a style of politics and a political strategy. For example, as a political strategy, populism has been associated with so-called **anti-party parties**, which have a combative, even insurrectionist, character, and reject conventional politics' obsession with compromise and centre-ground thinking. However, recent years have seen a growing tendency to adopt an ideational approach to populism, conceiving it essentially as a political ideology (Mudde and Kaltwasser, 2015 and 2017). From this perspective, populism is defined by its Manichean tendency to view the world in terms of conflict between good and evil, or 'us' and 'them', these antithetical forces being articulated through 'the people' and 'the **elite**', respectively. Nevertheless, populism is very clearly a thin-centred ideology, possessing only a limited range of core features. This affords populists considerable scope to draw on other political traditions, notably conservatism, nationalism and socialism, which act, in effect, as 'host' ideologies. Not only does this mean that there is no such thing as 'pure' populism, but also that populism can vary dramatically both in the forms can take and where it is located on the political spectrum. Like all ideologies, however, populism is associated with a distinctive set of ideas and beliefs. The most important of these are:

- the people

- the elite

- populist democracy.

The people

The key claim made by populists is that the people are the ultimate source of political authority. In that sense, they believe in the primacy of the people. But who are 'the people'? The people is among the vaguest and most contested concepts in political analysis. 'People' (without the definite article) refers, quite simply, to the human species, encompassing all its members, without restriction. By contrast, *'the* people' is a narrower and more specific concept, distinguishing those who are part of the people from those who are not. However, such boundaries can be drawn in at least three different ways (Canovan, 2005):

- First, the people are *citizens,* members of a political community (usually a state), who are endowed with formal rights and duties. This is the sense in which the term is used in the preamble to the US Constitution, which begins: 'We the people of the United States…' Thanks to the liberal quest to establish universal citizenship, this use of the term is highly inclusive, and only fails to encompass those who are 'aliens' or 'undocumented immigrants'.

- Second, the people are the *common people*, or the *masses*, those who are viewed as somehow downtrodden, exploited or marginalized, as opposed to those who possess wealth, power or social prestige.

- Third, the people is equivalent to the *nation*. In this sense, the people are defined in cultural and ethnic terms, distinguishing them clearly from those who do not share their national identity, whether they live in the same political community, or a different one.

Anti-party party: A party that sets out to subvert traditional party politics by rejecting parliamentary compromise and emphasizing a strategy based on popular mobilization.

Elite: A minority in whose hands power, wealth and prestige is concentrated.

While populists reject the notion of the people as citizens, on the grounds that it is incompatible with the people/elite divide, each of the other two definitions casts some light on the populist conception of the people. The assertion that the people are 'common', 'plain' or 'ordinary', in the sense that they are somehow disadvantaged, is helpful in that it captures the idea that power – who has it, and who lacks it – is vital to the distinction between the people and the elite. However, if the people encompasses *all* those who lack power and are socially disadvantaged, it threatens to include groups that populists may wish to exclude (such as ethnic or religious minorities). Moreover, to base the people/elite divide primarily on socio-economic factors is to come close to adopting a form of class analysis that only left-wing populists could accept, most populists subscribing to a 'post-class' approach to society. The same applies to the assertion that the people are equivalent to the nation. While this is the defining assumption of **national populism** (sometimes called 'cultural' or 'xenophobic' populism), it is not a position necessarily favoured by other populists.

National populism: A form of populism that prioritizes the culture and interests of the nation and embraces strident anti-internationalism.

PERSPECTIVES ON ... THE PEOPLE

LIBERALS embrace a disaggregated, even atomistic, notion of the people, underpinned by a belief in the supreme importance of the individual over any social group or collective body. The people are therefore a collection of autonomous and unique individuals, whose 'personhood' is reflected in their entitlement to equal legal and political rights.

CONSERVATIVES have traditionally understood the people in the context of hierarchy, the people, or masses, occupying the lower strata of society and benefiting from the support, leadership and guidance that is provided by their social 'betters'. This view of the people was most prominent among pre-democratic conservatives.

SOCIALISTS define the people in terms of social class, meaning that they share a similar socio-economic position. The people are identified as the working class, implying either that they are manual, or 'blue collar', workers, or, in the Marxist view, that they live off the sale of their labour power (the proletariat).

NATIONALISTS believe that the people is equivalent to the nation. It is thus a collection of people who are bound together by shared values and traditions, a common language, religion and history, and usually occupying the same geographical area.

FASCISTS view the people as an organically unified whole, forged out of an intense and militant sense of national identity. In its Nazi version, *Volksgemeinscaft* (people's community) places a strong emphasis on the racial unity of the German people, seen as the 'master race'.

POPULISTS portray the people – typically conceived of selectively as the 'real people' or 'true people' – in either socialist or nationalist terms, seeing their wishes and instincts also as the sole legitimate guide to political action.

The populist conception of the people is distinctive in two senses. In the first place, populists claim to represent not all the people but only those who are seen as the 'real', 'pure' or 'true' people. Only some of the people are therefore really the people (Muller, 2017). To be a proper member of the political community it is thus necessary to meet some standard of **authenticity**. This authenticity derives from the moral identity of the people, giving populism a distinctively moralistic character. The 'real' people are taken to be righteous, pure and fully unified, a **homogeneous** entity that is both innocent and entirely trustworthy. Second, although the people are viewed as the sole reliable source of political wisdom, this wisdom is not, strictly speaking, a product of active political engagement on the part of the people themselves. Rather, it arises through a process of populist agitation that awakens the people to their 'true' convictions and beliefs. In this sense, populist ideology bears the influence of Rousseau's idea of the 'general will' (Mudde and Kaltwasser, 2017). This is because populists conceive the people's will as the indivisible collective will of the entire community, as opposed to the actual views of living and breathing human beings. The people's will is therefore a construct rather than an empirical fact. It is, thus, not uncommon for populists to treat elections and voting as an unreliable guide to the voice of the people. During the 2016 US presidential election campaign, for example, Donald Trump persistently refused to commit himself to accepting the election result should he be defeated, claiming that such an outcome would not be legitimate.

The elite

Populism is deeply critical of the elite or the **establishment**. Populism therefore clashes sharply with all forms of normative elitism. As with the people, populists take the elite to be a single, homogeneous force, unified by a shared moral character. Whereas the people are righteous and morally pure, the elite are thoroughly corrupt and morally debased, making them the 'enemy of the people'. The corruption that resides in the heart of the elite is manifest in its determination to subdue, exploit and manipulate the people. However, populists are typically more eager to condemn the elite as corrupt than they are to explain the source of its corruption. Thus, although populists may appear to share with liberals the belief that power and corruption are intrinsically linked, they cannot accept that the elite are 'made' corrupt by the experience of holding political power, for this would be irreconcilable with the emphasis populists customarily place on leadership. Similarly, populists must reject the liberal belief that corruption ultimately stems from the egoism that resides within all individuals, as this would call the people's intrinsic moral purity into question.

Authenticity: The quality of being real or genuine.

Homogeneity: The quality of uniformity, in which all parts of an entity or structure are the same or similar.

Establishment: A term, often used loosely, that refers to a collection of people that exercises control over society by virtue of their entrenched institutional power.

KEY CONCEPT

ELITISM

Elitism is, broadly, a belief in, or practice of, rule by an elite or minority. However, there are at least three different types of elitist. *Classical* elitists – examples including Vilfredo Pareto (1884–1923), Gaetano Mosca (1857–1941) and Robert Michels (1876–1936) – criticize egalitarian beliefs such as socialism and democracy on the grounds that elite rule is an inevitable (and usually desirable) feature of social existence. *Normative* elitists emphasize the personal, moral and intellectual superiority of the elite over masses, the elite, in effect, being 'the highest', 'the best' or 'the excellent'. *Modern* elitists advance a social-scientific analysis of elite rule that is typically based on the assumption that it can and should be overthrown.

Although populists treat the elite as a single, unified entity, three elements within the elite are often singled out for particular criticism. These are the political elite, the economic elite and the cultural elite. The most prominent of these, the political elite, comprises key figures in mainstream party politics (the 'political class') and senior political office holders (presidents, prime ministers, prominent ministers, top civil servants, judges and the like). Its purpose is to harness political power to the interests of the wider elite, and, in the process, distance the people from the levers of governmental control. The economic elite, consisting, most significantly, of big business and banks, both supports and works in conjunction with the political elite. In this way, politics and wealth are bound closely together. The cultural elite, and especially 'establishment' media outlets such as the BBC, *The New York Times, Le Monde* and *la Repubblica* (often seen as the 'metropolitan' media elite), are routinely accused by populists of propagating elite (and invariably 'liberal') values. However, by no means do populists assume that factors such as institutional position, wealth or social standing always shape people's values and viewpoints. Inconsistencies are common and often striking. For example, Viktor Orban has retained his populist credentials despite being Hungary's longest serving prime minister; Donald Trump's lavish lifestyle and vast business empire did not prevent him from attracting significant support in 2016 in particular from less-prosperous voters in the so-called Rust Belt states; and the US media conglomerate Fox News, together with many tabloid newspapers and most 'shock jock' radio presenters articulate strongly anti-establishment views.

An additional aspect of elite power, according to many populists, is that it is exercised through practices that are somehow deceitful or 'shady'. This reflects the elite's ability to manipulate understanding, concealing its true (oppressive) purposes. Populists accuse the elite of inauthenticity or fakery of various kinds, whether this is through their supposed dissemination of 'fake news' (that is, flagrant lying by any other standard), or the workings of 'fake esquires', 'fake courts', 'fake parliaments' and so forth. In presenting the distinction between the people and the elite as one between authenticity and fakery, populists have indulged in the blanket condemnation of elite ideas and beliefs, not uncommonly supported by **conspiracy theories** of one kind or another. Examples of such theories include that the Covid-19 pandemic was caused by the roll-out of the 5G mobile phone network and that the 2020 US presidential election was 'stolen' from Trump by fraud.

Populist democracy

Its relationship to democracy is key to grasping the nature of populism, but this is an issue that is both complex and contested. On the one hand, populism has been portrayed as an essentially democratic force, based on the claim that, in common with democracy, populism endorses the principles of **popular sovereignty** and majority rule. Some, indeed, argue that populism operates as a corrective to democracy, insofar as it gives a voice to people or groups who feel that they are marginalized or ignored within the existing democratic process. Populists, therefore, commonly proclaim that the established democratic system is failing to live up to the democratic ideal. On the other hand, populism has been portrayed as a threat to democracy, even as a pathological political phenomenon. In this view, not only are populists at best bogus democrats, practised in the arts of **demagoguery**, but, by endorsing plebiscitary forms of democracy (see p. 176), they are also at odds with all forms of representative politics.

Conspiracy theory: A theory that places a central (and undue) emphasis on the role of sinister forces, clandestine maneuverings and secret plans.

Popular sovereignty: The principle that there is no higher authority than the will of the people, directly expressed.

Demagoguery: The rule of political leaders who manipulate the masses through inflammatory oratory that exploits their prejudices and/or ignorance.

KEY CONCEPT
PLEBISCITARY DEMOCRACY

Plebiscitary democracy is a form of rule that operates through an unmediated link between the rulers and the rule, typically established by plebiscites (or referendums). These allow the public to express their views on political issues directly. Supporters of plebiscitary democracy argue that its advantages are that it is a way of avoiding the deficiencies of representative democracy (including that representatives may develop interests separate from those of the public at large), while avoiding the impracticalities of full-scale direct democracy. Plebiscitary democracy has nevertheless been widely criticized, not least for the scope it provides for manipulation and personal leadership. Indeed, plebiscitary democracy may amount to little more than a system of mass acclamation that gives dictatorship a popular gloss.

It is, nevertheless, difficult to deny that there are deep tensions between populism and the dominant, liberal or representative model of democracy. This is because the populist assertion that the instincts and wishes of the people constitute the sole legitimate guide to political action implies that nothing should be allowed to stand in the way of the popular will. In holding that liberal democracy (see p. 44) is largely a sham, populist thinking on this matter parallels the modern elitist critique of democracy. In *The Power Elite* (1956), C. Wight Mills offered a portrait of a USA dominated by a triumvirate of big business (particularly defence-related industries), the US military and political cliques surrounding the president. However, what makes populist antagonism towards a liberal democracy distinctive is the assertion that constitutionalism (see p. 42) is the enemy of 'genuine' popular rule. Populists are thus likely to show, at best, qualified respect for the 'liberal' aspects of liberal democracy, those that are designed to uphold limited government, such as protections for individual and minority rights, the separation of powers, judicial independence, the rule of law and media freedom. This nevertheless also implies that the 'democratic' aspects of liberal democracy – including, vitally, its commitment to popular sovereignty – may be undermined. This was dramatically demonstrated in January 2021 by the assault on the US Capitol building by Trump supporters seeking to block the certification by Congress of the previous November's presidential election result, so reversing Trump's defeat.

In this light, it is unsurprising that populism has been associated with illiberal forms of democracy. Since 2014, Viktor Orban has committed himself to the construction in Hungary of an 'illiberal state', and, as such thinking spread to Poland and elsewhere, in 2018 he declared that 'the era of liberal democracy is over'. However, there is no single model of illiberal democracy. In the case of revolutionary illiberal democracy, an attempt is made to overthrow the values and structures of liberal democratic governance and replace them with an entirely different set of values and structures. Fascism and communism are the clearest examples of this. Populism, by contrast, is an example of reformist illiberal democracy, in that it seeks to constrain or curtail aspects of liberal democracy, rather than eradicate it altogether. In his pioneering account of the phenomenon, Fareed Zakaria (1997) thus described illiberal democracies as democratically elected regimes that routinely ignore constitutional limits on their power and deprive citizens of basic rights and freedoms. Populist rule is therefore commonly associated with at least some of the following:

- A system of regular elections that are sufficiently free and fair to contribute, albeit within limits, to the maintenance of legitimacy.

- The political process is typically characterized by personalized leadership, a strong state, weak opposition, and emaciated checks and balances.

● Political and civil rights are selectively suppressed, especially in relation to the media, although no attempt is made to control every aspect of human life.

● A disposition towards majoritarianism is reflected in a general intolerance of pluralism and, maybe, hostility towards ethnic, cultural or religious minorities.

KEY CONCEPT

MAJORITARIANISM

As a descriptive concept, majoritarianism refers to a rule of decision-making in which the preferences of the majority overrule those of the minority, although it is unclear whether this refers to an 'absolute' or 'simple' majority. As a normative concept, majoritarianism refers to the belief that the majority view *should* prevail over the minority, with the possible implication that the defeated minority is morally obliged to come into line with the views of the majority. In this case, the majority effectively becomes the people. Majoritarianism has been criticized for allowing the majority to ride roughshod over minority groups, and for failing to recognize that complex modern societies contain no single, cohesive majority but rather comprise a collection of minorities.

Finally, an alternative approach to the relationship between populism and democracy has been advanced by theorists such as Ernesto Laclau (2005) and Chantal Mouffe (2018). In this view, populism has an in-built disposition in favour of democracy. By using **radical democracy** to redress the defects of liberal democracy, populists foster the 'democratization of democracy'. This process involves the reintroduction of conflict into politics, brought about, in particular, through the mobilization of the 'underdog' against 'those in power'. One of the implications of this is that all democratic movements can, to a greater or lesser degree, be seen as populist.

TYPES OF POPULISM

Populism is marked by a revulsion against the ideological centre ground. This is for at least two reasons. First, centrist politics is typically associated with a liberalism that populists deride, not least because the liberal emphasis on individualism (see p. 24) differs starkly from the populist image of a society divided into rival homogeneous groups. Second, the ideological centre ground is an arena of compromise and fine balances between left- and right-wing beliefs, which offers little scope for the blanket moral judgements to which populists are drawn. The idea of a 'populism of the centre' therefore makes very little sense. Some, indeed, link this to the wider problem of locating populism anywhere on the political spectrum, given a tendency to blend policies and beliefs from both the left and the right. For example, Poland's Law and Justice party combines a conservative approach to social issues with a socialist stance on economic affairs, while the yellow vest (*gilets jaunes*) movement in France has campaigned on issues of economic justice that span the left/right divide, and attracted support from many who had previously backed far-left and far-right candidates. However, other populist parties and movements tend to have a more consistent ideological orientation, in line with contrasting sub-traditions.

Radical democracy: A form of democracy that favours decentralization and participation, the widest possible dispersal of political power.

● right populism

● left populism.

Right populism

The ideological complexion of right-wing populism is reflected in a fusion between key features of generic populism – such as anti-elitism, monism and moralism – and the socially conservative belief that, being composed of a fragile network of relationships, society urgently needs to be bolstered or upheld. This fusion has been founded either on the basis of nationalism or on the basis of authoritarianism (see p. 66). Right-wing populism therefore comprises two principal forms – national populism and **authoritarian populism** – although most right-wing populists are sympathetic towards both nationalism and authoritarianism, albeit usually to different degrees.

National populism

The central feature of national populism is that it defines the people in ethnic terms, meaning that the people is equivalent to the nation. National populists thus prioritize the culture and interests of the nation over all other considerations. They promise to give a voice to a national community that has been neglected, even held in contempt, by distant and corrupt elites (Eatwell and Goodwin, 2018). Such a conception of the people typically also has a historical and a territorial dimension. Paul Taggart (2000) conveyed this by arguing that populism always draws on the notion of an implicit or explicit '**heartland**', a version of the past that celebrates a hypothetical, uncomplicated and non-political territory of the imagination. From this 'place', the people draw both their values and their sense of themselves as unified, diligent and ordinary. The heartland therefore encapsulates an image of past national greatness which national populists commit themselves to restoring.

Authoritarian populism: A form of populism that fuses robust anti-elitism, the practice of government 'from above' and strict adherence to conventional moral norms.

Heartland: An ill-defined earlier time in which a 'virtuous and unified population' resided.

Assimilation: The process through which immigrant communities lose their cultural distinctiveness by adjusting to the values, allegiances and lifestyles of the majority group.

Repatriation: The act or process of returning property or a person – voluntarily or forcibly – to their country of origin.

Nativism: A political stance that (supposedly) reflects the needs and interests of native (or majority ethnic) inhabitants against those of immigrants.

National populism has been rising steadily since the late 1990s, gaining impetus from the emergence of a faster-moving, more open society (see 'open/closed' divide, p. 15), and giving rise to burgeoning cultural wars (see p. 179) between social liberals and social conservatives. It has become by far the most prevalent form of populism across the globe, being particularly strong in Europe and the USA. In 2016 and 2017, 18.4 per cent of Europeans voted for national-populist parties, an increase of 7 per cent compared with 2000. In states including Hungary, Poland, Serbia, Slovakia, Italy and Austria, national-populist parties have succeeded in winning, or sharing, government power. This surge in national populism has been linked to two key – and often overlapping – policy positions. First, and most crucially, national populists oppose immigration, a stance that was boosted in Europe by the refugee crisis that peaked in 2015 (see p. 179), and in the USA by the election of President Trump in 2016. Opposition to immigration has been expressed, variously, in bans, or at least the imposition of robust controls, on migrants, pressure on minority ethnic communities to **assimilate** into the culture of the 'host' society, and, most radically, forcible **repatriation**. Anti-immigration populism typically has a strong '**nativist**' character and is underpinned by the wider belief that ethnic diversity is irreconcilable with national cohesion and social stability. Immigration and multiculturalism (see Chapter 11) are thus portrayed as twin enemies of the people. (For a more detailed account of the conservative nationalism on which such thinking is based, see Chapter 7.)

KEY CONCEPT
CULTURE WAR

A culture war is a hyper-partisan style of politics, in which there is a clash of values between those who subscribe to social liberalism (progressives) and those who support social conservatism (traditionalists). Key 'wedge' issues in this respect include abortion, same-sex marriage (see p. 57), gender equality, trans rights, racial justice, immigration and environmental protection. The spread of culture wars originated in the USA in the 1990s, sparked by a combination of a right-wing backlash against the advance of liberal values in the 1960s and 1970s, and the desire to reinvigorate left-wing politics, disillusioned by the centrist drift in economic policy in the 1980s and 1990s. Other factors stoking culture wars include divisions that flow from the advance of globalization, and the tendency of social media to 'amplify' emotion-filled and simplistic political views.

POLITICAL IDEOLOGIES IN ACTION...

THE REFUGEE CRISIS IN EUROPE

EVENTS: In what was Europe's biggest refugee crisis since World War II, more than one million migrants (most of whom were asylum seekers) crossed into Europe in 2015. The vast majority arrived by sea but some migrants made their way overland, principally via Turkey and Albania. Mainly fleeing conflict in Syria, Afghanistan, Iraq and elsewhere, migrants headed into Europe in search of peace and improved economic prospects, many of them having friends or family who had already made the journey. The journey to Europe was often perilous. More than 3,770 migrants were reported to have died trying to cross the Mediterranean Sea in 2015, while more than 800 died in the Aegean Sea, crossing from Turkey to Greece. The number of migrants entering Europe subsequently fell; according to the European Parliament, the number of migrants granted asylum in 2017 by EU states was 25 per cent down on 2016.

SIGNIFICANCE: One approach to the refugee crisis was to see it as, essentially, a humanitarian crisis. This was reflected, for example, in the German Chancellor Angela Merkel's announcement in 2015 of an open-door policy towards Syrian refugees. A very different stance was adopted by national populists across Europe, however. This saw international migration as both a challenge to the state's ability to control its own borders, a vital manifestation of national sovereignty, and as a threat to social cohesion, in this case stemming from the fact that most recent migrants into Europe have come from Muslim countries. Evidence of growing support for such thinking was found in the success of far-right, anti-immigration parties such as Alternative for Germany, which won seats in the German parliament for the first

BalkansCat/iStock

time in 2017, and Sweden Democrats, which, having received growing support during 2010–14, became the third largest party in Sweden in 2018.

The most dramatic response to the migrant crisis nevertheless came from national populists in power. For example, in December 2015 the Fidesz government in Hungary speedily erected a razor-wire fence along its southern border with Serbia, Croatia and Romania, complete with heat sensors, cameras and loudspeakers, and with the capacity to deliver electric shocks to unwanted migrants. When Hungarian riot police fired teargas and water cannon across the newly-closed border with Serbia, as thousands of refugees tried to enter through a gate that connects the two countries, Serbia's prime minister described Hungary's behaviour as 'brutal' and 'non-European'. After the election in Italy in 2018 of a coalition government between the far-right League party and the Five Star Movement, Matteo Salvini, the deputy prime minister and the League's leader, committed himself to the repatriation of half a million migrants, and clamped down on migrant rescues in the Mediterranean, sometimes leaving migrants at sea for days.

The second key policy position commonly associated with national populism is a resistance to the influence of intergovernmental and supranational bodies, rooted in a deep scepticism towards internationalism (see p. 139). Populist anti-internationalism has two main sources, related, respectively, to national sovereignty and national identity. By insisting on unswerving respect for national sovereignty, populists seek to counter the influence of global elites and other transnational forces, ensuring, in the process, that political control rests firmly in the hands of the nation. Through their emphasis on national identity, populists have aimed to strengthen the nation and, in particular, resist the advance of cosmopolitanism (see p. 139). Populist anti-internationalism has been most apparent in Europe, where its principal target has been the European Union. This has been expressed through growing scepticism about the EU's founding goal of building 'an ever closer union'. For example, the Visegrad Four group (Hungary, Poland, Slovakia and the Czech Republic), together with other like-minded states, including Austria, Croatia, Bulgaria, Romania and Italy, have backed the idea of a much looser 'Europe of sovereign nations'. The 'Leave' victory in the UK's 2016 EU referendum, which set the country on a course to exit the EU, which was carried out in 2020, is sometimes seen as a manifestation of national populism. However, Brexit is better interpreted as a product of a combination of non-populist and populist forces. The former were articulated by the mainly Conservative official 'Vote Leave' campaign (even though its most prominent figure, Boris Johnson, later to become Conservative leader and prime minister, is widely classified as a populist), which focused primarily on economic arguments against EU membership. The latter were largely expressed by the unofficial 'Leave.UK' campaign, which, closely linked to the UK Independence Party and its then-leader, Nigel Farage, made more of immigration-related issues.

Authoritarian populism

Juan Perón's dictatorial rule in Argentina is usually seen as the classic example of authoritarian populism, defined, as it was, by an emphasis on obedience, order and national unity. Modern right-wing populists nevertheless typically embrace a form of authoritarianism that stops short of outright dictatorship. In this context, the link between populism and authoritarianism is rooted in a particular style of leadership. This leadership style is based on the fact that, despite their veneration of the people, populists rarely hold that the people can and do speak for themselves. Leadership, usually in the form of a single dominant figure, is therefore needed both to give the people a voice and to awaken them to their 'real' interests. Strictly speaking, populist leaders do not portray themselves as *representatives* of the people, for this would imply speaking for, or on behalf of, the people, as a separate, and perhaps superior, entity. Rather, populist leaders emphasize their affinity with the people, even sometimes casting themselves as an integral *part* of the people. In this light, the role of the populist leader is, in effect, to create or embody the people. The practical implication of this is to widen the leader's realm of unconstrained action, in part by eroding respect for institutions that mediate between the leader and people, such as parliaments and regional and local assemblies.

In its most advanced form, authoritarian populism has contributed to the emergence of the wider phenomenon of 'strongman' politics, exemplified by figures such as Viktor Orban, Recep Tayyip Erdogan and Philippines' president Rodrigo Duterte (although the gendered term is misleading when applied to populist leaders, as examples like Evita Peron, Marine Le Pen (see p. 182), Sarah Palin and Pauline Hanson demonstrate).

Strongman leaders operate in a 'grey zone' between democracy and authoritarianism, their distinctively 'strong' governing style being as much a strategy to maintain electoral support as it is a means of neutralizing political opposition. Strongman politics is defined most clearly by the tendency of leaders to conjure up the image of a vilified 'other', an enemy within or an enemy without, which is used to play on people's fears and stoke resentment. Whether this 'other' is migrants, rich elites, secular liberals or the bullying West, it allows the strongman to portray himself (or herself) as the defender of the nation and take bold and assertive action to that end. While many believe that strongman politics is driven essentially by personal ambition and tends towards tyranny and the flouting of conventional political norms, others argue that it satisfies a longing for more decisive leadership and amounts to a rejection of the politics of compromise and dithering.

KEY FIGURE

VIKTOR ORBAN (BORN 1963)

A Hungarian political leader, Viktor Orban has been the prime minister of Hungary since 2010, having previously served as premier during 1998–2002. A founding member in 1988 of the national conservative party, Fidesz, Orban has been the party's president since 1993, with a break between 2000 and 2003. In a controversial speech in 2014, Orban condemned 'Western' political systems based on liberal values and accountability, praising instead 'Eastern' systems based on a strong state, a weak opposition and limited checks and balances. While Orban's self-styled 'system of national cooperation' has attracted criticism, not least by the EU, for its failure adequately to protect individual rights and democratic controls, he has exerted influence within parts of the EU for a more robust stance on immigration, based, in part, on a defence of 'Christian civilization'. (See Chapter 12, for a discussion of the link between religion and ideology.)

Antoine Gyori/Corbis News/ Getty Images

The far-right

By virtue of its link to authoritarianism, right-wing populism is often seen to be part of the **far-right** (also sometimes called the radical right), placing it on the political spectrum between the mainstream right (conservatism) and the extreme right (fascism). However, the far-right encompasses tensions and internal divisions, and by no means are all of its manifestations populist in character. Far-right parties such as the Freedom Parties in Austria and the Netherlands, the Italian League and Alternative for Germany have a clear populist orientation based on the claim to support the 'common man'. Other parties, notably the Sweden Democrats and Marine Le Pen's National Rally in France, have consolidated their far-right identity by disavowing **extremism** and strengthening their commitment to electoral politics. In the USA, the far-right is associated with a disparate collection of groups commonly referred to as the alt-right (an abbreviation for 'alternative right'), which gained considerable impetus from Donald Trump's bid for the White House in 2016, as well as later clashes with the burgeoning rival movement for racial justice. Nevertheless, the tendency of alt-right groups such as the Proud Boys to reject mainstream conservatism outright and to support implicit or explicit racism (see p. 162), in the form of **white nationalism**, suggests that they may be more accurately classified as neo-fascists or neo-Nazis, rather than as populists.

Far-right: A right-wing ideological stance that is characterized by ethno-nationalism, *laissez-faire* capitalism (anti-socialism) and ultraconservative or reactionary moral values.

Extremism: A stance that goes significantly beyond what, in mainstream politics, is deemed to be reasonable or acceptable.

White nationalism: A form of nationalism which seeks to establish an ethno-state of, and for, white people; sometimes seen as a quest for white supremacy.

Chesnot/Getty Images
News/Getty Images

MARINE LE PEN (BORN 1968)

A French politician and lawyer, Marine Le Pen has been the president of the National Front (renamed the National Rally in 2018) since 2011, with a brief interruption in 2017. As part of a process of 'de-demonization', aimed at distancing the party from its racist and anti-Semitic past, in 2015 she expelled her father, Jean-Marie Le Pen, who had founded the party in 1972 and had served as its leader until 2011. This process also involved a modernization of the party's policies, including accepting unconditional abortion and same-sex partnerships, and dropping the death penalty. In 2017, Marine Le Pen succeeded in getting through to the run-off, second ballot of the presidential election, but she was beaten by Emmanuel Macron.

Left populism

Although most contemporary manifestations of populism, and especially incidences of populists winning or sharing government power, involve right-wing populists, populism also has a long-established left-wing tradition. In Latin America, indeed, left-wing populism has generally been more prevalent than right-wing populism. But how does left populism differ from right populism? In the first place, left-wing populists typically conceive the people, not in ethnic terms, but in class (and often in Latin America cross-class) terms. One of the implications of this is that left-wing populists tend to prioritize socio-economic concerns such as poverty, inequality and job security, over socio-cultural concerns. The people are therefore not just the common people, but the common *working* people – artisans, industrial or farm labourers, peasants and so on – with the experience of productive labour typically being seen as the source of their righteousness and moral purity. The left-wing populist view of the people thus tends to be more inclusive than that advanced by right-wing populists, encompassing, as it often does, ethnic and religious minorities and other marginalized groups.

TENSIONS WITHIN . . . POPULISM

Right populism	v.	Left populism
exclusivity	↔	inclusivity
ethnic view of the people	↔	class view of the people
cultural concerns	↔	economic concerns
migrant threat	↔	neoliberal threat
xenophobia	↔	egalitarianism
'liberal' elite	↔	'corporate' elite
neoconservatism	↔	neo-socialism

Second, while nationalism is central to right-wing populism, left-wing populists are inclined to treat working people in neighbouring states as natural allies, and so are not necessarily constrained by national borders. And yet, at the heart of the corrupt elite against which left-wing populists rail is a capitalist system that has a pronounced international character, comprising, among other things, transnational corporations, regional trade blocs and bodies such as International Monetary Fund and the World Trade Organization. It is therefore not uncommon for the internationalism embraced by left-wing populists to be qualified by calls to resist foreign influence in the domestic economy. Third, the links between, respectively, right-wing populism and conservatism, and left-wing populism and socialism, means that a marked value divide runs through populism. Whereas right populism is associated with tradition, authority and order, left populism allied to equality, social justice and progress.

The contemporary wave of left-wing populism emerged in response to the widespread shift towards neoliberalism, which began in the 1980s and 1990s and witnessed widening inequality linked to tax cuts for the better-off and the 'rolling back' of systems of social protection. The resurgence of left-wing populism first became apparent in Latin America, where market-based economic and social policies had been pursued with particular vigour. In a process initiated by the rise of Venezuela's Hugo Chavez in 1998, a succession of left-wing populist presidents came to power in states including Nicaragua, Bolivia and Ecuador in the following decade or more. Although the socialism these presidents preached differed from country to country, common features included burgeoning government spending, an expansion of state control and state ownership, and appeals to the poor through promises to redistribute wealth.

KEY FIGURE

HUGO CHAVEZ (1954–2013)

Miguel Tovar/LatinContent WO/Getty Images

A Venezuelan soldier and politician, Hugo Chavez was elected president of Venezuela in 1999 and remained in power until his death in 2013, with a brief interruption following a coup attempt in 2002. Once in office, Chavez quickly proceeded to widen executive power. He instituted the creation of a constitutional assembly, whose constitution was accepted in 1999 and greatly increased his position. In what he styled the 'Bolivarian revolution' (named after Simon Bolivar, the nineteenth-century South American independence hero), Chavez introduced economic and social reforms, including the nationalization of key industries and programmes to expand access to food, housing, health care and education, underpinned by an ideology known as Chavismo. His 'anti-imperialist' foreign policy aimed to reduce the influence of US-supported neoliberalism and promoted Latin American and Caribbean cooperation.

The basis for the rise of left-wing populism in Europe and USA was laid by the conversion, from the 1990s onwards, of many Western left-liberal and reformist socialist parties to neo-revisionism, leading to an acceptance of market economics and globalization. In many cases, this gave lower-income voters the impression that they had effectively been 'disenfranchised', abandoned by the parties that had traditionally represented them. However, this development only gained practical expression with the onset of the 'Great Recession'. Coming in the wake of the 2007–09 global financial crisis, this saw an extended period of falling or stagnant living standards, particularly in the Western world, often made more acute by the introduction of **austerity** policies. In this context, populist social movements sprang up in many parts of the world, articulating a far-left ideological agenda, at the heart of which was resistance to austerity. Examples of this included the

Austerity: Sternness or severity; as an economic strategy, austerity refers to public spending cuts designed to eradicate a budget deficit, underpinned by faith in market forces.

Indignados in Spain (also referred to as the 15-M Movement, and later superseded by Podemos) and Occupy Wall Street in the USA. As far as left-wing populist parties were concerned, Syriza in Greece had the greatest impact, having become the largest party in the Greek parliament in 2015, based on the promise to crack down on the Greek oligarchs and to counter pressure from the European Central Bank and the IMF to scale down public spending.

THE FUTURE OF POPULISM

The history of populism is marked by a broad pattern, and there is little reason to doubt that this will persist in the future. In short, populism comes in waves. Rather than being an enduring, if not permanent, part of the ideological landscape (as in the case of liberalism, conservatism, socialism, nationalism and so on), populism comes and goes. Populism has therefore historically had difficulty in sustaining itself over time. Why has this been the case? One reason is that, whatever form it may take, and whatever its political complexion, each populist project must choose between two political strategies, both of which have serious pitfalls. Populist parties and movements may either place a priority on consolidating support in their heartland, in which case they maintain their radicalism and continue to operate as political 'outsiders'; or they may look to extend support beyond their heartland, in which case they gravitate towards pragmatism (see p. 6) and look to cultivate 'respectability'. The pitfall of the first strategy is that it risks turning populism into little more than an instrument of protest, restricting its electoral appeal and confining it to the political fringe. The pitfall of the second strategy is that it risks provoking disillusionment, even a sense of betrayal, among heartland supporters, without a guarantee that this could be compensated for by breaking into the political mainstream.

However, although populism has conformed to a broad pattern of intermittent recurrence, each wave of populism is different. Each upsurge in populism is fuelled and, for a period at least, sustained by a particular complex of historical forces. These historical forces are nevertheless the subject of significant debate when it comes to contemporary populism. In one view, contemporary populism is essentially a cultural backlash against the advance of liberal values, a process that has seen the trajectory of social and cultural change depress key groups' level of subjective social status (Norris and Inglehart, 2019). This 'silent revolution' can be traced back to the 1960s and includes changing family structures, and especially changes in the role of women, the spread of post-material values and growing respect for minorities in general and multicultural rights in particular. A growing pool of people – in the case of Trump and Brexit often identified as the 'left behind': mainly middle-aged and older, white men without a college education – therefore became susceptible to the entreaties of populism, especially in its nationalist form. This analysis, however, can be used to suggest that the heralded 'age of populism' is likely to be short-lived, since it runs counter to long-term social trends such as the expansion of college or higher education and the remorseless impact of generational change.

In another view, though, the contemporary populist upsurge is unlikely to subside any time soon, and may even be getting stronger. From this perspective, populism is not just a politico-cultural phenomenon; it also has deep economic roots, linked to the dynamics of economic globalization (see p. 21), particularly as they affect the developed world. Although the West was, in many ways, the creative force behind the modern global economy, and the region in which open markets were most pervasive and entrenched, over time it may have become a 'victim' of economic globalization. This can be seen from the fact that rates of economic growth in Western Europe and the USA have dropped off in recent decades, with inevitable consequences for living standards. 'Real' living standards for middle-income families in the USA have, for example, hardly risen for over 30 years. Moreover, since the 1980s, most Western societies have experienced a marked increase in within-country inequality, helping to foster both resentment towards elites and disillusionment with a democratic system that no longer seems to 'work' for the less well-off. Such developments are difficult, and may be impossible, to reverse because they stem both from the inner workings of globalization itself (which, for instance, dictate the continuing export of manufacturing jobs from the developed to the developing world) and from the fact that even the most powerful state is unable to 'opt out' altogether from the processes of globalization.

◎ QUESTIONS FOR DISCUSSION

- To what extent do historical examples of populism have common origins?
- On what grounds can populism be regarded as an ideology?
- In what sense is the populist notion of 'the people' a construct?
- According to populists, how does the elite exercise power over the people?
- Is illiberal democracy a contradiction in terms?
- How and why do populists condemn centrist politics?
- Are all populists nationalists, or only some?

- With what forms of nationalism is populism compatible?
- What is the basis of the link between populism and authoritarianism?
- What is the relationship between populism and the far-right?
- Why and how does left-wing populism differ from right-wing populism?
- Is contemporary populism better explained in terms of economic factors or cultural factors?
- In what senses does populism pose a particular threat to liberalism?

◎ FURTHER READING

Eatwell, R. and Goodwin, M. *National Populism: The Revolt Against Liberal Democracy* (2018). An accessible and insightful account of the rise of national populism in the West, and its implications.

Kaltwasser, C., Taggart, P., Espejo, O. and Ostiguy, P. (eds) *The Oxford Handbook of Populism* (2017). A collection that provides state-of-the-art research and scholarship on various aspects of populism.

Moffit, B. *Populism* (2020). A strong theoretical introduction to the debates around defining and classifying populism, as well as its interactions without other major ideologies.

Norris, P. and Inglehart, R. *Cultural Backlash and the Rise of Populism: Trump, Brexit and Authoritarian Populism* (2019). An attempt to set out a general theory that explains polarization over the cultural cleavage dividing social liberals from social conservatives.

Team Populism https://populism.byu.edu. An academic collaboration studying populist politics, their website provides a wealth of links to relevant publications, studies, databases and other web resources.

CHAPTER 9

FEMINISM

PREVIEW

As a political term, 'feminism' was a twentieth-century invention and has only been a familiar part of everyday language since the 1960s. ('Feminist' was first used in the nineteenth century as a medical term to describe either the feminization of men or the masculinization of women.) In modern usage, feminism is linked to the goal of advancing the role of women, usually by reducing gender inequality, although it has come to be associated with the wider project of transforming gender relations.

Feminist ideology has traditionally been defined by two basic beliefs: that women are disadvantaged because of their gender; and that this disadvantage can and should be overthrown. In this way, feminists have highlighted what they see as a political relationship between the sexes, the supremacy of men and the subjection of women in most, if not all, societies. In viewing gender divisions as 'political', feminists challenged a 'mobilization of bias' that has traditionally operated within political thought, by which generations of male thinkers, unwilling to examine the privileges and power their sex had enjoyed, had succeeded in keeping the role of women off the political agenda.

Nevertheless, feminism has also been characterized by a diversity of views and political positions. The women's movement, for instance, has pursued goals that range from the achievement of female suffrage and an increase in the number of women in elite positions in public life, to the legalization of abortion, and sexual harassment and sexual assault of women. Similarly, feminist theory has both drawn on established political traditions and values, notably liberalism and socialism, and, in the form of radical feminism, rejected conventional political ideas and concepts. However, feminism has long since ceased to be confined to these 'core' traditions. Contemporary feminist thought is characterized by a more radical engagement with the politics of difference, as well as an encounter with modern approaches to gender and sexuality, such as intersectionality, trans theory and queer theory.

HISTORICAL OVERVIEW

Although the term 'feminism' may be of recent origin, feminist views have been expressed in many different cultures and can be traced back as far as the ancient civilizations of Greece and China. Christine de Pisan's *Book of the City of Ladies*, published in Italy in 1405, foreshadowed many of the ideas of modern feminism in recording the deeds of famous women of the past and advocating women's right to education and political influence. Nevertheless, it was not until the nineteenth century that an organized women's movement developed. The first text of modern feminism is usually taken to be Mary Wollstonecraft's (see p. 28) *A Vindication of the Rights of Woman* ([1792] 1967), written against the backdrop of the French Revolution. By the mid-nineteenth century, the women's movement had acquired a central focus: the campaign for female suffrage, the right to vote, which drew inspiration from the progressive extension of the franchise to men. This period is usually referred to as **first-wave feminism**, and was characterized by the demand that women should enjoy the same legal and political rights as men. Female suffrage was the principal goal of first-wave or **liberal feminism** because it was believed that if women could vote, all other forms of sexual discrimination or prejudice would quickly disappear.

The women's movement was strongest in those countries where political democracy was most advanced. The famous Seneca Falls convention, held in 1848, marked the birth of the US women's rights movement. It adopted a Declaration of Sentiments, written by Elizabeth Cady Stanton (1815–1902), which deliberately drew on the language and principles of the Declaration of Independence and called, among other things, for female suffrage. The National Women's Suffrage Association, led by Stanton and Susan B. Anthony (1820–1906), was set up in 1869 and merged with the more conservative American Women's Suffrage Association in 1890. Similar movements developed in other Western countries. In the UK, an organized movement developed during the 1850s and, in 1867, the House of Commons defeated the first attempt to introduce female suffrage, an amendment to the Second Reform Act, proposed by John Stuart Mill (see p. 25). The UK suffrage movement adopted increasingly militant tactics after the formation in 1903 of the Women's Social and Political Union, led by Emmeline Pankhurst (1858–1928) and her daughter Christabel (1880–1958). From their underground base in Paris, the Pankhursts coordinated a campaign of direct action in which 'suffragettes' carried out wholesale attacks on property and mounted a series of well-publicized public demonstrations.

Feminism's 'first-wave' ended with the achievement of female suffrage, introduced first in New Zealand in 1893. The Nineteenth Amendment of the US Constitution granted the vote to American women in 1920. The franchise was extended to women in the UK in 1918, but they did not achieve equal voting rights with men for a further decade. Ironically, in many ways, winning the right to vote weakened and undermined the women's movement. The struggle for female suffrage had united and inspired the movement, giving it a clear goal and a coherent structure. Furthermore, many activists naively believed that in winning suffrage rights, women had achieved full emancipation. It was not until the 1960s that the women's movement was regenerated, with the emergence of feminism's 'second wave'.

The publication in 1963 of Betty Friedan's *The Feminine Mystique* did much to relaunch feminist thought. **Second-wave feminism**, as it became

First-wave feminism: The early form of feminism which developed in the mid-nineteenth century and was based on the pursuit of sexual equality in the areas of political and legal rights, particularly suffrage rights.

Liberal feminism: A form of feminism that is grounded in the belief that sexual differences are irrelevant to personal worth, and calls for equal rights for women and men in the public sphere.

Second-wave feminism: The form of feminism that emerged in the 1960s and 1970s, and was characterized by a more radical concern with 'women's liberation', including, and perhaps especially, in the private sphere.

known, acknowledged that the achievement of political and legal rights had not solved the 'women's question'. Indeed, feminist ideas and arguments became increasingly radical, and at times revolutionary. Books such as Kate Millett's *Sexual Politics* (1970) and Germaine Greer's *The Female Eunuch* (1970) pushed back the borders of what had previously been considered to be 'political' by focusing attention on the personal, psychological and sexual aspects of female oppression. The goal of second-wave feminism was not merely political emancipation but 'women's liberation', reflected in the ideas of the growing Women's Liberation Movement. Such a goal could not be achieved by political reforms or legal changes alone, but demanded, modern feminists argued, a more far-reaching and perhaps revolutionary process of social change.

Since the first flowering of **radical feminism** in the late 1960s and early 1970s, feminism has developed into a distinctive and established ideology, whose ideas and values challenge the most basic assumptions of conventional political thought. Feminism has succeeded in establishing **gender** and gender perspectives as important themes in a range of academic disciplines, and in raising consciousness about gender issues in public life in general. By the 1990s, feminist organizations existed in all Western countries and most parts of the developing world. However, three processes have accompanied these developments. The first is a process of deradicalization, whereby there has been a retreat from the sometimes uncompromising positions that characterized feminism in the early 1970s. This led to the growing popularity of the idea of '**postfeminism**', suggesting that as feminist objectives have been largely achieved, the women's movement has moved 'beyond feminism'.

The second process is one of fragmentation. Instead of simply losing its radical or critical edge, feminist thinking has gone through a process of radical diversification, making it difficult, and perhaps impossible, any longer to identify 'common ground' within feminism. In addition to the 'core' feminist traditions – liberal feminism, **socialist feminism** and radical feminism – must now be added postmodern feminism, psychoanalytical feminism, black feminism, lesbian feminism and **transfeminism**, among others. The third, and related, process is the growing recognition of intersectionality (see p. 201) and of the tendency for women to have multiple social identities. Women, thus, do not have a straightforward gender-based identity but one in which, for instance, race, social class, ethnicity, age, religion, nationality and sexual orientation can overlap or 'intersect' with gender. This implies that women may be subject to interlocking systems of oppression and discrimination, as **sexism** becomes entangled with racism (see p. 162), xenophobia, homophobia and the like.

Radical feminism: A form of feminism that holds gender divisions to be the most politically significant of social cleavages, and believes that they are rooted in the structures of domestic life.

Gender: A social and cultural distinction between males and females, as opposed to sex, which refers to biological and therefore ineradicable differences between women and men.

Postfeminism: Either the perception that many or all of the goals of feminism have been achieved, or the loss of support for feminism among women.

Socialist feminism: A form of feminism that links the subordination of women to the dynamics of the capitalist economic system, emphasizing that women's liberation requires a process of radical social change.

Transfeminism: A form of feminism that rejects the idea of fixed identities and specifically avows sexual and gender ambiguity.

Sexism: Prejudice or discrimination based on sex; especially discrimination against women.

CORE THEMES

Until the 1960s, the idea that feminism should be regarded as an ideology in its own right would have been highly questionable. It is more likely that feminism would have been viewed as a subset of liberalism and socialism, the point at which the basic values and theories of these two ideologies can be applied to gender issues. The rise of radical feminism changed this, in that radical feminists proclaimed the central political importance of gender divisions, something that no conventional ideology could accept. Conventional ideologies were therefore viewed as inadequate vehicles for advancing the social role of women, and even, at times, criticized for harbouring patriarchal attitudes and assumptions. However, the emergent ideology of feminism was clearly a cross-cutting ideology, encompassing, from the outset, distinctive liberal, socialist and radical sub-traditions, as well as a range of hybrid or 'dual-system' feminisms (stemming from the attempt, for example, to blend radical feminism with certain Marxist ideas). Although this level of ideological diversity was intensified, particularly from the 1990s onwards, by a more radical engagement with the politics of difference and the emergence of new feminist tendencies, a number of 'common ground' themes can still be identified within feminism. The most important of these are:

- redefining 'the political'

- sex and gender

- patriarchy

- equality and difference.

Redefining 'the political'

Traditional notions of what is 'political' locate politics in the arena of public rather than private life. Politics has usually been understood as an activity that takes place within a 'public sphere' of government institutions, political parties, pressure groups and public debate. Family life and personal relationships have normally been thought to be part of a 'private sphere', and therefore to be 'non-political'. Modern feminists, on the other hand, insist that politics is an activity that takes place within all social groups and is not merely confined to the affairs of government or other public bodies. Politics exists whenever and wherever social conflict is found. Kate Millett, for example, defined politics as 'power-structured relationships, arrangements whereby one group of persons is controlled by another'. The relationship between government and its citizens is therefore clearly political, but so is the relationship between employers and workers within a firm, and also relationships in the family, between husbands and wives, and between parents and children.

KEY FIGURE

KATE MILLETT (BORN 1934)

A US feminist writer, political activist and artist, Millett developed a comprehensive critique of patriarchy in Western society and culture that had a profound impact on radical feminism. In *Sexual Politics* (1970), Millett analysed the work of male writers, from D. H. Lawrence to Norman Mailer, highlighting their use of sex to degrade and undermine women. In her view, such literature reflects deeply patriarchal attitudes that pervade culture and society at large, providing evidence that patriarchy is a historical and social constant.

Denver Post/Getty Images

The definition of what is 'political' is not merely of academic interest. Feminists argue that sexual inequality has been preserved precisely because the sexual division of labour that runs through society has been thought of as 'natural' rather than 'political'. Traditionally, the public sphere of life, encompassing politics, work, art and literature, has been the preserve of men, while women have been confined to an essentially private existence, centred on the family and domestic responsibilities, as illustrated in Figure 9.1. If politics takes place only within the public sphere, the role of women and the question of sexual equality are issues of little or no political importance. Women, restricted to the private role of housewife and mother, are in effect excluded from politics.

Feminists have therefore sought to challenge the divide between 'public man' and 'private woman' (Elshtain, 1993). However, they have not always agreed about what it means to break down the public/private divide, about how it can be achieved, or about how far it is desirable. Radical feminists have been the keenest opponents of the idea that politics stops at the front door, proclaiming instead that 'the personal is the political'. Female oppression is thus thought to operate in all walks of life, and in many respects originates in the family itself. Radical feminists have therefore been concerned to analyse what can be called 'the politics of everyday life'. This includes the process of conditioning in the family, the distribution of housework and other domestic responsibilities, and the politics of personal and sexual conduct. For some feminists, breaking down the public/private divide implies transferring the responsibilities of private life to the state or other public bodies. For example, the burden of child-rearing on women could be relieved by more generous welfare support for families or the provision of nursery schools or crèches at work. Socialist feminists have also viewed the private sphere as political, in that they have linked women's roles within the conventional family to the maintenance of the capitalist economic system. However, although liberal feminists object to restrictions on women's access to the public sphere of education, work and political life, they also warn against the dangers of politicizing the private sphere, which, according to liberal theory, is a realm of personal choice and individual freedom.

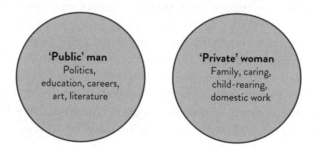

Figure 9.1   The sexual division of labour

Sex and gender

The most common of all anti-feminist arguments is that the gender division that runs through society is 'natural': women and men merely fulfil the social roles for which nature designed them. The fact that childbearing is unique to the female sex is thus seen to suit women for the responsibilities of motherhood: nurturing, educating and raising children by devoting themselves to home and family. In short, 'biology is destiny'. Feminists typically challenge such thinking by drawing a sharp distinction between sex and gender. 'Sex', in this sense, refers to biological differences between females and males; these differences are natural and therefore are unalterable. The most important sex differences are those that are linked to reproduction. 'Gender', on the other hand, is a cultural term; it refers to the different roles that society ascribes to women and men. Gender differences are typically imposed through contrasting stereotypes of 'masculinity' and 'femininity'.

As Simone de Beauvoir pointed out, 'Women are made, they are not born'. In denying that there is a necessary or logical link between sex and gender, feminists therefore emphasize that gender differences are socially, or even politically, constructed.

PERSPECTIVES ON ... GENDER

LIBERALS have traditionally regarded differences between women and men as being of entirely private or personal significance. In public and political life, all people are considered as individuals, gender being as irrelevant as ethnicity or social class. In this sense, individualism is 'gender-blind'.

CONSERVATIVES have traditionally emphasized the social and political significance of gender divisions, arguing that they imply that the sexual division of labour between women and men is natural and inevitable. Gender is thus one of the factors that gives society its organic and hierarchical character.

SOCIALISTS, like liberals, have rarely treated gender as a politically significant category. When gender divisions are significant it is usually because they reflect and are sustained by deeper economic and class inequalities.

FASCISTS view gender as a fundamental division within humankind. Men naturally monopolize leadership and decision-making, while women are suited to an entirely domestic, supportive and subordinate role.

FEMINISTS usually see gender as a cultural or political distinction, in contrast to biological and ineradicable sexual differences. Gender divisions are therefore a manifestation of male power. Difference feminists may nevertheless believe that gender differences reflect a psycho-biological gulf between female and male attributes and sensibilities.

FUNDAMENTALISTS have an ultra-conservative view of gender roles, typically characterized by male 'guardianship' over the family, the observation by women of a strict dress code, and restrictions on women's access to aspects of public life.

KEY FIGURE

SIMONE DE BEAUVOIR (1906–86)

A French novelist, playwright and social critic, de Beauvoir's work reopened the issue of gender politics and foreshadowed the ideas of later radical feminists. In *The Second Sex* (1949), she developed a complex critique of patriarchal culture, in which the masculine is represented as the positive or the norm, while the feminine is portrayed as the 'other' – fundamentally limiting women's freedom and denying them their full humanity. De Beauvoir placed her faith in rationality and critical analysis as the means of exposing this process.

Evening Standard/Hulton Archive/Getty Images

Most feminists believe that human nature is characterized by **androgyny**. All human beings, regardless of sex, possess the genetic inheritance of a mother and a father, and therefore embody a blend of both female and male attributes or traits. Such a view accepts that sex differences are biological facts of life but insists that they have no necessary social, political or economic implications. Women and men should thus not be judged by

Androgyny: The possession of both male and female characteristics; used to imply that human beings are sexless 'persons' in the sense that sex is irrelevant to their social role or political status.

their sex, but as individuals, as 'persons'. This implies that the central core of feminism is the achievement of genderless 'personhood'. Establishing a concept of gender that is divorced from biological sex had crucial significance for feminist theory in at least two senses. Not only does it highlight the possibility of social change – socially constructed identities can be reconstructed or even demolished – but it also draws attention to the processes through which women are 'engendered' and therefore oppressed.

Although most feminists have regarded the sex/gender distinction as empowering, others have attacked it. These attacks have been launched from two main directions. The first, advanced by so-called '**difference feminists**', suggests that there are profound and perhaps ineradicable differences between women and men. From this '**essentialist**' perspective, accepted by some but by no means all difference feminists, social and cultural characteristics are seen to reflect deeper biological differences. The second attack on the sex/gender distinction challenges the categories themselves. Postmodern feminists have questioned whether 'sex' is as clear-cut a biological distinction as is usually assumed. For example, the features of 'biological womanhood' do not apply to many who are classified as women: some women cannot bear children, some women are not sexually attracted to men, and so on. The categories 'female' and 'male' are therefore more or less arbitrary. An alternative approach to gender has been advanced by the trans movement. In seeing gender as essentially a matter of self-identification, this explodes the **binary** conception of gender, in which the human world is tidily divided into female and male parts. The implications of such thinking are examined later in the chapter, in connection with trans theory and feminism.

Patriarchy

Feminists use the concept of '**patriarchy**' to describe the power relationship between women and men. The term literally means 'rule by the father' (*pater* meaning father in Latin). Some feminists employ patriarchy only in this specific and limited sense, to describe the structure of the family and the dominance of the husband-father within it, preferring to use broader terms such as 'male supremacy' or 'male dominance' to describe gender relations in society at large. However, feminists believe that the dominance of the father within the family symbolizes male supremacy in all other institutions. Many would argue, moreover, that the patriarchal family lies at the heart of a systematic process of male domination, in that it reproduces male dominance in all other walks of life: in education, at work and in politics. Patriarchy is therefore commonly used in a broader sense to mean quite simply 'rule by men', both within the family and outside. Millett (1970), for instance described 'patriarchal government' as an institution whereby 'that half of the populace which is female is controlled by that half which is male'. She suggested that patriarchy contains two principles: 'male shall dominate female, elder male shall dominate younger'. A patriarchy is therefore a hierarchic society, characterized by both sexual and generational oppression.

Difference feminism: A form of feminism which holds that there are deep and possibly ineradicable differences between women and men, whether these are rooted in biology, culture or material experience.

Essentialism: The belief that biological factors are crucial in determining psychological and behavioural traits.

Binary: Composed of or involving two parts.

Patriarchy: Literally, rule by the father; often used more generally to describe the dominance of men and subordination of women in society at large.

The concept of patriarchy is, nevertheless, broad. Feminists may believe that men have dominated women in all societies, but accept that the forms and degree of oppression have varied considerably in different cultures and at different times. At least in Western countries, the social position of women improved significantly during the twentieth century as a result of the achievement of the vote and broader access to education, changes in marriage and divorce law, the legalization of abortion and so on. However, in parts of the developing world, patriarchy still assumes a cruel, even gruesome, form: tens of million women, mainly in Africa, are subjected to the practice of female genital mutilation; bride murders still occur in India; and the persistence of the dowry system ensures that female children are often unwanted and sometimes allowed to die. Nevertheless, by no means are the physical intimidation of women and sexual violence confined to developing societies, as the Me Too movement has highlighted (see p. 194).

Feminists do not have a single or simple analysis of patriarchy, however. Liberal feminists, to the extent that they use the term, use it primarily to draw attention to the unequal distribution of rights and entitlements in society at large. The face of patriarchy they highlight is therefore the under-representation of women in senior positions in politics, business, the professions and public life generally. Socialist feminists tend to emphasize the economic aspects of patriarchy. In their view, patriarchy operates in tandem with capitalism, gender subordination and class inequality being interlinked systems of oppression. Some socialist feminists, indeed, reject the term altogether, on the grounds that gender inequality is merely a consequence of the class system: capitalism, not patriarchy, is the issue. Radical feminists, on the other hand, place considerable stress on patriarchy. They see it as a systematic, institutionalized and pervasive form of male power that is rooted in the family. Patriarchy thus expresses the belief that the pattern of male domination and female subordination that characterizes society at large is, essentially, a reflection of the power structures that operate within domestic life, as illustrated in Figure 9.2.

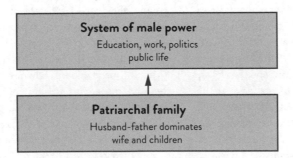

Figure 9.2   Radical feminist view of patriarchy

Equality and difference

Although the goal of feminism is the overthrow of patriarchy and the ending of sexist oppression, feminists have sometimes been uncertain about what this means in practice and how it can be brought about. Traditionally, women have demanded equality with men, even to the extent that feminism is often characterized as a movement for the achievement of sexual equality. However, the issue of equality has also exposed major fault lines within feminism: feminists have embraced contrasting notions of equality and some have entirely rejected equality in favour of the idea of difference. Liberal feminists champion legal and political equality with men. They have supported an equal rights

POLITICAL IDEOLOGIES IN ACTION...

THE ME TOO MOVEMENT

EVENTS: In 2006, the social activist and community organizer, Tarana Burke, first used the phrase 'Me Too' on the Myspace social network to indicate solidarity with sufferers of sexual violence, focusing especially on the threat posed to black women and women from low-income communities. Burke was later to be acknowledged as the leader of the Me Too movement. However, it was not until October 2017, when allegations surfaced of serial sexual misconduct by the Hollywood movie mogul, Harvey Weinstein, that the movement began to spread virally as a hashtag (#MeToo) on social media. This was encouraged by the US actor Alyssa Milano, who proposed that Twitter be used to gauge the magnitude of the problem. In 2020, Weinstein was convicted of rape and sentenced to 23 years in prison.

SIGNIFICANCE: Feminists have long worked to promote bodily autonomy and to protect girls and women from brutal crimes such as rape, sexual harassment and domestic violence. This focus, indeed, has sharpened since the 2010s, as issues such as sexual harassment in the workplace, campus sexual harassment, body shaming, sexist imagery in the media and online misogyny have attracted greater attention. In this context, #MeToo has both raised awareness of the extent of sexual abuse and provoked debate – among men as well as women – about the norms of personal, professional and sexual behaviour, helping, in the process, to strengthen legal protections for women and girls. #MeToo's impact in these respects stems significantly from the benefits of social media-based political

Johannes Eisele/Getty

activism and the media attention generated by high-profile cases.

However, #MeToo has also generated controversy within feminist circles. One source of tension derives from the allegedly declining emphasis on addressing the concerns of socially marginalized women, in view of the prominence that celebrities have assumed within the movement. A second source of tension focuses on differing understandings of sexism and how it should be challenged. On the one hand, those who support #MeToo typically assume that sexual harassment and assault are systemic problems, which can only be tackled by the transformation of society, using the power of empathy and solidarity. On the other hand, #MeToo's mainly liberal-feminist detractors claim that the movement fails to recognize individual women as moral agents, who must, at some level, take responsibility for the decisions they make. From this perspective, the goal of feminism is not so much to transform society as to better equip women to navigate their way within society.

agenda, which would enable women to compete in public life on equal terms with men, regardless of sex. Equality thus means equal access to the public realm. Socialist feminists, in contrast, argue that equal rights may be meaningless unless women also enjoy social equality. Equality, in this sense, has to apply in terms of economic power, and so must address issues such as the ownership of wealth, pay differentials and the distinction between waged and unwaged labour. Radical feminists, for their part, are primarily concerned about equality in family and personal life. Equality must therefore operate, for example, in terms of child care and other domestic responsibilities, the control of one's own body, and sexual expression and fulfilment.

TENSIONS WITHIN . . . FEMINISM (1)

↔

Equality feminism	v.	Difference feminism
androgyny	↔	essentialism
personhood	↔	sisterhood
human rights	↔	women's rights
gender equality	↔	sexual liberation
abolish difference	↔	celebrate difference
sex/gender divide	↔	sex equals gender
transcend biology	↔	embrace biology
pro-human	↔	pro-woman
men are redeemable	↔	men are 'the problem'
engagement with men	↔	feminist separatism

Despite tensions between them, these egalitarian positions are united in viewing gender differences in a negative light. **Equality feminism** links 'difference' to patriarchy, seeing it as a manifestation of oppression or subordination. From this viewpoint, the feminist project is defined by the desire to liberate women *from* 'difference'. However, other feminists champion difference rather than equality. Difference feminists regard the very notion of equality as either misguided or simply undesirable. To want to be equal to a man implies that women are 'male identified', in that they define their goals in terms of what men are or what men have. The demand for equality therefore embodies a desire to be 'like men'. Although feminists seek to overthrow patriarchy, many warn against the danger of modelling themselves on men, which would require them, for example, to adopt the competitive and aggressive behaviour that characterizes male society. For many feminists, liberation means achieving fulfilment as women; in other words, being 'female identified'.

Difference feminists are thus often said to subscribe to a '**pro-woman**' position, which accepts that sex differences have political and social importance. This is based on the essentialist belief that women and men are fundamentally different at a psycho-biological level. The aggressive and competitive nature of men and the creative and empathetic character of women are thought to reflect deeper hormonal and other genetic differences, rather than simply the structure of society. To idealize androgyny or personhood and ignore sex differences is therefore a mistake. Women should recognize and celebrate the distinctive characteristics of the female sex; they should seek liberation *through* difference, as developed and fulfilled women,

Equality feminism: A form of feminism that aspires to the goal of sexual equality, whether this is defined in terms of formal rights, the control of resources, or personal power.

'Pro-woman' feminism: A form of feminism that advances a positive image of women's attributes and propensities, usually stressing creativity, caring and human sympathy, and cooperation.

not as sexless 'persons'. In the form of **cultural feminism**, this has led to an emphasis on women's crafts, art and literature, and on experiences that are unique to women and promote a sense of 'sisterhood', such as childbirth, motherhood and menstruation.

TYPES OF FEMINISM

- traditional feminist theories
- modern approaches to gender and sexuality.

Traditional feminist theories

Until the early 1990s, feminist **discourse** still revolved predominantly around first- and second-wave themes and issues, although new approaches to feminism had been emerging for a decade or more. Debate within feminism therefore continued to be conducted largely between three 'core' traditions, namely:

- liberal feminism
- socialist feminism
- radical feminism.

Liberal feminism

Early feminism, particularly the 'first wave' of the women's movement, was deeply influenced by the ideas and values of liberalism. The first major feminist text, Wollstonecraft's *A Vindication of the Rights of Woman* ([1792] 1967), argued that women should be entitled to the same rights and privileges as men on the grounds that they are 'human beings'. She claimed that the 'distinction of sex' would become unimportant in political and social life if women gained access to education and were regarded as rational creatures in their own right. John Stuart Mill's *On the Subjection of Women* ([1869] 1970), written in collaboration with Harriet Taylor, proposed that society should be organized according to the principle of 'reason', and that 'accidents of birth' such as sex should be irrelevant. Women would therefore be entitled to the rights and liberties enjoyed by men and, in particular, the right to vote.

'Second-wave' feminism also has a significant liberal component. For instance, Betty Friedan (see p. 28) advanced a critique of the 'feminine mystique', by which she referred to the cultural myth that women seek security and fulfilment in domestic life and 'feminine' behaviour. This myth therefore serves to discourage women from entering employment, politics and public life in general. She highlighted what she called 'the problem with no name', the sense of despair and deep unhappiness that many women experienced because they were confined to a domestic existence and are thus unable to gain fulfilment in a career or through political life. In 1966, Friedan helped to found and became the first leader of the National Organization of Women (NOW), which has developed into a powerful pressure group and the largest women's organization in the world.

The philosophical basis of liberal feminism lies in the principle of individualism (see p. 24). This implies that individuals are entitled to

Cultural feminism: A form of feminism that emphasizes an engagement with a woman-centred culture and lifestyle, and is typically repelled by the corrupting and aggressive male world of political activism.

Discourse: Human interaction, especially communication: discourse may disclose or illustrate power relations.

equal treatment regardless of their gender, race, colour, creed or religion. If individuals are to be judged, it should be on rational grounds, on the content of their character, their talents, or their personal worth. Any form of discrimination against women that constrains their ability to participate in, or gain access to, public or political life should therefore be prohibited. Wollstonecraft, for example, insisted that education, in her day the province of men, should be opened up to women. J. S. Mill argued in favour of equal citizenship and political rights. Indeed, the entire suffrage movement was based on liberal individualism and the conviction that female emancipation would be brought about once women enjoyed equal voting rights with men. Liberal feminists have, nevertheless, usually assumed that women and men have different natures and inclinations, and therefore accept that, at least in part, women's leaning towards family and domestic life is influenced by natural impulses and so reflects a willing choice. In *The Second Stage* (1983) Friedan thus discussed the problem of reconciling the achievement of 'personhood', made possible by opening up broader opportunities for women in work and public life, with the need for love, represented by children, home and the family. Although such a stance has encouraged some liberal feminists to proclaim that women can 'have it all' – that is, a successful career as well as the satisfaction of motherhood and homemaking – radical feminists have criticised it for contributing to a 'mystique of motherhood'.

Finally, the demand for equal rights, which lies at the core of liberal feminism, has principally attracted those women whose education and social backgrounds equip them to take advantage of wider educational and career opportunities. For example, nineteenth-century feminists and the leaders of the suffrage movement were usually educated, middle-class women who had the opportunity to benefit from the right to vote, pursue a career or enter public life. Female emancipation, in the liberal sense, may mean that other forms of social disadvantage – for example, those linked to social class and race – are ignored. Liberal feminism may therefore reflect the interests of white, middle-class women in developed societies but fail to address the problems of working-class women, black women and women in the developing world.

Socialist feminism

Although some early feminists subscribed to socialist ideas, socialist feminism only became prominent in the second half of the twentieth century. In contrast to their liberal counterparts, socialist feminists have not believed that women simply face political or legal disadvantages that can be remedied by equal legal rights or the achievement of equal opportunities. Rather, they argue that the relationship between the sexes is rooted in the social and economic structure itself, and that nothing short of profound social change – some would say a social revolution – can offer women the prospect of genuine emancipation.

The central theme of socialist feminism is that patriarchy can only be understood in the light of social and economic factors. The classic statement of this argument was developed in Friedrich Engels' *The Origins of the Family, Private Property and the State* ([1884] 1976). Engels suggested that the position of women in society had changed fundamentally with the development of capitalism and the institution of private property. In pre-capitalist societies, family life had been communistic, and 'mother right' – the inheritance of property and social position through the female line – was widely observed. Capitalism, however, being based on the ownership of private property by men, had overthrown 'mother right' and brought about what Engels called 'the world historical defeat of the female sex'. Like many subsequent socialist feminists, Engels believed that female oppression operates through the institution of the 'bourgeois family'. The patriarchal character of such a family is ensured by the practice of patrilineality, through which descent is traced through the male line, together with the inheritance of property.

Most socialist feminists agree that the confinement of women to a domestic sphere of housework and motherhood serves the economic interests of capitalism. Some have argued that women constitute a 'reserve army of labour', which can be recruited into the workforce when there is a need to increase production, but easily shed and returned to domestic life during a depression, without imposing a burden on employers or the state. At the same time, women's domestic labour is vital to the health and efficiency of the economy. In bearing and rearing children, women are producing the next generation of capitalism's workers. Similarly, in their role as housewives, women relieve men of the burden of housework and child-rearing, allowing them to concentrate their time and energy on paid and productive employment. The traditional family provides the worker with a powerful incentive to find and keep a job because he has a wife and children to support. The family also provides male workers with a necessary cushion against the alienation and frustrations of life as 'wage slaves'. Male 'breadwinners' enjoy high status within the family and are relieved of the burden of 'trivial' domestic labour.

Although socialist feminists agree that the 'women's question' cannot be separated from social and economic life, they are profoundly divided about the nature of that link. Gender divisions clearly cut across class cleavages, creating tension within socialist feminist analysis about the relative importance of gender and social class, and raising particularly difficult questions for Marxist feminists. Orthodox Marxists insist on the primacy of class politics over sexual politics. This suggests that class exploitation is a deeper and more significant process than sexual oppression. It also suggests that women's emancipation will be a by-product of a social revolution in which capitalism is overthrown and replaced by socialism. However, many modern socialist feminists find it difficult to accept the primacy of class politics over sexual politics, in part because of the disappointing progress made by women in state-socialist societies such as the Soviet Union. Many of them, indeed, subscribe to a form of neo-Marxism, which accepts the interplay of economic, social, political and cultural forces in society. They therefore refuse to analyse the position of women in simple economic terms and have, instead, given attention to the cultural and ideological roots of patriarchy. This can be seen, for example, in Juliet Mitchell's (1971) assertion that women must achieve emancipation in four key areas: work, reproduction, sexuality and the socialization of children.

Radical feminism

The central feature of radical feminism is the belief that sexual oppression is the most fundamental feature of society and that other forms of injustice – class exploitation, racial hatred and so on – are merely secondary. Gender is thought to be the deepest social cleavage and the most politically significant; more important, for example, than social class, race or nation. Radical feminists have therefore insisted that society be understood as 'patriarchal' to highlight the central role of gender oppression. Such thinking was evident in the pioneering work of Simone de Beauvoir, and was developed by early radical feminists such as Eva Figes, Germaine Greer and Kate Millett.

Figes' *Patriarchal Attitudes* (1970) drew attention not to the more familiar legal or social disadvantages suffered by women, but to the fact that patriarchal values and beliefs pervade the culture, philosophy, morality and religion of society. In all walks of life and learning, women are portrayed as inferior and subordinate to men, a stereotype of 'femininity' being imposed on women by men. In *The Female Eunuch* (1970), Greer suggested that women are conditioned to a passive sexual role, which has repressed their true **sexuality** as well as the more active and adventurous side of their personalities. In effect, women have been 'castrated' and turned into sexless objects by the cultural stereotype of the 'eternal feminine'. In *Sexual Politics* (1970), Millett argued that the different roles of women and men have their origin in a process of 'conditioning': from an early age boys and girls are encouraged to conform to very specific gender identities. This process takes place largely within the family – 'patriarchy's chief institution' – but it is also evident in literature, art, public life and the economy. Millett proposed that patriarchy should be challenged through a process of '**consciousness-raising**', an idea influenced by the Black Power movement of the 1960s and early 1970s.

KEY FIGURE

GERMAINE GREER (BORN 1939)

An Australian writer, academic and journalist, Greer's *The Female Eunuch* (1970) helped to stimulate radical feminist theorizing. Its principal theme, the extent to which male domination is upheld by a systematic process of sexual repression, was accompanied by a call for women to re-engage with their libido, their faculty of desire and their sexuality. In *Sex and Destiny* (1985), Greer celebrated the importance of childbearing and motherhood, while *The Whole Woman* (1999) criticized 'lifestyle feminists' and the alleged right to 'have it all'.

David Levenson/Getty Images Entertainment/Getty Images

Radical feminists generally agree that the origins of patriarchy lie in the structures of family, domestic and personal life, and therefore that women's liberation requires a sexual revolution in which these structures are overthrown and replaced. However, radical feminism encompasses a number of divergent elements, some of which emphasize the fundamental and unalterable difference between women and men. An example of this is the 'pro-woman' position, particularly strong in France and the USA. This position extols the positive virtues of fertility and motherhood. Women should not try to be 'more like men'. Instead, they should recognize and embrace their sisterhood, the bonds that link them to all other women. The pro-woman position therefore accepts that women's attitudes and values are different from men's, but implies that in certain respects women are superior, possessing the qualities of creativity, sensitivity and caring, which men can never fully appreciate or develop. Such ideas have been associated in particular with ecofeminism, which is examined in Chapter 10.

The acceptance of deep and possibly unalterable differences between women and men leads some radical feminists to retreat from what they see as the corrupting and aggressive male world of political activism into an apolitical, woman-centred culture and lifestyle. Conversely, others become politically assertive and even revolutionary. This is based on the assumption that the roots of patriarchy reside within the male sex itself. 'All men' are thus physically and psychologically disposed to oppress 'all women'; in other words, 'men are the enemy'. This clearly leads in the direction of feminist separatism. Men constitute an oppressive 'sex-class' dedicated to aggression, domination and destruction; so the female 'sex-class' is therefore the 'universal victim'. For example, Susan Brownmiller's *Against Our Will* (1975) emphasized that men dominate women through a process

Sexuality: The capacity for erotic feeling, usually linked to sexual orientation or preference.

Consciousness-raising: Strategies to remodel social identity and challenge cultural inferiority by an emphasis on pride, self-worth and self-assertion.

TENSIONS WITHIN . . . FEMINISM (2)

Liberal feminism	v.	Radical feminism
female emancipation	↔	women's liberation
gender equality	↔	patriarchy
individualism	↔	sisterhood
conventional politics	↔	the personal is political
public/private divide	↔	transform private realm
access to public realm	↔	gender equality
equal rights/opportunities	↔	sexual politics
reform/gradualism	↔	revolutionary change
political activism	↔	consciousness-raising

of physical and sexual abuse. Men have created an 'ideology of rape', which amounts to a 'conscious process of intimidation by which all men keep all women in a state of fear'.

Feminists who have pursued this line of argument also believe that it has profound implications for women's personal and sexual conduct. Sexual equality and harmony is impossible because all relationships between women and men must involve oppression. Heterosexual women are therefore thought to be 'male identified', incapable of fully realizing their true nature and becoming 'female identified'. This has led to the development of political lesbianism, which holds that sexual preferences are an issue of crucial political importance for women. Only women who remain celibate or choose lesbianism can regard themselves as 'woman-identified women'. In the slogan attributed to Ti-Grace Atkinson: 'feminism is the theory; lesbianism is the practice' (Charvet, 1982). However, the issues of separatism and lesbianism have deeply divided the women's movement, the majority of radical feminists remaining faithful to the goal of constructing a non-sexist society, in which women and men live in harmony with one another.

Modern approaches to gender and sexuality

Since the 1990s, feminist discourse has moved beyond the campaigns and demands of the 1960s and 1970s women's movement. This has made it increasingly difficult to analyse feminism simply in terms of the threefold division into liberal, socialist and radical traditions. Not only have new forms of feminism emerged, but feminism has also been challenged as well as enriched by its encounter with new thinking about gender and sexuality. Among the themes that this has brought to the fore are the following:

- 'third-wave' thinking and intersectionality

- trans theory and feminism

- queer theory.

Third-wave thinking and intersectionality

The term 'third-wave feminism' was increasingly adopted from the 1990s onwards, becoming popular among feminist theorists for whom the concerns of the 1960s and 1970s women's movement seemed to lack relevance to their own lives. This was both because of the emergence of new issues in feminist politics and because of the political and social transformations that second-wave feminism has brought about (Heywood and Drake, 1997). If there was a unifying theme within third-wave feminism it was a more radical engagement with the politics of difference, especially going beyond those strands within radical feminism that emphasize that women are different *from* men by showing a greater concern with differences *between* women. In so doing, third-wave feminists tried to rectify an over-emphasis within earlier forms of feminism on the aspirations and experiences of middle-class, white women in developed societies, thereby illustrating the extent to which the contemporary women's movement is characterized by diversity, hybridity and what the US scholar and advocate, Kimberlé Crenshaw (born 1959), dubbed 'intersectionality'. This has allowed the voices of, among others, low-income women, women in the developing world, 'women of colour' and **LGBTIQ** people to be heard more effectively. Black feminism has been particularly effective in this respect, challenging the tendency within conventional forms of feminism to ignore racial differences and to suggest that women endure a common oppression by virtue of their gender. Especially strong in the USA, and developed in the writings of theorists such as bell hooks, black feminism portrays sexism and racism as linked systems of oppression, and highlights the particular and complex range of gender, racial and economic disadvantages that confront women of colour.

LGBTIQ: Lesbian, gay, bisexual, transgender, intersex and queer (or 'questioning').

KEY CONCEPT
INTERSECTIONALITY

Intersectionality is a framework for the analysis of injustice and social equality that emphasizes the multidimensional or multifaceted nature of personal identity and of related systems of domination. In this view, women do not just have a straightforward gender-based identity but rather one in which, for instance, race, social class, ethnicity, age, religion, nationality and sexual orientation can overlap, or 'intersect', with gender. This implies that women may be subject to interlocking systems of oppression and discrimination, as sexism becomes entangled with racism, xenophobia, homophobia, and so on.

KEY FIGURE

Karjean Levine/Archive Photos/Getty Images

BELL HOOKS (BORN 1952)

A cultural critic, feminist and writer, Gloria Jean Watkins (better known by her pen name, bell hooks) has emphasized that feminist theorizing must take account of intersectionality and be approached from the lenses of gender, race and social class. In her classic *Ain't I a Woman* (1985), hooks examined the history of black women in the USA. Arguing that, in the USA, racism takes precedence over sexism, she advanced a powerful critique of the implicit racism of the mainstream women's movement.

In being concerned about issues of 'identity', and the processes through which women's identities are constructed (and can be reconstructed), third-wave feminism also reflects the influence of **poststructuralism**. Influenced particularly by the French philosopher Michel Foucault (1926–84), poststructuralism has drawn attention to the link between power and systems of thought using the idea of discourse, or 'discourses of power'. In crude terms, this implies that knowledge is power. Poststructuralist or postmodernist feminists question the idea of a fixed female identity, also rejecting the notion that insights can be drawn from a distinctive set of women's experiences. From the poststructural perspective, even the idea of 'woman' may be nothing more than a fiction, as supposedly indisputable biological differences between women and men are, in significant ways, shaped by gendered discourses (not all women are capable of bearing children, for example). However, it is questionable whether the consistent application of poststructural or postmodern analysis is compatible with the maintenance of a distinctively feminist political orientation.

Trans theory and feminism

Poststructuralism: An intellectual tradition, related to postmodernism, which emphasizes that all ideas and concepts are expressed in language that itself is enmeshed in complex relations of power.

Genderqueer: Denoting or relating to people who do not conform to prevailing expectations about gender, usually by crossing over or moving between gender identities.

Transgender: Denoting or relating to people who do not conform to the sex they were assigned at birth, and who may seek to realign their gender and their sex through medical intervention.

Although **genderqueer** and **transgender** issues sometimes surfaced in the 1970s, often in connection with cultural feminism or lesbian separatism, trans theory (or transgenderism) has only been recognized as a specific area of politico-cultural debate since the 1990s. At the heart of trans theory lies a radically critical approach to thinking about gender. In particular, trans theorists reject the binary conception of gender, in which society allocates its members to one of two sets of identities, usually linked to biological or anatomical differences. In the binary view, the categories woman and man are meaningful and objectively based. Although trans theory is not associated with a single or simple conception of gender, its most influential belief is the idea of gender and sexual ambiguity, sometimes based on the idea of a gender continuum. Trans people are thus 'gender nonconforming'; they are neither women nor men (Beasley, 2005). From this non-binary perspective, gender is not something that is determined at birth or ascribed to individuals by society; instead, it is a matter of self-identity. People are therefore whatever gender they choose to be, based on their inner feelings. In this vein, Judith Butler's concept of gender as repeated social performance has been particularly influential. (Such thinking is discussed further in connection with queer theory.)

KEY FIGURE

JUDITH BUTLER (BORN 1956)

A US philosopher and gender theorist, Butler has challenged currents in feminist thinking that unwittingly enforce a binary view of gender identity, in which human beings are divided into two clear-cut groups: women and men. She rejects the idea that the sex/gender divide reflects an underpinning nature/culture divide, arguing instead that gender encompasses the discursive and cultural means whereby 'sexed nature', or 'a natural sex', is produced. Butler thus contends that not only gender but sex itself is, at least to some extent, a 'performative' social construct. Butler's most influential work is *Gender Trouble* ([1990] 2006).

Target Presse Agentur Gmbh/Getty Images News/Getty Images

The relationship between trans theory and feminism is both contested and controversial. While early encounters between feminism and the emergent trans movement were often marked by hostility, over time there has been a greater willingness among feminists to take on board issues raised by trans activists. Not only does this reflect widening support within feminism for a more personalized and nuanced approach to gender, but it also demonstrates a growing awareness of the parallels and overlaps that exist between sexism and **transphobia**. At the same time, supporters of the trans movement have increasingly recognized the extent to which its thinking may be applicable to all women (Scott-Dixon, 2006). Such an alignment of ideological forces has been recognized most acutely by transfeminist scholars and activists, whose objective is to advance the social role of trans women, together with those who are sympathetic to their needs.

Nevertheless, other feminists have viewed trans theory – and, with it, the notion of transfeminism – as deeply problematic. In part, this reflects the difficulty of reconciling feminism's stress on the distinctions between sex and gender, and between biology and culture, with a rejection of gender binaries of all kinds, a task that becomes yet more difficult if difference feminism is taken into account. Further concerns have flowed from the alleged clash between trans rights and women's rights. Some feminists argue, for example, that if anyone who self-identifies as a woman is a woman, this could allow male-bodied people to intrude into women's spaces, threatening to erode women's identities, safety and privacy. Supporters of the trans movement have nevertheless held that such views reflect the influence of a strain of anti-trans thinking within feminism, commonly termed 'trans-exclusionary radical feminism' (TERF), although its proponents prefer to call themselves 'gender critical'. TERF emerged in the 2000s but grew out of ideas developed within 1970s radical feminist circles. It is trans-exclusionary in the sense that it opposes trans rights generally and calls for the exclusion of trans women from spaces and organizations specifically designed for women. Such positions are underpinned by the core TERF belief that trans women are not women, a stance that is also commonly associated with conservatism.

Queer theory

The term 'queer theory' was coined in 1990 by the Italian-American feminist theorist Teresa de Lauretis. This reflected the tendency within the LGBTIQ community in the 1980s for 'queer' – once a term of homophobic abuse – to be reclaimed as a means of denoting a radical and unapologetic rejection of conventional sexual identities. The link between 'queer' and 'theory' was largely forged by the application of poststructuralism to the analysis of sexuality, especially in the writings of Michel Foucault. Being primarily concerned with the construction of the human subject, Foucault treated sexuality as a discursive social production rather than an essential and biologically rooted part of a human. From the perspective of queer theory, therefore, sexuality is not a natural, fixed, core identity, but something that is fluid, plural and continually negotiated. Although queer theory was built on foundations that had been shaped by feminism, and especially the encounter between lesbian feminism and the gay liberation front, many queer thinkers now believe that sexuality can and should be theorized independently from feminism. In that sense, queer theory has been said to go beyond gender, sexual identity being prioritized over gender identity.

Perhaps the defining feature of queer theory is robust opposition to **heteronormativity** (sometimes dubbed anti-heteronormativity). Heteronormativity establishes heterosexuality as the baseline for humankind, a

Transphobia: Prejudice against or dislike of people who do not conform to prevailing expectations about gender identity.

Heteronormativity: Institutional and other arrangements that present heterosexuality as the 'normal', natural and/or preferred way of life for human beings.

position sustained by cultural belief, religion and institutional arrangements, linked, among other things, to marriage, taxation and adoption rights. Even the practice of 'coming out' as gay assumes that people are straight to begin with. As such, heteronormativity systematically marginalizes – and 'invisibilizes' – gay people. Resistance to this can nevertheless be explained by reference to the concept of gender **performativity**, particularly as developed by Judith Butler (2006). To say that gender is performative is to say that how we understand gender, and how we position ourselves as gendered or sexual beings in relation to other, is a product of repeated words and actions. Gender and sexuality are therefore not an expression of what one *is* (identity), but of what one *does* (social action). A final aspect of queer theory is a general tendency to adopt an intersectional approach to analysis that refuses to view sexuality in isolation from other social structures, with a particular emphasis being placed on the interplay between sexuality and race.

THE FUTURE OF FEMINISM

The image of feminism as constantly beleaguered and in retreat, conjured up by the once-fashionable idea of 'postfeminism' is starkly misleading. Rather than being dead – or at least transformed into something else, which is not really feminist – feminism is alive and vibrant and shows every sign of continuing to be so (Walby, 2011). What has happened to feminism is that it has become less visible, or less easily noticed, but this may be more a reflection of feminism's widening influence than its incipient decline. This can be seen in at least two respects. First, feminism is no longer only (or mainly) an outsider protest movement. Instead, it has increasingly moved into the mainstream. This can, for example, be seen in the fact that initiatives to reduce gender inequality (a traditional concern of feminism, even though the initiatives are not necessarily labelled 'feminist') have increasingly become standard practice in the public services and across civil society. Further evidence of this can be found in the prominence feminist perspectives now enjoy in a growing range of fields of academic study. Second, the ideological orientation of feminism has been revised and broadened. Whereas feminism once focused on the relatively narrow goal of advancing the role of women by reducing gender inequality, it has come to address the issue of gender relations in general, reflecting on both how they are shaped and how they can be transformed. This has drawn feminists, together with those influenced by feminism but who do not self-define as feminists, into wider debates about gender and sexuality.

Feminism, nevertheless, is confronted by a number of enduring challenges. One of the most significant of these challenges is that feminism's successes threaten to weaken the women's movement, undermining its unity and sense of purpose. The achievement of votes for women, accomplished in many Western states in the early twentieth century, was thus followed by decades of decline, during which the women's movement often barely functioned. Similarly, the reforms of the 1960s and 1970s, which witnessed, among other things, the legalization of abortion, the introduction of equal pay and anti-discrimination legislation and wider access for women to education and political and professional life, led to a period of feminist de-radicalization. A further challenge is that the survival of the forces of anti-feminism seems to suggest that feminism will always

Performativity: Repeated actions or rituals through which a subject (gendered or otherwise) is constructed.

exist within a contested political environment. This was evident in the 1980s in a conservative backlash against feminism, which has been revived in the early decades of the twenty-first century, in association with the rise of right-wing populism.

QUESTIONS FOR DISCUSSION

- Why and how have feminists challenged conventional notions of politics?
- Why has the distinction between sex and gender been so important to feminist analysis?
- What role does patriarchy play in feminist theory?
- Why do some feminists reject the goal of gender equality?
- To what extent is feminism compatible with liberalism?
- In what sense is radical feminism revolutionary?

- Is socialist feminism a contradiction in terms?
- Are the differences within feminism greater than the similarities?
- Have the core liberal, socialist and radical feminist traditions been exhausted?
- To what extent, and how, can feminism engage with the politics of difference?
- Is feminism compatible with trans theory?
- What light does queer theory shed on our understanding of gender?

FURTHER READING

Bryson, V. *Feminist Political Theory: An Introduction*, 3rd edn (2016). A thorough introduction to the development of feminist theory.

Disch, L. & Hawkesworth, M. *The Oxford Handbook of Feminist Theory* (2016). The definitive survey of feminist scholarship across many applications of society and politics.

McCann, H. & Monaghan, W. *Queer Theory Now: From Foundations to Futures* (2020). An introductory textbook on the development of queer theory and its political implications.

Tong, R. & Botts, T. *Feminist Thought: A More Comprehensive Introduction*, 5th edn (2018). An in-depth survey of the key branches in feminist theory, particularly those emerging in recent decades.

Ms. Magazine www.msmagazine.com and the *Feminist Majority* www.feminist.org. Founded in 1971, *Ms.* is one of the longest running feminist publications, now published by the *Feminist Majority*. Both websites feature news, educational resources, commentary and media on feminist issues, politics, and history.

CHAPTER 10

ECOLOGISM

PREVIEW

The term 'ecology' was coined by the German zoologist Ernst Haeckel in 1866. Derived from the Greek *oikos*, meaning household or habitat, he used it to refer to 'the investigations of the total relations of the animal both to its organic and its inorganic environment'. Since the early years of the twentieth century, ecology has been recognized as a branch of biology that studies the relationship among living organisms and their environment. It has, however, increasingly been converted into a political term by the use made of it, especially since the 1960s, by the growing green or environmental movement.

As a political ideology, ecologism is based on the belief that nature is an interconnected whole, embracing humans and non-humans, as well as the inanimate world. This has encouraged ecological thinkers to question (but not necessarily reject) the anthropocentric, or human-centred, assumptions of conventional political ideologies, allowing them to come up with new ideas about, among other things, economics, morality and social organization. Nevertheless, there are different strains and tendencies within ecologism. Some ecologists are committed to 'shallow' ecology, which attempts to harness the lessons of ecology to human ends and needs. This provides the basis for a reformist, or 'modernist', approach to ecologism, sometimes dubbed environmentalism. It is also expressed through ecological theories that acknowledge that the relationship between humankind and nature has an important social dimension. These include eco-socialism and eco-anarchism. 'Deep' ecologists, on the other hand, completely reject any lingering belief that the human species is in some way superior to, or more important than, any other species. This is a stance that has also been embraced by some eco-feminist thinkers.

HISTORICAL OVERVIEW

Although modern environmental politics did not emerge until the 1960s and 1970s, ecological ideas can be traced back to much earlier times. Many have suggested that the principles of contemporary ecologism owe much to ancient pagan religions, which stressed the concept of an Earth Mother, and to eastern religions such as Hinduism, Buddhism and Daoism. However, to a large extent, ecologism was, and remains, a reaction against the process of industrialization. This was evident in the nineteenth century, when the spread of urban and industrial life created a profound nostalgia for an idealized rural existence, as conveyed by novelists such as Thomas Hardy and political thinkers such as the UK libertarian socialist William Morris (1834–96) and Peter Kropotkin (see p. 113). This reaction was often strongest in those countries that had experienced the most rapid and dramatic process of industrialization. For example, Germany's rapid industrialization in the nineteenth century deeply scarred its political culture, creating powerful myths about the purity and dignity of peasant life, and giving rise to a strong 'back to nature' movement among German youth. Such romantic **pastoralism** was most likely to surface during the twentieth century in right-wing political doctrines, not least the 'Blood and Soil' ideas of the German Nazis.

The growth of ecologism since the 1960s has been provoked by the further and more intense advance of industrialization and urbanization, linked to the emergence of postmaterial sensibilities among young people in particular. Environmental concern has become more acute because of the fear that economic growth is endangering both the survival of the human race and the very planet it lives on. Such anxieties have been expressed in a growing body of literature. Rachel Carson's *The Silent Spring* (1962) is often considered to have been the first book to draw attention to a developing ecological crisis. Other important early works included Ehrlich and Harriman's *How to Be a Survivor* (1971), Goldsmith *et al.*'s *Blueprint for Survival* (1972), the unofficial UN report *Only One Earth* (1972) and the Club of Rome's *The Limits to Growth* (1972).

KEY FIGURE

RACHEL CARSON (1907–1964)

A US marine biologist and conservationist, Carson did much through her writings to stimulate interest in scientific and environmental topics, contributing to the growth of the green movement. In her best-selling *The Silent Spring* (1962), she highlighted the malign consequences to humans, birds, fish and plant life of the widespread use of powerful toxic agents within US agriculture, reflecting the extent to which agri-business and state sponsorship threaten ecological balance and therefore sustainability.

Bettmann/Getty Images

A new generation of activist pressure groups has also developed – ranging from Greenpeace and Friends of the Earth to the non-violent civil disobedience group Extinction Rebellion, animal liberation activists and so-called 'eco-warrior' groups – campaigning on issues such as air, river and sea pollution, deforestation, animal experimentation and climate change and its associated challenges. Together with established and much larger groups, such as the Worldwide Fund for Nature, this has led to the emergence of a high profile and increasingly influential green movement. From the 1980s onwards, environmental questions have been kept high on the

Pastoralism: A belief in the virtues of rural existence: simplicity, community and a closeness to nature, in contrast to the allegedly corrupting influence of urban and industrialized life.

political agenda by green parties, which now exist in most industrialized countries, often modelling themselves on the pioneering efforts of the German Greens.

Since the turn of the twenty-first century greater urgency has been injected into the quest for environmental protection by the recognition that, in certain respects, the ecological crisis is getting more, not less, severe. This is particularly the case in relation to climate change. Although the United Nations formally acknowledged the seriousness of the issue in 1994, and attempts have been made to promote a coordinated international response to it, notably by the 1997 Kyoto Protocol and the 2015 Paris climate accord, the initial opportunity to tackle climate change has been blown by decades of denial. Indeed, as emerging economies such as China and India have dramatically increased their greenhouse gas emission, without a willingness on the part of developed states, especially the USA, to curtail theirs, the period since the mid-1990s became, in effect, the Golden Age of the carbon economy. As a result, there seemed to be little likelihood that the increase in the global average temperature during the twenty-first century could be kept below the UN's target of 2°C above pre-industrial levels. This, it is claimed, is the level at which climate change will have widespread and devastating consequences.

The onset of the Covid-19 pandemic in 2020 nevertheless sometimes raised more optimistic expectations. The adoption by many countries of a lockdown response to the pandemic caused economic activity and CO2 levels to fall dramatically, creating an opportunity to accelerate economic restructuring in line with the goal of neutral carbon usage, possibly underpinned by a reassessment of materialist priorities in society at large. However, the speed and eagerness with which lockdown was often relaxed and economies reopened suggests that any looked-for ecological benefits of the pandemic might be limited.

CORE THEMES

Thinking about the environment only acquired a fully ideological character through the rise of the green movement. By the end of the 1970s, ecologism or green thinking was widely viewed as an ideology in its own right, having gone beyond a mere pressure-group-like concern for the environment, commonly called '**environmentalism**'. However, ecologism takes ideological thinking in novel and challenging directions. Its starting point is largely or entirely ignored by other political ideologies: the idea of an intrinsic relationship between humankind and nature (or non-human nature, to avoid confusion with the notion of 'human nature'). Green theorists believe that conventional ideologies commit the sad, even comic, mistake of believing that humans are the centrepiece of existence. David Ehrenfeld (1978) called this the 'arrogance of **humanism**'.

Environmentalism: A concern about the natural environment and particularly about reducing environmental degradation: a policy orientation rather than an ideological stance.

Humanism: A philosophy that gives moral priority to the achievement of human needs and ends.

Instead of preserving and respecting the Earth and the diverse species that live on it, humans have sought to become, in the words of John Locke (see p. 29), 'the masters and possessors of nature'. Ecologism has therefore uncovered new ideological terrain. It differs from both the 'politics of material distribution', as practised by the classical ideologies (notably liberalism, conservatism and socialism) and 'identity politics' (see p. 232), as practised by most of the so-called 'new' ideologies that have emerged since the 1960s (such as second-wave feminism, ethnocultural nationalism, religious fundamentalism (see p. 246) and multiculturalism).

What makes ecologism deeper and, in a sense, more radical than other political ideologies is that it practises the 'politics of sensibilities'. By attempting to re-orientate people's relationship with and appreciation of 'the non-human' – the world 'out there' – ecologism sets out to do nothing less than transform human consciousness and, in the process, radically reconfigure our moral responsibilities. In order to give expression to this vision of interconnectedness, green thinkers have been forced to search for new concepts and ideas in the realm of science, or rediscover ancient ones from the realms of religion and mythology. The central themes of ecologism are:

- ecology

- systems thinking

- sustainability

- environmental ethics

- from having to being.

Ecology

The central principle of all forms of green thought is **ecology**. Ecology developed as a distinct branch of biology through a growing recognition that plants and animals are sustained by self-regulating natural **systems** – ecosystems – composed of both living and non-living elements. Simple examples of an ecosystem are a field, a forest or a pond. All ecosystems tend towards a state of harmony or equilibrium through a system of self-regulation. Biologists refer to this as **homeostasis**. Food and other resources are recycled, and the population size of animals, insects and plants adjusts naturally to the available food supply. However, such ecosystems are not 'closed' or entirely self-sustaining: each interreacts with other ecosystems. A lake may constitute an ecosystem, but it also needs to be fed with fresh water from tributaries, and receive warmth and energy from the sun. In turn, the lake provides water and food for species living along its shores, including human communities. The natural world is therefore made up of a complex web of ecosystems, the largest of which is the global ecosystem, commonly called the 'ecosphere' or 'biosphere'.

Scientific ecology radically challenged the conventional understanding of the natural world and of the place of human beings within it. Ecology conflicts with the notion of humankind as 'the master' of nature, and instead suggests that a delicate network of interrelationships that had hitherto been ignored sustains each human community, indeed the entire human species. Green thinkers argue that humankind currently faces the prospect of environmental disaster precisely because, in its passionate but blinkered pursuit of material wealth, it has upset the 'balance of nature' and endangered the very ecosystems that make human life possible. Ecologism thus favours **ecocentrism** and either rejects **anthropocentrism** altogether, or seeks to recast it in line with the principle of ecology. This draws attention

Ecology: The study of the relationship between living organisms and the environment; ecology stresses the network of relationships that sustains all forms of life.

System: A collection of parts that operate through a network of reciprocal interactions and thereby constitute a complex whole.

Homeostasis: The tendency of a system, especially the physiological systems of higher animals, to maintain internal equilibrium.

Ecocentrism: A theoretical orientation that gives priority to the maintenance of ecological balance rather than the achievement of human ends.

Anthropocentrism: A belief that human needs and interests are of overriding moral and philosophical importance; the opposite of ecocentrism.

to the most important distinction within the green movement; that is, the divide between what Arne Naess (see p. 222) termed '**shallow ecology**' and '**deep ecology**'.

The 'shallow' or 'humanist' perspective accepts the lessons of ecology but uses them essentially to further human needs and ends. In other words, it preaches that if we conserve and cherish the natural world, it will continue to sustain human life. This amounts to a form of 'light' or 'enlightened' anthropocentrism, and is reflected in a concern with issues such as cutting back on the use of finite, non-renewable resources and reducing pollution. While some regard such a stance as a form of 'weak' ecologism, others classify it as environmentalism to distinguish it more clearly from ecologism. The 'deep' perspective, however, advances a form of 'strong' ecologism that dismisses any lingering belief that the human species is in some way superior to, or more important than, any other species, or indeed nature itself. It is based on the more challenging idea that the purpose of human life is to help sustain nature, and not the other way around. (Deep ecology is discussed in greater detail later in the chapter.)

Shallow ecology: A green ideological perspective that harnesses the lessons of ecology to human needs and ends, and is associated with values such as sustainability and conservation.

Deep ecology: A green ideological perspective that rejects anthropocentrism and gives priority to the maintenance of nature, and is associated with values such as biocentric equality, diversity and decentralization.

PERSPECTIVES ON ... NATURE

LIBERALS see nature as a resource to satisfy human needs, and thus rarely question human dominion over it. Lacking value in itself, nature is invested with value only when it is transformed by human labour, or when it is harnessed to human ends.

CONSERVATIVES often portray nature as threatening, even cruel, characterized by an amoral struggle and harshness that also shapes human existence. Humans may be seen as part of nature within a 'great chain of being', their superiority nevertheless being enshrined in their status as custodians of nature.

SOCIALISTS, like liberals, have viewed and treated nature as merely a resource. However, a romantic or pastoral tradition within socialism has also extolled the beauty, harmony and richness of nature, and looks to human fulfilment through a closeness to nature.

ANARCHISTS have often embraced a view of nature that stresses unregulated harmony and growth. Nature therefore offers a model of simplicity and balance, which humans would be wise to apply to social organization in the form of social ecology.

FASCISTS have often adopted a dark and mystical view of nature that stresses the power of instinct and primal life forces, nature being able to purge humans of their decadent intellectualism. Nature is characterized by brutal struggle and cyclical regeneration.

FEMINISTS, notably ecofeminists, tend to view nature as creative and benign, qualities that they tend to share with women generally. In this view, the quest to counteract male domination should therefore see women aligning themselves – 'female nature', patriarchy and the environmental crisis being linked.

ECOLOGISTS, particularly deep ecologists, regard nature as an interconnected whole, embracing humans and non-humans as well as the inanimate world. Nature is sometimes seen as a source of knowledge and 'right living', human fulfilment coming from a closeness to and respect for nature, not from the attempt to dominate it.

TENSIONS WITHIN ... ECOLOGISM

'Shallow' ecology	v.	'Deep' ecology
environmentalism	↔	ecologism
'light' anthropocentrism	↔	ecocentrism
science	↔	mysticism
humankind	↔	nature
limited holism	↔	radical holism
instrumental value	↔	value-in-nature
modified humanism	↔	biocentric equality
animal welfare	↔	animal rights
sustainable growth	↔	anti-growth
personal development	↔	ecological consciousness

Systems thinking

Traditional political ideologies have typically assumed that human beings are the masters of the natural world, and have therefore regarded nature as little more than an economic resource, available to satisfy human ends. Fritjof Capra (1982) traced the origin of such thinking to the ideas of figures such as the French philosopher René Descartes (1596–1650) and the British scientist Isaac Newton (1642–1727). Instead of seeing the world as organic, Descartes and Newton portrayed it as a machine, implying that, like any other machine, it can be tinkered with, repaired, improved on or even replaced. Capra thus described nature, from this perspective, as the 'Newtonian world-machine'. Based on the application of scientific method, in which hypotheses are formulated and tested against empirical evidence, what became orthodox science enabled remarkable advances to be made in human knowledge and provided the basis for the development of modern industry and technology. So impressive were the fruits of science, that intellectual inquiry in the modern world has come to be dominated by **scientism**. However, green theorists argue that these benefits have come at a high cost. By encouraging human beings to think of themselves not as part of the natural world but as its master, the mechanistic world-view that lay at the heart of the 'Cartesian-Newtonian paradigm' fundamentally destabilized the relationship between humankind and nature.

This led to a search for a new, non-mechanistic paradigm, a search that has drawn green thinking into the spheres of both modern science and ancient myths and religions. One attempt do this was made through the notion of **holism**. The term 'holism' was coined in 1926 by Jan Smuts, a Boer general and twice prime minister of South Africa. He used it to describe the idea that the natural world could only be understood as a whole and not through its individual parts. Smuts believed that science commits the sin of reductionism: it reduces everything it studies to separate parts and tries to understand each part in itself. In contrast, holism suggests that

Scientism: The belief that scientific method is the only value-free and objective means of establishing truth, and is applicable to all fields of learning.

Holism: A belief that the whole is more important than its parts; holism implies that understanding is gained by studying relationships among the parts.

each part only has meaning in relation to other parts, and ultimately in relation to the whole. However, in twentieth-century science the holistic perspective became known as 'systematic', and the way of thinking it implied as '**systems thinking**' (sometimes called 'network' or 'contextual' thinking). Systems thinking concentrates not on individual building blocks, but on the principles of organization within a system. It therefore stresses the relationships within a system and the integration of its various elements within the whole. This is evident in the idea of an ecosystem, discussed earlier in the chapter. As an example of applied systems theory, a systems approach to medicine would consider not just physical ailments but would see these as a manifestation of imbalances within the patient as a whole, taking account of psychological, emotional, social and environmental factors.

Those green thinkers who look to modern science to provide a new paradigm for human thought typically emphasize the importance of twentieth-century developments in physics, particularly the emergence of the so-called 'new physics'. The breakthrough moment in this process came in the early twentieth century when the German-born US physicist Albert Einstein (1879–1955) advanced the theory of relativity. Moving significantly beyond the mechanistic and reductionist ideas of Newton, Einstein's work, among other things, fundamentally challenged the traditional concepts of time and space by putting forward the notion of a time-space continuum. Such thinking was taken further by quantum theory, developed by physicists such as Niels Bohr (1885–1952) and Verner Heisenberg (1901–76). In quantum theory the physical world is understood not as a collection of individual molecules, atoms or even particles, but as a system, or, more accurately, a network of systems.

Systems thinking: A way of thinking that treats living systems as integrated wholes, in which, ultimately, there are no parts but only patterns in an inseparable web of relationships.

System: A collection of parts that operate through a network of reciprocal interactions and thereby constitute a complex whole.

Gaia hypothesis: The hypothesis that the Earth is best understood as a living entity, which acts, above all, to maintain its own existence.

An alternative basis for systems thinking has been found in religion and ancient myths. For example, many in the green movement have been attracted by Eastern mysticism, seeing in it both a philosophy that gives expression to ecological wisdom and a way of life that encourages compassion for fellow human beings, other species and the natural world. Particular attention in this respect has focused on Hinduism, Daoism and Buddhism, in view of their stress on the unity or oneness of all things. Modern greens have, nevertheless, also looked back to pre-Christian spiritual ideas, especially the notion of an 'Earth Mother'. Such thinking has been most influential when it has been advanced through what James Lovelock termed the **Gaia hypothesis**. Gaia is the name of the Greek goddess of the Earth. The basis

KEY FIGURE

JAMES LOVELOCK (BORN 1919)

A UK atmospheric chemist, inventor and environmental thinker, Lovelock is best known as the inventor of the 'Gaia hypothesis'. This proposes that the Earth is best understood as a complex, self-regulating, living 'being', implying that the prospects for humankind are closely linked to whether the species helps to sustain, or threaten, the planetary ecosystem. Lovelock was also the first person to alert the world to the global presence of CFCs in the atmosphere, and he is, controversially, a supporter of nuclear power.

for the Gaia hypothesis is that the Earth's biosphere, atmosphere, oceans and soil exhibit precisely the same kind of self-regulating behaviour that characterizes other forms of life. The implication of this is that human beings must respect the health of the planet, and act to conserve its beauty and resources, the well-being of the planet being more important than that of any single species living on it at present.

Sustainability

Green thinkers argue that the ingrained assumption of conventional political creeds, articulated by virtually all mainstream political parties (so-called 'grey' parties), is that human life has unlimited possibilities for material growth and prosperity. Indeed, green thinkers commonly lump capitalism and socialism together, and portray them both as examples of 'industrialism'. A particularly influential metaphor for the environmental movement has been the idea of 'spaceship Earth', because this emphasizes the notion of limited and exhaustible wealth. The idea that Earth should be thought of as a spaceship was first suggested by Kenneth Boulding (1966). Boulding argued that human beings have traditionally acted as though they live in a 'cowboy economy', an economy with unlimited opportunities, like the American West during the frontier period. He suggested that this encourages, as it did in the American West, 'reckless, exploitative, and violent behaviour'. However, as a spaceship is a capsule, it is a 'closed' system. 'Open' systems receive energy or inputs from outside; for example, all ecosystems on Earth – ponds, forests, lakes and seas – are sustained by the Sun. However, 'closed' systems, as the Earth itself becomes when it is thought of as a spaceship, show evidence of **'entropy'**. All 'closed' systems tend to decay or disintegrate because they are not sustained by external inputs.

KEY CONCEPT
INDUSTRIALISM

The term 'industrialism', as used by environmental theorists, relates to a 'super-ideology' that encompasses capitalism and socialism, left-wing and right-wing thought. As an economic system, industrialism is characterized by large-scale production, the accumulation of capital and relentless growth. As a philosophy, it is dedicated to materialism, utilitarian values, absolute faith in science and a worship of technology. Many green thinkers thus see industrialism as 'the problem'. Ecosocialists, however, blame capitalism rather than industrialism (which ignores important issues such as the role of ownership, profit and the market), while ecofeminists argue that industrialism has its origins in patriarchy.

Not only have green thinkers argued that, in their economic activity, humans live beyond the constraints of a 'closed' ecosystem, but they have also been unwisely cavalier in plundering its resources. Garrett Hardin (1968) developed a particularly influential model to explain why over-exploitation of environmental resources has occurred, in the form of the **'tragedy of the commons'**. The idea of the tragedy of the commons draws parallels between global environmental degradation and the fate of common land before the introduction of enclosures. Common land or common fisheries stocks encourage individuals to act in rationally self-interested ways, each exploiting the resources available to satisfy their needs and the needs of their families and communities. However, the collective impact of such behaviour may be devastating, as the vital resources on which all depend become depleted, Thus, as Hardin put it,

Entropy: A tendency towards decay or disintegration, exhibited by all 'closed' systems.

Tragedy of the commons: A parable that shows that economic resources will be despoiled unless access to them is strictly constrained.

'Freedom in a commons brings ruin to all', an outcome that in his view could only be prevented by either stronger government or population control.

Nevertheless, green economics is not only about warnings and threats; it is also about solutions. Entropy may be an inevitable process; however, its effects can be slowed down or delayed considerably if governments and private citizens respect ecological principles. Green thinkers argue that the human species will only survive and prosper if it recognizes that it is merely one element of a complex biosphere, and that only a healthy, balanced biosphere will sustain human life. Policies and actions must therefore be judged by the principle of '**sustainability**'. Sustainability sets clear limits on human ambitions and material dreams because it requires that production does as little damage as possible to the fragile global ecosystem. This can be ensured not merely through the implementation of government controls or tax regimes to discourage the over-exploitation of natural resources, but, at a deeper level, by the adoption of an alternative approach to economic activity. This is what E. F. Schumacher sought to offer in his idea of 'Buddhist economics'. For Schumacher, this would involve humankind abandoning its obsession with wealth creation, and focusing instead on 'right livelihood', a transformation facilitated in large part by a shift to smaller-scale living and working arrangements.

Sustainability: The capacity of a system to maintain its health and continue in existence over a period of time.

Modernist ecology: A reformist tendency within green politics that seeks to reconcile ecology with the key features of capitalist modernity.

Limits to growth: The tendency for the environmental and other drawbacks of economic growth to expand to the point at which further increases in material prosperity are unachievable.

Social ecology: A broad tendency within green politics that links ecological sustainability to radical social change, or the eco-anarchist principle that human communities should be structured according to ecological principles.

Degrowth: A broad term that reflects the desire to move beyond the paradigm of economic growth for either or both practical or moral reasons.

There is nevertheless considerable debate about what sustainability implies in practice. Reformist or **modernist ecologists** support 'weak' sustainability, which tries to reconcile ecology with economic growth through getting richer but at a slower pace. This is often conveyed by the notion of **limits to growth**. However, radical ecologists, who include both **social ecologists** and deep ecologists, support (if to different degrees) 'strong' sustainability, which places far greater stress on preserving 'natural capital' and is more critical of economic growth. If, as some radical ecologists argue, the origin of the ecological crisis lies in materialism, consumerism and a fixation with economic growth, the solution would appear to lie in 'zero growth' and the construction of a 'postindustrial age' in which people live in small, rural communities and rely on craft skills. This could mean a fundamental and comprehensive rejection of industry and modern technology – literally a 'return to nature'. The idea of **degrowth** has become increasingly influential in environmental circles as a means of advancing a critique of

the ecological consequences of economic growth, based on the assumptions that growth is no longer desirable (as demonstrated by the fact that pre-industrial societies often flourished without it) and, being rooted in the drive for a surplus, growth is always linked exploitation (Kallis, 2017).

Environmental ethics

Ecologism, in all its forms, is concerned with extending moral thinking in a number of novel directions. This is because conventional ethical systems are clearly anthropocentric, orientated around the pleasure, needs and interests of human beings. In such philosophies, the non-human world is invested with value only to the extent that it satisfies human ends. An example of the novelty of environmental ethics can be found in the debate, raised by the 'Fridays for Future' school strikes, over whether young people's views on climate change should receive special consideration (see p. 216). An alternative approach to environmental ethics involves applying moral standards and values developed in relation to human beings to other species and organisms. This can be seen in the growth of **ethical veganism**, which goes far beyond the adoption of a plant-based diet. However, the most familiar attempt to extend moral standards to other species comes in the form of '**animal rights**'. In an argument that has had considerable impact on the animal liberation movement, Peter Singer (1976) claimed that an altruistic concern for the well-being of other species derives from the fact that, as sentient beings, they are capable of suffering. Drawing on utilitarianism (see p. 33), he pointed out that animals, like humans, have an interest in avoiding physical pain, and he therefore condemned any attempt to place the interests of humans above those of animals as '**speciesism**'.

Nevertheless, the moral stance of deep ecology goes much further, in particular by suggesting that nature has value in its own right; that is, intrinsic value. From this perspective, environmental ethics have nothing to do with human instrumentality and cannot be articulated simply through the extension of human values to the non-human world. Robert Goodin (1992), for instance, attempted to develop a 'green theory of value', which holds that resources should be valued precisely because they result from natural processes rather than human activity. However, since this value stems from the fact that the natural landscape helps people to see 'some sense and pattern in their lives' and to appreciate 'something larger' than themselves, it embodies a residual humanism that fails to satisfy some deep ecologists.

From having to being

Ecologism seeks not only to revise conventional moral thinking, but also to reshape our understanding of happiness and human well-being. In particular, green thinkers have advanced a critique of **materialism** and consumerism. Consumerism is a psycho-cultural phenomenon whereby personal happiness is equated with the consumption of material possessions, giving rise to what the German psychoanalyst and social philosopher Erich Fromm (1979) called a 'having' attitude of mind. For green theorists, 'having' – the disposition to seek fulfilment in acquisition and control – is deficient in at least two respects. First, it tends to undermine, rather than enhance, psychological and

Ethical veganism: The philosophical belief that cruelty and suffering to animals be avoided at all practical costs.

Animal rights: Moral entitlements that are based on the belief that as animals are non-human 'persons', they deserve the same consideration (at least in certain areas) as human beings.

Speciesism: A belief in the superiority of one species over other species, through the denial of their moral significance.

Materialism: An emphasis on material needs and their satisfaction, usually implying a link between pleasure or happiness and the level of material consumption.

emotional well-being. As modern advertising and marketing techniques tend to create ever-greater material desires, they leave consumers in a constant state of dissatisfaction because, however much they acquire and consume, they always want more. Consumerism thus works not through the satisfaction of desires, but through the generation of new desires, keeping people in an unending state of neediness, want and aspiration. Second, materialism and consumerism provide the cultural basis for environmental degradation. This occurs as the 'consumer society' encourages people to place short-term economic considerations ahead of longer-term ecological concerns, in which case nature is nothing other than a commodity or resource. In this light, ecologism can be seen to be associated with the ideas of postmaterialism (see p. 217) and anti-consumerism.

POLITICAL IDEOLOGIES IN ACTION . . .

SCHOOL CLIMATE STRIKES

EVENTS: In August 2018, a Swedish schoolgirl Greta Thunberg and other young activists sat in front of the Swedish parliament every school day for three weeks, to protest against political inaction on climate change. She posted what she was doing on Instagram and Twitter and the message soon went viral, creating an international movement ('Fridays for Future' or 'FFF') in which school students take time off from class on Fridays to raise awareness about the climate crisis and ecological destruction. A global strike in March 2019 attracted more than one million participants, with around 2,200 strikes taking place in some 125 countries. The Global Week of Climate Action in September 2019 gathered roughly four million protesters, many of them schoolchildren, making it probably the largest climate demonstration in history.

SIGNIFICANCE: The Fridays for Future movement is underpinned by the fact that anxieties about climate change have a marked future-looking character, meaning that moral obligations in relation to the issue are unequally distributed between the generations. Young people, and therefore schoolchildren, are entitled to greater consideration than older people on two grounds. First, the negative consequences of climate change (more and stronger storms, longer heatwaves, rising sea levels, melting ice caps and so on) are set to be felt for longer, and more severely, by children than by adults. Second, by contrast with their parents' and grandparents' generations, children are in no way culpable for the failure of ecological stewardship that allowed the

Ernesto Ruscio/Getty

climate crisis to escalate in the first place. If these arguments apply to the younger generation, they do so even more strongly to those yet to be born; that is, 'future generations'.

However, what can be called cross-generational justice has also been called into question. For example, the younger generation is not a fixed unchanging entity, distinguished, throughout their lives, by the same set of values and beliefs. Instead, as today's children are tomorrow's adults, the idealism of many young climate activists might be expected to fade over time. Similarly, to see the climate change debate very largely as a clash of generations is to ignore the impact on the climate of structural factors such as mechanistic and reductionist thinking and consumer capitalism. Finally, specifically in relation to future generations, because their size is unknown, living generations may either make sacrifices for the benefit of people who may prove to be much better off than themselves, or their sacrifices may be entirely inadequate to meet future needs.

KEY CONCEPT

POSTMATERIALISM

Postmaterialism is a theory that explains the nature of political concerns and values in terms of levels of economic development. It is based loosely on Abraham Maslow's (1908–70) 'hierarchy of needs', which places self-esteem and self-actualization above material or economic needs. Postmaterialism assumes that conditions of material scarcity breed egoistical and acquisitive values, meaning that politics is dominated by economic issues (who gets what). However, in conditions of widespread prosperity, individuals tend to express more interest in 'postmaterial' or 'quality of life' issues. These are typically concerned with morality, political justice and personal fulfilment, and include gender equality, world peace, racial harmony, ecology and animal rights.

In their search for an alternative model of human well-being, green theorists have generally emphasized the importance of 'quality of life' issues and concerns, thereby divorcing happiness from a simple link to material acquisition. Such thinking is taken most seriously by eco-anarchists, ecofeminists and especially deep ecologists. In line with Fromm, they have placed 'being' above 'having'. The key feature of 'being' as an attitude of mind is that it seeks to transcend the self, or individual ego, and to recognize that each person is intrinsically linked to all other living things, and, indeed, to the universe itself. The Australian philosopher Warwick Fox (1990) claimed to go beyond deep ecology in embracing 'transpersonal ecology', the essence of which is the realization that 'things are', that human beings and all other entities are part of a single unfolding reality. For Naess, self-realization is attained through a broader and deeper 'identification with others'. Such ideas have often been shaped by Eastern religions, most profoundly by Buddhism. One of the core features of Buddhism is the doctrine of 'no self', the notion that the individual ego is a myth or delusion, and that awakening or enlightenment involves transcending the self and recognizing the oneness of life.

TYPES OF ECOLOGISM

The key sub-traditions of ecologism are as follows:

- reformist ecologism

- eco-socialism

- eco-anarchism

- eco-feminism

- deep ecology.

Reformist ecology

Reformist or modernist ecology refers to the form of ecologism that is practised by most environmental pressure groups and by a growing range of mainstream political parties. It is reformist in that it seeks to advance ecological principles and promote 'environmentally sound' practices, but without rejecting the central features of capitalist modernity – individual self-seeking, materialism, economic growth and so on. It is thus very clearly a form of 'shallow' or humanist ecology. The key feature of reformist ecology is the recognition that there are environmental limits to growth, in the sense that pollution, increased CO_2 emissions, the exhaustion of non-renewable energy sources and other forms of environmental degradation ultimately threaten prosperity and economic performance. The watchword of this form of ecologism is therefore sustainable development (in the sense of 'weak' sustainability) or, more specifically, environmentally sustainable capitalism. As, in economic terms, this means 'getting richer more slowly', reformist ecology extends moral and philosophical sensibilities only in modest directions. Indeed, it is often condemned by more radical ecologists as hopelessly compromised: part of the problem rather than part of the solution.

The two main ideological influences on reformist ecology are liberalism and conservatism. Liberalism has, at best, an ambivalent relationship with ecologism. On the one hand, radical ecologists criticize individualism (see p. 24) as a stark example of anthropocentrism, and have serious reservations about utilitarianism, the moral philosophy that underpins much of classical liberalism, on the grounds that it equates happiness with material consumption. On the other hand, the stress found within modern liberalism on self-realization and developmental individualism can be said to sustain a form of 'enlightened' anthropocentrism, which encourages people to take into account long-term, and not merely short-term, interests, and to favour 'higher' pleasures (including an appreciation of the natural world) over 'lower' pleasures (such as material consumption). This can be seen, for example, in J. S. Mill's (see p. 25) condemnation of rampant industrialization and his defence of both a stationary population and a steady-state economy, grounded in the belief that the contemplation of nature is an indispensable aspect of human fulfilment.

KEY CONCEPT
SUSTAINABLE DEVELOPMENT

Sustainable development refers to 'development that meets the needs of the present without compromising the ability of future generations to meet their own needs' (Brundtland Report, 1987). It therefore embodies two concepts: (1) the concept of need, particularly the essential needs of the world's poor; and (2) the concept of limitations, especially related to the environment's ability to meet future as well as present needs. So-called *weak* sustainability takes economic growth to be desirable but simply insists that growth must be limited to ensure that ecological costs do not threaten its long-term sustainability, allowing 'human capital' to be substituted for 'natural capital'. *Strong* sustainability rejects the pro-growth implications of weak sustainability, and focuses just on the need to preserve and sustain 'natural capital'.

Green capitalism: The idea that a reliance on the capitalist market mechanism will deliver ecologically sustainable outcomes, usually linked to assumptions about capitalism's consumer responsiveness.

Consumer sovereignty: The notion, based on the theory of competitive capitalism, that consumer choice is the ultimately determining factor within a market economy.

Conservatives, for their part, have evinced a sympathy for environmental issues on two main grounds. First, ecoconservatism has drawn on a romantic and nostalgic attachment to a rural way of life threatened by the growth of towns and cities. It is clearly a reaction against industrialization and the idea of 'progress'. Such environmental sensibilities typically focus on the issue of conservation and on attempts to protect the natural heritage – woodlands, forests and so on – as well as the architectural and social heritage. The conservation of nature is therefore linked to a defence of traditional values and institutions. Second, conservatives have advocated market-based solutions to environmental problems, even espousing the idea of **'green capitalism'**. The theory of green capitalism is based on the assumption that the market mechanism can and will respond to pressure from more ecologically aware consumers by forcing firms to produce 'environmentally sound' goods and adopt 'green' technologies. Such thinking relies on the idea of **consumer sovereignty** and acknowledges the impact of the trend towards so-called 'responsible consumption'. Long-term corporate profitability can thus only be achieved in a context of sustainable development.

Ecosocialism

This is the socialist strand within the green movement, which has been particularly pronounced among the German Greens, many of whose leaders have been former members of far-left groups. Ecosocialism has drawn from the pastoral socialism of thinkers such as William Morris, who extolled the virtues of small-scale craft communities living close to nature. However, it has more usually been associated with Marxism. For example, Rudolph Bahro (1982) argued that the root cause of the environmental crisis is capitalism. The natural world has been despoiled by industrialization, but this is merely a consequence of capitalism's relentless search for profit. In this view, capitalism's anti-ecological bias derives from a number of sources. These include that private property encourages the belief that humans are dominant over nature; that the market economy 'commodifies' nature, in the sense that it turns it into something that only has exchange-value and so can be bought and sold; and that the capitalist system breeds materialism and consumerism, and so leads to relentless growth. From this perspective, 'green capitalism' is a contradiction in terms.

The core theme of ecosocialism is thus the idea that capitalism is the enemy of the environment, while socialism is its friend. However, as with socialist feminism, such a formula embodies tension between two elements, this time between 'red' and 'green' priorities. If environmental catastrophe is nothing more than a by-product of capitalism, environmental problems are best tackled by abolishing capitalism, or at least taming it. Therefore, ecologists should not form separate green parties or set up narrow environmental organizations, but work within the larger socialist movement and address the real issue: the economic system. On the other hand, socialism has also been seen as another 'pro-production' political creed: it can be seen to espouse exploiting the wealth of the planet, albeit for the good of humanity, rather than just the capitalist class. Nevertheless, although socialist parties continue to base their electoral appeal primarily on the promise of economic growth, and are therefore reluctant to subordinate the green to the red, few of them now fail to treat ecological issues as a mainstream concern.

Eco-anarchism

Perhaps the ideology that has the best claim to being environmentally sensitive is anarchism. Some months before the publication of Rachel Carson's *The Silent Spring*, Murray Bookchin brought out *Our Synthetic Environment* ([1962] 1975). Many in the green movement also acknowledge a debt to nineteenth-century anarcho-communists, particularly Peter Kropotkin. Bookchin (1977) suggested that there is a clear correspondence between the ideas of anarchism and the principles of ecology, articulated in the idea of social ecology, based on the belief that ecological balance is the surest foundation for social stability. Anarchists believe in a stateless society, in which harmony develops out of mutual respect and social solidarity among human beings. The richness of such a society is founded on its variety and diversity. Green thinkers also believe that balance or harmony develops spontaneously within nature, in the form of ecosystems, and that these, like anarchist communities, require no external authority or control. The anarchist rejection of government within human society thus parallels the green thinkers' warnings about human 'rule' within the natural world. Bookchin therefore likened an anarchist community to an ecosystem, and suggested that both are distinguished by respect for the principles of diversity, balance and harmony.

MURRAY BOOKCHIN (1921–2006)

A US anarchist social philosopher and environmentalist, Bookchin was a leading proponent of the idea of 'social ecology'. As an anarchist, Bookchin emphasized the potential for non-hierarchic cooperation within conditions of post-scarcity and radical decentralization. Arguing that ecological principles should be applied to social organization, he linked the environmental crisis to the breakdown of the organic fabric of both society and nature. His major works in this field include *The Ecology of Freedom* (1982) and *Re-enchanting Humanity* (1995).

Debbie Bookchin/
Wikimedia Commons

Anarchists have also advocated the construction of decentralized societies, organized as a collection of communes or villages, a social vision to which many deep ecologists are also attracted. Life in such communities would be lived close to nature, each community attempting to achieve a high degree of self-sufficiency. Such communities would be economically diverse; they would produce food and a wide range of goods and services, and therefore contain agriculture, craftwork and small-scale industry. Self-sufficiency would make each community dependent on its natural environment, spontaneously generating an understanding of organic relationships and ecology. In Bookchin's view, decentralization would lead to 'a more intelligent and more loving use of the environment'. Although such thinking has been eagerly embraced by the radical wing of the green movement, it marks a clear divide between anarchism and mainstream ecologism, which sees government and state agencies as the principal means through which environmental issues should be addressed.

Ecofeminism

The idea that feminism offers a distinctive and important approach to green issues has grown to such a point that ecofeminism has developed into one of the major philosophical schools of environmentalist thought, its key theorists including Karen Warren, Vandana Shiva and Carolyn Merchant. The basic theme of ecofeminism is that ecological destruction has its origins in patriarchy: nature is under threat not from humankind but from men and the institutions of male power. Feminists who adopt an androgynous or sexless view of human nature argue that patriarchy has distorted the instincts and sensibilities of men by divorcing them from the 'private' world of nurturing, home-making and personal relationships. The sexual division of labour thus inclines men to subordinate both women and nature, seeing themselves as 'masters' of both. From this point of view, ecofeminism can be classified as a particular form of social ecology. However, many ecofeminists subscribe to essentialism, in that their theories are based on the belief that there are fundamental and ineradicable differences between women and men.

Such a position is adopted, for instance, by Mary Daly in *Gyn/Ecology* (1979). Daly argued that women would liberate themselves from patriarchal culture if they aligned themselves with 'female nature'. The notion of an intrinsic link between women and nature is not a new one. Pre-Christian religions and 'primitive' cultures often portrayed the Earth or natural forces as a goddess, an idea resurrected in the Gaia hypothesis.

KEY FIGURE

Robert Holmgren/
ESPM UC Berkeley

CAROLYN MERCHANT (BORN 1936)

A US ecofeminist philosopher and historian of science, Merchant's work has highlighted links between gender oppression and the 'death of nature'. Merchant developed a feminist critique of a scientific revolution that explained environmental degradation ultimately in terms of the application by men of a mechanistic view of nature. On this basis, she argued that a global ecological revolution requires a radical restructuring of gender relations. Some of Merchant's works include *The Death of Nature* (1983), *Radical Ecology* (1992) and *Autonomous Nature* (2015).

Modern ecofeminists, however, highlight the biological basis for women's closeness to nature, in particular the fact that they bear children and suckle babies. The fact that women cannot live separate from natural rhythms and processes in turn structures their politico-cultural orientation. Traditional 'female' values therefore include reciprocity, cooperation and nurturing, values that have a 'soft' or ecological character. The idea that nature is a resource to be exploited or a force to be subdued is more abhorrent to women than men, because they recognize that nature operates in and through them, and intuitively sense that personal fulfilment stems from acting with nature rather than against it. The overthrow of patriarchy therefore promises to bring with it an entirely new relationship between human society and the natural world, meaning that ecofeminism shares with deep ecology a firm commitment to ecocentrism.

Deep ecology

The term 'deep ecology' was coined in 1973 by Arne Naess. For Naess, deep ecology is 'deep' because it persists in asking deeper questions concerning 'why' and 'how', and is thus concerned with fundamental philosophical questions about the impact of the human species on the biosphere. The key belief of deep ecology is that ecology and anthropocentrism (in all its forms, including 'enlightened' anthropocentrism) are simply irreconcilable; indeed, anthropocentrism is an offence against the principle of ecology.

This rejection of anthropocentrism has had profound moral and political implications. Deep ecologists have viewed nature as the source of moral goodness. Nature thus has 'intrinsic' or inherent value, not just 'instrumental' value deriving from the benefits it brings to human beings. A classic statement of the ethical framework of deep ecology is articulated in Aldo Leopold's *Sand County Almanac* ([1948] 1968) in the form of the 'land ethic': 'A thing is right when it tends to preserve the integrity, stability and beauty of the biotic community. It is wrong when it tends otherwise'. Such a moral stance implies '**biocentric equality**'. Naess (1989) expressed this in the idea that all species have an 'equal right to live and bloom', reflecting the benefits of **biodiversity**. Such ecocentric ethical thinking has been accompanied by a deeper and more challenging philosophical approach that amounts to nothing less than a new **metaphysics**, a new way of thinking about and understanding the world. In addressing metaphysical issues, deep ecology

Biocentric equality: The principle that all organisms and entities in the biosphere are of equal moral worth, each being an expression of the goodness of nature.

Biodiversity: The range of species within a biotic community, often thought to be linked to its health and stability.

Metaphysics: The branch of philosophy that is concerned with explaining the fundamental nature of existence, or being.

is radical in a way and to a degree that does not apply elsewhere in ideological thought. Deep ecology calls for a change in consciousness, specifically the adoption of 'ecological consciousness', or 'cosmological consciousness'. At the heart of this is an 'inter-subjective' model of selfhood that allows for no distinction between the self and the 'other', thereby collapsing the distinction between humankind and nature.

KEY FIGURE

ARNE NAESS (1912–2008)

A Norwegian philosopher, writer and mountaineer, Naess has been described as the 'father' of deep ecology. His philosophy, Ecosophy T (the 'T' is for the Tvergastein hut in which he lived in solitude high on a Norwegian mountain), which was influenced by the ideas of Spinoza, Gandhi's ethic of non-violence and Taoist thought, was based on the assertion that 'the Earth does not belong to human beings', as all creatures have an equal right to live and bloom.

PA Images/Alamy Stock Photo

Deep ecology is also associated with a distinctive analysis of environmental degradation and how it should be tackled. Instead of linking the environmental crisis to particular policies or a specific political, social or economic system (be it industrialization, capitalism, patriarchy or whatever), deep ecologists argue that it has more profound cultural and intellectual roots. The problem lies in the mechanistic world-view that has dominated the thinking of Western societies since about the seventeenth century, and which subsequently came to affect most of the globe. Above all, this dominant paradigm is dualistic: it understands the world in terms of distinctions (self/other, humankind/nature, individual/society, mind/matter, reason/emotion and so on) and thus allows nature to be thought of as inert and valueless in itself, a mere resource for satisfying human ends. In this light, nothing less than a paradigm change – a change in how we approach and think about the world – will properly address the challenge of environmental degradation.

In addition to its moral and philosophical orientation, deep ecology has been associated with a wider set of goals and concerns. These include:

- *Wilderness preservation.* Deep ecologists seek to preserve nature 'wild and free', based on the belief that the natural world, unspoilt by human intervention, is a repository of wisdom and morality. **Preservationism** is nevertheless different from conservationism, in that the latter is usually taken to imply protecting nature in order to satisfy long-term human ends. The 'wilderness ethic' of deep ecology is often linked to the ideas of Henry David Thoreau (see p. 119), whose quest for spiritual truth and self-reliance led him to flee from civilized life and live for two years in virtual solitude, close to nature, an experience described in *Walden* ([1854] 1983).

Preservationism: The disposition to protect natural systems, often implying keeping things 'just as they are' and restricting the impact of humans on the environment.

- *Population control.* Although greens from many traditions have shown a concern about the exponential rise in the human population, deep ecologists have placed a particular emphasis on this issue, often arguing that a substantial decrease in the human population is the only way of ensuring the flourishing of non-human life. To this end, some deep ecologists have rejected aid to the developing world; called for a reduction in birth rates, especially in the developing world; or argued that immigration from the developing world to the developed world should be stopped.

- *Simple living*. Deep ecologists believe that humans have no right to reduce the richness and diversity of nature except, as Naess put it, to satisfy vital needs. This is a philosophy of 'walking lighter on the Earth'. It certainly implies an emphasis on promoting the quality of life ('being') rather than the quantity of possessions ('having'), and is often linked to a postmaterial model of self-realization, commonly understood as **self-actualization**. This implies being 'inwardly rich but outwardly poor'.

- *Bioregionalism*. This is the idea that human society should be reconfigured in line with naturally-defined regions, each 'bioregion', in effect, being an ecosystem. **Bioregionalism** is clearly at odds with established territorial divisions, based on national or state borders. Although deep ecologists seldom look to prescribe how humans should organize themselves within such bioregions, there is general support for self-reliant, self-supporting, autonomous communities.

THE FUTURE OF ECOLOGISM

The future prospects for ecologism would appear to be firmly linked to the state of the environmental crisis and the general level of understanding about environmental issues and problems. As evidence of the blight of nature accumulates – through climate change, reduced levels of male fertility caused by pollution, the eradication of animal and plant species, and so on – the search for an alternative to growth-obsessed industrialism will surely intensify. The fluctuating fortunes of green parties and single-issue environmental groups provide no reliable indication of the strength of ecological ideas and values. One of the problems confronting green parties is that their mainstream and much larger rivals have often take up 'eco-friendly' positions that were once exclusively theirs. Similarly, the membership and activist base of environmental groups does not reflect the number of 'fellow-travellers' in society at large, nor the wider adoption of ecological practices such as recycling, the consumption of organic food and the adoption of vegan diets. In this light, we can expect growing numbers of people to 'turn green' in an attempt to reverse the policies and practices that have brought both the human species and the natural world close to destruction.

Significant problems nevertheless confront ecologism. In the first place, it is difficult to see how ecologism can become a genuinely global ideology. As far as developing-world states are concerned, the strictures of ecologism appear to deny them the opportunity to catch up materially with the West, ruling out large-scale industrialization, the exploitation of finite resources and uncontrolled pollution. Second, industrialism and its underlying values, such as competitive individualism and consumerism, have become more deeply entrenched, in part as a result of the advance of economic globalization. Third, difficulties surround the anti-growth or degrowth message of ecologism. The politics of zero or even sustainable growth may be so electorally unattractive to populations that it proves to be politically impossible. This was perhaps demonstrated by the Covid-19 pandemic, and the speed with which states re-prioritized economic growth each time they believed the public health crisis had passed. Fourth, ecologism may simply be an urban fad, a form of postindustrial

Self-actualization: An 'inner', even quasi-spiritual, fulfilment that is achieved by transcending egoism and materialism.

Bioregionalism: The belief that the territorial organization of economic, social and political life should take into account the ecological integrity of bioregions.

romanticism. This suggests that environmental awareness is merely a temporary reaction to industrial progress and is likely to be restricted to the young and the materially affluent. Finally, perhaps the most daunting challenge confronting ecologism is the very scale of the changes it calls for. It does not merely demand economic transformation or the reordering of political power; it seeks to establish nothing less than a new mode of being, a different way of experiencing and understanding existence.

QUESTIONS FOR DISCUSSION

- How does an ecocentric perspective challenge conventional approaches to politics?
- Is 'enlightened' anthropocentrism a contradiction in terms?
- Why have ecological thinkers been ambivalent about science?
- Should all thinking strive to be 'systematic'?
- What are the features of a sustainable economy?
- How has ecologism extended conventional moral thinking?
- Do we have obligations to young people and future generations, and if so, how far do they extend?

- Why and how have green theorists rethought the nature of human fulfilment?
- Which political ideologies are most compatible with ecological thinking, and why?
- To what extent can the goals of ecologism only be achieved through radical social change?
- Does deep ecology constitute the philosophical core of green political thought?
- Can ecologism ever be electorally and politically viable?

FURTHER READING

Carter, N. *The Politics of the Environment: Ideas, Activism, Policy*, 3rd edn (2018). An excellent general introduction to environmental politics and its application in activism and government.

Dobson, A. *Green Political Thought* (2007). An accessible and useful account of the ideas behind green politics; a classic text on the subject.

Dyzek, J. & Schlosberg, D. *Debating the Earth: The Environmental Politics Reader*, 2nd edn (2005). A broad collection of readings highlighting key issues, debates and perspectives within environmental political discourse.

Gabrielson, T. *et al. The Oxford Handbook of Environmental Political Theory* (2016). The most authoritative text compiling the latest scholarship and research on green ideology, and its interactions with other ideologies.

Solutions Journal www.thesolutionsjournal.com. This open access peer-reviewed journal profiles environmental policy solutions as well as commentary and ideas on contemporary issues from a green standpoint.

CHAPTER 11

MULTICULTURALISM

PREVIEW

Although multicultural societies have long existed – examples include the Ottoman empire, which reached its peak in the late sixteenth and early seventeenth centuries, and the USA from the early nineteenth century onwards – the term 'multiculturalism' is of relatively recent origin. It was first used in 1965 in Canada to describe a distinctive approach to tackling the issue of cultural diversity. In 1971, multiculturalism, or 'multiculturalism within a bilingual framework', was formally adopted as public policy in Canada, providing the basis for the introduction of the Multiculturalism Act in 1988. Australia also officially declared itself multicultural and committed itself to multiculturalism in the early 1970s. However, the term 'multiculturalism' has only been prominent in wider political debate since the 1990s.

Multiculturalism is more an arena for ideological debate than an ideology in its own right. As an arena for debate, it encompasses a range of views about the implications of growing cultural diversity and, in particular, about how cultural difference can be reconciled with civic unity. Its key theme is therefore diversity within unity. A multiculturalist stance implies a positive endorsement of communal diversity, based on the right of different cultural groups to recognition and respect. In this sense, it acknowledges the importance of beliefs, values and ways of life in establishing a sense of self-worth for individuals and groups alike. Distinctive cultures thus deserve to be protected and strengthened, particularly when they belong to minority or vulnerable groups. However, there are a number of competing models of a multicultural society. These draw on, variously, the ideas of liberalism, pluralism and cosmopolitanism, each offering a different model of the balance between togetherness and difference.

HISTORICAL OVERVIEW

The 1960s and 1970s witnessed a trend towards growing political assertiveness among minority groups, sometimes manifest in the form of **ethnocultural nationalism**. This development affected parts of Asia, Africa and Latin America, but it had a particular impact in North America, Australasia and Western Europe, where it was typically expressed through a quest for cultural or ethnic recognition within a liberal-democratic framework. This was, for example, evident among the French-speaking people of Quebec in Canada, in the rise of Scottish and Welsh nationalism in the UK, and in the growth of separatist movements in Catalonia and the Basque region in Spain, Corsica in France, and Flanders in Belgium. A trend towards ethnic assertiveness was also found among the Native Americans in Canada and the USA, the aboriginal peoples in Australia, and the Maoris in New Zealand. In response to these pressures, a growing number of countries adopted 'official' multiculturalism policies, the 1988 Canadian Multiculturalism Act being perhaps the classic example. This Act acknowledges the freedom of all members of Canadian society to preserve, enhance and share their cultural heritage, and endorses the principle of **bilingualism**.

A common theme among these emergent forms of ethnic politics was the desire to challenge economic and social marginalization, and sometimes racial oppression. In this sense, ethnic politics was a vehicle for political liberation, its enemy being structural disadvantage and ingrained inequality. For black communities in North America and Western Europe, for instance, the establishment of an ethnic identity provided a means of confronting a dominant white culture that had traditionally emphasized their inferiority and demanded subservience.

Apart from growing assertiveness among established minority groups, multicultural politics has also been strengthened by trends in international migration since 1945 that have significantly widened cultural diversity in many societies. Migration rates rose steeply in the early post-1945 period, both as people tried to escape from poverty by looking to economic opportunities abroad, and Western as states sought to recruit workers from abroad to help in the process of postwar reconstruction. This saw, for example, massive migration to the Middle East from India, Bangladesh and Pakistan, and a growing number of Chinese migrants in Africa. In the case of European states, migration routes were often shaped by links to former colonies. Immigration into the UK thus came mainly from the West Indies and the Indian subcontinent, while immigration in France came largely from Algeria, Morocco and Tunisia. In the case of West Germany, immigrants were *Gastarbeiter* (guest workers), usually recruited from Turkey or Yugoslavia. These trends have nevertheless intensified in the post-Cold War period, fuelled by a combination of an upsurge in war, ethnic conflict and political upheaval, and deepening economic fault-lines exposed by the advance of globalization (see p. 21). More and more societies are, as a result, characterized by ethnic diversity, meaning that the monocultural nation-state has become very much the exception and not the rule.

Ethnocultural nationalism: A form of nationalism that is fuelled primarily by a keen sense of ethnic and cultural distinctiveness and the desire to preserve it.

Bilingualism: The ability to speak two languages, or the widespread practice in society of speaking two languages.

By the early 2000s, a growing number of Western states, including virtually all the member states of the European Union, had responded to such developments by incorporating multiculturalism in some way into public policy. This has been particularly evident in countries such as Belgium, Finland, Greece, Ireland, Norway, Portugal, Spain and Sweden. Nevertheless, the tide may have turned against multiculturalism. It has become increasingly fashionable, particularly in Europe, to claim that multiculturalism has somehow 'gone too far', or even 'failed'. Such protestations have often been linked to the rise of populist nationalism, as discussed in Chapter 8.

CORE THEMES

The term 'multiculturalism' has been used in a variety of ways, both descriptive and normative. As a descriptive term, it refers to cultural diversity that arises from the existence within a society of two or more groups whose beliefs and practices generate a distinctive sense of collective identity. Multiculturalism, in this sense, is invariably reserved for communal diversity that arises from racial, ethnic and language differences. The term can also be used to describe governmental responses to such communal diversity, either in the form of public policy or in the design of institutions. Multicultural public policies, whether applied in education, health care, housing or other aspects of social policy, are characterized by a formal recognition of the distinctive needs of particular cultural groups and a desire to ensure **equality of opportunity** between and among them. Multicultural institutional design goes further than this by attempting to fashion the apparatus of government around the ethnic, religious and other divisions in society. In the form of **consociationalism**, it has shaped political practice in states such as the Netherlands, Switzerland and Belgium; it has also been applied in the form of 'power sharing' in Northern Ireland and in multilevel governance in post-conflict Bosnia-Herzegovina.

As a normative term, multiculturalism implies a positive endorsement, even celebration, of communal diversity, typically based on either the right of different cultural groups to respect and recognition, or to the alleged benefits to the larger society of moral and cultural diversity. However, multiculturalism is more an ideological 'space' than a political ideology in itself. Instead of advancing a comprehensive world-view which maps out an economic, social and political vision of the 'good society', multiculturalism is, rather, an arena within which increasingly important debates about the balance in modern societies between cultural diversity and civic unity are conducted. Nevertheless, a distinctive multiculturalist ideological stance can be identified. The most significant themes within multiculturalism are:

- postcolonialism
- politics of recognition
- culture and identity
- minority rights
- togetherness in difference.

Postcolonialism

The political and intellectual foundations of multiculturalism were laid by the postcolonial theories that developed out of the collapse of the European empires in the early post-World War II period. Postcolonialism originated as a trend in literary and cultural studies that sought to address the cultural conditions characteristic of newly-independent societies. Its purpose has been primarily to expose and overturn the cultural and psychological dimensions of colonial rule, recognizing that 'inner' subjugation can persist

Equality of opportunity: Equality defined in terms of life chances or the existence of a 'level playing-field'.

Consociationalism: A form of power sharing involving a close association among a number of parties or political formations, typically used in deeply divided societies.

long after the political structures of colonialism have been removed. A major thrust of postcolonial theory has been to establish the legitimacy of non-Western and sometimes anti-Western political ideas. Postcolonialism has therefore sought to give the developing world a distinctive political voice separate from the universalist pretensions of liberalism and socialism. (In an educational context, such thinking provides the basis for growing calls to 'decolonize the curriculum' (see p. 12).)

KEY CONCEPT

COLONIALISM

Colonialism is the theory or practice of establishing control over a foreign territory and turning it into a 'colony'. Colonialism is thus a particular form of imperialism. Colonialism is usually distinguished by settlement, dispossession and economic domination.

As typically practised in Africa and Southeast Asia, colonial government was exercised by a settler community from a 'mother country'. In contrast, neo-colonialism is essentially an economic phenomenon based on the export of capital from an advanced country to a less developed one (for example, so-called US 'dollar imperialism' in Latin America).

In one of the most influential works of postcolonial theory, Edward Said, developed the notion of '**Orientalism**' to highlight the extent to which Western cultural and political hegemony over the rest the world, but over the Orient in particular, has been maintained through elaborate stereotypical fictions that belittle and demean non-Western people and cultures. Examples of such stereotypes include ideas such as the 'mysterious East', 'lustful Turks' and 'Asian inscrutability'. In this way, Said delineated the structures of the discourse of Orientalism, treating Orientalism as a manifestation of the wider phenomenon of **Eurocentrism**.

KEY FIGURE

Bettmann/Getty Images

EDWARD SAID (1935–2003)

A Jerusalem-born US academic and literary critic, Said was a prominent advocate of the Palestinian cause and a founding figure of postcolonial theory. He developed, from the 1970s onwards, a humanist critique of the Western Enlightenment that uncovered its link to colonialism and highlighted 'narratives of oppression', cultural and ideological biases that disempower colonized peoples. He thereby condemned Eurocentrism's attempt to remake the world in its own image. Said's key works include *Orientalism* (1978) and *Culture and Imperialism* (1993).

Orientalism: Stereotypical depictions of 'the Orient' or Eastern culture generally which are based on distorted and invariably demeaning Western assumptions.

Eurocentrism: The application of values and theories drawn from European culture to other groups and peoples, implying a biased or distorted world-view.

Black nationalism in the USA and elsewhere was one of the early offshoots of postcolonialism. Aimed at promoting black consciousness, black nationalism dates back to the early twentieth century and the rise of the 'back to Africa' movement inspired by figures such as Marcus Garvey (see p. 136). Black politics nevertheless gained greater prominence in the 1960s with an upsurge in both the reformist and revolutionary wings of the movement. In its reformist guise, the movement took the form of a struggle for civil rights that reached national prominence in the USA under the leadership of Martin Luther King (1929–68). The strategy of non-violent civil disobedience was nevertheless rejected by the Black Power movement.

This constituted a loose collection of groups committed to a separatist creed, which included the Black Panthers and the Black Muslims (now the Nation of Islam) and was associated with figures such as Kwame Ture (formally Stokely Carmichael) (1941–98). The idea of black consciousness has nevertheless been revived by the Black Lives Matter (BLM) movement, founded in 2013. Initially committed to anti-racist advocacy and protest focused primarily around the issue of police violence, particularly since 2020 Black Lives Matter has developed into a genuinely global organization concerned with, among other things, the decolonization of culture, education and society.

Politics of recognition

Multiculturalists argue that minority cultural groups are disadvantaged in relation to majority groups, and that remedying this involves significant changes in society's rules and institutions. As such, multiculturalism, in common with many other ideological traditions (not least socialism and feminism), is associated with the advancement of marginalized, disadvantaged or oppressed groups. However, multiculturalism draws from a novel approach to such matters, one that departs from conventional approaches to social advancement. Three contrasting approaches can be adopted, based, respectively, on the ideas of rights, redistribution and recognition (see Figure 11.1).

Approach	Main obstacle to advancement	Key theme	Reforms and policies
Politics of rights (republicanism)	Legal and political exclusion	Universal citizenship	• Formal equality (legal and political rights) • Ban discrimination • Prohibit ethical/cultural/racial profiling
Politics of redistribution (social reformism)	Social disadvantage	Equality of opportunity	• Social rights • Welfare and redistribution • Positive discrimination
Politics of recognition (multiculturalism)	Cultural-based marginalization	Group self-assertion	• Right to respect and recognition • Minority rights • Group self-determination

Figure 11.1 **Contrasting approaches to social advancement**

The notion of the 'politics of rights' is rooted in the ideas of republicanism (see p. 230), which are associated by many (but by no means all) with liberalism. Republicanism is concerned primarily with the problem of legal and political exclusion, the denial to certain groups of rights that are enjoyed by their fellow citizens. Republican thinking was, for example, reflected in first-wave feminism, in that its campaign for female emancipation focused on the struggle for votes for women and equal access for women and men to education, careers and public life in general. The republican stance can, in this sense, be said to be 'difference-blind': it views difference as 'the problem' (because it leads to discriminatory or unfair treatment) and proposes that difference be banished or transcended in the name of equality. Republicans therefore believe that social advancement can be brought about largely through the establishment of **formal equality**.

The contrasting idea of the 'politics of redistribution' is rooted in a social reformist stance that embraces, among other traditions, modern liberalism and social democracy. It arose out of the belief that universal **citizenship** and formal equality are not sufficient, in themselves, to tackle the problems of subordination and marginalization. People are held back not merely by legal and political exclusion, but also, and more importantly, by social disadvantage – poverty, unemployment, poor housing, lack of education and so on. The key idea of social reformism is the principle of equal opportunities, the belief in a 'level playing-field' that allows people to rise or fall in society strictly on the basis of personal ability and their willingness to work. This implies a shift from legal egalitarianism to social egalitarianism, the latter involving a system of social engineering that redistributes wealth so as to alleviate poverty and overcome disadvantage. In such an approach, difference is acknowledged as it highlights the existence of social injustice. Nevertheless, this amounts to no more than a provisional or temporary acknowledgement of difference, in that different groups are identified only in order to expose unfair practices and structures, which can then be reformed or removed.

KEY CONCEPT
REPUBLICANISM

Republicanism refers, most simply, to a preference for a republic over a monarchy. However, the term 'republic' suggests not merely the absence of a monarch but, in the light of its Latin root, *res publica* (meaning common or collective affairs), it implies that the people should have a decisive say in the organization of the public realm. The central theme of republican political theory is a concern with a particular form of freedom, sometimes seen as 'freedom as non-domination' (Pettit, 1999). This combines liberty, in the sense of protection against arbitrary or tyrannical rule, with active participation in public and political life. The moral core of republicanism is expressed in a belief in civic virtue, understood to include public-spiritedness, honour and patriotism (see p. 125).

Multiculturalism, for its part, developed out of the belief that group marginalization often has even deeper origins. It is not merely a legal, political or social phenomenon but is, rather, a cultural phenomenon, one that operates through stereotypes and values that structure how people see themselves and are seen by others. In other words, universal citizenship and equality of opportunity do not go far enough. Egalitarianism has limited value, in both its legal and social forms, and may even be part of the problem (in that it conceals deeper structures of cultural marginalization). In this light, multiculturalists have been inclined to emphasize difference rather than equality. This is reflected in the 'politics of recognition', which involves a positive endorsement, even a celebration, of cultural difference, allowing marginalized groups to assert themselves by reclaiming an authentic sense of cultural identity.

Formal equality: Equality based on people's status in society, especially their legal and political rights (legal and political equality).

Citizenship: Membership of a state: a relationship between the individual and the state based on reciprocal rights and responsibilities.

Culture and identity

Multiculturalism's politics of recognition is shaped by a larger body of thought which holds that **culture** is basic to political and social identity. Multiculturalism, in that sense, is an example of the politics of cultural self-assertion. In this view, a pride in one's culture, and especially a public acknowledgement of one's cultural identity, gives people a sense of social and historical rootedness. In contrast, a weak or fractured sense of cultural identity can leave people feeling isolated and confused. In its extreme form, this can result in what has been called 'culturalism' – as practised by thinkers such as the French political philosopher Montesquieu (1689–1775) and J. G. Herder (see p. 135) – which portrays human beings as culturally defined creatures. In its modern form, cultural politics has been shaped by two main forces: communitarianism and identity politics (see p. 232).

Communitarianism advances a *philosophical* critique of liberal universalism – the idea that, as individuals, people in all societies and all cultures have essentially the same 'inner' identity. In contrast, communitarians champion a shift away from universalism to particularism, reflecting an emphasis less on what people share or have in common and more on what is distinctive about the groups to which they belong. Identity, in this sense, links the personal to the social, and sees the individual as 'embedded' in a particular cultural, social, institutional or ideological context.

Only groups and communities can give people a genuine sense of identity and moral purpose. During the 1980s and 1990s, a major debate raged in philosophy between liberals and communitarians. However, one of the consequences of this debate was a growing willingness among many liberal thinkers to acknowledge the importance of culture. This, in turn, made liberalism more open to the attractions of multiculturalism, helping to give rise to the tradition of **liberal multiculturalism**.

> **Culture:** Beliefs, values and practices that are passed on from one generation to the next through learning; culture is distinct from nature.
>
> **Liberal multiculturalism:** A form of multiculturalism that is committed to toleration and seeks to uphold freedom of choice in the moral sphere, especially in relation to culture or religion.
>
> **Pluralist multiculturalism:** A form of multiculturalism that is committed to 'deep' diversity, based on the alleged benefits of culture entrenchment and the need to resist cultural imperialism.

KEY CONCEPT
COMMUNITARIANISM

Communitarianism is the belief that the self or person is constituted through the community, in the sense that individuals are shaped by the communities to which they belong and thus owe them a debt of respect and consideration – there are no 'unencumbered selves'. Though clearly at odds with liberal individualism, communitarianism nevertheless has a variety of political forms. *Left-wing* communitarianism holds that community demands unrestricted freedom and social equality (for example, anarchism). *Centrist* communitarianism holds that community is grounded in an acknowledgement of reciprocal rights and responsibilities (for example, social democracy/Tory paternalism). *Right-wing* communitarianism holds that community requires respect for authority and established values (for example, neoconservatism (see p. 67)).

Identity politics is a broad term that encompasses a wide range of political trends and ideological developments, ranging from ethnocultural nationalism and religious fundamentalism to second-wave feminism and **pluralist multiculturalism**. What all forms of identity politics nevertheless have in common is that they advance a *political* critique of liberal universalism. Liberal universalism is a source of oppression, even a form of cultural imperialism, in that it tends to marginalize and demoralize subordinate groups and peoples. It does this because, behind a façade of universalism, the culture of liberal societies is constructed in line with the values and interests of its dominant groups:

PERSPECTIVES ON . . . CULTURE

LIBERALS have sometimes been critical of traditional or 'popular' culture, seeing it as a source of conformism and a violation of individuality. 'High' culture, however, especially in the arts and literature, may nevertheless be viewed as a manifestation of, and stimulus to, individual self-development. Culture is thus valued only when it promotes intellectual development.

CONSERVATIVES place a strong emphasis on culture, emphasizing its benefits in terms of strengthening social cohesion and political unity. Culture, from this perspective, is strongest when it overlaps with tradition and therefore binds one generation to the next. Conservatives support monocultural societies, believing that only a common culture can inculcate the shared values that bind society together.

SOCIALISTS, and particularly Marxists, have viewed culture as part of the ideological and political 'superstructure' that is conditioned by the economic 'base'. In this view, culture is a reflection of the interests of the ruling class, its role being primarily ideological. Culture thus helps to reconcile subordinate classes to their oppression within the capitalist class system.

FASCISTS draw a sharp distinction between rationalist culture, which is a product of the Enlightenment and is shaped by the intellect alone, and organic culture, which embodies the spirit or essence of a people, often grounded in blood. In the latter sense, culture is of profound importance in preserving a distinctive national or racial identity and in generating a unifying political will. Fascists believe in strict and untrammelled monoculturalism.

POPULISTS, especially right-wing populists, view culture as a key battleground in the conflict between the people and the elite, expressed though the notion of a 'culture war'. While the elite is bound to liberal or progressive values, the people are attached to conservative or traditionalist values, key wedge issues including gender equality, racial justice, same-sex marriage and trans rights.

FEMINISTS have often been critical of culture, believing that, in the form of patriarchal culture, it reflects male interests and values and serves to demean women, reconciling them to a system of gender oppression. Nevertheless, cultural feminists have used culture as a tool of feminism, arguing that, in strengthening distinctive female values and ways of life, it can safeguard the interests of women.

MULTICULTURALISTS view culture as the core feature of personal and social identity, giving people an orientation in the world and strengthening their sense of cultural belonging. They believe that different cultural groups can live peacefully and harmoniously within the same society because the recognition of cultural difference underpins, rather than threatens, social cohesion. However, cultural diversity must in some way, and at some level, be balanced against the need for common civic allegiances.

KEY CONCEPT
IDENTITY POLITICS

Identity politics is an orientation towards social or political theorizing, rather than a coherent body of ideas with a settled political character. It seeks to challenge and overthrow oppression by reshaping a group's identity through what amounts to a process of politico-cultural self-assertion. This reflects two core beliefs. (1) Group marginalization operates through stereotypes and values developed by dominant groups that structure how marginalized groups see themselves and are seen by others. These inculcate a sense of inferiority, even shame. (2) Subordination can be challenged by reshaping identity to give the group concerned a sense of pride and self-respect (e.g. 'black is beautiful' or 'gay pride'). Embracing or proclaiming a positive social identity is thus an act of defiance or liberation.

men, whites, the wealthy and so on. Subordinate groups and peoples are either consigned an inferior or demeaning stereotype, or they are encouraged to identify with the values and interests of dominant groups (that is, their oppressors). However, identity politics does not only view culture as a source of oppression; it is also a source of liberation and empowerment, particularly when it seeks to cultivate a 'pure' or 'authentic' sense of identity. Embracing such an identity is therefore a political act, a statement of intent, and a form of defiance. This is what gives identity politics its typically combative character and imbues it with psycho-emotional force.

Minority rights

The advance of multiculturalism has gone hand in hand with a willingness to recognize minority rights, sometimes called 'multicultural' rights. Minority rights are 'special' rights, in that they are specific to the groups to which they belong, each cultural group having different needs for recognition based on the particular character of its religion, traditions and way of life. The most systematic attempt to identify such rights was undertaken by Will Kymlicka. Kymlicka (2000) identified three kinds of minority rights:

- *Self-government* rights belong to what are classified as so-called national minorities, indigenous or tribal peoples who are territorially concentrated, possess a shared language and are characterized by a 'meaningful way of life across the full range of human activities'. Examples include Native Americans and the First Nations, Inuits and Metis peoples in Canada. In these cases, the right to self-government involves the devolution of political power, often through federalism (see p. 43), to political units that are substantially controlled by their members, although it may extend to the right of secession and, therefore, to sovereign independence.

- *Polyethnic* rights are rights that help ethnic groups and religious minorities, which have developed through immigration, to express and maintain their cultural distinctiveness. This would, for instance, provide the basis for legal exemptions, such as the exemption of Jews and Muslims from animal slaughtering laws, and the exemption of Muslim girls from school dress codes.

- Special *representation* rights attempt to redress the under-representation of minority or disadvantaged groups in education and in senior positions in political and public life. Kymlicka justified 'reverse' or **'positive' discrimination** in such cases, on the grounds that it is the only way of ensuring the full and equal participation of all groups in the life of their society, thus ensuring that public policy reflects the interests of diverse groups and peoples, and not merely those of traditionally dominant groups.

Minority rights have been justified in a variety of ways. First, they have been viewed, particularly by liberal multiculturalists, as a guarantee of individual freedom and personal autonomy. In this view, culture is a vital tool that enables people to live autonomous lives. Charles Taylor (see p. 234) thus argues that individual self-respect is intrinsically bound up with cultural membership. As people derive an important sense of who they are from their cultures, individual rights cannot but be entangled with minority rights.

Positive discrimination: Preferential treatment towards a group designed to compensate its members for past disadvantage or structural inequality.

WILL KYMLICKA (BORN 1962)

A Canadian political philosopher, Kymlicka is often seen as the leading theorist of liberal multiculturalism. In *Multicultural Citizenship* ([1995] 2000), he argued that certain 'collective rights' of minority cultures are consistent with liberal-democratic principles, but acknowledged that no single formula can be applied to all minority groups, particularly as the needs and aspirations of immigrants differ from those of indigenous peoples. For Kymlicka, cultural identity and minority rights are closely linked to personal autonomy. His other works in this area include *Multicultural Odysseys* (2007).

dpa picture alliance/Alamy Stock Photo

Second, in many cases minority rights are seen as a way of countering oppression. In this view, societies can 'harm' their citizens by trivializing or ignoring their cultural identities – harm, in this case, being viewed as a 'failure of recognition' (Taylor, 1994). Minority groups are always threatened or vulnerable because the state, despite its pretence of neutrality, is inevitably aligned with a dominant culture, whose language is used, whose history is taught, and whose cultural and religious practices are observed in public life. Of particular importance in this respect is the issue of **'offence'** and the idea of a right not to be offended. This in particular concerns religious groups which consider certain beliefs to be sacred, and are therefore especially deserving of protection. To criticize, insult or even ridicule such beliefs is thus seen as an attack on the group itself. This can be seen in relation to the phenomenon of 'cultural appropriation' (see p. 235).

CHARLES TAYLOR (BORN 1931)

A Canadian academic and political philosopher, Taylor drew on communitarian thinking to construct a theory of multiculturalism as 'the politics of recognition'. Emphasizing the twin ideas of equal dignity (rooted in an appeal to people's humanity) and equal respect (reflecting difference and the extent to which personal identity is culturally situated), Taylor's multiculturalism goes beyond classical liberalism, while also rejecting particularism and moral relativism. His most influential work in this area is *Multiculturalism and 'The Politics of Recognition'* (1994).

Brent N. Clarke/WireImage/ Getty Images

Offence: (In this sense) to feel hurt, even humiliated; an injury against one's deepest beliefs.

Affirmative action: Policies or programmes that are designed to benefit disadvantaged minority groups (or, potentially, women) by affording them special assistance.

Third, minority rights have been supported on the grounds that they redress social injustice. In this view, minority rights are a compensation for unfair disadvantages and for under-representation, usually addressed through a programme of 'positive' discrimination. This has been particularly evident in the USA, where the political advancement of African-Americans has, since the 1960s, been associated with so-called **'affirmative action'**. For example, in the case of *Regents of the University of California* v. *Bakke* (1978), the Supreme Court upheld the principle of 'reverse' discrimination in educational admissions, allowing black students to gain admission to US universities with lower qualifications than white students.

POLITICAL IDEOLOGIES IN ACTION ...

CULTURAL APPROPRIATION

EVENTS: In January 2020, the Japanese fashion brand Comme des Garçons issued a 'deep and sincere' apology after sending white models wearing cornrow wigs – a protective hairstyle strongly linked to black culture – down the catwalk at Paris Fashion Week. Claiming to have drawn inspiration from the style of an 'Egyptian prince', the fashion brand was accused of 'cultural appropriation'. In September 2019, Canada's prime minister Justin Trudeau faced a storm of criticism, almost wrecking his chances of re-election, after images emerged of him wearing black make-up when he was in his late teens and early 20s. Other alleged examples of cultural appropriation include the sporting of Native American headdresses at festivals, the singing of the slave anthem 'Swing Low, Sweet Chariot' by England rugby fans and the widespread commercialization of yoga.

TASS/Getty

SIGNIFICANCE: Cultural appropriation (or 'cultural misappropriation', to emphasize its negative character) refers to the adoption of the customs, practices or ideas of one culture by members of another and typically more dominant culture. This form of cultural borrowing is considered undesirable and offensive by various groups and individuals, including indigenous peoples and disadvantaged or minority cultures. The reason for this is that these marginalized cultures are harmed by stereotypical portrayals that demean, insult or trivialize aspects of their heritage, preserving ignorance and undermining self-esteem in the process. At the same time, more dominant cultures are encouraged to treat less dominant ones as objects of amusement or a means of satisfying their appetite for the 'exotic'. As such, cultural appropriation sustains and entrenches imbalances in power.

The concept of cultural appropriation has also been the target of criticism, however. In the first place, it fails to recognize the extent to which cultures are not separate and discrete, but fluid, multifarious and overlapping entities. Second, cultural appropriation may be a positive, not always a negative thing. Thus whereas, at one extreme, adopting blackface is now almost universally considered to be blatantly insulting, other forms of cultural borrowing may be based on admiration for, and a sincere desire to learn from, other cultures. The fact of cultural borrowing may therefore be less important than the motive behind it – that is, whether or not it is done respectfully. Third, some argue that representations of other people's culture, however insensitive or demeaning they may be, do not meaningfully constitute social harm, and so do not genuinely provide a basis for offence.

Finally, multiculturalists such as Kymlicka believe that indigenous peoples or national minorities are entitled to rights that go beyond those of groups that have formed as a result of immigration. This can be sustained on the grounds that indigenous peoples have been dispossessed and subordinated through a process of colonization and settlement. In no way did they choose to give up their culture or distinctive way of life; neither did they consent to the formation of a new state. In these circumstances, minority rights are, at least potentially, 'national' rights. In contrast, as migration involves some level of choice and voluntary action (even allowing for the possible impact of factors such as poverty and persecution), immigrant groups can be said to be under an obligation to accept the core values and governmental arrangements of their country of settlement. Migration and settlement can therefore be seen as a form of implicit consent.

However, although the movement on behalf of indigenous peoples shares much in common with anti-colonial nationalism, its political goals are typically more modest. Rather than aspiring to establish sovereign independence, indigenous peoples seek to maintain certain traditional practices while participating on their own terms in wider social, economic and political arrangements. According to James Tully, such a development would involve constitutional remodelling to both protect cultural diversity and expand the rights of indigenous peoples, especially in areas such as hunting and fishing in particular territories, land ownership on the part of the majority community, and the enforcement of traditional family law.

KEY FIGURE

JAMES TULLY (BORN 1946)

A Canadian political theorist, Tully has championed a plural form of political society that accommodates the needs and interests of indigenous peoples. He portrayed modern constitutionalism, which stresses sovereignty and uniformity, as a form of imperialism that denies indigenous modes of self-government and land appropriation. In its place, he advocated 'ancient constitutionalism', which respects diversity and pluralism, and allows traditional values and practices to be accepted as legitimate. Tully's key works in this area are *Strange Multiplicity* (1995) and *Public Philosophy in a New Key* (2008).

University of Victoria

Controversy nevertheless surrounds the rights of minority cultural groups when it comes to their implications for vulnerable group members, particularly women (Okin, 1999). This happens when minority rights and the politics of recognition serve to preserve and legitimize patriarchal and traditionalist beliefs that systematically disadvantage women, an argument that may equally be applied to those of the LGBTQ community, and is sometimes seen as the 'minorities within minorities' problem. Cultural practices such as dress codes, family structures and access to elite positions have thus been seen to establish structural gender biases. Multiculturalism may therefore be little more than a concealed attempt to bolster male power. However, contemporary liberal political philosophers have strived to resolve the 'paradox of multicultural vulnerability' by trying to take account of the need to reduce injustice between minority groups and the wider society, while, at the same time, enhancing justice within minority groups (Shachar, 2001).

Togetherness in difference

Multiculturalism has much in common with nationalism. Both emphasize the capacity of culture to generate social and political cohesion, and both seek to bring political arrangements into line with patterns of cultural differentiation. Nevertheless, whereas nationalists believe that stable and successful societies are ones in which nationality, in the sense of a shared cultural identity, coincides with citizenship, multiculturalists hold that cultural diversity is compatible with, and perhaps provides the best basis for, political cohesion. Multiculturalism is characterized by a steadfast refusal to link diversity to conflict or instability. All forms of multiculturalism are based on the assumption that unity and diversity – or 'togetherness in difference' (Young, 1995) – can, and should, be blended with one another: they are not opposing forces. In this sense, multiculturalists accept that people can have multiple identities and multiple loyalties; for instance, to their country of origin and their country of settlement. Indeed, multiculturalists argue that cultural recognition underpins political stability. People are willing and able to participate in society precisely because they have a firm and secure identity, rooted in their own culture. From this perspective, the denial of cultural recognition results in isolation and powerlessness, providing a breeding ground for extremism and the politics of hate.

Multiculturalists do not just believe that diversity is possible; they believe it is also desirable and should be celebrated. Apart from its benefits to the individual in terms of a stronger sense of cultural identity and belonging, multiculturalists believe that diversity is of value to society at large. This can be seen, in particular, in terms of the vigour and vibrancy of a society in which there are a variety of lifestyles, cultural practices, traditions and beliefs. Multiculturalism, in this sense, parallels ecologism, in drawing links between diversity and systemic health. Cultural diversity is seen to benefit society in the same way that biodiversity benefits an ecosystem. An additional advantage of diversity is that, by promoting cultural exchange between groups that live side by side with one another, it fosters cross-cultural **toleration** and understanding, and therefore a willingness to respect 'difference'. Diversity, in this sense, is the antidote to social polarization and prejudice.

Nevertheless, multiculturalism has sometimes been criticized for endorsing diversity at the *expense* of unity. This has been reflected growing interest in what is called '**interculturalism**', seen either as an alternative to multiculturalism or as an updated version of multiculturalism. Viewed as a response to how to live *in*, rather than *with*, *diversity,* interculturalism is based on three key assumptions. First it rejects the idea that cultures are fixed and unchanging, instead emphasizing that they are fluid and internally differentiated. Dialogue thus takes place within cultures as well as between them. Second, contest, debate and argument are seen to be intrinsically worthwhile, reflecting an underlying faith in reason. Third, cultures are taken to be distinguished more by what they have in common than by what divides them. However, some multiculturalists hold that interculturalism is a political and moral dead end. This is because they fear that by encouraging cultural exchange and prioritizing mutual understanding, it risks blurring the contours of group identity and creating a kind of 'pick-and-mix', melting-pot society in which individuals have but a 'shallow' sense of social and historical identity.

TYPES OF MULTICULTURALISM

All forms of multiculturalism advance a political vision that claims to reconcile cultural diversity with civic cohesion. However, multiculturalism is not a single doctrine in the sense that there is no settled or agreed view of how multicultural society should operate. Indeed, multiculturalism is another example of a cross-cutting ideology that draws on a range of other political traditions and encompasses a variety of ideological stances. Multiculturalists disagree both about how far they should go in positively endorsing cultural diversity, and about how civic cohesion can best be brought about. In short, there are competing models of multiculturalism, each offering a different view

Toleration: Forbearance; a willingness to accept views or actions with which one is in disagreement.

Interculturalism: An approach to diversity that strongly emphasizes the benefits of dialogue and interaction between cultures.

of the proper balance between diversity and unity. The three main types of multiculturalism are as follows:

- liberal multiculturalism
- pluralist multiculturalism
- cosmopolitan multiculturalism.

Liberal multiculturalism

There is a complex and, in many ways, ambivalent relationship between liberalism and multiculturalism. Some view liberalism and multiculturalism as rival political traditions, the former emphasizing individualism (see p. 24) and freedom of choice, while the latter stresses collectivism (see p. 80) and group identity. Since the 1970s, however, liberal thinkers have taken the issue of cultural diversity increasingly seriously, and have developed a form of liberal multiculturalism. This is sometimes seen to reflect a shift within liberalism, from an emphasis on universalism to a stress on pluralism (see p. 240). The cornerstone aspect of liberal multiculturalism is an unswerving commitment to toleration and a desire to uphold freedom of choice in the moral sphere, especially in relation to matters that are of central concern to particular cultural or religious traditions. This has contributed to the idea that liberalism is 'neutral' in relation to the moral, cultural and other choices that citizens make. John Rawls (see p. 39), for example, championed this belief in arguing that liberalism strives to establish conditions in which people can establish the good life as each defines it ('the right'), but it does not prescribe or try to promote any particular values or moral beliefs ('the good'). Liberalism, in this sense, is 'difference-blind': it treats factors such as culture, ethnicity, race, religion and gender as, in effect, irrelevant, because all people should be evaluated as morally autonomous individuals.

However, toleration is not morally neutral, and only provides a limited endorsement of cultural diversity. In particular, toleration extends only to views, values and social practices that are themselves tolerant; that is, ideas and actions that are compatible with personal freedom and autonomy. Liberals thus cannot accommodate **'deep' diversity**. For example, liberal multiculturalists may be unwilling to endorse practices such as female genital mutilation, forced (and possibly arranged) marriages and female dress codes, however much the groups concerned may argue that these are crucial to the maintenance of their cultural identity. The individual's rights, and particularly his or her freedom of choice, must therefore come before the rights of the cultural group in question.

The second feature of liberal multiculturalism is that it draws an important distinction between 'private' and 'public' life. It sees the former as a realm of freedom, in which people are, or should be, free to express their cultural, religious and language identity, whereas the latter must be characterized by at least a bedrock of shared civic allegiances. Citizenship is thus divorced from cultural identity, making the latter essentially a private matter. Such a stance implies that multiculturalism is compatible with civic nationalism. This can be seen in the so-called 'hyphenated nationality' that operates in the USA, through which people view themselves as African-Americans, Polish-Americans, German-Americans and so on. In this tradition, integration, rather than diversity, is emphasized in the public sphere. The USA, for instance, stresses proficiency in English and a knowledge of US political history as preconditions for gaining citizenship.

Deep diversity: Diversity that rejects the idea of objective or 'absolute' standards and so is based on moral relativism.

The third and final aspect of liberal multiculturalism is that it regards liberal democracy (see p. 44) as the sole legitimate political system. In this view, the virtue of liberal democracy is that it ensures that government is based on the consent of the people, and, in providing guarantees for personal freedom and toleration, it provides a political space for the expression of diverse views and values. This, nevertheless, does not lead to a free-for-all, in which any views and values can be expressed. Liberal democracy is its own gatekeeper: groups and political movements may be prohibited if their goals and beliefs are incompatible with key liberal-democratic principles. Groups are therefore only entitled to toleration and respect, if they, in turn, are prepared to tolerate and respect other groups.

Pluralist multiculturalism

Pluralism provides firmer foundations for a politics of difference than does liberalism. For liberals, as has been seen, diversity is endorsed but only when it is constructed within a framework of toleration and personal autonomy, amounting to a form of **'shallow' diversity.** This is the sense in which liberals 'absolutize' liberalism (Parekh, 2005). Isaiah Berlin (see p. 240) nevertheless went beyond liberal toleration in endorsing the idea of **value pluralism**. This holds, in short, that people are bound to disagree about the ultimate ends of life, as it is not possible to demonstrate the superiority of one moral system over another. As values clash, the human predicament is inevitably characterized by moral conflict. In this view, liberal or Western beliefs, such as support for personal freedom, toleration and democracy, have no greater moral authority than illiberal or non-Western beliefs. Berlin's ([1958] 1969) stance implies a form of live-and-let-live multiculturalism, or what has been called the politics of *in*difference. However, as Berlin remained a liberal to the extent that he believed that only within a society that respects individual liberty can value pluralism be contained, he failed to demonstrate how liberal and illiberal cultural beliefs can co-exist harmoniously within the same society. Nevertheless, once liberalism accepts moral pluralism, it is difficult to contain it within a liberal framework. John Gray (1995b), for instance, argued that pluralism implies a 'post-liberal' stance, in which liberal values, institutions and regimes are no longer seen to enjoy a monopoly of legitimacy (see Figure 11.2).

Shallow diversity: Diversity that is confined by the acceptance of certain values and beliefs as 'absolute' and therefore non-negotiable.

Value pluralism: The theory that there is no single, overriding conception of the 'good life', but rather a number of competing and equally legitimate conceptions.

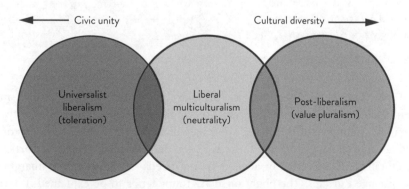

Figure 11.2   **Liberalism and cultural diversity**

An alternative basis for pluralist multiculturalism has been advanced by Bhikhu Parekh (2005). In Parekh's (see p. 241) view, cultural diversity is, at heart, a reflection of the dialectic or interplay between human nature and culture. Although human beings are natural creatures, who possess a common species-derived physical and mental structure, they are also culturally constituted in the sense that their attitudes, behaviour and ways of life are shaped by the groups to which they belong. A recognition of the complexity of human nature, and the fact that any culture expresses only part of what it means to be truly human, therefore provides the basis for a politics of recognition and thus for a viable form of multiculturalism. Such a stance goes beyond liberal multiculturalism in that it stresses that Western liberalism gives expression only to certain aspects of human nature.

KEY FIGURE

ISAIAH BERLIN (1909–97)

A Riga-born UK historian of ideas and a philosopher, Berlin developed a form of liberal pluralism that was grounded in a lifelong commitment to empiricism. Basic to Berlin's philosophical stance was the idea that conflicts of values are intrinsic to human life, a position that has influenced 'postliberal' thinking about multiculturalism. A fierce critic of totalitarianism, Berlin's best-known political work is *Four Essays on Liberty* ([1958] 1969), in which he extolled the virtues of 'negative' freedom over 'positive' freedom.

Sophie Bassouls/Sygma/
Getty Images

KEY CONCEPT

PLURALISM

Pluralism, in its broadest sense, is a belief in or commitment to diversity or multiplicity, the existence of many things. As a descriptive term, pluralism may denote the existence of party competition (*political* pluralism), a multiplicity of ethical values (*moral* or value pluralism), a variety of cultural beliefs (*cultural* pluralism) and so on. As a normative term it suggests that

diversity is healthy and desirable, usually because it safeguards individual liberty and promotes debate, argument and understanding. More narrowly, pluralism is a theory of the distribution of political power. As such, it holds that power is widely and evenly dispersed in society, not concentrated in the hands of an elite or ruling class. In this form, pluralism is usually seen as a theory of 'group politics', implying that group access to government ensures broad democratic responsiveness.

Beyond pluralist multiculturalism, a form of 'particularist' multiculturalism can be identified. Particularist multiculturalists emphasize that cultural diversity takes place within a context of unequal power, in which certain groups have customarily enjoyed advantages and privileges that have been denied to other groups. Particularist multiculturalism is very clearly aligned to the needs and interests of marginalized or disadvantaged groups. The plight of such groups tends to be explained in terms of the corrupt and corrupting nature of Western culture, values and lifestyles, which are either believed to be tainted by the inheritance of colonialism and racism (see p. 162) or associated with 'polluting' ideas such as materialism and permissiveness. In this context, an emphasis on cultural distinctiveness amounts to a form of political resistance, a refusal to succumb to repression or corruption. However, such an emphasis on cultural 'purity', which may extend to an unwillingness to engage in cultural exchange, raises concerns about the prospects for civic cohesion: diversity may be stressed at the expense of unity. Particularist multiculturalism may thus give rise to ingrained social fragmentation, as each cultural group gravitates towards an undifferentiated communal ideal, which has less and less in common with the ideals of other groups.

KEY FIGURE

BHIKHU PAREKH (BORN 1935)

An Indian political theorist, Parekh has developed an influential defence of cultural diversity from a pluralist perspective. In *Rethinking Multiculturalism* (2005), he rejected universalist liberalism on the grounds that what is reasonable and moral is embedded in and mediated by culture, which, in turn, helps people to make sense of their lives and the world around them. 'Variegated' treatment, including affirmative action, is therefore required to put ethnic, cultural or religious minorities on an equal footing with the majority community.

Roger Harris/
Wikimedia Commons

TENSIONS WITHIN ... MULTICULTURALISM ⟷

Liberal multiculturalism	v.	Pluralist multiculturalism
toleration	⟷	difference
fundamental values	⟷	value pluralism
individual rights	⟷	cultural rights
'shallow' diversity	⟷	'deep' diversity
cultural fluidity	⟷	cultural embeddedness
liberal-democratic framework	⟷	plural political forms
universalism	⟷	particularism

Cosmopolitan multiculturalism

Cosmopolitanism (see p. 139) and multiculturalism can be seen as entirely distinct, even conflicting, ideological traditions. Whereas cosmopolitanism encourages people to adopt a global consciousness which emphasizes that ethical responsibility should not be confined by national borders, multiculturalism appears to particularize moral sensibilities, focusing on the specific needs and interests of a distinctive cultural group. However, for theorists such as Jeremy Waldron (see p. 242), multiculturalism can effectively be equated with cosmopolitanism. Cosmopolitan multiculturalists endorse cultural diversity and identity politics, but they view them as essentially transitional states in a larger reconstruction of political sensibilities and priorities. This position celebrates diversity on the grounds of what each culture can learn from other cultures, and because of the prospects for personal self-development that are offered by a world of wider cultural opportunities and options. This results in what has been called a 'pick-and-mix' multiculturalism, in which interculturalism and cultural mixing are positively encouraged. People, for instance, may eat Italian food, practise yoga, enjoy African music and develop an interest in world religions.

KEY FIGURE

Chip Somodevilla/ GettyImages News/ Getty Images

JEREMY WALDRON (BORN 1953)

A New Zealand legal and political theorist, Waldron has developed a 'cosmopolitan' understanding of multiculturalism that stresses the rise of 'hybridity'. Waldron's emphasis on the fluid, multifarious and often fractured nature of the human self provided the basis for the development of cosmopolitanism as a normative philosophy that challenges both liberalism and communitarianism. It rejects the 'rigid' liberal perception of what it means to lead an autonomous life, as well as the tendency within communitarianism to confine people within a single 'authentic' culture.

Culture, from this perspective, is fluid and responsive to changing social circumstances and personal needs; it is not fixed and historically embedded, as pluralist or particularist multiculturalists would argue. A multicultural society is thus a 'melting pot' of different ideas, values and traditions, rather than a 'cultural mosaic' of separate ethnic and religious groups. In particular, the cosmopolitan stance positively embraces **hybridity**. This recognizes that, in the modern world, individual identity cannot be explained in terms of a single cultural structure, but rather exists, in Waldron's (1995) words, as a 'melange' of commitments, affiliations and roles. Indeed, for Waldron, immersion in the traditions of a particular culture is like living in Disneyland and thinking that one's surroundings epitomize what it is for a culture to exist. If we are all now, to some degree, cultural 'mongrels', multiculturalism is as much an 'inner' condition as it is a feature of modern society. The benefit of this form of multiculturalism is that it broadens moral and political sensibilities, ultimately leading to the emergence of a 'one world' perspective. However, multiculturalists from rival traditions criticize the cosmopolitan stance for stressing togetherness

Hybridity: A condition of social and cultural mixing in which people develop multiple identities.

	Liberal multiculturalism	Pluralist multiculturalism	Cosmopolitan multiculturalism
Key themes	• Communitarianism • Minority rights • Diversity strengthens toleration and personal autonomy	• Identity politics • Cultural embeddedness • Diversity counters group oppression	• Cosmopolitanism • Cultural mixing • Hybridity
Core goal	Cultural diversity within a liberal-democratic framework	'Strong' diversity, recognizing legitimacy of non-liberal and liberal values	Fluid and multiple identities provide the basis for global citizenship

Figure 11.3 Types of multiculturalism

at the expense of difference. To treat cultural identity as a matter of self-definition, and to encourage hybridity and cultural mixing, is, arguably, to weaken any genuine sense of cultural belonging.

THE FUTURE OF MULTICULTURALISM

In some respects, multiculturalism may turn out to be *the* ideology of the twenty-first century. One of the chief features of the modern world, thanks to the perhaps irresistible forces generated by globalization, is a substantial increase in geographical, and particularly cross-border, mobility. More and more societies have, as a result, accepted cultural diversity as an irresistible fact of life. Not only is the relatively homogeneous nation-state a receding memory in many parts of the world, but attempts to reconstruct it – through, for example, strict immigration controls, enforced **assimilation** or pressure to repatriate – increasingly appear to be politically fanciful. If this is the case, just as nationalism was the major ideological force in world politics during the nineteenth and twentieth centuries, helping to reshape the contours of political authority as well as the relationship between different societies, multiculturalism may be its successor. The major ideological issue for our time, and for succeeding generations, may therefore be the search for ways in which people with different moral values and from different cultural and religious traditions can find a way of living together without civil strife or violence. Multiculturalism is not only the ideology that most squarely addresses this question, but it also offers solutions, albeit tentative ones.

It is more common, nevertheless, for multiculturalism to be seen as an idea whose time has gone, not come. Once seen as a fine idea, which gave dignity to difference and provided minority voices with a political platform, some argue the price that has been paid for these benefits has been just too great. From this perspective, the central flaw of multiculturalism is that it tends always to gravitate more towards diversity than unity, favouring segregation rather than integration. For the Indian welfare economist and philosopher Amartya Sen (2006), this stems from the 'solidaristic' assumptions that underpin multiculturalism (particularly in its pluralist and particularist forms), which suggests that human identities are formed by membership of a *single* social group. This, Sen argued, not only leads to the 'miniaturization' of humanity, but also encourages people to identify only with their own monoculture and fail to recognize the rights and integrity of people from other cultural groups. Multiculturalism thus breeds a kind of '**ghettoization**'. The most strident critique of multiculturalism nevertheless stems from the conservative tradition. Conservatives object to multiculturalism on the grounds that shared values and a common culture are a necessary precondition for a stable and successful society. The basis for such a view is the belief that human beings are drawn to others who are similar to themselves. Critics of multiculturalism therefore often claim that a fear or distrust of strangers or foreigners is 'natural' and unavoidable, in which case multicultural societies are inherently flawed and conflict ridden.

Assimilation: The process through which immigrant communities lose their cultural distinctiveness by adjusting to the values, allegiances and lifestyles of the 'host' society.

Ghettoization: A process of segregating a body of people, as in a ghetto (a walled area in a mediaeval European city).

QUESTIONS FOR DISCUSSION

- How does postcolonialism provide the basis for multiculturalist thinking?
- How and why is multiculturalism linked to the politics of recognition?
- Is multiculturalism a form of communitarianism?
- What is the justification for minority or multicultural rights?
- Is multiculturalism compatible with the idea of individual rights?
- Why do multiculturalists believe that diversity provides the basis for a politically stable society?

- Why have liberals supported diversity, and when do they believe that diversity is 'excessive'?
- How does pluralism go 'beyond' liberalism?
- Are Western cultures tainted by the inheritance of colonialism and racism?
- Can multiculturalism be reconciled with any form of nationalism?
- To what extent is there tension between cultural rights and women's rights?
- What impact does multiculturalism have on the politics of redistribution?
- Could multiculturalism lead to cosmopolitanism?

FURTHER READING

Cordeiro-Rodrigues, L. & Simendic, M. *Philosophies of Multiculturalism: Beyond Liberalism* (2017). Diverse commentaries on how multiculturalism interacts with other political ideologies, particularly in non-Western contexts.

Ivison, D. *Ashgate Research Companion to Multiculturalism* (2016). A broad collection of essays from leading scholars on multiculturalism and its wider philosophical and political implications.

Murphy, M. *Multiculturalism: A Critical Introduction* (2012). An accessible general introduction to multiculturalism as a societal philosophy.

Parekh, B. *Rethinking Multiculturalism: Cultural Diversity and Political Theory*, 2nd edn (2005). A comprehensive defence of the pluralist perspective on cultural diversity that also discusses the practical problems confronting multicultural societies.

Tremblay, A. *Diversity in Decline? The Rise of the Political Right and the Fate of Multiculturalism* (2019). A timely book exploring the place of multicultural ideas in the context of increasingly right-leaning politics.

FUNDAMENTALISM

PREVIEW

The word 'fundamentalism' derives from the Latin *fundamentum*, meaning base. The term was first used in debates within American Protestantism in the early twentieth century. Between 1910 and 1915, evangelical Protestants published a series of pamphlets entitled *The Fundamentals*, upholding the inerrancy, or literal truth, of the Bible in the face of 'modern' interpretations of Christianity.

The term 'fundamentalism' is highly controversial. It is commonly associated with inflexibility, dogmatism, authoritarianism, even violence. As a result, many of those who are classified as fundamentalists reject the term as simplistic or demeaning, preferring instead to describe themselves as 'traditionalists', 'conservatives', 'evangelicals', 'revivalists' and so forth. However, unlike alternative terms, fundamentalism has the advantage of conveying the idea of a religio-political movement or project, rather than simply the assertion of the literal truth of sacred texts (although this remains a feature of certain forms of fundamentalism). Religious fundamentalism is thus characterized by a rejection of the distinction between religion and politics. Politics, in effect, *is* religion. This implies that religious principles are not restricted to personal or 'private' life, but are seen as the organizing principles of 'public' existence, including law, social conduct and the economy as well as politics. As such, fundamentalist tendencies can be identified in all the world's major religions – Christianity, Islam, Hinduism, Judaism, Buddhism and Sikhism. Nevertheless, although some forms of religious fundamentalism co-exist with pluralism (for example, Christian fundamentalism in the USA and Jewish fundamentalism in Israel), because their goals are limited and specific, other forms of religious fundamentalism are revolutionary (notably Islamic fundamentalism), in that they aim to construct a theocracy, in which the state is reconstructed on the basis of religious principles, and political position is linked to one's place within a religious hierarchy.

HISTORICAL OVERVIEW

Despite its backward-looking emphasis and evident anti-modernism, religious fundamentalism is very much a creature of the modern world. Indeed, most commentators treat it as a distinctively modern phenomenon and deny that it has historical parallels. Possible exceptions to this include the German preacher and Anabaptist, Thomas Müntzer (1489–1525), who led the Peasants' War, and the French Protestant reformer, Jean Calvin (1509–64), who founded a theocracy (see p. 247) in Geneva that allowed him to control almost all the city's affairs. Similarly, the Puritans, a loose collection of anti-episcopal Presbyterians, played a major role in initiating the English Revolution of the seventeenth century, and demonstrated their 'this-worldly' concern to establish a new political and social system by sailing to North America to found a New England. Oliver Cromwell (1599–1658), the leader of the New Model Army and a convinced Puritan, abolished the English monarchy and established, in its place, the Commonwealth, which became for a while the head and champion of Protestant Europe.

KEY CONCEPT

RELIGIOUS FUNDAMENTALISM

The word 'fundamentalism' derives from the Latin *fundamentum*, meaning 'base'. The core idea of religious fundamentalism is that religion cannot and should not be confined to the private sphere, but finds its highest and proper expression in the politics of popular mobilization and social regeneration. Although often related, religious fundamentalism should not be equated with scriptural literalism, as the 'fundamentals' are often extracted through a process of 'dynamic' interpretation by a charismatic leader. Religious fundamentalism also differs from ultraorthodoxy, in that it advances a programme for the moral and political regeneration of society in line with religious principles, as opposed to a retreat from corrupt secular society into the purity of faith-based communal living.

Subsequently, this style of fundamentalist **religion** went into decline, as, in Europe in particular, Christianity entered a period characterized by its gradual, long-term withdrawal from the public or political sphere. This was in line with the so-called **secularization thesis**. At its minimum, secularization was reflected in the decline of the prestige and power of religious teachers. It also typically involved the decline or end of, among other things, state support for religious bodies, religious teaching in national schools and legislative protection for religious doctrines. Over time, in many cases secularism came to be backed up with legal or constitutional force, a lead being taken by the First Amendment of the US Constitution, which, in guaranteeing freedom of religious worship, ensures that the state cannot encroach on religious matters. This process reached its peak in the twentieth century, most notably in communist states such as the Soviet Union and China, where systematic attempts were made to suppress religion in all its forms.

Secularization thesis: The theory that modernization is characterized by the spread of worldly or rationalist ideas and values in the place of religious or sacred ones.

Religion: A body of beliefs about some kind of, usually 'other worldly', transcendent reality; religions may be monotheistic, pantheistic or nontheistic.

Nevertheless, there has been distinct evidence of a revival of religion in the period since the late twentieth century. New, and often more assertive, forms of religiosity have emerged, and religious movements have gained a renewed potency. Moreover, in its fundamentalist guise, this religious revivalism has assumed an overtly political form. This shift in emphasis was most dramatically demonstrated by the 1979 'Islamic Revolution' in Iran, which

KEY CONCEPT
THEOCRACY

Theocracy (literally 'rule by God') is the principle that religious authority should prevail over political authority. A theocracy is therefore a regime in which government posts are filled on the basis of people's position in the religious hierarchy. Theocratic rule is illiberal in two senses. First, it violates the public/private divide, in that it takes religious rules and precepts to be the guiding principles of both personal life and political conduct. Second, it invests political authority with potentially unlimited power because, as temporal power derived from spiritual wisdom, it cannot be based on popular consent, or be properly constrained within a constitutional framework. Strict theocratic rule is therefore a form of autocracy, while limited theocratic rule may co-exist with democracy and constitutionalism (see p. 42).

brought the Ayatollah Khomeini (see p. 248) to power as the leader of the world's first Islamic state. It soon became clear, however, that the fundamentalist upsurge was not an exclusively Islamic development. Christian fundamentalists, led by political organizations such as the Moral Majority, played a prominent role in the 1980s in US politics, campaigning for changes in public policy in such areas as abortion, homosexuality and school prayers. What became, in effect, the evangelical wing of the Republican Party forged close links to the Ronald Reagan presidency (1981–89), as it did with Donald Trump's presidency (2017–21) (see p. 249). During the 1980s and 1990s, fundamentalist movements also arose within Hinduism and Sikhism in India and within Buddhism in Sri Lanka and Myanmar. Interest in fundamentalism nevertheless peaked in the aftermath of the September 11, 2001 terrorist attacks on Washington and New York, and the initiation of the so-called 'war on terror', events which were interpreted by some as marking the beginning of a global struggle between Islam and the **West**, in line with Samuel Huntington's idea of a 'clash of civilization'.

KEY CONCEPT
CLASH OF CIVILIZATIONS

The 'clash of civilizations' thesis suggests that the twenty-first-century global order will be characterized by growing tension and conflict, but that this conflict will be cultural in character, rather than ideological, political or economic. According to Huntington (1996), the rise of culture as the key factor in world politics has occurred as ideology has faded in significance in the post-Cold War world and globalization has weakened the state's ability to generate a sense of civic belonging. Civilizations inevitably 'clash' because they are based on incommensurate values and meanings, with tension between China and the USA and between Islam and the West being particularly likely. The thesis may nevertheless underestimate both the complex and fluid nature of civilizations and their capacity for peaceful co-existence.

CORE THEMES

Fundamentalism is an untypical political ideology. Not only does it, in its religious guise, draw inspiration from sacred, spiritual or 'other-worldly' matters, but it also cuts across a variety of, or perhaps all, religions, regardless of their doctrinal and structural differences. To study religious fundamentalism as a single, coherent entity is to treat as secondary the substantial differences that divide the religions of the world – whether they believe in a single god, many small gods or no god at all; whether they have a holy book, a variety of scriptures or place faith in an oral tradition; how they view morality and social conduct, and so on. Moreover, while some fundamentalisms have been associated with violence and anti-constitutional political action, others have supported law-abiding and peaceful behaviour.

West: The parts of the world that are distinguished *culturally* by common Greco-Roman and Christian roots, *socially* by the dominance of industrial capitalism, and *politically* by the prevalence of liberal democracy.

Such differences draw attention to the fact that religious fundamentalism is essentially a *style* of political thought rather than a substantive collection of political ideas and values. To the extent that religious fundamentalism's central or core themes can be identified, they follow from its tendency to recognize certain principles as essential or unchallengeable 'truths', regardless of their content. This, in turn, implies that religion has a profoundly 'this-worldly' orientation; indeed, that it is the very stuff of politics itself. As a programme for the comprehensive restructuring of society on religious lines and according to religious principles, fundamentalism deserves to be classified as an ideology in its own right. Nevertheless, it is difficult to deny that in certain cases religious fundamentalism constitutes a form of ethnic nationalism (as discussed in Chapter 6). However, at least in its more radical forms, religious fundamentalism goes well beyond the reassertion of national or ethnic distinctiveness, and in the case of Islam in particular it has a marked transnational dimension. The characteristic themes of religious fundamentalism are:

- religion as politics
- essential truths
- anti-modernism
- militancy.

Religion as politics

The core theme of fundamentalism is a rejection of the distinction between religion and politics. In effect, in Ayatollah Khomeini's words, 'Politics is religion.' Religion may be the basis of politics, but what is religion? In its most general sense a religion is an organized community of people bound together by a shared body of beliefs concerning some kind of transcendent reality, usually expressed in a set of approved activities and practices. What 'transcendent' means here is difficult to define, for it may refer to anything from a supreme being, a creator God, to the experience of personal liberation, as in the Buddhist concept of nirvana, the 'extinction' of the personal self.

KEY FIGURE

AYATOLLAH KHOMEINI (1900–89)

An Iranian cleric and political leader, Khomeini was the architect of the 'Islamic Revolution' and leader of Iran (1979–89). Khomeini's world-view was rooted in a clear division between the oppressed (understood largely as the poor and excluded of the developing world) and the oppressors (seen as the twin Satans: the USA and the Soviet Union, capitalism and communism). In Khomeini's Shia fundamentalism, Islam was a theo-political project aimed at regenerating the Islamic world by ridding it of occupation and corruption from outside.

ullstein bild/Getty Images

The impact of religion on political life has been restricted progressively by the spread of liberal culture and ideas, a process that has been particularly prominent in the West. Nevertheless, liberal secularism is by no means an *anti*-religious tendency. Rather, it is concerned to establish a 'proper' sphere and role for religion. A key feature of liberal culture is the maintenance of a public/private divide, a strict separation between a 'public' sphere of life regulated by collective rules and subject to political authority, and a 'private' sphere in which people are free to do as they like. The great virtue of this distinction, from a liberal perspective, is that it guarantees individual liberty by constraining government's ability to interfere in personal or private affairs. However, it also has important implications for religion, which is fenced into a private arena, leaving public life to be organized on a strictly secular basis. In bringing about the 'privatization of religion', secularism has extended the public/private divide into a distinction between politics and religion.

POLITICAL IDEOLOGIES IN ACTION . . .

DONALD TRUMP AND THE CHRISTIAN RIGHT

EVENT: On 25 May 2020, George Floyd, an unarmed black man, was killed by the police in the US city of Minneapolis, sparking a wave of protests and civil unrest across the country and beyond. Seven days later, President Donald Trump issued his symbolic response to these developments. Having delivered a speech on law and order, Trump marched from the White House to Lafayette Park (from which peaceful demonstrators had just been cleared with teargas and rubber bullets) and stood outside St John's Episcopal Church, which had been damaged in unrest the previous night. Silently, he then held up a copy of the Bible, posing for the cameras for a full eight minutes.

Brendan Smialowski/Getty

one, only to be told that the Bible is full of stories about people who appear to be imperfect vessels for carrying out God's will.

SIGNIFICANCE: This incident underlined President Trump's desire to shore up support among evangelical Christians, with whom he had forged a powerful ideological alliance. Trump had been hailed by leaders of the new Christian right in the USA as God's appointed on Earth. Some even interpreted his election in 2016 as evidence of the Rapture, an 'end of days' event, in which Christ would return to Earth and escort qualified believers into heaven. Trump, for his part, made a commitment to a conservative religious agenda a key qualification for political appointment. His cabinet was, for example, stacked with devout Christians, among them Mike Pompeo, the secretary of state, and Vice-President Mike Pence. Many, nevertheless, pointed out that the alliance between Trump – a thrice-married man, often accused of misogynistic behaviour towards women and not a regular church goer – and the evangelical Christian movement was an unlikely

And yet, the relationship between Donald Trump and the evangelical movement may be better explained in transactional terms than ideological ones. For Trump, the endorsement of evangelical Christian leaders was what made his bid for the White House electorally viable. Close to one-quarter of the US electorate describe themselves as 'born again' Christians, and turnout levels among such voters are typically high. The 81 per cent of white evangelical votes that went to Trump in 2016 was therefore probably decisive in ensuring his victory over Hillary Clinton. Trump, in turn, repaid the loyalty of evangelical Christians by providing robust support for their favoured conservative moral agenda, in which opposition to abortion, same-sex marriage and transgender rights featured prominently. Trump delivered on these issues largely by consistently making conservative, or 'anti-choice', appointments to the Supreme Court and the federal judiciary.

Much of the spirit of religious fundamentalism is captured in its rejection of the public/private divide. On one level, fundamentalism is a manifestation of identity politics (see p. 232). The expansion of a public realm, organized on a secular and rationalistic basis, has gradually weakened traditional social norms, textures and values and has left many bereft of identity, or, as Eric Hobsbawm (1994) put it, as 'orphans' in the modern world. The intensity and zeal that typically characterizes fundamentalism establishes religion as the primary collective identity, giving its members and supporters a rootedness and sense of belonging that they would otherwise lack. On a deeper level, religious fundamentalism's refusal to accept that religion is merely a private or personal matter invests it with a radical political character and ideological potency. To treat religion *only* as a personal or private issue is to invite evil and corruption to stalk the public domain, hence the spread of permissiveness, materialism, corruption, greed, crime and immorality. The fundamentalist solution is simple: the world must be made anew, and existing structures must be replaced with a comprehensive system founded on religious principles and embracing law, politics, society, culture and the economy.

PERSPECTIVES ON . . . RELIGION

LIBERALS see religion as a distinct 'private' matter linked to individual choice and personal development. Religious freedom is thus essential to civil liberty and can only be guaranteed by a strict division between religion and politics, and between church and state.

CONSERVATIVES regard religion as a valuable (perhaps essential) source of stability and social cohesion. As it provides society with a set of shared values and the bedrock of a common culture, overlaps between religion and politics, and church and state, are inevitable and desirable.

SOCIALISTS have usually portrayed religion in negative terms, as at best a diversion from the political struggle and at worst a form of ruling-class ideology (leading in some cases to the adoption of state atheism). In emphasizing love and compassion, religion may nevertheless provide socialism with an ethical basis.

ANARCHISTS generally regard religion as an institutionalized source of oppression. Church and state are invariably linked, with religion preaching obedience and submission to earthly rulers while also prescribing a set of authoritative values that rob the individual of moral autonomy.

FASCISTS have sometimes rejected religion on the grounds that it serves as a rival source of allegiance or belief, and that it preaches 'decadent' values such as compassion and human sympathy. Fascism nevertheless seeks to function as a 'political religion', embracing its terminology and internal structure – devotion, sacrifice, spirit, redemption and so on.

FEMINISTS have tended to view nearly all religious traditions as patriarchal at root, one of their key purposes being that they serve to control women; they do this by legitimizing often starkly unequal gender roles, typically through the promotion of 'family values'.

FUNDAMENTALISTS view religion as a body of 'essential' and unchallengeable principles, which dictate not only personal conduct but also the organization of social, economic and political life. Religion cannot and should not be confined to the 'private' sphere, but finds its highest and proper expression in the politics of popular mobilization and social regeneration.

However, the perceived corruption of the secular public realm may give rise to one of two responses. The first, sometimes called 'passive' fundamentalism, takes the route of withdrawal and attempts to construct communities of believers untainted by the larger society. Groups such as the Amish in the USA and the Haredim, the ultra-**orthodox** Jews of Israel, undoubtedly believe that religion dictates social, economic and political principles, but they are generally more concerned with their own observation of these principles than with the comprehensive regeneration of society. The second response is 'active' fundamentalism, which takes the route of opposition and combat, and which alone should be considered an ideology, on the grounds that only it adopts an overtly political stance. However, the notion of politics it embraces is a distinctly conventional one. In marked contrast to feminists, who have also challenged the public/private divide, religious fundamentalists view politics in terms of government policy and state action. Far from regarding politics as inherently corrupt, they usually look to seize, or at least exert influence over, the modern state, seeing it as an instrument of moral regeneration. Critics of fundamentalism nevertheless argue that it is precisely this determination to remove the distinction between religion and politics that invests in fundamentalism a tendency towards totalitarianism (see p. 159). A state founded on religious principles is, almost by definition, unencumbered by constraints that arise out of the public/private divide. However, the degree to which particular fundamentalisms have succumbed to this totalitarian impulse varies greatly.

Essential truths

Fundamentalism is a style of thought in which certain principles are recognized as essential 'truths' that have unchallengeable and overriding authority, regardless of their content. Substantive fundamentalisms therefore have little or nothing in common, except that their supporters tend to evince an earnestness or fervour born out of doctrinal certainty. Fundamentalism can therefore be seen as the opposite of **relativism**. By this standard, certain political ideologies, notably fascism and communism, can be placed nearer the fundamentalist end of the fundamentalism–relativism spectrum, while liberalism in particular, disposed as it is towards scepticism by its commitment to reason and toleration, can be placed near the relativist end (see Figure 12.1). All ideologies, however, contain elements of fundamentalism. In the sense that fundamentalism implies keeping faith with original or 'classical' ideas, it is also possible to classify some traditions within an ideology as fundamentalist and others not. In this respect, fundamentalism is the opposite of revisionism. Classical Marxism, which aimed to abolish and replace capitalism, has thus been seen as a form of fundamentalist socialism, while social democracy is portrayed as revisionist socialism by virtue of having modified its opposition to private property, the market, material incentives and so on.

In the case of religious fundamentalism, the 'fundamentals' have usually, but not always, been derived from the content of sacred texts, supported by the assertion of their literal truth. Indeed, **scriptural literalism** was

Orthodoxy: Strict adherence to an established or traditional view, usually enjoying 'official' sanction or support.

Relativism: A belief that moral or factual statements can only be judged in relation to their contexts, because there are no objective or 'absolute' standards.

Scriptural literalism: A belief in the literal truth of sacred texts, which, as the revealed word of God, have unquestionable authority.

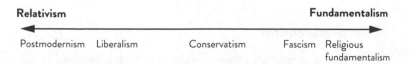

Figure 12.1   Relativism–fundamentalism spectrum

a central feature of American Protestant fundamentalism, which, for example, has continued to preach creationism or 'creation science', the belief that humankind was created by God, as described in the Book of Genesis, and the outright rejection of the Darwinian theory of evolution. Such tendencies can be found in all three 'religions of the book' – Christianity, Islam and Judaism – each of which possesses sacred texts that have been claimed to express the revealed word of God. Nevertheless, though often related, religious fundamentalism should not be equated with scriptural literalism. In the first place, all sacred texts contain a complex and diverse range of ideas, doctrines and principles. To treat a sacred text as a political ideology, as a moral and political programme for the regeneration of society and the mobilization of the masses, it is necessary to extract its 'fundamentals'. These are a set of simple and clean principles that provide an exact and unambiguous definition of religious identity. In John Garvey's (1993) words, fundamentalism constitutes 'a kind of stripped-down religion that travels light and fast'.

Second, in contrast with the ultra-orthodox, whose principal goal is to 'live by the book', fundamentalists have supported an 'activist' reading of texts that enables them to reduce the complexity and profundity of scripture to a **theo-political** project. In Islam, this is described as 'dynamic interpretation'. Selectivity and interpretation, however, create the problem of how one version of a scripture or doctrine can be upheld over other versions. Fundamentalists have usually resolved this problem by reflecting on *who* is doing the interpreting. In this respect, clerical position and religious office may be of secondary importance; more significantly, the 'true' interpreter must be a person (invariably male) of deep faith and moral purity, as well as an activist whose spiritual insight has been deepened through the experience of struggle. This is why religious fundamentalism is invariably associated with charismatic leadership, which gives it, critics argue, an implicitly authoritarian character.

The great strength of fundamentalism, as demonstrated by the proliferation of fundamentalist movements since the late twentieth century, is its capacity to generate political activism and mobilize the faithful. Fundamentalism thus operates on both psychological and social levels. Psychologically, its appeal is based on its capacity to offer certainty in an uncertain world. Being religious, it addresses some of the deepest and most perplexing problems confronting humankind; being fundamentalist, it provides solutions that are straightforward, practical and, above all, absolute. Socially, while its appeal has extended to the educated and professional classes, religious fundamentalism has been particularly successful in addressing the aspirations of those who feel economically and politically marginalized. Together with offering a secure identity and the prospect of social order, in the developing world in particular, it has displaced socialism as the creed of political renewal and social justice. However, among the limitations of fundamentalism is the fact that its simplicity and stripped-down character prevent it from dealing with complex problems or developing comprehensive solutions. In that sense, parallels can be drawn between religious fundamentalism and populism.

Anti-modernism

Theo-political: A mode of politics in which God or a deity is deemed to be the civil ruler.

The most prominent image of religious fundamentalism is that it turns its back dramatically on the modern world. Modernization appears to be equated with decline and decay, typified by the spread of godless secularism, and regeneration can only be brought about by returning to the spirit and traditions of some long-past 'golden age'. Unfortunately, however, this image is simplistic, and in certain respects misleading. Religious fundamentalism is selectively traditional but also selectively modern; a mixture of resentment and envy characterizes its relationship to modernity. One face of fundamentalism is undoubtedly its strident anti-modernism. Its traditionalism is evident in what amounts to a form of moral conservatism. Western societies, having succumbed to the cult of the individual and a passion for personal gratification, are seen as amoral at best and thoroughly degenerate at worst. Permissiveness, adultery, prostitution, homosexuality and pornography are only some of the symptoms of this moral pollution. Nothing less than a moral gulf divides liberal individualism (see p. 24) from religious fundamentalism: the former encourages people to make their own moral choices, while the latter demands that they conform to a prescribed and divinely ordained moral system. Islamic fundamentalists therefore call for the reintroduction of ancient **Sharia** law, and Christian fundamentalists attempt to combat the spread of permissiveness and materialism by a return to 'family' or 'religious' values.

Fundamentalism should not be mistaken for conservatism or traditionalism, however. Despite overlaps between conservatism and fundamentalism and the ease with which they have sometimes constructed alliances, notably in the USA through organizations such as the Moral Majority and within the Republican Party, the two differ in terms of both temper and aspirations. Conservatism is modest and cautious, where fundamentalism is strident and passionate; conservatism is disposed to protect elites and defend hierarchy, while fundamentalism embodies populist and egalitarian inclinations; conservatism favours continuity and tradition, while fundamentalism is radical and may be revolutionary. Fundamentalism has little in common with traditionalism, in that it favours 'novel' interpretations of religious teachings and calls for comprehensive social regeneration. There is a closer affinity between fundamentalism and the reactionary radicalism of the new right. Nevertheless, fundamentalism is more clearly reactive than reactionary: behind the rhetoric of moral traditionalism, it is perhaps orientated more towards a purified future than an idealized past. The tendency within fundamentalism towards populism, charismatic leadership and psycho-social regeneration has also led some to suggest parallels with fascism. However, this risks ignoring the degree to which fundamentalism may be animated by genuinely religious passions.

The clearest evidence that fundamentalists are not just dyed-in-the-wool reactionaries is found in their enthusiasm for particular aspects of modernity. For instance, fundamentalists across the globe have shrewdly exploited the advantages of modern techniques of mass communication, not least in the case of the 'televangelists' of the USA, and more recently through the use of social media. This contrasts markedly with revivalist and ultra-orthodox movements that have turned their backs on the 'unredeemed' world. Nevertheless, the fundamentalist accommodation with modernity is not merely a cynical or tactical exercise. The willingness to use the Internet and other new media, the machinery of the modern state and even to accept nuclear weapons suggests sympathy for the spirit of modernity, and respect for 'this-worldly' rationalism rather than a descent into 'other-worldly' mysticism. Early interest in Iran, for instance, in the idea of 'Islamic science' quickly gave way to an acceptance of conventional, and therefore Western, science. Similarly, the search for 'Islamic economics' soon developed into the application of market principles derived from economic liberalism. Finally, it is significant that fundamentalists

Sharia: (Arabic) Literally, the 'way' or 'path'; divine Islamic law, based on principles expressed in the Koran.

advance an essentially modernist view of religion, relying more heavily on 'dynamic' interpretation than on faith in inherited structures and traditions. As Parekh (1994) put it, fundamentalism 'reconstitutes religion within the limits of modernity, even as it copes with modernity within the limits of religion'.

Militancy

While religious fundamentalists have embraced a conventional, state-centred view of politics, they have pursued a highly distinctive style of political activity: one that is vigorous, militant and sometimes violent. Fundamentalists are usually happy to see themselves as militants, in the sense that **militancy** implies passionate and robust commitment. Fundamentalist militancy derives from a variety of sources. In the first place, there is a tendency for conflicts involving religion to be intense, because religion deals with core values and beliefs. Those who act in the name of religion are often inspired by what they believe to be a divinely ordained purpose, which clearly takes precedence over all other considerations. This perhaps helps to explain why religious wars have been so common throughout history.

A second factor is that fundamentalism in particular is a form of identity politics: it serves to define who a people are and gives them a collective identity. All forms of politics of identity, whether based on social, national, ethnic or religious distinctiveness, tend to be based on divisions between 'them' and 'us', between an 'out-group' and an 'in-group'. Certainly, religious fundamentalism has been associated with the existence of a hostile and threatening 'other', which serves both to create a heightened sense of collective identity and to strengthen its oppositional and combative character. This demonized 'other' may take various guises, from secularism and permissiveness to rival religions, Westernization, the USA, Marxism and imperialism. A third and related factor is that fundamentalists generally embrace a Manichaean world-view, one that emphasizes conflict between light and darkness, or good and evil. If 'we' are a chosen people acting according to the will of God, 'they' are not merely people with whom we disagree, but a body actively subverting God's purpose on Earth. They, in short, represent nothing less than the 'forces of darkness'. Political conflict, for fundamentalists, is therefore a battle or war, and ultimately either the believers or the infidels must prevail.

One of the consequences of this militancy is a willingness to engage in extra-legal, anti-constitutional political action. Nevertheless, although God's law outranks human law, fundamentalists do not necessarily disregard the latter, as the new Christian right's firm support for law and order demonstrates. The most controversial issue, however, is the fundamentalist use of violence. While the popular image of fundamentalists as suicide bombers and terrorists is unbalanced and misleading, as it ignores the fact that fundamentalist protest is overwhelmingly peaceful and usually legal, it is impossible to deny a link with **terrorism** and violence. Examples of this include the assassinations of the Egyptian president, Anwar Sadat, by Islamic fundamentalists in 1981, the Indian prime minister, Indira Gandhi, by militant Sikhs in 1984, and the Israeli prime minister, Yitzak Rabin, by a Jewish fanatic in 1995; as well as the Sri Lankan Civil War (1983–2009) against the Liberation Tigers of Tamil Elam and the forcible displacement of Rohingya Muslims in Myanmar since 2012, both fuelled by Buddhist nationalism.

Militancy: Heightened or extreme commitment; a level of zeal and passion typically associated with struggle or war.

Terrorism: The use of terror for furthering political ends; terrorism seeks to create a climate of fear and apprehension.

The most common fundamentalist justification for such acts is that, as they are intended to eradicate evil, they fulfil the will of God. Islamic suicide bombers, for example, believe that in sacrificing their lives in the cause of Allah they will immediately be dispatched to heaven. The incidence of violence among fundamentalist groups is almost certainly increased by a link between fundamentalist belief and **millenarianism**. Other ideologies that have endorsed violence and the use of terror, such as fascism and sometimes anarchism, have been viewed as forms of political millenarianism. However, religion adds an extra dimension to this, in that it creates the heightened expectations and revolutionary fervour of **apocalypticism**.

TYPES OF FUNDAMENTALISM

Fundamentalism comes in a number of forms. These include the following:

- Islamism
- Christian fundamentalism
- other fundamentalisms.

Islamism

Islam and Protestant Christianity have been the most likely religious traditions to throw up fundamentalist or fundamentalist-type movements. This is because both are primarily based on a single sacred text and hold that believers have direct access to spiritual wisdom, rather than this being concentrated in the hands of accredited representatives (Parekh, 1994). In addition, both provide a means of achieving comprehensive political renewal, making them particularly attractive to marginalized or oppressed peoples. In the case of Islam, it is not merely a religion but a total and complete way of life. It provides guidance in every sphere of human existence – individual and social, material and moral, legal and cultural, economic and political, national and international. In Islam, then, politics and religion are two sides of the same coin. However, the notion of a fusion between Islam and politics has assumed a more radical and intense character due to the rise, since the early twentieth century, of Islamism. As far as the notion of fundamentalism in Islam is concerned, this does not mean a belief in the literal truth of the Koran, for this is rarely questioned within Islam, even though differences of interpretation do exist. Instead, fundamentalism (if the term is used at all within Islam) means an intense and militant faith in Islamic beliefs as the overriding principles of social life and politics, as well as of personal morality.

Millenarianism: A belief in a thousand year period of divine rule; political millenarianism offers the prospect of a sudden and complete emancipation from misery and oppression.

Apocalypticism: A belief in the imminent end of the world (as we know it), often associated with the return of a supreme or god-like figure, denoting final salvation and purification.

KEY CONCEPT
ISLAMISM

Islamism (also called 'political Islam', radical Islam' or 'activist Islam') is a politico-religious ideology, as opposed to a simple belief in Islam. Although Islamist ideology has no single creed or political manifestation, certain common beliefs can be identified. These include: (1) that society should be reconstructed in line with the religious principles and ideals of Islam; (2) that the modern secular state should be replaced by an 'Islamic state', in which religious principles and authority have primacy over political principles and authority; and (3) that the West and Western values are corrupt and corrupting, justifying, for some, the notion of a *jihad* against them. However, distinctive Sunni and Shia versions of Islamism have developed, the former linked to Wahhabism, and the latter to Iran's 'Islamic Revolution'.

Modern Islamism emerged in the context of the collapse and carve-up of the once-powerful Ottoman empire in the aftermath of World War I. As the Middle East fell into stagnation, new ways of thinking about both Islam and politics spread. The Muslim Brotherhood was founded in 1928 in Ismailia, Egypt, by Hassan al Banna (1906–49). The world's most enduringly influential Islamist movement, the Brotherhood pioneered a model of political, and sometimes militant, activism combined with Islamic charitable works that has subsequently been embraced across the Muslim world. However, Islamism only emerged as a powerful political force during the post-World War II period, and especially from the 1980s onwards. The war in Afghanistan against the Soviet Union, during 1979–89, led to the growth of the Mujahideen, a loose collection of religiously inspired resistance groups, out of which developed a collection of new *jihadi* organizations, the most important of which was al-Qaeda, founded in 1988. The 2003 US-led invasion of Iraq fomented bitter sectarian rivalry between Sunni and Shia (or Shi'ite) Muslims, which both spread across the region and contributed to the emergence of the Islamic State of Iraq and al-Sham, or ISIS (also called Islamic State, or IS), whose influence expanded due to the protracted Syrian civil war.

Islamism is perhaps characterized most of all by a strident rejection of the West. This applies because Islamism developed not through isolation from the West but through encounters with the West, and these encounters invariably had a bruising character. The revolt against the West was expressed by figures such as Sayyib Qutb. Qutb, who was radicalized during a two-year study visit to the USA, 1948–50, expressed a profound distaste for the materialism, immorality and sexual licentiousness he claimed to have encountered there. Qutb's world-view highlighted the barbarism and corruption that Westernization had inflicted on the world, with a return to strict Islamic practice in all aspects of life offering the only possibility of salvation. He argued that Islam was confronted with two possible relations with the rest of the world: 'peace with a contractual agreement, or war'. This Islamist conception of a global civilizational struggle between Islam and the non-Islamic world (not just the West) was later taken up by groups such as al-Qaeda and ISIS, especially once, during the 1990s, the object of Islamist hostility shifted from the 'near enemy' ('un-Islamic' or **apostate** leaders or regimes) and came to encompass the 'far enemy' (the USA and the West in general).

Islamism is centrally concerned with the issue of political order and the construction of an 'Islamic state'. Although the Islamic state is often

Jihad: (*Arabic*) An Islamic term literally meaning 'struggle'; includes the struggle against one's own soul and external, physical effort or even 'holy war'.

Apostasy: The abandonment of one's religious faith, sometimes applied to cause, a set of principles or a political faction.

Caliphate: A system of government by which, under the original custom of Islam, the faithful were ruled by a caliph who stood in the Prophet's stead.

KEY FIGURE

Historic Collection/Alamy Stock Photo

SAYYID QUTB (1906–66)

An Egyptian writer and religious leader, Qutb is sometimes seen as the 'father' of modern political Islam. A leading member of the Muslim Brotherhood, Qutb recoiled from what he saw as the moral and sexual corruption of the West, but, influenced by Maududi, highlighted the condition of *jihiliyyah* ('ignorance of divine guidance') into which the Muslim world had fallen. In the face of this, Qutb advocated Islam as a comprehensive political and social system that would both ensure social justice and sweep away corruption, oppression and luxury.

portrayed as a restoration of the **caliphate**, significant differences exist between traditional forms of Islamic administration and the Islamic state as conceived by modern Islamists. As the caliphs possessed Mohammed's authority, but not his direct access to divine revelation, they were inclined to consult with and consider the views of the scholars, seen as the guardians of the law. Over time, however, the Islamic state came increasingly to be defined by the predominance given to the enforcement of the *Sharia*, so much so that the Islamic state has come, in effect, to be a *Sharia* state.

The most controversial aspect of Islamism is nevertheless its association with militancy and violence. Although the vast majority of Islamist parties and groups are engaged in democratic or at least electoral politics, and many of those who subscribe to Islamist beliefs, even their radical guides, eschew violence in principle, militant Islamism is a prominent tendency within the larger Islamist movement. The chief doctrinal basis of Islamist militancy lies in the doctrine of *jihad*. *Jihad* literally means to 'struggle' or 'strive'; it is used to refer to the religious duty of Muslims. However, the term is used in at least two contrasting ways. In the form of the 'greater' *jihad*, struggle is understood as an inner or spiritual quest to overcome one's own sinful nature. In the form of the 'lesser' *jihad*, it is understood more as an outer or physical struggle against the enemies of Islam. This is the sense in which *jihad* is translated (often unhelpfully) as 'holy war', sometimes seen as *'jihad* by the sword'.

Salafism

Salafism is the main form of Islamism that has emerged out of the majority Sunni sect within Islam. It is closely related to Wahhabism, the official version of Islam in Saudi Arabia, the world's first fundamentalist Islamic state. Wahhabism advocates a return to the Islam of the first-generation and opposes everything that has been added since. Among other things, Wahhabis ban pictures, photographs, musical instruments, singing, videos and television, celebrations of Mohammed's birthday and the cult of Mohammed as the perfect man. Salafism developed as a school of Islamic thought in the second half of the nineteenth century, largely in reaction to the spread of European ideas and influences. Its chief focus was to expose the roots of modernity within Western civilization, with a view to eradicating them. However, whereas Wahhabism continued to represent staunch conservatism, Salafism was drawn in an increasingly activist and revolutionary direction. The *jihadi* groups that emerged out of, or drew inspiration from, the Afghan war in the 1980s transformed Salafism into an ideology of anti-Western struggle, giving rise to 'jihadist Salafism', or 'Salafi-jihadism'. The most influential militant Salafi groups have been al-Qaeda, ISIS and the Taliban in Afghanistan. However, only after the outbreak of the Arab Spring in 2011 did openly Salafi parties and groups enter the political arena, usually offering a radical alternative to Muslim Brotherhood-linked groups in North Africa and elsewhere.

Shia Islamism

Shia Islamism stems from the distinctive temper and doctrinal character of the Shia sect in contrast to the Sunni sect. Sunnis have tended to see Islamic history as a gradual movement away from the ideal community, which existed during the life of Mohammed and his four immediate successors. Shias, though, believe that divine guidance is about to re-emerge into the world with the return of the 'hidden imam', or the arrival of the mahdi, a leader directly guided by God. They see history moving towards the goal of an ideal community, not away from it. Such ideas of revival or imminent salvation have given the Shia sect a messianic and emotional quality that is not enjoyed by the traditionally more sober Sunnis. Shia Islam has also traditionally been more political than Sunni Islam. It has proved especially attractive to the poor and the downtrodden, for whom the re-emergence of divine wisdom into the world has represented the purification of society, the overthrow of injustice and liberation from oppression. The politico-religious propensities of Shia Islam were particularly clearly illustrated by the popular demonstrations that in Iran precipitated the overthrow of the Shah and prepared the way for the creation of an Islamic Republic under Ayatollah Khomeini.

The Iranian's system of government is a complex mix of theocracy and democracy. The Supreme Leader (currently Ali Khamenei) presides over a system of institutionalized clerical rule that operates through the Islamic Revolutionary Council, a body of 15 senior clerics. Although a popular elected president (currently Hassan Rouhani, a pragmatic conservative) and parliament have been established, all legislation is ratified by the Council for the Protection of the Constitution, which ensures conformity to Islamic principles. *Sharia* law continues to be strictly enforced throughout Iran as both a legal and moral code. Iran is engaged in a regional power struggle with Saudi Arabia, which increasingly threatens to divide the Middle East on Sunni/Shia lines, its standing being bolstered by its association with groups such as Hamas and Hezbollah, and its influence over Iraq, Syria and Yemen.

Moderate or conservative Islamism

Not all forms of Islamism are militant and revolutionary, however. Although much confusion surrounds the idea of 'moderate' (as opposed to 'radical') Islamism, there is a school of Islamist thought that is distinguished by the attempt to reconcile political Islam with democratic elections and party pluralism. The issue of democracy has been particularly problematic in this respect, since it appears to place popular sovereignty ahead of the will of God, a possibility that has encouraged most democratic Islamists to insist those core Islamic principles are entrenched in constitutional law. Political developments in modern Turkey provide a particularly telling example of the relationship between Islamism and democracy in the sphere of practical politics. This is because tensions have existed between the military, committed to the strict secular principles on which the state of Turkey was established, and a growing Islamist movement. The Justice and Development Party (AKP), which has been in power since 2003, attempts to balance a moderate conservative politics based on Islamic values with an acceptance of Turkey's secular democratic framework. Critics have nevertheless warned the AKP plans to overturn the secular nature of the Turkish state, possibly establishing any Iranian-style Islamic republic through a process of 'Islamification'. In 2016, deepening tension between elements in the military and the AKP government headed by President Tayyip Erdogan resulted in a failed coup. In the aftermath of the coup, over 4,000 institutions were shut down and tens of thousands of public servants were removed, as the Erdogan government solidified its control over the police, the military, the judiciary, the media and the education system.

Christian fundamentalism

Although all Christians acknowledge the authority of the Bible, three main divisions have emerged: the Catholic, Orthodox and Protestant churches. Roman Catholicism is based on the temporal and spiritual leadership of the pope in Rome, seen as unchallengeable since the promulgation of the doctrine of **papal infallibility** in 1871. Eastern Orthodox

Christianity emerged from the split with Rome in 1054 and developed into a number of autonomous churches, the Russian Orthodox Church and the Greek Orthodox Church being the most significant. Protestantism embraces a variety of movements that, during the Reformation of the sixteenth century, rejected Rome's authority and established reformed national versions of Christianity. Although there are many doctrinal divisions among Protestants, Protestantism tends to be characterized by the belief that the Bible is the sole source of truth and the idea that it is possible for people to have a direct, personal relationship with God.

Since the Reformation, the political significance of Christianity has declined markedly. The advance of liberal constitutionalism (see p. 42) was in part reflected in the separation of church and state, and in the thoroughgoing secularization of political life. Christianity, at least in the developed West, adjusted to these circumstances by becoming increasingly a personal religion, geared more to the spiritual salvation of the individual than to the moral and political regeneration of society. This, in turn, has helped to shape the character of Christian fundamentalism since the late twentieth century. Confronted by stable social, economic and political structures, rooted in secular values and goals, fundamentalists have been content to work mainly within a pluralist and constitutional framework. Rather than seeking to establish a theocracy, they have usually campaigned around single issues, or concentrated their attention on moral crusading.

One of the causes that Christian fundamentalism has helped to articulate is ethnic nationalism. This has been evident in Northern Ireland, where an upsurge in evangelical Protestantism was one of the consequences of 'The Troubles', the period of low-level warfare that broke out in the late 1960s and is usually deemed to have ended with the Good Friday Agreement of 1998. Largely expressed through the Free Presbyterian Church, set up in 1951 by the Northern Irish loyalist politician and Protestant religious leader Ian Paisley Sr (1926–2014), and organized politically by the Democratic Unionist Party (DUP), Ulster fundamentalism equates the idea of a united Ireland with the victory of Catholicism and Rome. Although Paisley himself never actively promoted violence, he warned that, should reunification go ahead, it would lead to armed resistance by the Protestant community. By appealing to working-class Protestants as well as fundamentalists, Paisley and his supporters succeeded in keeping 'the iron in the soul of Ulster unionism' and blocking political moves that might ultimately have led to the establishment of a united Ireland (Bruce, 1993). However, the theological basis of Paisleyite resistance drew heavily from the USA, the birthplace of evangelical Protestantism and home of the most influential Christian fundamentalist movement, the new Christian right.

The new Christian right

In terms of the number of church-going Christians, the USA is easily the most religious of Western countries. This largely reflects the fact that, from its earliest days, the USA provided a refuge for religious sects and movements wishing to escape from persecution. During the nineteenth century, a fierce battle was fought within American Protestantism between modernists, who adopted a liberal view of the Bible, and conservatives (later 'fundamentalists') who took a literal view of it. Nevertheless, such religious passions and views were largely confined to the private world of the family and the home. Religious groups were rarely drawn into active politics, and when they were, they were rarely successful. The

Papal infallibility: The Catholic doctrine that, being God's spokesperson on Earth, the Pope's teachings are infallible and therefore unquestionable.

introduction of prohibition, 1920–33, was a notable exception to this. The new Christian right, which emerged in the late 1970s, was therefore a novel development, in that it sought to fuse religion and politics in attempting to 'turn America back to Christ'.

Two main factors explain the emergence of the new Christian right. The first is that in the post-World War II period the USA, as elsewhere, experienced a significant extension of the public sphere. For instance, in the early 1960s the Supreme Court ruled against the use of prayers in US schools, and, particularly as part of Lyndon Johnson's 'Great Society' initiative, there was a proliferation of welfare, urban development and other programmes. The result of this was that many 'God-fearing' Southern conservatives felt that their traditional values and way of life were being threatened, and that the Washington-based liberal establishment was to blame. The second factor was the increasingly political prominence of groups representing blacks, women and homosexuals, whose advance threatened traditional social structures, particularly in rural and small-town USA. The new Christian right campaigned for the restoration of 'traditional family values', its particular targets included 'affirmative action' (positive discrimination in favour of blacks), feminism and the gay rights movement. In the 1980s and 1990s, this politics of morality coalesced increasingly around the anti-abortion issue.

A variety of organizations emerged to articulate these concerns, often mobilized by noted televangelists. These included the Religious Round Table, Christian Voice, American Coalition for Traditional Values and the most influential of all, the Moral Majority, formed by Jerry Falwell Sr in 1979. Although Catholics were prominent in the anti-abortion movement, new Christian right groups were drawn in particular from the ranks of evangelical Protestants, who as 'Bible believers' subscribed to scriptural inerrancy, and often claimed to be 'born again', in the sense that they had undergone a personal experience of conversion to Christ. Divisions nevertheless exist among evangelicals. For instance, there are those who style themselves as fundamentalists and tend to keep apart from non-believing society, and those who call themselves charismatics or evangelicals, who believe that the Holy Spirit can operate through individuals, by giving them gifts of prophecy and healing. Since the 1980s, the Moral Majority and other such groups have provided campaign finance and organized voter-registration drives with a view to targeting liberal or 'pro-choice' Democrats, and encouraging Republicans to embrace a new social and moral agenda based on opposition to abortion and calls for the restoration of prayers in US schools. Ronald Reagan's willingness to embrace this agenda in the 1980s meant that the new Christian right became an important component of a new Republican

KEY FIGURE

Mike Slaughter/Toronto Star/
Getty Images

JERRY FALWELL (1933–2007)

A US preacher, televangelist and lobbyist, Falwell was the co-founder of Moral Majority and a prominent figure in the Southern Baptist Movement. Falwell articulated a combination of biblical and political ultraconservatism that embraced a 'pro-life, pro-family, pro-moral and pro-American' stance. Under his leadership, Moral Majority engaged in a cultural war against liberal values in their various forms, with gay rights, feminism, welfare recipients, black activists and 'peaceniks' attracting particular vitriol.

coalition that placed as much emphasis on moral issues as it did on traditional ones such as the economy and foreign policy.

Since the end of the Reagan era, the influence of the new Christian right has fluctuated significantly. Reagan's successor, George Bush Sr, was not 'one of them' (until 1980, for instance, he supported abortion) and broke his campaign promise not to put up taxes. This prompted the Christian right to put up its own candidate for the presidency, leading to Pat Robertson's unsuccessful 1992 bid for the Republican nomination. However, the Christian right received a major boost from the election of George W. Bush in 2000. Not only were a number of members of Bush's cabinet, including Bush himself and his vice-president, Dick Cheney, 'born again' Christians, but a leading evangelical, John Ashcroft, was appointed attorney general. Fundamentalist influence on the Bush administration was clearest in relation to foreign policy, particularly in the aftermath of the September 11 terrorist attacks. This was evident in, among other things, stronger US support for Israel. The importance of Israel for the US evangelical right stems from the belief, sometimes called Christian Zionism, that the creation of the state of Israel in 1948 fulfilled the Bible prophecy that the return of Jews to the Holy Land prepared the way for the Second Coming of Jesus Christ. The peak of support for Christian Zionism nevertheless came after the election of Donald Trump in 2016, and was reflected in support for the idea of 'Greater Israel' (and the effective abandonment of the two-state solutions to the Palestinian-Israeli problem), an end to condemning Israel for allowing settlements to be built on Palestinian land, and the recognition of Jerusalem as the capital of Israel.

Other fundamentalisms

Instead of advancing comprehensive programmes of political renewal, other forms of fundamentalism have typically been concerned more narrowly with helping to clarify or redefine national or ethnic identity. In this sense, many fundamentalist movements can be seen as sub-varieties of ethnic nationalism. This has usually occurred in response to the emergence of rival ethnic or religious groups, or to actual or threatened territorial change. In this context, religion can exert a powerful appeal, since it provides a basis for group identity that is supposedly primordial and seemingly unchangeable. The fundamentalism of Ulster Protestants – whose religion gives their national identity, their 'Britishness', an ethnic substance – is thus very different from the fundamentalism of US evangelicals, which has little bearing on their ethnicity. Hindu, Sikh, Jewish and Buddhist fundamentalism also resemble forms of ethnic mobilization.

Hindu fundamentalism

Hinduism, the principal religion of India, appears on the surface to be relatively inhospitable to fundamentalism. It is the clearest example of an ethnic religion, in which an emphasis is placed on custom and social practice rather than formal texts or doctrines. Nevertheless, a fundamentalist movement emerged out of the struggle for Indian independence, achieved in 1947, although this was modest by comparison with the support for the secular Congress Party. However, it has flourished in India since the decline of Congress and the collapse of the Nehru-Gandhi dynasty in the mid-1980s, a key point in this process coming with the demolition of the Babri Masjid (Mosque) in Ayodhya in 1992. The core goal of fundamentalist Hinduism is to challenge the multicultural, multi-ethnic mosaic of India by making Hinduism the basis of national identity. This is not expressed in demands for the expulsion of 'foreign' religions and culture so much as in a call for the 'Hinduization' of Sikh, Jain and especially Muslim communities. The World Hindu Council, on the radical wing of the fundamentalist movement, preaches 'India for the Hindus', while its parent body, the Rashtriya Swayamsevak Sangh. or RSS, aims to create a 'Greater India', stretching from Myanmar to Iraq, and to establish India's geopolitical dominance across central Asia. Hindu fundamentalism's breakthrough to mainstream politics nevertheless came when the Bharatiya Janata Party (BJP), an exponent of Hindu nationalism with a strong appeal to the newly prosperous Indian middle class, won a landslide victory in the 2014 elections, its leader, Narendra Modi, becoming prime minister. After winning re-election in 2019, the Modi government consolidated the shift towards Hinduization by measures such as the imposition of direct rule on Kashmir, India's only Muslim-majority state, and the passage of the citizenship law, a law that offers a fast-track to Indian citizenship for refugees of all faiths except Muslims.

KEY FIGURE

NARENDRA MODI (BORN 1950)

An Indian politician, Modi was born into a deeply religious, lower-middle class Gujarati family. Having an association with the Hindu nationalist volunteer organization, the RSS, that dates back to childhood, he became a full-time worker for the body at the age of 21, and was assigned to the BJP, the political wing of the Hindu nationalist movement, four years later. Modi served as chief minister of Gujarat from 2001 to 2014, when he led his party to victory in the Lok Sabha (lower chamber of the Indian parliament), after which he was sworn in as prime minister of India. Apart from other things, Modi has stressed that the practice of yoga is intrinsic to Hindu identity, promoting it through major public events and social media.

Mike Slaughter/Toronto Star/Getty Images

Sikh fundamentalism

Sikh fundamentalism is different, in that it is associated with the struggle to found an independent nation-state, not with the remaking of a national identity within an existing one. As such, it overlaps with the concerns of liberal nationalism, and is distinguished from the latter only by its vision of the nation as an essentially religious entity. Sikh nationalists thus look to establish 'Khalistan', located in present-day Punjab, with Sikhism as the state religion and its government obliged to ensure its unhindered flourishing. Just

KEY FIGURE

JARNAIL SINGH BHINDRANWALE (1947–84)

A militant Sikh activist, Bhindranwale was the leader of the religious group Damdami Taksal, and was best-known for his part in the seizure of the Golden Temple in Amritsar in 1984. Bhindranwale's key goal was the creation of a separate Sikh state called Khalistan ('The Land of the Pure'), located in the Punjab. His nationalism was enmeshed with Sikh revivalism, generating both an ethical system and a social programme, and implying resistance to Hinduism and therefore the influence of India.

Bettmann/Getty Images

as Hindu nationalism has a markedly anti-Islamic character, Sikh nationalism is in part defined by its antipathy towards Hinduism. This was evident in the seizing of the Golden Temple in Amritsar in 1982 by the Damdami Taksal, under its militant leader, Jarail Singh Bhindranwale, and in the assassination of Indira Gandhi two years later, following the storming of the temple. The separate upsurges in Hindu, Sikh and Islamic fundamentalism in the Indian subcontinent are undoubtedly interconnected developments. Not only have they created a chain reaction of threats and resentments, but they have also inspired one another by closely linking ethnic identity to religious fervour.

Jewish fundamentalism

Both Jewish and Buddhist fundamentalisms are also closely linked to the sharpening of ethnic conflict. In contrast with the ultra-orthodox Jews, some of whom have refused to accept Israel as the Jewish state prophesized in the Old Testament, Jewish fundamentalists have transformed Zionism into a defence of the 'Greater Land of Israel', characterized by territorial aggressiveness. In the case of Israel's best-known fundamentalist group, Gushmun Emunim (Bloc of the Faithful), this has been expressed in a campaign to build Jewish settlements in territory occupied during the Six Day War of 1967 and then formally incorporated into Israel. More radical groups such as Katch (Thus) proclaim that Jews and Arabs can never live together and so look to the expulsion of all Arabs from what they see as the 'promised land'. Although small, Israel's collection of ultra-orthodox parties tend to exert disproportional influence because their support is usually necessary for either of the major parties, Likud and Labour, to form a government. Under the leadership of Benjamin Netanyahu, Likud has held power since 2009, as it had previously done from 1996 to 1999, thanks to a rock-solid alliance with the Haredi, groups within orthodox Judaism characterized by strict allegiance to *Halacha* (Jewish religious law) and tradition.

KEY CONCEPT

ZIONISM

Zionism (*Zion* is Hebrew for the Kingdom of Heaven) is the movement for the establishment of a Jewish homeland, usually seen as being located in Palestine. The idea was first advanced in 1897 by Theodore Herzl (1860–1904) at the World Zionist Congress in Basel, as the only means of protecting the Jewish people from persecution. Early Zionists had secularist and nationalistic aspirations, often associated with socialist sympathies. Since the foundation of the state of Israel in 1948, however, Zionism has come to be associated both with the continuing promise of Israel to provide a home for all Jews, and with attempts to promote sympathy for Israel and defend it against its enemies. In the latter sense, it has been recruited to the cause of fundamentalism, and, according to Palestinians, it has acquired an expansionist, anti-Arab character.

Buddhist fundamentalism

The spread of Buddhist nationalism in Sri Lanka has largely occurred as a result of growing tension between the majority and largely Buddhist Sinhalese population and the minority Tamil community, comprising Hindus, Christians and Muslims. Although on the surface – by virtue of its commitment to individual responsibility, religious toleration and non-violence – Buddhism is the least fundamentalist of the major religions (Dalai Lama, 1996), the Theravada Buddhism of Southern Asia has supported fundamentalist-type developments when nationalism and religious revivalism have been intertwined. In Sri Lanka, the drive for the 'Sinhalization' of national identity, advanced by militant groups such as the People's Liberation Front, has been expressed in the demand that Buddhism be made a state religion. Such pressures, however, merely fuelled Tamil separatism, giving rise to a terrorist campaign by the so-called Tamil Tigers, which began in the late 1970s and continued through to the Tigers' military defeat in 2009.

THE FUTURE OF FUNDAMENTALISM

The question of the future of fundamentalism conjures up two starkly different scenarios. The first raises doubts about the long-term viability of any religiously based political creed in the modern world, and highlights the particular limitations of fundamentalism as a political project. In this view, fundamentalist religion is essentially a symptom of the difficult adjustments that modernization brings about, but it is ultimately doomed because it is out of step with the principal thrust of the modernization process. Modernization is essentially a Westernizing process, and it is destined to prevail because it is closely associated with both the trend towards economic globalization and the spread of liberal democracy. This suggests that religion will be restored to its 'proper' private domain, and that public affairs will once again be contested by secular political creeds. This analysis suggests the politico-cultural project that lies at the heart of fundamentalism will gradually fade, with religious groups (if they retain any political significance) being absorbed into broad nationalist movements whose major elements are secular. While civic nationalism, orientated around the cornerstone principle of self-determination, is destined to survive, there would appear to be little future for militant ethnic nationalist movements, especially when they are based on religious distinctiveness. If fundamentalist undercurrents continue to exist in any shape or form they are unlikely to amount to more than a politics of protest, devoid of a clear political programme or a coherent economic philosophy.

In the rival scenario, fundamentalism offers a glimpse of the 'postmodern' future. From this perspective, it is secularism and liberal culture, rather than fundamentalist religion, that are in crisis. Their weakness, dramatically exposed by the rise of fundamentalism, is their failure to address deeper human needs and their inability to establish authoritative values that give social order a moral foundation. Far from the emerging global system fostering uniformity modelled on Western liberal democracy, it is more likely that as the current century unfolds, it will be characterized, as Huntington (1996) predicted, by a clash of civilizations. Competing transnational power blocs will emerge, and religion is likely to provide them with a distinctive politico-cultural identity. Fundamentalism, in this version, is seen to have strengths rather than weaknesses. Religious fundamentalists have already demonstrated their adaptability by embracing the weapons and spirit of the modern world, and the fact that they are not encumbered by tradition but travel 'fast and light' enables them to reinvent their creeds in response to the challenges of postmodernity.

QUESTIONS FOR DISCUSSION

- Why is fundamentalism often considered to be a pejorative term?
- Do all political ideologies harbour fundamentalist tendencies?
- What are the key features of fundamentalist religion?
- Is secularism compatible with religious belief?
- Is the rise of religious fundamentalism evidence of a 'clash of civilizations'?
- Is religious fundamentalism necessarily based on a belief in the literal truth of sacred texts?
- Are religious fundamentalists always anti-modern?

- Is fundamentalism implicitly totalitarian and prone to violence?
- In what sense is Islamism fundamentalist in character?
- To what extent is Christian fundamentalism compatible with constitutionalism and political pluralism?
- What is the relationship between religious fundamentalism and ethnic nationalism?
- Why and how does fundamentalism resemble populism?
- Does religious fundamentalism have a future?

FURTHER READING

Almond, G., Appleby, R.S. & Sivan, E. *Strong Religion: The Rise of Fundamentalisms around the World* (2003). Exploring the rise in fundamentalist movements internationally in the twenty-first century, and its implications for politics and society. Part of the excellent Fundamentalism Project.

Fox, J. *An Introduction to Religion and Politics: Theory and Practice*, 2nd edn (2018). A solid general introduction to religion in modern politics, including fundamentalist ideas.

Dowland, S. *Family Values and the Rise of the Christian Right* (2018). An excellent overview of the emergence of Christian fundamentalist politics in the United States and its continuing impact in Western politics.

Mandaville, P. *Islam and Politics* (2014). A comprehensive survey of the development of political Islamism and its major national or sectional variations, as well as its influence in contemporary global politics.

Political Theology Network www.politicaltheology. com. A well-maintained hub of commentary, debates and other media on the intersections between religion and politics.

CHAPTER 13

WHY POLITICAL IDEOLOGIES MATTER

PREVIEW

In this concluding chapter, we return to the issue of the nature of political ideologies. However, whereas the purpose of Chapter 1 was to provide a general introduction to the subject, by examining, for example, debates over the meaning of ideology, the relevance of the left/right divide, the rise of so-called 'new' ideologies and the idea of 'end of ideology', the present chapter reflects on the impact of ideology – for good or ill – on the wider political process. Why do political ideologies matter?

We need political ideologies for a number of reasons. Mostly importantly, they provide politicians, parties and other political actors with an intellectual framework which helps them to make sense of the world in which they live. Ideologies are not systematic delusions (as many commentators have claimed) but, rather, rival versions of the political world. Each ideology illuminates particular aspects of a complex and multifaceted reality. In that sense, ideologies operate as paradigms: they guide the process of intellectual enquiry by providing a set of values, theories and assumptions within which the search for knowledge is conducted. Ideologies play a number of other roles. These include ensuring that politics has an ethical or emotional dimension, in that what 'is' is always linked to what 'ought to be'; and helping to forge a sense of the collective, by embedding the individual within a social context. However, there is a sense in which political ideologies may matter *too* much. Each use of political ideology may, in some way, be abused. For example, paradigms that structure and inform our search for knowledge may also foster tunnel vision and even become intellectual prisons. For a variety of reasons, it may be difficult, and perhaps impossible, to think 'outside' or 'beyond' our favoured ideological tradition. Moreover, because ideologies tend to blur the distinction between truth and falsehood, there is, in the final analysis, no reliable way of 'proving' that one political ideology is better than any other ideology. Finally, in the process of forging a sense of collective belonging, political ideologies typically conjure up the image of a distrusted, feared or hated 'other', bringing conflict and polarization in its wake.

WHY WE NEED POLITICAL IDEOLOGIES

Although the world of political ideologies does not stand still, but fluctuates in response to ever-changing social and historical circumstances, we continue to live in the age of ideology. Ideology constitutes the vital link between theory and practice in politics. But why, specifically, do we need political ideologies? What role or roles do ideologies play? These include the following:

- making sense of the world
- investing politics with moral purpose
- forging the collective.

Making sense of the world

The most significant role performed by political ideologies is to widen and/or deepen our perceptual field, and, in the process, to make better sense of the world in which we live. In this sense, ideologies are 'lenses' through which we seek political understanding, sometimes referred to as 'world-views'. This relates to the first key feature of political ideology: advancing a critical account of the existing order (see Figure 1.1, p. 000). If we try to see the world simply 'as it is' – that is, without the benefit of political ideology – we will see only what we expect to see, what we *think* we will see. The chief benefit of political ideologies is therefore that they alert us to relationships, processes and structures of which we may previously have been unaware. For example, looking at the world through a 'feminist lens' not only means rectifying the traditional 'invisibility' of women in the spheres of politics, art, literature, culture and so on, but it also allows us to see how the world might look if women's values and concerns were treated as matters of central importance. In the same way, political ideologies help to expose 'hidden' prejudices and biases. This makes them a device for promoting critical self-reflection, a means of uncovering 'taken-for-granted' assumptions and understandings about the established order. In the case of feminist ideology, this is reflected in our attempts to expose the ways in which mainstream thinking about social and political affairs is '**gendered**'.

In this approach, ideologies are treated as paradigms (see p. 268), in the sense employed by Thomas Kuhn in his pioneering *The Structure of Scientific Revolutions* (1962). As defined by Kuhn, a paradigm is 'the entire constellation of beliefs, values, techniques and so on shared by members of a given community'. Although Kuhn developed the concept of paradigm specifically in relation to the natural sciences, it has come to be widely applied to the social sciences. The value of paradigms is that they help us to make sense of what would otherwise be an impenetrably complex reality. They define what is important to study and highlight significant trends, patterns and processes. In so doing, they draw attention to relevant questions and lines of enquiry, as well as indicate how the results of intellectual enquiry might be interpreted. Nevertheless, as the search for knowledge always takes place *within* a paradigm, this implies that rival paradigms – and therefore rival political ideologies – are **incommensurable**. Political ideologies, thus, do not provide competing accounts of the *same* world; in effect, they 'see' *different* worlds, and, in some respects, use different languages to describe

Gendered: The tendency to reflect the experiences, prejudices or orientations of one gender more than the other; bias in favour of one's own gender.

Incommensurability: An inability to compare or judge between rival policies or propositions because of the absence of common features.

those worlds. This explains why the issues that divide ideologies from one another can never be resolved simply through a process of debate and discussion; ideologies, if you like, 'talk past one another'.

KEY CONCEPT
PARADIGM

A paradigm is, in a general sense, a pattern or model that highlights relevant features of a particular phenomenon. As used by Kuhn (1962), however, it refers to an intellectual framework comprising interrelated values, theories and assumptions, within which the search for knowledge is conducted.

In this view, what Kuhn termed 'normal' science is conducted within an established intellectual framework; in 'revolutionary' science, by contrast, an attempt is made to replace an old paradigm with a new one. The radical implication of this theory is that 'truth' and 'falsehood' cannot be finally established. They are only provisional judgements operating within an accepted paradigm that will, eventually, be replaced.

Investing politics with moral purpose

An additional source of ideology's survival and success deals less with our ability to 'make sense' of events, developments and circumstances, and more with how we should react to them in ethical or emotional terms. This relates to the second key feature of political ideology: outlining a model of a desired future, a vision of the 'good society'. Ideologies are the principal source of meaning and idealism in politics; they touch those aspects of politics that other political forms cannot reach. A post-ideological age would therefore be an age without hope, without vision. If politicians cannot cloak the pursuit of power in ideological purpose, they risk being seen simply as power-seeking pragmatists, whose policy programmes lack coherence and direction. This is evident in the case of modern, 'de-ideologized' party politics, in which, as parties of both left and right become detached from their ideological roots, they struggle to provide members and supporters alike with a basis for emotional attachment. As parties come to sell 'products' (leaders or policies) rather than hopes or dreams, party membership and voter turnout both fall, and politicians become increasingly desperate to re-engage with the 'vision thing'. By creating an appetite for the resurgence of ideology, post-ideological politics contains the seeds of its own destruction, a tendency that helps to explain, for instance, the rise of both right- and left-wing populism in the period since the 2007–09 global financial crisis. For this, if for no other reason, political ideology is destined to be a continuing and unending process.

Forging the collective

A further advantage of political ideologies is that they give people a reason to believe in something larger than themselves. This is important because people's personal narratives only make sense when they are situated within a broader socio-historical narrative. This relates to the third key feature of political ideology: acting as a form of social cement, providing social groups, and indeed whole societies, with a set of unifying beliefs and values. This has been evident in the common association of political ideologies with particular social classes – for example, liberalism with the middle classes, conservatism with the wealthy or aristocracy, socialism with the working class, and so on. These ideological traditions are capable of reflecting the life experiences, interests and aspirations of a social class, and thereby help to forge a sense of belonging and solidarity. However, political ideologies can also bind together divergent groups and interests within the same society. For instance, liberalism fosters a collection of bedrock values, including individual rights, democracy and constitutionalism (see p. 42), while nationalism inculcates a common set of political allegiances and cultural affiliations (see Chapter 6). In providing society with a unifying political culture, ideologies deliver order and social stability. Nevertheless, a unifying set of political ideas and values can develop naturally within a society, or it can be imposed on it in an attempt to manufacture obedience and exercise control. The clearest example of this latter tendency is the 'official' ideologies that have emerged in communist and fascist regimes (see Chapters 4 and 7, respectively).

DO IDEOLOGIES MATTER TOO MUCH?

Throughout its history, stretching back at least to the 1789 French Revolution, political ideology has been subject to criticism and attack. This has often been expressed through predictions of its imminent (and usually welcome) demise. However, rather than countenancing the eradication of ideology as something that is possible or desirable, most commentators see ideology as a mixed blessing. In short, political ideologies can be used but they can also be abused. Their dangers associated with political ideology include the following:

● imprisoning the mind

● distorting 'truth'

● pitting 'us' against 'them'.

Imprisoning the mind

The notion that ideologies, as paradigms, serve the interests of political understanding fails to acknowledge that they may also promote tunnel vision, or even act as intellectual prisons. Instead of widening and deepening our perceptual field, paradigms may allow us to 'see' only what their account of political reality allows us to see. By generating conformity among those who subscribe to them, ideologies come to resemble political religions, sets of values, theories and doctrines that demand faith and commitment from 'believers', who are unable to think 'outside' or 'beyond' their chosen world-view. Such a tendency can be further explained by a range of cognitive dispositions. **Sunk cost fallacy**, for instance, stops us giving up on a cause because we do not want to admit that we were wrong to invest in it in the first place. We fall foul of this mental habit not just when we invest financially but when we invest ourselves in an idea, strategy or ethical position. **Confirmation bias** is the tendency to seek out, interpret, judge and remember information so that it reinforces one's pre-existing beliefs and values. It also explains why people rarely access websites, blogs, journals, books and newspapers that contain material that challenges their established views. **Cognitive entrenchment theory**

> **Sunk cost fallacy:** The disposition to continue a behaviour or endeavour as a result of costs that have already been incurred and cannot be recovered.

> **Confirmation bias:** The disposition to give more weight to information that confirms people's beliefs and to undervalue information that could disprove them.

suggests that the greater a person's familiarity with, and knowledge of, a particular issue, the harder it is for them to approach the issue in an open-minded and self-critical manner. This implies that there is always a trade-off in intellectual activity between expertise and flexibility.

Distorting 'truth'

A second problem with political ideologies is that they have, seemingly unavoidably, an unreliable relationship with truth. Indeed, to suggest that ideologies can be deemed to be either true or false is to miss the vital point that they embody values, dreams and aspirations that are, by their very nature, not susceptible to scientific analysis. No one can 'prove' that one theory of justice is preferable to any other, any more than rival conceptions of human nature can be tested by surgical intervention to demonstrate once and for all that human beings possess rights, are entitled to freedom, or are naturally selfish or naturally sociable. Ideologies are embraced less because they stand up to scrutiny and logical analysis, and more because they help individuals, groups and societies to deal with the world in which they live. As Andrew Vincent (2009) put it, 'We examine ideology as fellow travellers, not as neutral observers'. Nevertheless, ideologies undoubtedly embody a claim to uncover truth; in this sense, they can be seen, in Michel Foucault's (1991) words, as 'regimes of truth'. As 'regimes of truth', ideologies are always linked to power. In a world of competing truths, values and theories, ideologies seek to prioritize certain values over others, and to invest legitimacy in particular theories or sets of meanings. However, this is never done on the basis of a standard of truth that has an objective character. Although all ideologies may have an unreliable relationship with truth, 'truth decay' has become more prominent due to the rise of populism, particularly through its emphasis on conspiracy theories.

Pitting 'us' against 'them'

Although political ideologies build within people a sense of collective belonging, this is often accomplished through a deepening of conflict and division. In some cases, the link within an ideology between conflict and the collective is stark and unmistakable. Marxism, for instance, embraces the doctrine of class war, while fascists extol the virtues of the national community while also believing in a conception of life as 'unending struggle'. Nevertheless, the association between conflict and the collective may have a wider application, and perhaps taints all ideological traditions. Theorists in the field of social psychology have argued that there is a basic tendency for people to divide the world into an in-group ('us'), consisting, in this case, of those who support one's own ideological beliefs, and an out-group ('them'), consisting of those who support rival political ideologies. In a process of negative integration, our sense of 'us' is strengthened by the existence of 'them' – sometimes seen as the 'other' – who we come to distrust, fear or even hate. It is, nevertheless, widely argued that the tendency for the ideological landscape to be structured according to the 'us/them' divide has become more prominent since the 1990s, as issues related to identity, and thus who we *are*, displace more conventional socio-economic issues. This is evident in the growing prevalence of 'culture wars' (see p. 179).

Cognitive entrenchment theory: The theory that people's beliefs become more rigid the greater the degree to which they are immersed in their domain of expertise.

CHOOSING BETWEEN IDEOLOGIES

In the discussion above, political ideologies were portrayed very much as a mixed blessing. For example, while ideologies may constitute an essential road to political understanding, this road may also promote tunnel vision and distort truth. However, the balance between understanding and distortion may not be uniform across the ideological landscape; rather, it may differ from ideology to ideology, certain ideologies proving to be more reliable or more insightful than others. In that sense, some ideologies may matter more than others. This may be evident in a number of ways. One of these is that ideologies vary in the extent to which they correspond to 'the facts' and succeed in explaining real-world events and developments. Socialism, for instance, has widely been viewed as a less reliable and insightful political ideology, as a result of the declining significance of social class since the 1970s. A widening gap thus developed between ideological belief (reflected in the socialist assumption that social classes are the principal actors in history) and reality.

However, the correspondence-to-reality approach to evaluating political ideologies is not without its difficulties. In particular, it is rooted in the confident belief that facts have an objective existence separate from our values and assumptions. The notion of a distinction between facts and values is nevertheless foreign to the thrust of ideological thought, which is concerned not just with understanding the world, but with doing so for a purpose: namely, remaking the world for the better (whatever that may mean in practice). When we choose between political ideologies, then, we are not evaluating rival intellectual frameworks so much as selecting the most compelling vehicle for ethical and emotional engagement in politics.

◎ QUESTIONS FOR DISCUSSION

- In what sense can political ideologies be thought of as paradigms?
- Is it possible to resolve differences between ideologies through a process of debate and discussion?
- Are modern 'de-ideologized' political parties sustainable in the long run?
- How, and how effectively, do political ideologies forge a sense of the collective?
- Why, and with what implications, have ideologies been portrayed as political religions?

- Is it possible to avoid confirmation bias? And if so, how can this be done?
- To what extent are political ideologies susceptible to scientific analysis?
- How and why do modern ideological rivalries so often take the form of culture wars?
- Are some ideologies more reliable and insightful than others?
- Can political ideologies ever be judged by how far they correspond to reality?

BIBLIOGRAPHY

Acton, Lord (1956) *Essays on Freedom and Power*. London: Meridian.

Adams, I. (1989) *The Logic of Political Belief: A Philosophical Analysis*. London and New York: Harvester Wheatsheaf.

Adib-Moghaddam, A. (ed.) (2014) *Introduction to Khomeini*. New York: Cambridge University Press.

Adonis, A. and Hames, T. (1994) *A Conservative Revolution? The Thatcher– Reagan Decade in Perspective*. Manchester: Manchester University Press.

Adorno, T., Frenkel-Brunswik, E., Levinson, D. and Sandford, R. (1950) *The Authoritarian Personality*. New York: Harper.

Ahmed, R. (2001) *Jihad: The Rise of Militant Islam in Central Asia*. New Haven, CT: Yale University Press.

Ali, T. (2003) *The Clash of Fundamentalism: Crusades, Jihads and Modernity*. London: Verso.

Almond, G., Appleby, R.S. and Sivan, E. (2003) *Strong Religion: The Rise of Fundamentalisms around the World*. Chicago: University of Chicago Press.

Anderson, B. (1983) *Imagined Communities: Reflections on the Origins and Spread of Nationalism*. London: Verso.

Arblaster, A. (1984) *The Rise and Decline of Western Liberalism*. Oxford: Basil Blackwell.

Arendt, H. (1951) *The Origins of Totalitarianism*. London: Allen & Unwin.

Aristotle (1962) *The Politics*, trans. T. Sinclair. Harmondsworth: Penguin (Chicago, IL: University of Chicago Press, 1985).

Aughey, A., Jones, G. and Riches, W. T. M. (1992) *The Conservative Political Tradition in Britain and the United States*. London: Pinter.

Bahro, R. (1982) *Socialism and Survival*. London: Heretic Books.

Bahro, R. (1984) *From Red to Green*. London: Verso/ New Left Books.

Bakunin, M. (1973) *Selected Writings*, ed. A. Lehning. London: Cape.

Bakunin, M. (1977) 'Church and State', in G. Woodcock (ed.), *The Anarchist Reader*. London: Fontana.

Ball, T., Dagger, R. and O'Neill, D. (2016) *Political Ideologies and the Democratic Ideal*. Abingdon and New York: Routledge.

Ball, T., Dagger, R. and O'Neill, D. (2019) *Ideals and Ideologies: A Reader*, 11th edn. New York: Routledge.

Baradat, L. P. (2003) *Political Ideologies: Their Origins and Impact*, 8th edn. Upper Saddle River, NJ: Prentice Hall.

Barber, B. (2003) *Jihad vs. the World: How Globalism and Tribalism Are Reshaping the World*. London: Corgi Books.

Barker, R. (1997) *Political Ideas in Modern Britain: In and After the 20th Century*, 2nd edn. London and New York: Routledge.

Barry, B. (2002) *Culture and Equality*. Cambridge and New York: Polity Press.

Barry, J. (1999) *Rethinking Green Politics*. London and Thousand Oaks, CA: Sage.

Barry, N. (1987) *The New Right*. London: Croom Helm.

Baumann, Z. (1999) *In Search of Politics*. Cambridge and Malden, MA: Polity Press.

Baxter, B. (1999) *Ecologism: An Introduction*. Edinburgh: Edinburgh University Press.

Beasley, C. (1999) *What Is Feminism?* London: Sage.

Beasley, C. (2005) *Gender and Sexuality: Critical Theories and Critical Thinkers*. London and Thousand Oaks, CA: Sage Publications.

Beauvoir, S. de (1968) *The Second Sex*, trans. H. M. Parshley. New York: Bantam.

Beck, U. (1992) *Risk Society: Towards a New Modernity*. London and New York: Sage.

Bell, D. (1960) *The End of Ideology*. Glencoe, IL: Free Press.

Bellamy, R. (1992) *Liberalism and Modern Society: An Historical Argument*. Cambridge: Polity Press.

Benn, T. (1980) *Arguments for Democracy*. Harmondsworth: Penguin.

Bentham, J. (1970) *Introduction to the Principles of Morals and Legislation*, ed. J. Burns and H. L. A. Hart. London: Athlone Press and Glencoe, IL: Free Press.

Berki, R. N. (1975) *Socialism*. London: Dent.

Berlin, I. ([1958] 1969) 'Two Concepts of Liberty', in *Four Essays on Liberty*. London: Oxford University Press.

Berman, P. (2003) *Terror and Liberalism*. New York: W. W. Norton.

Bernstein, E. ([1898] 1962) *Evolutionary Socialism*. New York: Schocken.

Black, A. (2011) *History of Islamic Political Thought: From the Prophet to the Present*. Edinburgh: Edinburgh University Press.

Blakeley, G. and Bryson, V. (eds) (2002) *Contemporary Political Concepts: A Critical Introduction*. London: Pluto Press.

Bobbio, N. (1996) *Left and Right: The Significance of a Political Distinction*. Oxford: Polity Press.

Bobbitt, P. (2002) *The Shield of Achilles*. New York: Knopf and London: Allen Lane.

Bookchin, M. ([1962] 1975) *Our Synthetic Environment*. London: Harper & Row.

Bookchin, M. (1977) 'Anarchism and Ecology', in G. Woodcock (ed.), *The Anarchist Reader*. London: Fontana.

Bosworth, R. (ed.) (2012) *The Oxford Handbook of Fascism*. Oxford: Oxford University Press.

Boulding, K. (1966) 'The Economics of the Coming Spaceship Earth', in H. Jarrett (ed.), *Environmental Quality in a Growing Economy*. Baltimore, MD: Johns Hopkins Press.

Bourne, R. (1977) 'War Is the Health of the State', in G. Woodcock (ed.), *The Anarchist Reader*. London: Fontana.

Bracher, K. D. (1985) *The Age of Ideologies: A History of Political Thought in the Twentieth Century*. London: Methuen.

Bramwell, A. (1989) *Ecology in the Twentieth Century: A History*. New Haven, CT and London: Yale University Press.

Bramwell, A. (1994) *The Fading of the Greens: The Decline of Environmental Politics in the West*. New Haven, CT and London: Yale University Press.

Browers, M. (2015) 'Islamic Political Ideologies', in M. Freeden, L. T. Sargent, and M. Stears (eds), *The Oxford Handbook of Political Ideologies*. Oxford and New York: Oxford University Press.

Brown, D. (2000) *Contemporary Nationalism: Civic, Ethnocultural and Multicultural Politics*. London: Routledge.

Brownmiller, S. (1975) *Against Our Will: Men, Women and Rape*. New York: Simon & Schuster.

Bruce, S. (1993) 'Fundamentalism, Ethnicity and Enclave', in M. Marty and R. S. Appleby (eds), *Fundamentalism and the State*. Chicago, IL and London: Chicago University Press.

Bruce, S. (2008) *Fundamentalism*. Cambridge: Polity Press.

Bruilly, J. (ed.) (2013) *The Oxford Handbook of the History of Nationalism*. Oxford: Oxford University Press.

Bryson, V. (2003) *Feminist Political Theory: An Introduction*, 2nd edn. London: Red Globe Press.

Bryson, V. (2016) *Feminist Political Theory: An Introduction*, 3rd edn. London: Red Globe Press.

Burke, E. ([1790] 1968) *Reflections on the Revolution in France*. Harmondsworth: Penguin.

Burke, E. ([1790] 1975) *On Government, Politics and Society*, ed. B. W. Hill. London: Fontana.

Burnham, J. (1960) *The Managerial Revolution*. Harmondsworth: Penguin and Bloomington, IN: Indiana University Press.

Buruma, I. and Margalit, A. (2004) *Occidentalism: A Short History of Anti-Westernism*. London: Atlantic Books.

Butler, C. (2002) *Postmodernism: A Very Short Introduction*. Oxford and New York: Oxford University Press.

Butler, J. (2006) *Gender Trouble*. Abingdon and New York: Routledge.

Canovan, M. (2005) *The People*. Cambridge: Cambridge University Press.

Capra, F. (1975) *The Tao of Physics*. London: Fontana.

Capra, F. (1982) *The Turning Point*. London: Fontana (Boston, MA: Shambhala, 1983).

Capra, F. (1997) *The Web of Life: A New Synthesis of Mind and Matter*. London: Flamingo.

Carson, R. (1962) *The Silent Spring*. Boston, MA: Houghton Mifflin.

Carter, A. (1971) *The Political Theory of Anarchism*. London: Routledge & Kegan Paul.

Carter, N. (2018) *The Politics of the Environment: Ideas, Activism, Policy*, 3rd edn. Cambridge: Cambridge University Press.

Castells, M. (2000) *The Rise of the Network Society*. Oxford and Malden, MA: Blackwell.

Cecil, H. (1912) *Conservatism*. London and New York: Home University Library.

Chamberlain, H. S. ([1899] 1913) *Foundations of the Nineteenth Century*. New York: John Lane.

Charvet, J. (1982) *Feminism*. London: Dent.

Charvet, J. (2018) *Liberalism: The Basics*. London: Routledge.

Chesterton, G. K. (1908) *Orthodoxy*. London: John Lane, The Bodley Head.

Chomsky, N. (1999) *The New Military Humanism*. Monroe, ME: Common Courage Press.

Chomsky, N. (2003) *Hegemony and Survival: America's Quest for Global Domination*. New York: Henry Holt & Company.

Chomsky, N. (2013) *Anarchism*. New York: The New Press.

Christoyannopoulos, A. (2011) *Religious Anarchism: New Perspectives*. Newcastle upon Tyne: Cambridge Scholars Publishing.

Club of Rome. See Meadows *et al.* (1972).

Coakley, J. (2012) *Nationalism, Ethnicity and the State*. Thousand Oaks, CA: SAGE.

Collins, P. (1993) *Ideology after the Fall of Communism*. London: Bowerdean.

Constant, B. (1988) *Political Writings*. Cambridge: Cambridge University Press.

Conway, D. (1995) *Classical Liberalism: The Unvanquished Ideal*. London and New York: Palgrave Macmillan.

Coole, D. (1993) *Women in Political Theory: From Ancient Misogyny to Contemporary Feminism*, 2nd edn. Hemel Hempstead: Harvester Wheatsheaf.

Cordeiro-Rodrigues, L. and Simendic, M. (2017) *Philosophies of Multiculturalism: Beyond Liberalism*. New York: Routledge.

Costa, M. D. and James, S. (1972) *The Power of Women and the Subordination of the Community*. Bristol: Falling Wall Press.

Crick, B. (1962) *A Defence of Politics*. Harmondsworth: Penguin.

Critchley, T. A. (1970) *The Conquest of Violence*. London: Constable.

Crosland, C. A. R. (1956) *The Future of Socialism*. London: Cape (Des Plaines, IL: Greenwood, 1977).

Curran, G. (ed.) (2007) *21st Century Dissent: Anarchism, Globalization and Environmentalism*. London: Palgrave Macmillan.

Dahl, R. (1961) *Who Governs? Democracy and Power in an American City*. New Haven, CT: Yale University Press.

Dalai Lama (1996) *The Power of Buddhism*. London: Newleaf.

Daly, H. (1974) 'Steady-state Economics vs Growthmania: A Critique of Orthodox Conceptions of Growth, Wants, Scarcity and Efficiency', *Policy Sciences*, vol. 5, pp. 149–67.

Daly, M. (1979) *Gyn/Ecology: The Meta-Ethics of Radical Feminism*. Boston, MA: Beacon Press.

Darwin, C. ([1859] 1972) *On the Origin of Species*. London: Dent.

Dickinson, G. L. (1916) *The European Anarchy*. London: Allen & Unwin.

Disch, L. and Hawkesworth, M. (2016) *The Oxford Handbook of Feminist Theory*. Oxford: Oxford University Press.

Dobson, A. (1991) *The Green Reader*. London: André Deutsch.

Dobson, A. (2007) *Green Political Thought*, 4th edn. London and New York: Routledge.

Dolgoff, D. (1974) *The Anarchist Collective: Workers' Self-Management in the Spanish Revolution, 1936–1939*. Montreal, Quebec: Black Rose Books.

Dowland, S. (2018) *Family Values and the Rise of the Christian Right*. Philadelphia: University of Pennsylvania Press.

Downs, A. (1957) *An Economic Theory of Democracy*. New York: Harper & Row.

Dworkin, A. (1976) *Woman Hating: A Radical Look at Sexuality*. Harmondsworth: Penguin.

Dworkin, A. and K. MacKinnon (1988) *Pornography and Civil Rights*. Minneapolis, MN: Organizing Against Pornography.

Dworkin, R. (2000) *Sovereign Virtue: The Theory and Practice of Equality*. Cambridge, MA: Harvard University Press.

Dyzek, J. and Schlosberg, D. (2005) *Debating the Earth: The Environmental Politics Reader*, 2nd edn. Oxford: Oxford University Press.

Eagleton, T. (1991) *Ideology: An Introduction*. London and New York: Verso.

Eatwell, R. (2003) *Fascism: A History*. London: Vintage.

Eatwell, R. and Goodwin, M. (2018) *National Populism: The Revolt Against Liberal Democracy*. London: Pelican.

Eatwell, R. and O'Sullivan, N. (eds) (1989) *The Nature of the Right: European and American Politics and Political Thought since 1789*. London: Pinter.

Eatwell, R. and Wright, A. (eds) (1999) *Contemporary Political Ideologies*, 2nd edn. London: Pinter.

Eccleshall, R. *et al.* (2003) *Political Ideologies: An Introduction*, 3rd edn. London and New York: Routledge.

Eckersley, R. (1992) *Environmentalism and Political Theory: Towards an Ecocentric Approach*. London: UCL Press.

Edgar, D. (1988) 'The Free or the Good', in R. Levitas (ed.) *The Ideology of the New Right*. Oxford: Polity Press.

Egoumenides, M. (2014) *Philosophical Anarchism and Political Obligation*. London: Bloomsbury.

Ehrenfeld, D. (1978) *The Arrogance of Humanism*. Oxford: Oxford University Press.

Ehrlich, P. and Ehrlich, A. (1970) *Population, Resources and Environment: Issues in Human Ecology*. London: W. H. Freeman.

Ehrlich, P. and Harriman, R. (1971) *How to Be a Survivor*. London: Pan.

Elshtain, J. B. (1993) *Public Man, Private Woman: Women in Social and Political Thought*. Oxford: Martin Robertson and Princeton, NJ: Princeton University Press.

Enayat, H. (1982) *Modern Islamic Political Thought*. London: Macmillan Press.

Engels, F. ([1884] 1976) *The Origins of the Family, Private Property and the State*. London: Lawrence & Wishart (New York: Pathfinder, 1972).

Etzioni, A. (1995) *The Spirit of Community: Rights, Responsibilities and the Communitarian Agenda*. London: Fontana.

Eysenck, H. (1964) *Sense and Nonsense in Psychology*. Harmondsworth: Penguin.

Faludi, S. (1991) *Backlash: The Undeclared War Against American Women*. New York: Crown.

Fanon, F. (1965) *The Wretched of the Earth*. Harmondsworth: Penguin (New York: Grove-Weidenfeld, 1988).

Faure, S. ([1925] 1977) 'Anarchy–Anarchist', in G. Woodcock (ed.), *The Anarchist Reader*. London: Fontana.

Fawcett, E. (2015) *Liberalism: The Life of an Idea*. Princeton, NJ: Princeton University Press.

Fawcett, E. (2018) *Liberalism: The Life of an Idea*, 2nd edn. Princeton, NJ:Princeton, NJ: Princeton University Press.

Fawcett, E. (2020) *Conservatism: The Fight for a Tradition*. Princeton, NJ:Princeton, NJ: Princeton University Press.

Feldman, N. (2012) *The Fall and Rise of the Islamic State*. Princeton, NJ: Princeton University Press.

Festenstein, M. and Kenny, M. (eds) (2005) *Political Ideologies: A Reader and Guide*. Oxford and New York: Oxford University Press.

Figes, E. (1970) *Patriarchal Attitudes*. Greenwich, CT: Fawcett.

Firestone, S. (1972) *The Dialectic of Sex*. New York: Basic Books.

Foley, M. (1991) *American Political Ideas: Tradition and Usages*. Manchester: Manchester University Press.

Foucault, M. (1991) *Discipline and Punishment: The Birth of the Prison*. London: Penguin.

Fox, J. (2018) *An Introduction to Religion and Politics: Theory and Practice,* 2nd edn. London: Routledge.

Fox, W. (1990) *Towards a Transpersonal Ecology: Developing the Foundations for Environmentalism*. Boston, MA: Shambhala.

Freeden, M. (1996) *Ideologies and Political Theory: A Conceptual Approach*. Oxford and New York: Oxford University Press.

Freeden, M. (2001) *Reassessing Political Ideologies: The Durability of Dissent*. London and New York: Routledge.

Freeden, M. (2004) *Ideology: A Very Short Introduction*. Oxford and New York: Oxford University Press.

Freeden, M., Sargent, L. T. and Stears, M. (eds) (2015) *The Oxford Handbook of Political Ideologies*. Oxford: Oxford University Press.

Freedman, J. (2001) *Feminism*. Buckingham and Philadelphia, PA: Open University Press.

Friedan, B. (1963) *The Feminine Mystique*. New York: Norton.

Friedan, B. (1983) *The Second Stage*. London: Abacus (New York: Summit, 1981).

Friedman, D. (1973) *The Machinery of Freedom: Guide to a Radical Capitalism*. New York: Harper & Row.

Friedman, M. (1962) *Capitalism and Freedom*. Chicago, IL: University of Chicago Press.

Friedman, M. and Friedman, R. (1980) *Free to Choose*. Harmondsworth: Penguin (New York: Bantam, 1983).

Friedrich, C. J. and Brzezinski, Z. (1963) *Totalitarian Dictatorships and Autocracy*. New York: Praeger.

Fromm, E. (1979) *To Have or To Be*. London: Abacus.

Fromm, E. (1984) *The Fear of Freedom*. London: Ark.

Fukuyama, F. (1989) 'The End of History?', *National Interest*, Summer.

Fukuyama, F. (1992) *The End of History and the Last Man*, Harmondsworth: Penguin.

Gabrielson, T., Hall, C., Meyer, J. and Schlosberg, D. (2016) *The Oxford Handbook of Environmental Political Theory*. Oxford: Oxford University Press.

Galbraith, J. K. (1992) *The Culture of Contentment*. London: Sinclair Stevenson.

Gallie, W. B. (1955–6) 'Essentially Contested Context', in *Proceedings of the Aristotelian Society*, vol. 56.

Gamble, A. (1994) *The Free Economy and the Strong State*, 2nd edn. London: Red Globe Press.

Gandhi, M. (1971) *Selected Writings of Mahatma Gandhi*, ed. R. Duncan. London: Fontana.

Garvey, J. H. (1993) 'Fundamentalism and Politics', in Martin E. Marty and R. Scott Appleby (eds), *Fundamentalisms and the State*. Chicago, IL and London: University of Chicago Press.

Gasset, J. Ortega y ([1930] 1972) *The Revolt of the Masses*. London: Allen & Unwin.

Gellner, E. (1983) *Nations and Nationalism*. Oxford: Blackwell.

Geoghegan, V. and Wilford, R. (eds) (2014) *Political Ideologies: An Introduction*. Abingdon and New York: Routledge.

Giddens, A. (1994) *Beyond Left and Right: The Future of Radical Politics*. Cambridge: Polity Press.

Giddens, A. (1998) *The Third Way: The Renewal of Social Democracy*. Cambridge: Polity Press.

Giddens, A. (2000) *The Third Way and Its Critics*. Cambridge: Polity Press.

Gillis, S., Howie, G. and Mumford, R. (eds) (2007) *Third Wave Feminism: Critical Exploration*. London and New York: Palgrave Macmillan.

Gilmour, I. (1978) *Inside Right: A Study of Conservatism*. London: Quartet Books.

Gilmour, I. (1992) *Dancing with Dogma: Britain under Thatcherism*. London: Simon & Schuster.

Gobineau, J.-A. (1970) *Gobineau: Selected Political Writings*, ed. M. D. Biddiss. New York: Harper & Row.

Godwin, W. ([1793] 1971) *Enquiry Concerning Political Justice*, ed. K. C. Carter. Oxford: Oxford University Press.

Goldman, E. (1969) *Anarchism and Other Essays*. New York: Dover.

Goldsmith, E. (1988) *The Great U-Turn: De-industrialising Society*. Totnes: Green Books.

Goldsmith, E., Allen, R. and others (eds) (1972) *Blueprint for Survival*. Harmondsworth: Penguin.

Goodhart, D. (2004) 'The Discomfort of Strangers', *Prospect*, February.

Goodhart, D. (2017) *The Road to Somewhere: The New Tribes Shaping British Politics*. London: Penguin.

Goodin, R. E. (1992) *Green Political Theory*. Oxford: Polity Press.

Goodman, P. (1977) 'Normal Politics and the Psychology of Power', in G. Woodcock (ed.), *The Anarchist Reader*. London: Fontana.

Goodwin, B. (1997) *Using Political Ideas*, 4th edn. London: John Wiley & Sons.

Gorz, A. (1982) *Farewell to the Working Class*. London: Pluto Press (Boston, MA: South End Press, 1982).

Gould, B. (1985) *Socialism and Freedom*. London: Macmillan (Wakefield, NH: Longwood, 1986).

Gramsci, A. ([1935] 1971) *Selections from the Prison Notebooks*, ed. Q. Hoare and G. Nowell-Smith. London: Lawrence & Wishart.

Gray, J. (1995a) *Enlightenment's Wake: Politics and Culture at the Close of the Modern Age*. London: Routledge.

Gray, J. (1995b) *Liberalism*, 2nd edn. Milton Keynes: Open University Press.

Gray, J. (1996) *Post-liberalism: Studies in Political Thought*. London: Routledge.

Gray, J. (1997) *Endgames: Questions in Late Modern Political Thought*. Cambridge and Malden, MA: Blackwell.

Gray, J. (2000) *Two Faces of Liberalism*. Cambridge: Polity Press.

Gray, J. and Willetts, D. (1997) *Is Conservatism Dead?* London: Profile Books.

Green, T. H. (1988) *Works*, ed. R. Nettleship. London: Oxford University Press (New York: AMS Press, 1984).

Greenfeld, L. (2019) *Nationalism: A Short History*. Washington, D.C.: Brookings Institution.

Greenleaf, W. H. (1983) *The British Political Tradition: The Ideological Heritage*, Vol. 2. London: Methuen.

Greer, G. (1970) *The Female Eunuch*. New York: McGraw-Hill.

Greer, G. (1985) *Sex and Destiny*. New York: Harper & Row.

Greer, G. (1999) *The Whole Woman*. London: Doubleday.

Gregor, A. J. (1969) *The Ideology of Fascism*. New York: Free Press.

Griffin, R. (1993) *The Nature of Fascism*. London: Routledge.

Griffin, R. (2018) *Fascism*. Cambridge: Polity.

Griffin, R. (ed.) (1995) *Fascism*. Oxford and New York: Oxford University Press.

Griffin, R. (ed.) (1998) *International Fascism: Theories, Causes and the New Consensus*. London: Arnold and New York: Oxford University Press.

Hadden, J. K. and Shupe, A. (eds) (1986) *Prophetic Religions and Politics: Religion and Political Order*. New York: Paragon House.

Hall, J. A. (1988) *Liberalism: Politics, Ideology and the Market*. London: Paladin.

Hall, S. and Jacques, M. (eds) (1983) *The Politics of Thatcherism*. London: Lawrence & Wishart.

Hamid. S. (2016) *Islamic Exceptionalism*. New York: St. Martin's Press.

Hardin, G. (1968) 'The Tragedy of the Commons', *Science*, vol. 162, pp. 1243–8.

Hardt, M. and Negri, A. (2000) *Empire*. Cambridge, MA: Harvard University Press.

Harrington, M. (1993) *Socialism, Past and Future*. London: Pluto Press.

Harvey, D. (2003) *The New Imperialism*. Oxford: Oxford University Press.

Harvey, D. (2005) *A Brief History of Neoliberalism*. Oxford and New York: Oxford University Press.

Hayek, F. A. von (1944) *The Road to Serfdom*. London: Routledge & Kegan Paul (Chicago, IL: University of Chicago Press, 1956, new edn).

Hayek, F. A. von (1960) *The Constitution of Liberty*. London: Routledge & Kegan Paul.

Hayward, T. (1998) *Political Theory and Ecological Values*. Cambridge: Polity Press.

Hearn, J. (2006) *Rethinking Nationalism: A Critical Introduction*. London: Red Globe Press.

Heath, A., Jowell, R. and Curtice, J. (1985) *How Britain Votes*. Oxford: Pergamon.

Heffernan, R. (2001) *New Labour and Thatcherism*. London: Palgrave.

Hegel, G. W. F. (1942) *The Philosophy of Right*, trans. T. M. Knox. Oxford: Clarendon Press.

Heywood, L. and J. Drake (eds) (1997) *Third Wave Agenda: Being Feminist, Doing Feminism*. Minneapolis, MN: University of Minnesota Press.

Hiro, D. (1988) *Islamic Fundamentalism*. London: Paladin.

Hitler, A. ([1925] 1969) *Mein Kampf*. London: Hutchinson (Boston, MA: Houghton Mifflin, 1973).

Hobbes, T. ([1651] 1968) *Leviathan*, ed. C. B. Macpherson. Harmondsworth: Penguin.

Hobhouse, L. T. (1911) *Liberalism*. London: Thornton Butterworth.

Hobsbawm, E. (1983) 'Inventing Tradition', in E. Hobsbawm and T. Ranger (eds), *The Invention of Tradition*. Cambridge: Cambridge University Press.

Hobsbawm, E. (1992) *Nations and Nationalism since 1780: Programme, Myth and Reality*, 2nd edn. Cambridge: Cambridge University Press.

Hobsbawm, E. (1994) *Age of Extremes: The Short Twentieth Century, 1914–1991*. London: Michael Joseph.

Hobsbawm, E. (2011) *How to Change the World: Tales of Marx and Marxism*. London: Little, Brown.

Hobson, J. A. (1902) *Imperialism: A Study*. London: Nisbet.

Hoffman, J. and P. Graham (2006) *Introduction to Political Ideologies*. London: Pearson Education.

Holden, B. (1993) *Understanding Liberal Democracy*, 2nd edn. Hemel Hempstead: Harvester Wheatsheaf.

Holland, T. (2015) 'In Search of the True Prophet', *The Sunday Times*, 31 May.

Honderich, T. (1991) *Conservatism*. Harmondsworth: Penguin.

Honderich, T. (2005) *Conservatism: Burke, Nozick, Bush, Blair?* London and Ann Arbor, MI: Pluto Press.

Honneth, A. (2016) *The Idea of Socialism: Towards a Renewal*. Cambridge: Polity.

Huemer, M. (2013) *The Problem of Political Authority: An Examination of the Right to Coerce and the Duty to Obey*. London: Palgrave Macmillan.

Huntington, S. (1993) 'The Clash of Civilizations', *Foreign Affairs*, vol. 72, no. 3.

Huntington, S. (1996) *The Clash of Civilizations and the Remaking of World Order*. New York: Simon & Schuster.

Hutchinson, J. and Smith, A. D. (eds) (1994) *Nationalism*. Oxford and New York: Oxford University Press.

Hutton, W. (1995) *The State We're In*. London: Jonathan Cape.

Ingersoll, D., Matthews, R. and Davison, A. (2016) *The Philosophic Roots of Modern Ideology*, 5th edn. Cornwall on Hudson, NY: Sloan.

Ivison, D. (ed.) (2016) *The Ashgate Research Companion to Multiculturalism*. Abingdon: Routledge.

Jefferson, T. (1972) *Notes on the State of Virginia*. New York: W. W. Norton.

Jefferson, T. (1979) 'The United States Declaration of Independence', in W. Laqueur and B. Rubin (eds), *The Human Rights Reader*. New York: Meridian.

Jones, C. and Vernon, R. (2018) *Patriotism*. Cambridge: Polity.

Jost, J., Kruglanski, A. and Sulloway, F. (2003) 'Political Conservatism as Motivated Social Cognition', *Psychological Bulletin*, p. 129.

Journal of Political Ideologies. Abingdon, UK and Cambridge, MA: Carfax.

Kallis, A. (ed.) (2003) *The Fascism Reader*. London: Routledge.

Kallis, G. (2017) *Degrowth*. Newcastle upon Tyne: Agenda Publishing Limited.

Kaltwasser, C., Taggart, P., Espejo, O. and Ostiguy, P. (eds) (2017) *The Oxford Handbook of Populism*. Oxford: Oxford University Press.

Kant, I. (1991) *Kant: Political Writings*, ed. Hans Reiss, trans. H. B. Nisbet. Cambridge: Cambridge University Press.

Kautsky, K. (1902) *The Social Revolution*. Chicago: Kerr.

Keddi, N. (1972) *Sayyid Jamal ad-Din 'Al-Afghani'*. Berkeley, CA: California University Press.

Kelly, P. (2005) *Liberalism*. Malden, MA and Cambridge: Polity Press.

Kepel, G. (2006) *Jihad: The Trail of Political Islam*. London: I. B. Tauris.

Keynes, J. M. ([1936] 1963) *The General Theory of Employment, Interest and Money*. London: Palgrave Macmillan (San Diego: Harcourt Brace Jovanovich, 1965).

Kingdom, J. (1992) *No Such Thing as Society? Individualism and Community*. Buckingham, UK and Philadelphia, PA: Open University Press.

Kinna, R. (2009) *Anarchism: A Beginner's Guide*. Oxford: Oneworld Publications.

Kinna, R. (2020) *The Government of No One: The Theory and Practice of Anarchism*. London: Pelican.

Kinna, R. (ed.) (2014) *The Bloomsbury Companion to Anarchism*. New York: Bloomsbury.

Kropotkin, P. ([1902] 1914) *Mutual Aid*. Boston, MA: Porter Sargent.

Kuhn, T. (1962) *The Structure of Scientific Revolutions*. Chicago, IL: Chicago University Press.

Kymlicka, W. (2000) *Multicultural Citizenship*. Oxford: Oxford University Press.

Laclau, E. (2005) *On Populist Reason*. London: Verso.

Laclau, E. and Mouffe, C. (2014) *Hegemony and Socialist Strategy*. London: Verso.

Lamb, P. (2019) *Socialism*. Cambridge: Polity.

Lane, D. (1996) *The Rise and Fall of State Socialism*. Oxford: Polity Press.

Laqueur, W. (ed.) (1979) *Fascism: A Reader's Guide*. Harmondsworth: Penguin.

Larrain, J. (1983) *Marxism and Ideology*. London: Macmillan.

Layard, R. (2011) *Happiness: Lessons from a New Science*. Harmondsworth and New York: Penguin Books.

Leach, R. (2002) *Political Ideology in Britain*. London: Red Globe Press.

Lenin, V. I. ([1902] 1988) *What Is to Be Done?* Harmondsworth and New York: Penguin.

Lenin, V. I. ([1916] 1970) *Imperialism, the Highest Stage of Capitalism*. Moscow: Progress Publishers.

Lenin, V. I. ([1917] 1964) *The State and Revolution*. Peking: People's Publishing House.

Leopold, A. (1968) *Sand County Almanac*. Oxford: Oxford University Press.

Letwin, S. R. (1992) *The Anatomy of Thatcherism*. London: Fontana.

Lewis, B. (2004) *The Crisis of Islam: Holy War and Unholy Terror*. London and New York: Random House.

Lindblom, C. (1977) *Politics and Markets*. New York: Basic Books.

Locke, J. (1962) *Two Treatises of Government*. Cambridge: Cambridge University Press.

Locke, J. (1963) *A Letter Concerning Toleration*. The Hague: Martinus Nijhoff.

Lovelock, J. (1979) *Gaia: A New Look at Life on Earth*. Oxford and New York: Oxford University Press.

Lovelock, J. (1988) 'Man and Gaia', in E. Goldsmith and N. Hilyard (eds), *The Earth Report*. London: Mitchell Beazley.

Lyotard, J.-F. (1984) *The Postmodern Condition: The Power of Knowledge*. Minneapolis, MN: University of Minnesota Press.

MacIntyre, A. (1981) *After Virtue*. London: Duckworth.

Macmillan, H. ([1938] 1966) *The Middle Way*. London: Macmillan.

Macpherson, C. B. (1973) *Democratic Theory: Essays in Retrieval*. Oxford: Clarendon Press.

Maistre, J. de ([1817] 1971) *The Works of Joseph de Maistre*, trans. J. Lively. New York: Schocken.

Mandaville, P. (2014) *Islam and Politics*, 2nd edn. London: Routledge.

Mann, M. (2004). *Fascists*. Cambridge: Cambridge University Press.

Mannheim, K. ([1929] 1960) *Ideology and Utopia*. London: Routledge & Kegan Paul.

Manning, D. (1976) *Liberalism*. London: Dent.

Marcuse, H. (1964) *One Dimensional Man: Studies in the Ideology of Advanced Industrial Society*. Boston, MA: Beacon.

Maritain, J. ([1936] 1996) *Integral Humanism*. Notre Dame, IN: University of Notre Dame Press.

Marquand, D. (1988) *The Unprincipled Society*. London: Fontana.

Marquand, D. (1992) *The Progressive Dilemma*. London: Heinemann.

Marquand, D. and Seldon, A. (1996) *The Ideas that Shaped Post-War Britain*. London: Fontana.

Marshall, P. (1995) *Nature's Web: Rethinking Our Place on Earth*. London: Cassell.

Marshall, P. (2007) *Demanding the Impossible: A History of Anarchism*. London: Fontana.

Marshall, P. (2009) *Demanding the Impossible: A History of Anarchism*. Oakland, CA: PM Press.

Martell, L. (2001) *Social Democracy: Global and National Perspectives*. London and New York: Palgrave Macmillan.

Martin, R. C. and Barzegar, A. (eds) (2009) *Islamism: Contested Perspectives on Political Islam*. Redwood City, CA: Stanford University Press.

Marty, M. E. (1988) 'Fundamentalism as a Social Phenomenon', *Bulletin of the American Academy of Arts and Sciences*, vol. 42, pp. 15–29.

Marty, M. E. and Appleby, R. S. (eds) (1993) *Fundamentalisms and the State: Remaking Polities, Economies, and Militance*. Chicago, IL and London: University of Chicago Press.

Marx, K. and Engels, F. ([1846] 1970) *The German Ideology*. London: Lawrence & Wishart.

Marx, K. and Engels, F. ([1848] 1967) *The Communist Manifesto*. Harmondsworth: Penguin Books.

Marx, K. and Engels, F. (1968) *Selected Works*. London: Lawrence & Wishart.

McCann, H. and Monaghan, W. (2020) *Queer Theory Now: From Foundations to Futures*. London: Red Globe Press.

McLellan, D. (1980) *The Thought of Karl Marx*, 2nd edn. London: Macmillan.

McLellan, D. (1995) *Ideology*, 2nd edn. Milton Keynes: Open University Press.

McLellan, D. (2007) *Marxism after Marx*, 4th edn. London: Palgrave Macmillan.

Mead, W. R. (2006) 'God's Country?', *Foreign Affairs*, vol. 85, no. 5.

Meadows, D. H., Meadows, D. L., Randers, D. and Williams, W. (1972) *The Limits to Growth*. London: Pan (New York: New American Library, 1972).

Michels, R. (1958) *Political Parties*. Glencoe, IL: Free Press.

Miliband, R. (1969) *The State in Capitalist Society*. London: Verso (New York: Basic Books, 1978).

Miliband, R. (1995) *Socialism for a Sceptical Age*. Oxford: Polity Press.

Mill, J. S. ([1859] 1972) *Utilitarianism, On Liberty and Consideration on Representative Government*. London: Dent.

Mill, J. S. ([1869] 1970) *On the Subjection of Women*. London: Dent.

Miller, D. (1984) *Anarchism*. London: Dent.

Millett, K. (1970) *Sexual Politics*. New York: Doubleday.

Mills, C. W. (1956) *The Power Elite*. New York: Oxford University Press.

Mintz, F. (2012) *Workers' Self-Management in Revolutionary Spain*. Oakland, CA and Edinburgh: AK Press.

Mitchell, J. (1971) *Women's Estate*. Harmondsworth: Penguin.

Mitchell, J. (1975) *Psychoanalysis and Feminism*. Harmondsworth: Penguin.

Modood, T. (2013) *Multiculturalism*. Cambridge and Malden, MA: Polity Press.

Moffit, B. (2020) *Populism*. Cambridge: Polity.

Montesquieu, C. de ([1748] 1969) *The Spirit of Laws*. Glencoe, IL: Free Press.

More, T. ([1516] 1965) *Utopia*. Harmondsworth: Penguin (New York: Norton, 1976).

Morland, D. (1997) *Demanding the Impossible: Human Nature and Politics in Nineteenth-Century Social Anarchism*. London and Washington, DC: Cassell.

Mosca, G. (1939) *The Ruling Class*, trans. and ed. A. Livingstone. New York: McGraw-Hill.

Moschonas, G. (2002) *In the Name of Social Democracy – The Great Transformation: 1945 to the Present*. London: Verso.

Mouffe, C. (2018) *For a Left Populism*. London: Verso.

Mudde, C. and Kaltwasser, C. (2015) 'Populism', in M. Freeden, L. T. Sargent and M. Stears (eds) (2015) *The Oxford Handbook of Political Ideologies*. Oxford and New York: Oxford University Press.

Mudde, C. and Kaltwasser, C. (2017) *Populism: A Very Short Introduction*. Oxford and New York: Oxford University Press.

Muller, J. (ed.) (1997) *Conservatism: An Anthology of Social and Political Thought from David Hume to the Present*. Princeton, NJ: Princeton University Press.

Muller, J.-W. (2017) *What is Populism?* London: Penguin.

Murphy, M. (2012) *Multiculturalism: A Critical Introduction*. Abingdon: Routledge.

Murray, C. (1984) *Losing Ground: American Social Policy: 1950–1980*. New York: Basic Books.

Murray, C. and Herrnstein, R. (1995) *The Bell Curve: Intelligence and Class Structure in American Life*. New York: Free Press.

Naess, A. (1973) 'The Shallow and the Deep, Long-range Ecology Movement: A Summary', *Inquiry*, vol. 16.

Naess, A. (1989) *Community and Lifestyle: Outline of an Ecosophy*. Cambridge: Cambridge University Press.

Neocleous, M. (1997) *Fascism*. Milton Keynes: Open University Press.

Newman, M. (2005) *Socialism: A Very Short Introduction*. Oxford and New York: Oxford University Press.

Nietzsche, F. ([1884] 1961) *Thus Spoke Zarathustra*, trans. R. J. Hollingdale. Harmondsworth: Penguin (New York: Random, 1982).

Nolte, E. (1965) *Three Faces of Fascism: Action Française, Italian Fascism and National Socialism*. London: Weidenfeld & Nicolson.

Norris, P. and Inglehart, R. (2019) *Cultural Backlash and the Rise of Populism: Trump, Brexit and the Rise of Authoritarian Populism*. Cambridge and New York: Cambridge University Press.

Nozick, R. (1974) *Anarchy, State and Utopia*. Oxford: Blackwell (New York: Basic Books, 1974).

O'Hara, K. (2011) *Conservatism*. London: Reaktion Books.

O'Sullivan, N. (1976) *Conservatism*. London: Dent and New York: St Martin's Press.

O'Sullivan, N. (1983) *Fascism*. London: Dent.

Oakeshott, M. (1962) *Rationalism in Politics and Other Essays*. London: Methuen (New York: Routledge Chapman & Hall, 1981).

Ohmae, K. (1989) *Borderless World: Power and Strategy in the Interlinked Economy* (London: HarperCollins).

Okin, S. M. (1999) *Is Multiculturalism Bad for Women?* Princeton, NJ: Princeton University Press.

Osman, T. (2016) *Islamism: What it Means for the Middle East and the World*. New Haven, CT and London: Yale University Press.

Özkirimli, U. (2017) *Theories of Nationalism*, 3rd edn. London: Red Globe Press.

Pappas, T. (2019) *Populism and Liberal Democracy: A Comparative and Theoretical Analysis*. Oxford and New York: Oxford University Press.

Parekh, B. (1994) 'The Concept of Fundamentalism', in A. Shtromas (ed.), *The End of 'isms'? Reflections on the Fate of Ideological Politics after Communism's Collapse*. Oxford, UK and Cambridge, MA: Blackwell.

Parekh, B. (2005) *Rethinking Multiculturalism: Cultural Diversity and Political Theory*, 2nd edn. London: Red Globe Press.

Pareto, V. (1935) *The Mind and Society*. London: Cape and New York: AMS Press.

Passmore, K. (2014) *Fascism: A Very Short Introduction*. Oxford and New York: Oxford University Press.

Pettit, P. (1999) *Republicanism: A Theory of Freedom and Government*. Oxford: Oxford University Press.

Pierson, C. (1995) *Socialism After Communism*. Cambridge: Polity Press.

Plato (1955) *The Republic*, trans. H. D. Lee. Harmondsworth: Penguin (New York: Random House, 1983).

Popper, K. (1945) *The Open Society and Its Enemies*. London: Routledge & Kegan Paul.

Popper, K. (1957) *The Poverty of Historicism*. London: Routledge.

Porritt, J. (2005) *Capitalism as if the World Matters*. London: Earthscan.

Poulantzas, N. (1968) *Political Power and Social Class*. London: New Left Books (New York: Routledge Chapman & Hall, 1987).

Proudhon, P.-J. ([1840] 1970) *What Is Property?*, trans. B. R. Tucker. New York: Dover.

Proudhon, P.-J. ([1851] 1923) *General Idea of Revolution in the Nineteenth Century*, trans. J. B. Robinson. London: Freedom Press.

Przeworski, A. (1991) *Democracy and the Market: Political and Economic Reforms in Eastern Europe and Latin America*. Cambridge and New York: Cambridge University Press.

Pugh, J. (ed.) (2009) *What Is Radical Politics Today?* London: Palgrave Macmillan.

Purkis, J. and Bowen, J. (1997) *Twenty-First Century Anarchism: Unorthodox Ideas for a New Millennium*. London: Cassell.

Purkis, J. and Bowen, J. (eds) (2004) *Changing Anarchism: Anarchist Theory and Practice in a Global Age*. Manchester: Manchester University Press.

Qutb, S. ([1962] 2007) *Milestones*. New Delhi: Islamic Book Services.

Ramsay, M. (1997) *What's Wrong with Liberalism? A Radical Critique of Liberal Political Philosophy*. London: Leicester University Press.

Randall, V. (1987) *Women and Politics: An International Perspective*, 2nd edn. London: Red Globe Press.

Rawls, J. (1970) *A Theory of Justice*. Oxford: Oxford University Press (Cambridge, MA: Harvard University Press, 1971).

Rawls, J. (1993) *Political Liberalism*. New York: Colombia University Press.

Regan, T. (1983) *The Case for Animal Rights*. London: Routledge & Kegan Paul.

Robins, A. and Jones, A. (eds) (2009) *Genocide of the Oppressed*. Bloomington, IN: Indiana University Press.

Roemer, J. (ed.) (1986) *Analytical Marxism*. Cambridge: Cambridge University Press.

Rorty, R. (1989) *Contingency, Irony and Solidarity*. Cambridge: Cambridge University Press.

Rothbard, M. (1978) *For a New Liberty*. New York: Macmillan.

Rousseau, J.-J. ([1762] 1913) *The Social Contract and Discourse*, ed. G. D. H. Cole. London: Dent (Glencoe, IL: Free Press, 1969).

Roussopoulos, D. (ed.) (2002) *The Anarchist Papers*. New York and London: Black Rose Books.

Ruthven, M. (2007) *Fundamentalism: A Very Short Introduction*. Oxford and New York: Oxford University Press.

Said, E. ([1978] 2003) *Orientalism*. Harmondsworth: Penguin.

Sandel, M. (1982) *Liberalism and the Limits of Justice*. Cambridge: Cambridge University Press.

Sandel, M. (2020) *The Tyranny of Merit: What's Become of the Common Good?* London and New York: Allen Lane.

Sassoon, D. (2013) *One Hundred Years of Socialism*. London: Fontana.

Schneir, M. (1995) *The Vintage Book of Feminism: The Essential Writings of the Contemporary Women's Movement*. London: Vintage.

Scholte, J. A. (2005) *Globalization: An Introduction*, 2nd edn. London: Red Globe Press.

Schumacher, E. F. (1973) *Small Is Beautiful: A Study of Economics as if People Mattered*. London: Blond & Briggs (New York: Harper & Row, 1989).

Schumpeter, J. (1976) *Capitalism, Socialism and Democracy*. London: Allen & Unwin (Magnolia, MA: Peter Smith, 1983).

Schwarzmantel, J. (1991) *Socialism and the Idea of the Nation*. Hemel Hempstead: Harvester Wheatsheaf.

Schwarzmantel, J. (1998) *The Age of Ideology: Political Ideologies from the American Revolution to Post-Modern Times*. London: Red Globe Press.

Scott-Dixon, K. (ed.) (2006) *Trans/Forming Feminism: Transfeminist Voices Speak Out*. Canadian Scholars' Press: Toronto.

Scruton, R. (2001) *The Meaning of Conservatism*, 3rd edn. London: Palgrave Macmillan.

Scruton, R. (2018) *Conservatism: An Invitation to the Great Tradition*. New York: St. Martin's.

Seabright, P. (2004) *The Company of Strangers*. Princeton, NJ: Princeton University Press.

Sedgewick, M. (2019) *Key Thinkers of the Radical Right: Behind the New Threat to Liberal Democracy*. Oxford: Oxford University Press.

Seliger, M. (1976) *Politics and Ideology*. London: Allen & Unwin (Glencoe, IL: Free Press, 1976).

Sen, A. (1999) *Development as Freedom*. Oxford: Oxford University Press.

Sen, A. (2006) *Identity and Violence*. London: Penguin.

Shachar, A. (2001) *Multicultural Jurisdictions: Cultural Difference and Women's Rights*. Cambridge: Cambridge University Press.

Shtromas, A. (ed.) (1994) *The End of 'isms'? Reflections on the Fate of Ideological Politics after Communism's Collapse*. Oxford and Cambridge, MA: Blackwell.

Sil, R. and Katzenstein, P. J. (2010) *Beyond Paradigms: Analytic Eclecticism in the Study of World Politics*. London: Red Globe Press.

Singer, P. (1976) *Animal Liberation*. New York: Jonathan Cape.

Singer, P. (1993) *Practical Ethics*, 2nd edn. Cambridge: Cambridge University Press.

Smart, B. (1993) *Postmodernity*. London and New York: Routledge.

Smiles, S. ([1859] 1986) *Self-Help*. Harmondsworth: Penguin.

Smith, A. ([1776] 1976) *An Enquiry into the Nature and Causes of the Wealth of Nations*. Chicago, IL: University of Chicago Press.

Smith, A. D. (1986) *The Ethnic Origins of Nations*. Oxford: Blackwell.

Smith, A. D. (1991) *National Identity*. Harmondsworth: Penguin.

Smith, A. D. (2001) *Nationalism: Theory, Ideology, History*. Cambridge and Malden, MA: Polity Press.

Sorel, G. ([1908] 1950) *Reflections on Violence*, trans. T. E. Hulme and J. Roth. New York: Macmillan.

Spencer, H. ([1884] 1940) *The Man versus the State*. London: Watts & Co.

Spencer, H. (1967) *On Social Evolution: Selected Writings*. Chicago, IL: University of Chicago Press.

Spencer, P. and Wollman, H. (2002) *Nationalism: A Critical Introduction*. London and Thousand Oaks, CA: Sage.

Squires, J. (1999) *Gender in Political Theory*. Cambridge, UK and Malden, MA: Polity Press.

Stelzer, I. (ed.) (2004) *Neoconservatism*. London: Atlantic Books.

Stirner, M. ([1845] 1971) *The Ego and His Own*, ed. J. Carroll. London: Cape.

Sumner, W. (1959) *Folkways*. New York: Doubleday.

Surowiecki, J. (2004) *The Wisdom of Crowds*. New York: Doubleday.

Sydie, R. A. (1987) *Natural Women, Cultured Men: A Feminist Perspective on Sociological Theory*. Milton Keynes: Open University Press.

Taggart, P. (2000) *Populism*. Buckingham: Open University Press.

Talmon, J. L. (1952) *The Origins of Totalitarian Democracy*. London: Secker & Warburg.

Tam, H. (1998) *Communitarianism: A New Agenda for Politics and Citizenship*. London: Palgrave Macmillan.

Tawney, R. H. (1921) *The Acquisitive Society*. London: Bell (San Diego: Harcourt Brace Jovanovich, 1955).

Tawney, R. H. (1969) *Equality*. London: Allen & Unwin.

Taylor, C. (1994) *Multiculturalism and 'The Politics of Recognition'*. Princeton, NJ: Princeton University Press.

Taylor, C. (ed.) (1995) *Multiculturalism: Examining the Politics of Recognition*. Princeton, NJ: Princeton University Press.

Thoreau, H. D. ([1854] 1983) *Walden and 'Civil Disobedience'*. Harmondsworth: Penguin.

Thoreau, H. D. (1983) 'Civil Disobedience', in *Walden and Civil Disobedience*. Harmondsworth: Penguin Books.

Tibi, B. (2012) *Islamism and Islam*. New Haven, CT and London: Yale University Press.

Tocqueville, A. de (1968) *Democracy in America*. London: Fontana (New York: McGraw, 1981).

Tong, R. and Botts, T. (2018) *Feminist Thought: A More Comprehensive Introduction*, 5th edn. New York: Routledge.

Traub, J. (2019) *What Was Liberalism? The Past, Present, and Promise of a Noble Idea*. New York: Basic Books.

Tremblay, A. (2019). *Diversity in Decline? The Rise of the Political Right and the Fate of Multiculturalism*. Cham, CH: Palgrave Macmillan.

Vincent, A. (2009) *Modern Political Ideologies*, 2nd edn. Oxford: Blackwell.

Walby, S. (2011) *The Future of Feminism*. Cambridge: Polity Press.

Waldron, J. (1995) 'Minority Cultures and the Cosmopolitan Alternative', in W. Kymlicka (ed.), *The Rights of Minority Cultures*. London and New York: Open University Press.

Wall, S. (ed.) (2015) *The Cambridge Companion to Liberalism*. Cambridge: Cambridge University Press.

Wallerstein, I. (1974) *The Modern World System*. New York: Academic Press.

Wallerstein, I. (1984) *The Politics of the World Economy: States, Movements and Civilizations*. Oxford: Polity Press.

Walter, N. (1999) *The New Feminism*. London: Virago.

Walter, N. (2010) *Living Dolls: The Return of Sexism*. London: Virago.

Walters, M. (2005) *Feminism: A Very Short Introduction*. Oxford and New York: Oxford University Press.

Ward, B. and Dubois, R. (1972) *Only One Earth*. Harmondsworth: Penguin.

Ward, C. (2004) *Anarchism: A Very Short Introduction*. Oxford and New York: Oxford University Press.

Weber, M. ([1904–5] 2011) *The Protestant Ethic and the Spirit of Capitalism*. Oxford and New York: Oxford University Press.

White, S. (ed.) (2001) *New Labour: The Progressive Future?* London and New York: Palgrave Macmillan.

Willetts, D. (1992) *Modern Conservatism*. Harmondsworth: Penguin.

Wolf, N. (1994) *Fire with Fire: The New Female Power and How to Use It*. New York: Fawcett.

Wolff, R. P. (1998) *In Defence of Anarchism*, 2nd edn. Berkeley, CA: University of California Press.

Wollstonecraft, M. ([1792] 1967) *A Vindication of the Rights of Woman*, ed. C. W. Hagelman. New York: Norton.

Woodcock, G. (1992) *Anarchism: A History of Libertarian Ideas and Movements*. Harmondsworth and New York: Penguin.

Woolf, S. J. (1981) (ed.) *European Fascism*. London: Weidenfeld & Nicolson.

Wright, A. (1996) *Socialisms: Theories and Practices*. Oxford and New York: Oxford University Press.

Young, I. (1995) *Justice and the Politics of Difference*. Princeton, NJ: Princeton University Press.

Zakaria, F. (1997) 'The Rise of Illiberal Democracy', *Foreign Affairs*, 76.

INDEX

Note: page numbers that are in **bold** type refer to figures, tables and boxes; page numbers that are in *italics* refer to on-page definitions.